WORLDS OF PRODUCTION

WORLDS OF PRODUCTION

The Action Frameworks of the Economy

Michael Storper and Robert Salais

HARVARD UNIVERSITY PRESS

Cambridge, Massachusetts

London, England

1997

A somewhat different version of this book was published as *Les Mondes de Production: Enquête sur l'Identité Economique de la France* by Editions de l'Ecole des Hautes Etudes en Sciences Sociales, copyright 1993 by Robert Salais and Michael Storper.

Library of Congress Cataloging-in-Publication Data
Salais, Robert.
   [Mondes de production. English]
   Worlds of production : the action frameworks of the economy /
Michael Storper, Robert Salais.
      p. cm.
   Rev. translation of: Les mondes de production : enquête sur
l'identité économique de la France / Robert Salais et Michael
Storper.
   Includes bibliographical references and index.
   ISBN 0-674-96203-6 (alk. paper)
   1. Industries—France. 2. Industrial policy—France.
3. Production (Economic theory) 4. Industries—Italy.
5. Industries—United States. I. Storper, Michael. II. Title.
HC276.S24513   1997
338.0944—dc21   96-48228

.... ▬▬ ....

PREFACE

This book aims to explain economic processes in a way that deliberately mixes economic reasoning with other types of thought. Much has been written recently about the role of "non-economic" forces, such as institutions, cultures, and social practices, in economic life. We intend to take those forces as central to the economic process and no longer consider them as "non-economic." They take the form of conventions—largely implicit rules of action and coordination, generated by humans and routinized—which come together into what we call frameworks of economic action. We explore in detail four basic frameworks of action, which we call "possible worlds of production" in this book. Such frameworks underpin the mobilization of economic resources, the organization of production systems and factor markets, patterns of economic decision-making, and forms of profitability. The economic problem for actors is to couple such frameworks to products and production technologies in coherent ways. Our case studies examine how these possible worlds act to support innovative production complexes in a variety of sectors in several countries.

Much of economic analysis, even in contemporary institutionalist versions, expresses puzzlement at the "difficulty" of economic adjustments, the "paradoxical," "perverse," "unexpected" outcomes of economic policies or changes in the economic environment. When attempts to design policies go wrong, it is because the "subjects" of those policies do not "react" appropriately to the "stimulus" applied. In many situations, it has become increasingly difficult to get large numbers of people to agree on what constitutes appropriate economic ends and means. The premise of this book is that economic actors coordinate with each other and interpret what others are doing in ways that are constructed by convention. Actors are capable of generating systematic practices in the economy because these practices are rooted in convention. Unless we understand their conventional frameworks of action, we cannot figure out why these individuals and collectivities act as they do. In this book we try to show that different pathways to economic development, whether competitively successful or not, can be internally coherent for the people participating in them in ways often not understood by normal economic theory, nor even by much existing institutional analysis. These pathways are deeply tied into the economic identities of nations and regions; that is, the action frameworks deployed by economic actors identify actors to each other and to the outside world through the products that emerge from their activities.

We deliberately maintain a tension between analysis from without and close attention to the interpretations of actors within the situations of economic action. Thus in some respects we are like ethnographers, but we also step outside the actors' immediate context. Economies must make products, and markets have a disciplining force; by modeling the coherence among conventions, products, and production technologies, in light of their performance in markets, we can show that even when the conventions (and institutions) of a production system have a strong coherence for the actors themselves, they do not necessarily have the highest degree of coherence in the more traditional sense of competitiveness. One central mystery of these economic identities, and the development that accompanies them, is that feedback from external tests of performance to internal tests is much less straightforward, much more complex, than is admitted in most economic thought. In social theory terms, our approach essentially abandons the cleavage between structure and agency. An economy of conventions is an economy of constructed structures, the result of an ongoing encounter between social forces and habits of mind which shapes particular economic practices.

The principal challenge to economic policy today is to reconcile internal tests, as they are understood by those who make up economic systems—especially in jurisdictions where governments can act upon economic activity—and the external tests of product and financial markets, which tend increasingly to escape jurisdictional borders. There is no single model of growth and efficiency that brings these two sides together around the world today, even in narrowly defined product markets. An economy composed of conventions is one of a multiplicity of worlds of production; the world economy today is one of diversity, heterogeneity, and unevenness, even among the success stories. The paradox, which we think is underappreciated by social science today, is that if politics and policies are to cope with an increasingly unified global system of flows of commodities, money, and people, they must be situated in, and respectful of, the diverse, economically viable action frameworks found in different industries, regions, and nations.

We would like to thank the many agencies whose support made it possible to carry out the research leading to the production of this book. In the United States, our thanks go to the German Marshall Fund of the United States for a fellowship provided to Michael Storper in 1988–89; to the Council for International Exchange of Scholars (Fulbright Commission) and the Commission Franco-Américaine d'Echanges Culturels et Universitaires; at UCLA, to the International Studies and Overseas Programs, the Institute of Industrial Relations, the Center for International Business and Education Research (CIBER) at the Anderson Graduate School of Management, and the Lewis Center for Regional Policy Studies; and to the Center for German and European Studies, University of California at Berkeley.

In France, our warmest thanks go to the Institut National de la Statistique et des Etudes Economique (INSEE); the Conseil National de la Recherche Scientifique (CNRS), and within it the Programme Interdisciplinaire Travail-Technologie-Modes de Vie (PIRTTEM); the Ministère de la Recherche et de l'Espace; and the Commissariat Général du Plan, which supported the CNRS research group "Institutions, Emploi et Politique Économique" (IEPE), under whose auspices Robert Salais conducted his research for this book. The contribution of these institutions has taken many forms, including logistical and financial. Financial support for analyzing the Fonds National de l'Emploi data was also provided by the Ministère du Travail, de l'Emploi, et de la Formation professionnelle.

In Italy, the NOMISMA, Società di Studi Economici, Bologna, provided support and an institutional home, for which we are very grateful. We benefited, as well, from contact with a number of research projects funded by the Italian Centro Nazionale di Ricerche (CNR).

Too many individuals have assisted us in planning research, conducting interviews, preparing data, and in other tasks to be acknowledged individually here. Some, however, must be mentioned, and they include the following.

At UCLA, Michael Storper is grateful for the consistent support, both material and moral, of Richard Weinstein, former Dean of the Graduate School of Architecture and Urban Planning. His graduate student research assistants not only assisted with research tasks but also, in a number of seminars, helped the author develop his ideas and priorities; among these, Ahmed Enany and (now Professor) Jane Pollard played especially important roles. Along the way, Vanessa Dingley administered everything brilliantly.

The project was encouraged at its outset by the invaluable support of Chuck Sabel, and had roots in some of the pioneering work done by Sabel, Michael Piore, and Jonathan Zeitlin, as well as others in the United States who have opened our eyes to the importance of institutions and social practices in the economy, though none is in any way to be held responsible for the theoretical and empirical directions we have taken. The detailed critiques of Phil Scranton and Gary Herrigel were especially valuable in rewriting the manuscript.

Our interactions with the "Grenoble crowd," including Michel Bernardy de Sigoyer, Jacques Joly, and Claude Courlet, as well as Pierre Frappat, Rene Videcoq, and others, were extremely valuable, as was the counsel of Anna di Lellio of Columbia University. The "Florentine School" of economists and geographers has been a constant source of inspiration, stimulation, and information, as well as material aid; among them we cite Professor Giacomo Becattini, Fabio Sforzi, Marco Bellandi, Gabi Dei Ottati, and Maria Tinacci Mosello. The same may be said of the Bologna School, where we thank Patrizio Bianchi, Francesca Pasquini, Vittorio Cappecchi, Giuseppina Gualtieri, and Fabio Nuti. In Modena, Sebastiano Brusco, Mario Pezzini (via Paris), Tiziano Bursi, and many others have been central to this intellectual effort, and the work of Margherita Russo was inspiring. Many individuals, such as Daniella Martino of the Carpi Textile Center (CITER) and Marco Romagnolo in Prato, introduced us to the way industrial policy functions at a regional level in Italy. In Geneva, Werner Sengenberger and Frank Pyke organized a community of researchers and stimulated fruitful dialogue.

Robert Salais has worked, over the last few years, as part of a network of researchers in France interested in questions of conventions, rules, and frameworks of action in economic coordination. Their work has been published in a number of collections and scholarly journals, including the *Révue Economique,* the *Cahiers du Centre d'Études de l'Emploi,* and in publications of the Centre de Recherche en Épistémologie Appliquée (CREA). Much of this work has its origins in work on the history and social construction of statistics conducted at INSEE at the end of the 1970s. Those in this milieu include, among others, Alain Desrosieres, François Eymard-Duvernay, Olivier Favereau, and Laurent Thévenot. The principal themes of this book could not have been developed without this group. We wish also to thank colleagues in the research group IEPE for their intellectual support, advice, and friendship: Claude Didry, Francis Kramarz, Michel Margairaz, Dorothée Rivaud-Danset, and Alain Supiot read various versions of the manuscript and gave us pertinent feedback. Finally, thanks to Jacques Revel and two anonymous referees of the manuscript in French, in association with its publication in Paris by the École des Hautes Etudes en Sciences Sociales (EHESS). Their critiques and suggestions were of incalculable help. The final organization of the book owes much to the suggestions of Edmond Blanc.

In France as well, administrative assistance figured prominently in our ability to coordinate research and production of the book. Claude Morey, the secretary of IEPE, was able to take on this work—with smiles, patience, perseverance, and efficiency—while administering the research group as a whole.

We thank the following individuals for assisting in the preparation of case studies in France: Anne Moysan, Patrick Plein, and Luc Tessier.

We also wish to thank Peter Solomon for his extraordinary talent and dedication in editing the English version of the text; Aaron Shonk for producing the tables and figures; and Michael Aronson and Jeff Kehoe at Harvard University Press for seeing the project through to completion.

Finally, Michael Storper would like to thank Michel Rétiveau (1948–1996), to whom he dedicates his contribution, for his love and support during the preparation of this book.

CONTENTS

Contents

........——........

FIGURES AND TABLES

Figures

Tables

I

THEORIZING ECONOMIC DIVERSITY AND ECONOMIC ACTION

1

ACTION AND DIVERSITY VERSUS MODELS OF GROWTH

The Old Model of Economic Growth

Advanced capitalist economies enjoyed a kind of "Golden Age" in the 1950s and 1960s: in the countries of Western Europe and North America, there were twenty or thirty years of high growth, high profits, low inflation, low unemployment, and rapid rises in productivity, real wages, and incomes. As a consequence, standards of living rose steadily, as did expectations that such a trend would continue.

Somewhere around the end of the 1960s or the beginning of the 1970s, however, growth and profits started to fall, inflation and unemployment rose, increases in productivity and incomes slowed, and real wages actually declined in some sectors. Since then, the performance of the major capitalist economies in recovery periods—from the stagflation years of 1973–1982 to the recoveries of the mid-1980s; from the severe recession of the late 1980s and early 1990s to the halting comeback of the mid-1990s—has failed to equal performance during the recoveries of the Golden Age. Growth has become a mixed bag, accompanied in some countries by high unemployment, meager increases in real wages and incomes, and uneven profit performance. Long-term unemployment has become more prevalent in Europe, as has working poverty in the United States. High levels of public and private indebtedness are widespread, and social spending can no longer keep up with demand. In short, the indicators have—for almost two decades—refused to move together in the coherent fashion defined by the growth pattern of the Golden Age. Policymakers in these countries—on the left and the right—are generally lacking any substantive programs for solving simultaneously the problem of wages/incomes and that of unemployment: all their programs involve a tradeoff between the two.

These circumstances can be approached in two ways. The first, which is not our approach, is to ask what is missing today with respect to the past. Those who think along these lines have made a number of ambitious attempts to construct comprehensive, coherent explanations of the Golden Age, describing the ensemble of structures that made the variables behave as they did.[1] The 1960s, for example, are frequently characterized as a decade in which national macroeconomic policies were based on Keynesian demand management; the United States dominated the international order with its strong currency and a stable set of monetary rules in the form of the Bretton Woods Treaty; the paradigm of mass production, characterized by standardized products and long production runs, served as a motor of growth because of its steadily rising productivity levels, while oligopolistic industrial firms in stable markets enjoyed persistently high profit rates; and, finally, the rules of the game at the micro level included oligopolistic mark-up of prices, institutionalized wage determination via union contracts, internal labor markets, and widespread wage-pattern effects.[2]

In the 1980s, case studies of industrial change concentrated on the dimensions of production systems which were thought to represent an across-the-board break with the postwar industrial system: production without buffer stocks, using communication and information networks; decentralization, vertical disintegration, and externalization of activities; the growth of indirect labor ("roundaboutness"); increasing dependence on financing from outside the firm; integration of services with material production; the tendency to use continuous processes, more accurate market forecasting, and more frequent product changeovers; the internationalization of production and marketing; and the decline of the stable, in-house workforce.[3]

Yet these claims of a clean break with postwar mass production and its associated economic institutions are poorly posed insofar as they imply the existence of a single new alternative growth paradigm. In contrast, the notion explored in this book is that of a durable and concrete diversity of forms of economic coordination at intra- and inter-sectoral levels, not that of a unified model of economic growth. We explain the unevenness, diversity, and heterogeneity of economic life through the theoretical concept of multiple *possible worlds of production*. These are frameworks of economic action, centered on conventions among economic actors, which enable them to coordinate, in coherent fashion, ensembles of economic practices leading to successful products.

International Specialization and the Economic Identities of Nations and Regions

When we speak of diversity and complexity in the emerging world economy, we mean, at the most basic level, that different regions and nations make different things using different methods. This may seem to be an extraordinary claim at a time when internationalization of economic relations has proceeded so rapidly. Between 1955 and 1989, the world GDP index grew from 100 to 350, while the world export index increased to almost 1100. The share of trade in output thus increased from 6% to 22%. This rise in trade can be seen in an extraordinary variety of sectors. Trade in goods (excluding energy) increased from about 8% to 12% of total world output, and trade in services from about 1.5% to 2.5%.[4] Further, within the goods-producing sectors, the increase is surprisingly widespread; *filières* (commodity chains) with a stable or increasing share of world trade include metalworking, machinery, motor vehicles, electronics, chemicals, textiles, woodworking, and paper. The dramatic rise in trade is also associated with widespread increases in specialization of the world's advanced industrial economies. A high level of commodity disaggregation is necessary to appreciate this specialization: when statistics are highly aggregated, one sees instead a trend toward convergence in broad sectoral patterns of specialization of different countries, in part because consumption patterns among advanced economies tend to converge, and in part because intra-industry exchanges account for an increasing share of trade (up to 70% in the case of some European countries). Running counter to this, however, is an increase in intra-industry product specialization, that is, differentiation of production within the same broad sectors.[5] Thus, when one examines trade at the level of 5-digit SITC (Standard International Trade Classification) products, one sees that export vectors of the main industrial countries have become steadily less similar since 1978.[6] This should not be surprising: industrial production is organized around the making of particular *products;* it is in specific product markets that competition takes place. Moreover, this specialization is not a function of differential access to major production process technologies:[7] as Pavitt and Patel show, major firms in advanced countries have access to a wide and similar range of *production technologies* but stick to a much narrower range of *products.*[8]

THE INCREASE IN TRADE SPECIALIZATION:
WHAT THEORY HAS TO SAY

Three explanations can be offered for the growth of trade among countries of similar overall levels of development: factor cost differentials, economies of scale, and technological mastery. A large, and growing, share of world trade consists of exchanges that cannot be explained by the first of these, which is the traditional theory of comparative advantage. In the standard Ricardian understanding, comparative advantage is the result of either the range of natural resources available in a given place, or reductions in relative costs of production that flow from choosing activities best adapted to the local factor mix. In today's world, however, there is ample reason to expect that when a product is subject to the conditions of perfect competition, upon which the standard theory rests, it would cease to be an object of international trade. Ricardian trade theory was once criticized for ignoring differences in technology or capital endowments between countries, but we now live in a very different world, where factors of production for technologically stable products are not *endowed,* but *produced* (as intermediate inputs). Almost any developed country can become as efficient as the next country in a technologically stable manufacturing sector. As Vernon intimated,[9] the time required for diffusion of standardized technologies has progressively diminished. This is due in part to global corporations whose networks have spread and deepened over the past few decades, and in part to inter-firm and inter-country technological imitation. This has been confirmed by Amendola, Guerrieri, and Padoan,[10] who examined technologies by looking at patents and found that aggregate technological efficiency among major countries tended to diminish rapidly and steadily following major technological revolutions. Basic technologies thus become a sort of common knowledge of the developed (and a number of developing) economies, and this leads to rapidly converging costs of production for standardized or generic products. This runs quite opposite to the predictions of Ricardian theory.

A second current explanation, the "new trade theory," argues that trade patterns are largely consequences of economies of scale in production, and therefore that many markets are imperfectly competitive.[11] The global economy as a whole is characterized by much greater product variety than formerly, and the increasing complexity, specialization, and differentiation of many products mean that economies of scale in both final outputs and intermediate outputs overwhelm even the biggest national markets. As a result, according to new trade theory, many broad industrial markets have become contested through international invasion since the end of the 1960s, even though factor prices are similar and technological improvements rapidly diffused. Indeed, worldwide market concentration has tended to fall in many industries, despite the fact that in many sectors and countries domestic production is concentrated in fewer hands than ever before.

This explanation is powerful, and there is little reason to doubt that it applies to certain standardized products differentiated by segmented demands, as well as to trade between highly interdependent neighboring economies (as in Europe). It is nonetheless incomplete in certain respects. First, it is widely thought that minimal optimal scale economies in the production of many goods are either stable or falling, owing to the increasing flexibility (programmability in particular) of capital equipment;[12] this offsets some of the need for scale in intermediate outputs referred to above. Yet trade is rising in a number of markets affected by this phenomenon, such as automobile parts. Second, trade appears to be rising even in product markets where economies of scale have traditionally been quite low (most evidently in traditional industries such as clothing and textiles). Third, there is a critical ambiguity with respect to the significance of economies of scale in the case of small, open economies. Consider, for instance, the situation where a nation's citizens demand high quantities and very specific qualities of a certain good, and where that nation's economy is small and open—for example, Belgium, where the degree of openness is 45% (in comparison, that of the United States is about 12%). Belgium might produce a certain kind of beer for the specialized tastes of Belgians; but if minimal optimal scale economies are greater than domestic demand, Belgium might then export some of its production. If Belgium's exports are a very small share of world trade in that sector, then its trade specialization in beer has to do with economies of scale. But if that same quantity of exports amounts to a relatively high share of the world's production of certain kinds of beer, Belgium's trade specialization cannot be attributed exclusively to economies of scale; scale reasons might have "pushed" the Belgians into external markets in the first place, but world market demand for their output now "pulls" production along, because of the qualities of the Belgian product. Thus, in some circumstances, the mere existence of scale economies explains little about why trade specialization appears and persists. In markets without high barriers to entry, or in markets where barriers are present but trade specialization is stable or increasing, a product must have qualities that provide some kind of advantage in the face of rapid imitation by potential competitors.

This advantage is technological mastery, due to locally superior process or product technology. Product technology appears particularly important, as noted earlier, because of the increasing speed of diffusion of process technologies and their increasing flexibility with respect to output mix over time. Thus technological mastery is more and more reflected in the range and speed of product innovation, so that at any given moment certain centers of scarce outputs exist, giving rise to trade. These "economies of variety over time" depend on the ability of a specialized production system to generate a changing array of outputs in its product field, so it can outrun the catch-up effect from ever more rapid imitation and convergent productivity levels. This can be accomplished with or without the usual economies of variety (that is, making many products at the same time). The process, simultaneously "intellectual" and "material," that continually generates such products, which are not fully standardized or directed to generic markets, is the process of *technological and organizational learning.*[13] This means the ability to reinvent, differentiate, improve, and reconfigure products continuously through a dynamic redeployment of specialized production skills and equipment.

Learning is not the only form of technological *change;* rapidly changing average production or product technologies may come through imitating others, as well as by the kind of innovation discussed here, and the two processes may complement each other. But it is one thing to buy equipment or even knowledge, another to learn how to use it and apply it to real problems. Moreover, the market share advantages due to imitation are likely to be shorter-lived than those due to learning, because by definition imitators are subject to rapid competition from elsewhere, that is, to the spread of a catch-up process which is already in motion. (Learning can concern processes other than those based in product innovation; but the latter forms of learning have the most economic interest for our purposes.)

The existing literature on technological innovation and evolutionary economics is overwhelmingly oriented toward the engineering and science-intensive industries and their principal oligopolistic firms, but product-based technological and organizational learning is important across the economy. If learning-based dynamic economies of variety were truly so limited, it would be easy to claim that the contemporary surge in trade and specialization is an ephemeral phenomenon related to the electronics revolution and its application to other sectors. In this view, microelectronics, by destandardizing knowledge and production processes for a short time, permits a few countries that master state-of-the-art base technologies and applications to gain world market shares. But this "infant industry" perspective also predicts that the transition from the postwar mass production economy to a new system will be achieved when standardization, imitation, and convergence return. In other words, learning would only be a one-time advantage for the first movers in the microelectronics age. This view converges nicely with standard comparative advantage theory, of course, since such advantage, in the form of imperfect competition, would be just a temporary deviation from the "normal" course of economic history.

We argue instead that the contemporary microelectronics revolution (among other forces, including the increasing openness of world markets, shifting consumption patterns related to sociological and demographic changes, and so on) has brought to certain sectors the technological possibility of *beginning* a long-run process of ongoing *respecialization and redefinition* of outputs. World trade is rising even in traditional industries where microelectronics does not revolutionize production; trade is declining as a share of world output only in the non-energy resource and agricultural sectors, and certain materials processing sectors such as steel.

It appears that we have entered a period in the development of capitalism in which trade and specialization are driven by the supply-side learning behavior of specializers. Such behavior has become a broad characteristic of the logic of "best practice" in advanced capitalist economies. This ongoing differentiation of products has the effect of continually unsettling the division of labor through dynamic economies of variety, leading to what Freeman[14] suspects may be a "permanent shift in industrial structure and behavior." We thus come full circle, viewing trade as a handmaiden rather than as an autonomous engine of growth. Supply-side learning behaviors become the focus of attempts to understand emerging patterns of trade and the growth which stems from successful dynamic specialization. The question is why certain places build up advantages that permit them—over and over—to turn out products that cannot be easily and rapidly imitated.

UNDERSTANDING DIVERSITY AND COMPLEXITY: HUMAN ACTION IN THE ECONOMY

Economic theory in general is not well equipped to account in a positive way for the diversity of products and ways of making them found in contemporary advanced economies. The beauty of the standard theory is its simplicity: the allocation of a series of stock and flow variables optimized by the decision maker.[15] More empirically-minded approaches emphasize the diffusion of advanced technologies and convergence (through imitation) on so-called "best practices." Efficient (that is, optimizing) within-sector diversity is related to different factor endowments or market configurations; inefficient diversity results from obstacles to the diffusion of best practice—obstacles engendered by managerial failure, vested institutionalized interests, protective banking and trade legislation, and the like.

Such narrowly economistic views, however, underestimate the positive, and potentially efficient, sources of diversity arising from what is made and how it is made. The signals which may lead to success are much more complex than "weak" allocative market signals and the constrained optimality they incite. Firms receive at least two other important kinds of signals in capitalist economies: those based on technological opportunities ("Schumpeterian" signals) and those based on growth opportunities which cannot be reduced to the standard growth equation.[16] These two kinds of signals are the basis for "strong"[17] growth and change processes in capitalism, where actions taken to respond to, and to reshape, those signals lead to significant endogenous effects.[18] They give actors a wide margin of maneuver in developing products and the organization of production.

Think of the product as the *technology of the output,* where the precise ways in which the output is designed will generate its particular mix of *qualities.*[19] Innovation, as is now widely recognized, is not principally the result of attempts to economize on factors when their relative prices are rising. It depends on all kinds of independent forces, including the development of knowledge, sensibilities, and interests. Most important, innovations result from asymmetric information held by the innovator and are frequently motivated by the super-normal profits (quasi-rents) the innovator may earn. Innovative product differentiation and design (called development of the product's *qualities* throughout this book), and process innovation, vitiate the neat allocative effects of markets, at least in the short- and medium-term. Moreover, as the evolutionary theory of economic and technological change has shown, truly superior technologies are governed by the rules of absolute, rather than comparative, advantage in markets.[20] Absolute advantage exists when no set of alternative factor prices would suffice to generate a competitive short-term substitute product or process.[21] In practical terms, this means that "best practices" are the results of conventional market failures, and are developed in response to signals and opportunities quite at odds with the allocational efficiency suggested by the standard approach.[22]

Where do the means to carry out such strong competition come from? The development of asymmetric information (whether formalized as science or in the form of traditional skills and uncodified practices) and the reaction to it by actors (firms, individuals, social groups, governments) is one of the central mysteries of economic and social life.[23] We do know that such information has a localized, endogenous character; otherwise every Third World country, given a little capital, would be able to produce the finest goods, and there would be no problem of technological diffusion whatsoever between firms, regions, and industries.[24] An even greater mystery is the finding that certain forms of widely available abstract, codified knowledge are taken up more rapidly by some firms, regions, or industries than others, even when the potential direct economic payoffs for adopting such innovations are equalized. In other words, the application of knowledge to product development (in effect, the transformation of this information into an embodied asymmetric form) seems to depend on different routines of actors in relationship to signals. The capacities of actors to "see" and to "process" information are highly variable.[25]

These processes are collective. They take the form of actions and interactions between persons. A more orthodox way of stating this is that they depend on externalities, including

> untraded interdependencies between sectors, technologies and firms . . . Technological complementarities, untraded technological interdependencies, and information flows . . . do not correspond entirely to the flow of commodities; all represent a structured set of technological externalities which is in a sense a collective asset . . . [these are] context conditions which are (1) country specific, region specific, or even company specific; (2) a fundamental ingredient in the innovative process; and (3) as such, determine different opportunities/ stimuli/constraints on the innovation process for any given set of strictly economic signals.[26]

Moreover, these positive externalities have durable effects on the pathway of economic development. Technological choices are not perfectly reversible, in the sense that interdependencies between basic technologies and applications, or between patterns of end-uses, have a cumulative character: multiple interconnections, growing numbers of users, and rising investments in productive capital generate significant external economies of use for products and processes.[27] This is by no means absolute: existing interconnections can be swept away by radical new base innovations (as well as by intermediate choices and incremental modifications). Rather, it means that the present shapes the future in two important ways. First, within a product or process technology, previous possibilities are foreclosed, by increasing efficiencies of technologies which are adopted. This is the notion of "technological trajectory" developed by contemporary evolutionary economics.

A pathway of development is more than a narrowly *technological* trajectory, however, so the present also shapes the future in the sense that activities and actions develop and absorb asymmetric information, generating new "sprouts" on the evolutionary tree, opening up new options, new uncertainties, whose future depends on subsequent choices.[28] The recent histories of so-called technologically "mature" industries suggest very strongly that path dependency is fully compatible with the "continuation of history." These histories are constructed sequences of events, where functional organizational and technological interdependencies become temporal interdependencies, both creating and foreclosing options. They have recently been formalized as "neo-Austrian" or "out of equilibrium" developmental pathways.[29]

Absolute advantages are in many ways "structurally at the core of the signalling and allocative mechanisms of our economic system."[30] The conditions of price competition, exchange, and investment flows through capital markets do represent strong allocative mechanisms; but the parameters and possible effects of these mechanisms are not bounded by technologies. The latter are formed by the creative "strong" forms of competition which confer absolute advantage.

Yet most of the modern theory of economic growth is rather unhelpful in explaining these impulses; it describes growth as a process without "substance."[31] The economy consists of mechanisms but is without practices; there is no concrete content to what is made, how people make it, or how they think about and react to the world around them in so doing.[32] We shall argue in this book that product qualities and the organization of production systems, and thus growth, are inherently bound up with the "substantive" conditions that allow economies to select themselves into configurations of absolute and comparative advantages. Selection, in this case, means not only choosing from a menu of existing options for products and processes, but creating those options. Development is the consequence of strategic and reflexive action taken to generate multiple options for survival and growth. The range of possible "efficient" choices, the choice sets, and the rules of choice evolve together. The substance of the process is human action, and production systems are humanly constructed orders of routines, cognitive frameworks, institutions, practices, and objects.

Beyond the Structure-Action Dichotomy

A rich literature on comparative industrialization suggests that economic growth is the product of particular, often localized, institutional and political structures and cultures. In one version, the problem is formulated in terms of tradeoffs between the overall rate of economic growth and the political structures (such as stability of rules and property rights) which provide for such growth, as in the contrast between southern Europe's "Catholic capitalism" and northern Europe's "Protestant capitalism."[33] More recent work on comparative industrialization looks to differences not only in the rate of growth, but in product specialization and in methods of organizing the production process at the micro level;[34] the "politics of production" at all levels, from state to industry to firm to region to workplace, are seen to affect profoundly the evolution of production. Capitalism has cultural foundations: groups of individuals with different rationalities have different time preferences and utility functions, and hence select themselves into different activities and organize those activities in a wide variety of more or less efficient ways.

These perspectives exist in a kind of tension with more economistic approaches to industrial organization, for just as the non-economic must shape the actions of economic agents in important ways, so there must be some limits to the influence of the political inside the production system. Thus, the response to the deficiencies of orthodox approaches is not simply to replace a focus on optimization with a focus on supposedly "non-economic" forces as central to development. Instead, we must develop conceptions of economic activity that allow us to define both the creative side of that activity (the problem of action) and the ways in which it is subject to external tests of markets and competitiveness (the problem of structure). The task becomes more complicated if such structures, that is, economic tests, are thought to be developed endogenously in the socioeconomic process, and to have important margins of variation. This approach is neither a "politics of economics," nor an economics "founded on politics,"[35] but rather an attempt to reformulate the question.

This reformulation involves departures from orthodox economics and its underlying social theory, but it departs from neo-institutionalist social theory as well. In so doing, we are forced up against the central problems of social theory: is action an individually generated source of structure (pattern, institution, process), or does structure "precede" human agency and have a causally superior status? Modern social theory itself does not provide much help with this problem of economic action: virtually its entire corpus opposes methodological individualism and atomistic individuals to collectivist or holist visions of society in which individuals become bearers of structures. Neither position shows much interest in the problem of action: the former carries a belief in universal, rational utilitarianism; the latter a belief in the power of external norms. Modern social theory is peopled by calculating machines or bearers of structures.

The problem of reconciling true structure with true agency, giving real weight to both terms, has been the subject of some recent work, notably by Anthony Giddens, Pierre Bourdieu, and others, but rather little of this has reached economics. This cleavage should be rejected.

> At the top of the agenda is the requirement to circumvent the perennial dualisms that split social scientific thought and mutilate our grasp of reality: those between subject and object, choice and constraint, consent and coercion, or between purposive and meaningful activity through which agents construct their world on the one hand, and the impersonal compulsion and limits that the gravity of social structures impose on them on the other.[36]

The way to reject this dualism is to reconstruct our definition of human action in the economy. Rather than attempting to isolate human actions analytically, and either seeking the universal intentions and rationalities behind them or seeking the structures (norms, interests, and so forth) which generate specific intentions and rationalities, we can simply accept that in any given pragmatic situation, an actor subject to uncertainty must make an effort to determine how to coordinate successfully with other actors to deal with the situation at hand. This makes the central problem one of producing coordination among actors. Such coordination, we argue, is the product neither of atomism nor of norms and structures, but of actions undertaken so as to proceed effectively in situations of interdependence with other actors. That is, the emergence of economic practices from actions is the central phenomenon to be explained.

INDUSTRIAL DIVERSITY: PRAGMATICS

Since it is not fruitful to isolate individual actions and then ask for their underlying intentions or rationalities or for the governing norms and external rules, we begin with the actors' pragmatic needs and problems. The practical common purpose of economic actors is to make and exchange *products;* it is the product that embodies and thus realizes the potentialities of the resources of action.[37] The product, in its diversity and particularity, is the critical strategic space of the economy for actors.

As social theorists, our methodological stance with respect to describing the situations of actors is to try, at least at the outset, to impose the bare minimum of categories that the actors themselves do not use. This scarcity of presuppositions is based on our profound skepticism with respect both to structuralist and functionalist sociology and to the presuppositions of neoclassical economics. In this sense, we pursue the notion of doing archaeology or genealogies of economic situations (without accepting any of the baggage that weighs down those methods), to avoid enclosing our understanding in narrow disciplinary constructions. We can take seriously the complexity and diversity of pragmatic problems, including the ways actors themselves describe their situations, cataloging the objects they use much as an ethnographer would, observing the real ways in which actors organize their interactions—precisely as the starting point for modeling the nature of the economy.

To understand what economic actors do, we must examine quite closely the situations in which they find themselves. Even when actors describe their own actions in terms of laws (as in the everyday use of the language of the market), our theories do not have to accept those descriptions as "truthful" (or lawful)—nor do they authorize rejecting them as irrelevant falsehoods. Instead, we must analyze the extent to which actors actually use such descriptions or hypotheses to represent their practical problems, and how, as forms of lived social life, the descriptions affect the real course of economic action, irrespective of their "truthfulness." Our starting point is therefore the individual's interpretative effort, a strong form of action in and of itself.

CONVENTION

What happens in pragmatic situations? The making of products generates diverse situations of complex social activity—that is, situations founded on interdependence with other actors—and therefore necessarily involves for each actor a diffused and radical kind of *uncertainty* with respect to the performance and expectations of other actors. The particular form and nature of that uncertainty vary according to the contours of the particular situation, as do the sets of ways to resolve it so as to go forward and succeed in the collective activity of production. In other words, the making of each kind of product is characterized by a particular set of uncertainties among the actors involved.

The different pragmatic tasks of any economy require coordination between the individuals who engage in them, and this coordination can only come about when their interpretations lead to a sort of "agreement" about what is to be done—in the sense that what each person does meets the expectations of the others on whom he or she depends. Such agreement—specific to the pragmatic situation at hand—is required between buyers and sellers of a commodity, between input-supplier and purchaser, between one worker and another on the shop floor, between manager and worker; without it, the collective, mutually interdependent activity cannot go forward.

Of course, this is not an "agreement" in the sense of a formal contract or explicit rule, but rather in the sense of a *common context:* a set of points of reference which goes beyond the actors as individuals but which they nonetheless build and understand in the course of their actions. These points of reference for evaluating a situation and coordinating with other actors are essentially established by *conventions* between persons. Conventions emerge both as responses to and as definitions of uncertainty; they are attempts to order the economic process in a way that allows production and exchange to take place according to expectations which define efficiency. Conventions resemble "hypotheses" formulated by persons with respect to the relationship between their actions and the actions of those on whom they must depend to realize a goal. When interactions are reproduced again and again in similar situations, and when particular courses of action have proved successful, they become incorporated in routines and we then tend to forget their initially hypothetical character. Conventions thus become an intimate part of the history incorporated in behaviors.

The formal notion of convention as elaborated by David Lewis[38] is as follows:

A regularity, R, in the behavior of members of a population P, when they act in a recurrent situation, S, is a convention, if and only if, for each example of S, for the members of P:
Each conforms to R;
Each anticipates that all others will conform to R;
Each prefers to conform to R on the condition that others do so.
Since S is a problem of coordination, the general conformity to R results in a coordination equilibrium.[39]

Lewis's definition shows us that coordination by convention may develop between members of a defined population and in light of a common objective. It supposes also that each identifies, at least for herself or himself, R as a regularity, as well as the nature of the situations S, their recurrent character, and the relationship between S and R.

The word "convention" is commonly understood to suggest at one and the same time: a rule which is taken for granted and to which everybody submits without reflection, the result of an agreement (a contract), or even a founding moment (such as the Constitutional Convention). Thus convention refers to the simultaneous presence of these three dimensions: (a) rules of spontaneous individual action, (b) constructing agreements between persons, and (c) institutions in situations of collective action; each has a different spatio-temporal extent, and they overlap in complex ways at any given moment in any given situation. In practice, it is only by initially *assuming* the existence of a common context and by formulating expectations with respect to the actions of others that it is possible to engage in coordinated collective action: these are the dimensions of inherited, *longue durée* conventions, some of which take the form of formal institutions and rules. But at any given moment, the context is evaluated and re-evaluated, reinterpreted, by the individual who must choose to practice or not practice according to a given convention. Common contexts are therefore not the same things as norms or structures, and the points of reference thus do not appear as results of the encompassing social order, but rather through the built-up coordination of situations and the ongoing resolution of differences of interpretation into new or modified common contexts of action.[40]

THE EMERGENCE AND EVOLUTION OF CONVENTIONS

A theory of collective action rooted in convention offers the potential for a richer analysis than orthodox approaches precisely because it accepts as central the tension between action and structure that people live with in the course of ordinary economic life. This is far from both a neoclassical conception of contract (in which two individuals endowed with equal optimizing rationality execute a complete contingent claims contract) and from its sociological opposite, which sees agreement as the result of persons submitting to exogenous norms (social institutions, laws, and so forth). We choose to explore a theory which maintains the tension between these two extremes.

There are critical differences between our analysis of convention and the way Lewis and other analytical philosophers deploy it. Convention does not emerge automatically under specific external conditions, in "a given situation," such that whenever such a situation exists, the convention will be found.[41] A situation may itself be identified (interpreted) in many different ways, and thus it may lead to quite different actions from one moment to another. It follows that coordination among actors depends not on correct application of unambiguous decision rules, but on interpretation in the course of action. Even though in daily life we proceed *as if* certain things were agreed upon, there is no structural guarantee of this.

Our conception differs from that which can be found in much contemporary game theory as well.[42] The assumptions necessary to do game-theoretic analysis are too restrictive, the definition of the actor's "interest" typically too narrow and the role of interest too preponderant, and the equilibrium solutions are too far from reality, as well as having too great a role in determining the questions which can be asked.

As noted, conventions emerge as something like rebuttable hypotheses put forward by actors, which then become second nature through practice. They are subject to many possible sources of change, ranging from their failure in the face of external tests to a reinterpretation of circumstances by actors themselves. The microanalytics of the emergence and evolution of conventions is one of the most complex and challenging areas of the social science of conventions, and we do not advance a complete theory in this book. The history, negotiation, and evolution of conventions may be found in the empirical material in this book, as well as in several analytical generalizations we make about transformation of conventions.

THE ECONOMY AS A HYBRID OBJECT

The processes by which actors interpret their situations and then enter into pragmatic forms of coordination with other actors constitute the work of constructing the economy. Actors select and build meaningful courses of action in production by engendering routinized, largely implicit forms of coordination, which we call conventions. It is in generating conventions, and then drawing on them in practical activity, that the creative, out-of-equilibrium pathways of development are constructed. There is a great diversity of possible conventions for organizing productive activity, and also a great diversity of possible, conventionally agreed-upon economic tests of whether an activity is economically viable or "efficient."

Thus, in the economy, in production itself, actors contribute to determining the very "structure" in which they work. To say this is in no way to diminish the importance of structure, for the agency to which we refer is also socially structured. The choices of individuals "are systematically oriented by mental and corporeal schema resulting from the internalization of objective patterns of their extant social environment."[43] In a given pragmatic situation of productive activity, the objects, information, and previous expectations of actors tend to guide or channel such actions. The point, then, is that both structures and agencies are *social constructions*, both objectified in things, people, and routines. Seeking deep structure independent of agency is pointless; seeking true human freedom independent of structure is equally fruitless. Production systems and whole economies are constructed fields in this sense, fields with no a priori borders between laws and freedom, but only construction of both the kinds of laws which do exist and the kinds of human action undertaken. We shall show that in modern economies the concrete forms of "laws" vary enormously from product to product and place to place, according to the ways actors interpret the uncertainty they face and coordinate with others in order to resolve it. This action, the fundamental action in an economy, involves ceding autonomy to a social process—which is the creation of conventions.

In defining what pragmatic problem they face, and in resolving uncertainty through interpretative effort, there is little reason to believe that actors see a clear separation between the economic and non-economic dimensions. Such separations could be achieved and believed in as matters of particular doctrines or conventions, and then appear as necessary preconditions of economic efficiency (as in the case of liberalism). But this is a particular and not a general case; in many cases, we shall see that efficient economic coordination requires an *absence* of such separation and the coherence of multiple—"economic" and "non-economic"—dimensions of action.[44] It is in this sense that we reformulate the question of politics, culture, and institutions in relation to economics. In the end, the object of economic analysis, as for all social analysis, is a hybrid in which categories of action and structure, in this case the non-economic and the economic, disappear into fields of constructed objects and routines. Production systems and economies are such hybrid objects.

Possible Worlds of Production: Frameworks of Collective Action

The subject of our pragmatics is productive activity; its key dimensions are such things as technology, tools of work, work activity, and markets, for each specific type of product. Because these pragmatic dimensions of action are extremely heterogeneous, and because their successful coordination involves interpretation, precedent, and convention, it follows that there are multiple forms of efficient economic coherence for production systems, but that the possibilities for a given pragmatic situation are limited to coherent patterns of coordination or agreement.[45] We call these patterns "possible worlds of production."

A possible world of production constitutes for economic actors (individuals and firms) the expected coordination of activities in production and exchange, where the expectations are the result of convention, which is in turn rooted in recurrence or precedent. The common context of each possible world of production—that set of points of reference defined by convention—is thus a *framework of foreseeable action* for an economic actor.[46]

We see a multiplicity of worlds of production, a view based on the existence, for individuals, of different frameworks of action associated with the diverse product qualities of a complex modern economy, and the ways these frameworks permit the coordination of varying mixtures of human and physical resources for such products. Approaching production as a problem of collective action frameworks enables us to account, positively, for diversity, unevenness, and complexity in modern economies.

Here, in brief, are the worlds of production in terms of the types of products and their associated elementary frameworks of action.

The Interpersonal World is one of specialized and dedicated products, that is, products made according to the desires of the buyers. In this world, relationships between buyers and producers rest on conventions of confidence, reputation, and specificity of image; competition between producers centers on product quality. Contemporary examples of this are fashion-, design-, and craft-intensive industries,[47] and more generally, certain manufactures which are services-intensive. In the seventeenth, eighteenth, and nineteenth centuries, this world was represented by thousands of urban craft communities. It has had a certain resurgence of late, and we shall try to ascertain its possibilities, limits, and characteristics.

The Market World is that of standardized but now differentiated (what we call "dedicated") products. The user (that is, buyer) defines his particular needs in the universalizing language of standardization, so these needs can be translated into objective, codified norms. Competition between those producers who can respond to the demand, often relatively few in number, turns on price and rapidity of response. Conventions reduce each individual to an objective interest-seeker; each individual is thus socially constructed as being rational and opportunistic in the ways normally defined by economic theory. But rather than assuming these behaviors to be universal, we show how they are tied to the particular construction of this possible world, with only limited and contingent application in space and time. The contemporary restructured and flexible firm is close to this possible world today; historical examples include the industrial merchant of the nineteenth century who had at his disposition a network of home-workers.

The Industrial World is familiar to us as the world of mass production. Its internal crises and its difficulties with respect to other worlds have been unfolding since the early 1970s. As in the Market World, outputs of this world are the results of conventions, which define products as interchange-able objects for the consumer via objective codified norms for producers. Unlike that world, however, its products have broad rather than particular markets. Generic uses for standardized outputs allow firms to plan for the medium term, and to optimize short-run use of resources. In contrast to much economic thinking, however, we see this form of economic coordina-tion via the mediation of objects as just one of many forms of efficiency, not the culmination of all modern economic practice.

The World of Intellectual Resources is the world of creation: new technologies are created in a multiplicity of forms, including new materi-als, new production methods, and entirely new kinds of products. The key dynamic of this world is to take a specific kind of knowledge and make it generic, in the sense of widely applicable; the tension between novelty and acceptance is central. Conventions coordinate actors via scientific and professional rules.

Real Worlds of Production

All production must, in reality, survive a test of economic coherence. For contemporary advanced (that is, high wage and high cost) economies, such coherence is more and more attributable to their ability continuously to reinvent, differentiate, and reconfigure products so as to place themselves at the technological frontier (in the sense of product qualities, which they may also be responsible for defining) in a given sector. Coherence, in this sense, means creating the absolute advantages that propel economic spe-cialization. We define the systems of productive activity that succeed in doing this as "real worlds of production."

This "test" of coherence is neither fully endogenous nor mechanically exogenous, but a complex articulation of the two, of action and structure. In real worlds of production, firms and other actors have succeeded in constructing forms of coordination which allow them to generate a pathway of ongoing development of product qualities. Not all economic tissues are real worlds of production; many production systems have a lesser status—they are composite groups of resources and actions which do not reflect a *common existence* for their actors. These mere juxtapositions of resources have economic performance which is inferior to that of real worlds of production.

Two criteria for identifying real worlds are explored in this book. For the firm, profitability is the essential measure of performance. Profitability is both an endogenous and an exogenous criterion; and its composition differs from one world to another, as the objective pragmatic constraints differ from product to product. As a result, there are durable profit rate differentials in the modern economy, and these are the endogenous dimensions of profitability. Within any domain of activity, however, external circumstances dictate profit rate norms, and successful firms show the way to the best possible composition of profitability in that world; these are external dimensions of profitability.

The second criterion for identifying real worlds of production is international market share for traded products. As noted earlier, in a global economy, increasing specialization due to absolute advantage revolves around the endogenous innovative power of particular firms, and of national or regional production systems. But such power is subject to a test, and that is, fundamentally, their share of international markets over the medium run.

The possibilities of constructing real worlds of production based principally on products of the Industrial World have receded in recent years, precisely because of the essentially imitatable and diffusible qualities of those products. They have not disappeared—certain firms and nations have realized growing employment and market share in products of this world—but their situation has become structurally much more difficult. By contrast, real worlds of production based more on the Interpersonal, Intellectual, and Market World action frameworks present regional and national economies with increased possibilities for economic growth in the context of growing global interdependence, offering economic actors the possibility of constructing economic identities which position them favorably in the world economy.

By characterizing the problem of successful economic development as one of coordinating action frameworks in the form of real worlds of production, we mean to redefine the question of competitiveness. There are many routes to success, and unified theories of competitiveness (as we shall show in Part III) cannot account for this diversity.

GETTING INTO REAL WORLDS: PARTICIPATION AND IDENTITY

What makes real worlds of production develop? And why are different real worlds present in different nations and regions, often in similar product markets? Why are individuals and collectivities motivated to generate, for themselves, particular competences: what frameworks constrain their actions? What competences and precedents provide access to certain worlds and not to others, make certain worlds coherent and others incoherent? Additional conventions define the economic environment of specific places: conventions of *identity* and *participation*.

Conventions of identity refer to the taken-for-granted roles assigned to certain people by others in the context of productive activity; such conventions aggregate people into economic groups. We can draw from Gadamer's definition of hermeneutics to explain the notion of identity as a convention. A convention of identity is somewhat like sedimented significations regarding the competences and characteristics of groups of people—that is, cast in terms of external qualities or reference points used by others to form expectations about their abilities and behaviors. They are like hypotheses: new reflections based on past experience, where in each new situation we attempt to categorize according to precedent. The hypothesis is routine, but it is falsifiable.

Conventions of participation refer to the ways in which people thus identified conventionally interact. Participation refers to the roles, legitimate scope of action, and forms of action that each group is normally expected to have in its interaction with other, identified groups in the economy. This is a vast subject, much studied in the social sciences. Recasting participation as a convention, however, provides new insights into the variety of routinized ways actors are brought together into productive activity, and shows how they live this interaction as a set of expectations about their own behavior and about the reactions of other groups in a given pragmatic situation. We shall argue (in Chapter 9) that the importance of identity and participation is that together they confer or deny access to different frameworks of action and coordination.

Patterns of participation in real worlds also involve coordination among actors within often intricate technical divisions of labor inside firms and complex social divisions of labor between firms, through input-output relations as well as untraded interdependencies. Such participation relationships frequently involve the coordination of actors in different elementary action frameworks, different possible worlds of production. This is why the construction of a real world is difficult, but it is also why real worlds frequently involve positive spillover effects on their economies, as the conventions of identity and participation apply to groups of firms inserted into many different commodity chains. Real worlds rarely involve single "champion" firms, although such firms may play important roles. The analysis of real worlds of production thus takes place at the level of the *branch* of production (that is, a coherent "space" of productive activity, sometimes involving parts of several industries), not at the level of individual firms or establishments. Firms are important organizations within these tissues, but there is no reason to make the firm the central focus of economic analysis.

Plan of the Book

Our aim is to characterize possible worlds of production in an analytical way and then to show how firms, industries, regions, and nations combine different possible worlds into real worlds, according to their conventional competences. Chapters 2 and 3 are devoted to theory. They construct the four worlds of production in detail, showing the possible forms of coordination between persons, types of products, elementary frameworks of action, forms of uncertainty which actors confront. They define, for each possible world, the nature of production models of firms and their labor conventions, and the particular problems of innovation. Chapter 4 shows how worlds of production can be measured, and thus how our theory can be made empirically tractable. A sample of French firms in the 1980s reveals a variety of restructuring tendencies with a general movement away from the Industrial World into the other worlds of production.

Part II of the book, Chapters 5 through 9, sets the theoretical framework into motion with studies of production systems in France, the United States, and Italy. The emerging specializations of these countries are very different from one another, and this heterogeneity can be traced, at least in part, to their self-selection into different real worlds in the 1980s, based on their particular configurations of production conventions, resource mobilization, and the participation and identity of key groups of actors.

Part III examines institutions, the State, and public policies in light of the theory of worlds of production. In Chapter 10 we argue that the State is basically a convention for the citizens of each nation, and that the possible kinds of policies the State can implement, as well as their prospects for success, are tied into conventional expectations of the State as an actor in each economic context. If the development of real worlds of production is given priority, then both the traditional European conception of the interventionist State and the Anglo-American focus on "states versus markets" must be seriously questioned. This chapter also offers a critique of contemporary theories of competitiveness in light of the theory of the economy as a collection of action frameworks. Chapter 11 explores economic policies based on the notions of autonomy, plurality, and decentralization—policies "situated" in contexts of action. But policies called for by contemporary institutionalism, which emphasize contracting rules and debureaucratization, must also be questioned. In Chapter 12 we define the policy problems faced by the real worlds of production studied in this book and argue that we need policies situated in possible and real action frameworks, used by participants in economic life, rather than a new unified model of growth. Such policies could complement the resources present and desired by these participants, enabling them to transform resources, on an ongoing basis, into a diversity of real worlds of production.

Part IV returns to theory. Chapter 13 examines the theoretical foundations of economic development which follow from the New Institutional Economics and contemporary Institutional Analysis, to show that, although they open up extremely interesting questions, they lack a substantively defensible theory of economic life. In Chapter 14 we outline a research program on conventions, action frameworks, and institutions.

As noted, one of our major concerns is the history, negotiation, and evolution of conventions, a concern that is found throughout the book. The history and emergence of conventions are recounted in case studies of worlds of production, which can be found in Chapters 6, 7, and 8. Subsequently, in Chapter 11, there is a detailed study of the formation, renegotiation, and consolidation of labor conventions in twentieth-century France. In Chapter 9 we describe patterns of change observed in our case studies and make some analytical generalizations about pathways of transformation of conventions in production systems. Finally, Chapter 14 sets out categories of action, and the selection and feedback relationships which influence the emergence and change of conventions.

2

POSSIBLE WORLDS OF PRODUCTION

An Unorthodox Approach to Economic Organization

In this chapter we define four possible worlds of production, frameworks of action in which producers and users of products are inscribed and which permit them to coordinate their activities in an economically successful way. In the process of producing and exchanging, each person confronts uncertainty with respect to his or her own actions and those of others. This uncertainty takes radically different forms for each type of product, posing different dilemmas for actors with respect to others, but it must be resolved for production to succeed. This means that, for a given type of product, each actor must have the particular competence and resources needed to get around uncertainty by acting in ways expected and understood by others involved in the same productive effort. The result is a process of economic coordination.

In more concrete terms, each world of production is distinguished by fundamentally different routines for abating uncertainty; hence each world is organized according to different principles rather than by a set of choices founded on a single principle of optimization, as in orthodox theory. This framework of action is not necessarily a shared set of interests: we can differ in interests but still expect others to act in a certain way and can ourselves act according to mutually established guidelines in meeting their expectations.

Notice that we do not define a world in terms of the standard trade-off between structure and action, but as both the observable routines and the cognitive framework; this is because each world is continuously evaluated, interpreted, and reconstructed by its actors. Further, the conventions which make up the framework of action are not norms. We call certain worlds "possible" because they are ideal types of coherent action frameworks for the basic kinds of products found in a modern industrial economy. By ideal types, we mean that they express, in theoretical terms, the pragmatic coherence sought by actors themselves. We identify only four such worlds, and not five, six, or an infinity, because the basic dimensions of production pragmatics yield these four basic situations for economic actors. Later we will show that these action frameworks can be combined and syncretized in complex ways.

Forms of Economic Coordination

All economic theory turns essentially, if implicitly, on the problem of coordinating actors, and on the requirements for and consequences of different forms of coordination. In orthodox theory, coordination is essentially considered a problem facing the producer. It is most often treated in terms of price-setting under perfect competition; even in situations of imperfect competition, the question is whether rational action leads to market clearing, which is supposed to occur in the presence of appropriate or complete information. Though orthodox theory sometimes distinguishes between contexts of market certainty and those of uncertainty, it does not appreciate the possible diversity of relationships between producers and markets. Elements of just such a reflection, largely ignored today, may be found in Knight.[1]

THE MARKET: RISK VERSUS UNCERTAINTY

In terms of its impact on economic coordination, the market can be considered as a temporal structure of anticipations which guide production and investment decisions. All markets have fluctuations in demand involving both quantities and qualities of products. The problem for actors is to characterize these fluctuations for themselves in a way that allows them to act. Knight distinguished between uncertainty and risk:

> We may use the term "risk" to designate measurable uncertainty and the term "uncertainty" for unmeasurable uncertainty . . . The practical difference between the two categories risk and uncertainty is that in the former, the distribution of the outcome in a group of instances is known (either through calculation a priori or from statistics of past experience) while in the case of uncertainty this is not true, the reason being in general that it is impossible to form a group of instances, because the situation dealt with is in a high degree unique.[2]

27

In a world filled with objects or persons too numerous to be known individually, constructing a workable knowledge of some portion of the world requires concepts for identifying similar things, that is, things which have an invariant identity and always behave in the same fashion over time or in different circumstances. This is called "consolidation."[3] Consolidation means classification: we infer, on the basis of similarities observed in their behaviors, that certain objects or persons will behave similarly in ways which are not immediately observable. The producer who consolidates individual demands characterizes market fluctuations differently from one who does not: if consolidation is the strategy, then the producer adds individual demands together, estimates a mean and deviations from that mean, and so transforms fluctuations into probabilistic risks. These figures can then be incorporated in medium- and long-term forecasts and medium-term investment programs, and coupled to short-term adjustments. "Risk" and "certainty" belong to the same family of circumstances: certainty is merely one particular form of predictability and risk another.

Consolidation is impossible, however, in a context of true uncertainty. In such a case, the producer must limit the irreversibility of its investment: short-term adjustments have no medium-term guide, as they do with risk; there is no way to define the upper and lower bounds of adjustments that might be needed. Thus the producer must attempt to keep future options open, in terms of both qualities and quantities of output (and therefore in terms of production process and technology).

The same set of circumstances can be examined from the standpoint of the consumer's action framework. Consolidation is for Knight a manifestation that

> the primary phase of economic organization is the production of goods for a *general* market and not upon direct order of the consumer. But the consumer does not even contract for his goods in advance, generally speaking . . . The main reason is that he does not know what he will want, and how much, and how badly; consequently, he leaves it to producers to create goods and hold them ready for his decision when the time comes. The clue to the apparent paradox is, of course, the "law of large numbers," the consolidation of risks (or uncertainties). The consumer is, to himself, only one; to the producer he is a mere multitude in which *individuality* is lost. It turns out that an outsider can *foresee* the wants of a multitude with

more ease and accuracy than an individual can attain with respect of his own.[4]

Consolidation is thus a convention which corresponds to what we will call, following Knight, *generic* products. These are defined in advance by the producer without considering the consumers as individuals. This does not mean that consumers' needs are ignored, but simply that these needs are defined in a particular way. As Knight puts it, they disappear within the multitude of demands, where all individuality is lost. At the opposite extreme are products defined by a convention in which each demand is unique for the producer, not comparable to any other. For each individual demand, there is a particular product; such a product is *dedicated*. These two conventions also operate for the consumer (demander): in a world of generic products, consumers search the market for products that satisfy their demands without directly contacting particular producers, since the products available are conceived for a multitude; among products of similar quality, they will choose according to price. In a world of dedicated products, however, the consumer is uncertain: is there, somewhere, a producer able to satisfy the consumer's demands? In these highly individualized exchanges, the quality of the product, not only its price, is central.

We now have the first conventional criterion for separating action frameworks: those in which producers classify similar demands and consolidate them, and those in which they do not. Such distinctions are not automatically imposed by an external, objective reality; markets are—at least in part—constructed by the actors themselves, in an evolutionary process involving product design, production technique, and the social construction of consumers' rationalities, habits, and identities.

To head off any possible confusion, we should make it clear that we use the terms "generic" or "dedicated" to refer to the product-market relationship, not to the more common distinction between "general-purpose" or "dedicated" production equipment. For example, a generic product is often produced with dedicated equipment, but it has wide or generic applications in markets. A dedicated product, on the other hand, is dedicated to the consumer's specific needs.

PRODUCTIVE ACTION: SPECIALIZATION VERSUS STANDARDIZATION

The problem of defining frameworks exists also with respect to critical resource inputs to production. At one extreme, each human or material input is unique; at the other extreme, these inputs are identical and interchangeable. The first principle is *specialization* of resources; the second is *standardization*.

Specialization is considered in the literature as the counterpart of unique personal knowledge; as Polanyi put it, "a personal knowledge like industrial arts, craftsmanship in which skills are so embedded in the experienced workforce that they can be known or inferred by others only with great difficulty, if at all."[5] This is also what Marschak refers to as "idiosyncratic assets," which he contrasts to standardized goods: "There exist almost unique, irreplaceable research workers, teachers, administrators: just as there exist unique choice locations for plants and harbors. The problem of unique or imperfectly standardized goods . . . has been neglected."[6] For the employer, the concept of idiosyncratic tasks, utilized by Alfred Marshall, is tied to the existence of quasi-rents which make price formation less dependent on production costs.[7] That is, when products incorporate specialized assets, the market provides them not merely a payment or normal return, but a quasi-rent consolidation, as the "main principle for dealing with uncertainty." The advantage, from the standpoint of economic organization, is that "the specialist knows more about the problems with which he deals than would a venturer who dealt with them only occasionally."[8] Uncertainty is reduced when the quality of judgment improves; collective uncertainty is reduced when certain persons accumulate knowledge in areas unknown to or uncertain for other persons. Thus, Knight suggests that the confidence we place in specialists is a central element in economic coordination.

The fact that individuals are unique means that we cannot know their competences, and hence cannot be certain about their future behavior. In other words, this uncertainty stems from individuality within the necessarily collective activity of production. One person's specialization may be recognized as valuable in a given situation, but to gain access to this utility, that person must be treated as an individual, and not as an object or an interchangeable actor; communication is essential in order to understand the value of the specialist's "mysteries." Hayek called this initial lack of information and the effort to overcome it "the only interesting dimension of economic organization."[9]

When a convention of specialization is in use, work activity, the tools and objects upon which it depends, and the product are all strongly identified with persons—a given individual or a specific type of worker, skill, or production community.[10] With standardization, in contrast, organization is founded on eliminating the idiosyncratic character of activity and of individual competences. The product must owe nothing to its makers' individuality or personalities; it is defined by its general, objective characteristics. As with consolidation, standardization creates equivalence: between individual work actions, between individuals in the same line of work, or between different work situations having as their outcome the same kind of product. A convention of standardization thus makes possible interchangeable and reproducible resources, as when the labor process is broken down into elementary tasks or a product is assembled from components or modules. It was Taylor, of course, who built the most elaborate theory of work equivalence through standardization of tasks, but he erred in elevating it to the status of a teleology of economic life.

Coordination between consumers and producers also differs according to these two conventions. For example, the producer-consumer relationship is entirely different when buying a car than when remodeling a kitchen. In a world of standardized products, the consumer considers all producers making the same standardized product as roughly equivalent; in a world of specialized products, however, the consumer has a kind of ex ante uncertainty with respect to the different producers' products: an uncertainty about whether he has correctly identified his own needs and about whether the product ordered will satisfy them.

TECHNOLOGICAL PRINCIPLES: ECONOMIES OF
SCALE VERSUS ECONOMIES OF SCOPE-VARIETY

Industrial economics tends to see the problem of coordination as a problem of technology: every product with its associated production process has definite technological contours. Manufacturing an automobile dashboard is different from making a transmission, and their technologies confer a particular character on each production process. Technology here means not just the development of general knowledge, but also forms of specific know-how (often called "technique"—in standard economics, the choice along an isoquant);[11] it is also inseparable from the conventions which make it possible to embody knowledge in technique, in the coordinated forms of rules, equipment, and products.

The two conventions which link the product to its market, which we have named standardization or specialization, correspond to two classical images of technology in industrial economics: economies of scale and economies of variety.

The scale of production reflects the possibilities for standardization, and most high-scale technologies resemble one another in a number of ways (they tend to be capital-intensive and incorporate high levels of automation, for example), as do low-scale technologies (which have a low level of capital intensity and do not lend themselves readily to automation). High-scale production is associated with long series, designed to reduce unit costs of standardized products subject to strong price competition. To change product design in this organizational context implies heavy capital investment, and the nature of the equipment used requires that the idiosyncrasy of work activity be reduced to a minimum; hence the workers' personal identities become unimportant.[12]

"Economies of variety" refers to the range of products within a given production unit. In general, there is an inverse relation between the variety of products and the ease of standardizing or automating the production process.[13] Though the question has been little studied, it seems clear that there is a direct, close relationship between specialization of persons as an organizational principle and economies of variety as a technological principle.[14] The typical case here is the artisanal labor process which draws on a particular kind of "non-Smithian" know-how and turns out a family of specialized products, but economies of variety are also found in high technology industries or even in large firms seeking to differentiate and enlarge the range of their generic products.[15]

Four Possible Worlds of Production

FOUR COMBINATIONS OF CONVENTIONS

Each producer takes two elementary types of action: first, constructing the market (consolidation versus irreducible demands) and with it the choice of generic or dedicated product qualities; second, constructing the technology (scale versus variety) and with it the choice of standardized or specialized product qualities which reflect the kind of critical skills invested in production. This yields four possible combinations.

Figure 2.1 summarizes the four worlds, using the categories developed above.

The Industrial World. "Standardized-generic" products are conceived through the convention of consolidation, for a general market (one composed of undifferentiated demands), and fabricated according to a convention of standardization of critical resources and competences, which includes the labor process, technology, and the product itself.

The convention of standardization also coordinates producers and consumers. Producers compete on the basis of price; at any given moment, the consumer faces an established list of similar products, produced with interchangeable technologies. And a convention of standardization is also embodied for producers in the fixed character of their investments in

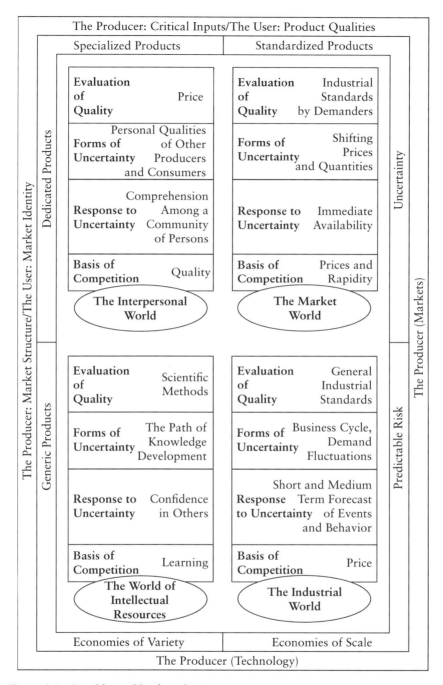

The Producer: Critical Inputs/The User: Product Qualities

	Specialized Products	Standardized Products	
Dedicated Products	**Evaluation of Quality** — Price	**Evaluation of Quality** — Industrial Standards by Demanders	Uncertainty
	Forms of Uncertainty — Personal Qualities of Other Producers and Consumers	**Forms of Uncertainty** — Shifting Prices and Quantities	
	Response to Uncertainty — Comprehension Among a Community of Persons	**Response to Uncertainty** — Immediate Availability	
	Basis of Competition — Quality	**Basis of Competition** — Prices and Rapidity	
	The Interpersonal World	The Market World	

The Producer: Market Structure/The User: Market Identity — The Producer (Markets)

	Specialized Products	Standardized Products	
Generic Products	**Evaluation of Quality** — Scientific Methods	**Evaluation of Quality** — General Industrial Standards	Predictable Risk
	Forms of Uncertainty — The Path of Knowledge Development	**Forms of Uncertainty** — Business Cycle, Demand Fluctuations	
	Response to Uncertainty — Confidence in Others	**Response to Uncertainty** — Short and Medium Term Forecast of Events and Behavior	
	Basis of Competition — Learning	**Basis of Competition** — Price	
	The World of Intellectual Resources	The Industrial World	

Economies of Variety	Economies of Scale

The Producer (Technology)

Figure 2.1   Possible worlds of production.

33

equipment. We call this the Industrial World because it corresponds to the mainstream image of modern business as it is constructed by industrial economists and business historians.[16]

In the Industrial World, fabrication of products rests on the social construction of uncertainty as predictable risk. Norms of product quality and production technology are codified. Production is organized around material objects (equipment, tools, production environments) designed to maximize economies of scale. Successful deployment of these instruments depends on routines such as risk management, production planning, widening of markets—and recourse to worker layoffs when such techniques miss their mark. Material objects have a particular "industrial" character: substitutability; that is, they may be transferred from one person to another, from one history to another, from one place to another. In other words, their particular character is to have no individual character. Think of a factory or an office situation in which established conventions are, to some extent, inscribed in the equipment present, the layout of the place, its work stations. This is one way to stabilize conventions of standardization. Each of us has an image of the assembly line where every worker must execute the same prescribed tasks in the same order: tighten this or that bolt, feed identical pieces at a certain pace and in a certain way into a given machine, and so on. This is far from being an instance of technological determinism; it is a way of acknowledging the power of convention to endow itself with a material reality.

In activities that depend on a great deal of equipment (objects), such as an automobile assembly line, the method itself is geared to make the individual worker unimportant. If a semi-skilled worker sometimes fails to carry out an assigned task in the division of labor as expected—forgetting to tighten a screw, say—it will not for the most part have any significant impact on the fundamental, "normal" qualities of the final product.[17] The line will continue to move; other workers will perform their tasks without considering themselves responsible for perceiving a problem. Instead, statistical quality control at the end of the line is supposed to recognize and eliminate these individual glitches. Obviously, there is a wide range of intermediate cases, including those in which the smallest defect means that a part will not fit (for example, in a high quality watch or in high technology manufacturing), but the nature of the objects is still impersonal. The presence of such objects does not completely eliminate uncertainty, but it does circumscribe the forms it can take.

The Market World. Certain products are made according to a convention of standardization, but each particular production run is dedicated to a specific client's demand. The convention of standardization is incorporated in the language clients use to define their particular demands; thus, even though two different clients will have different demands, they express them (construct them) in terms of combinations of standardized specifications of the available product, not in the language of uniqueness or customization inherent to artisanry.

By using the language of standardization, buyers in effect impose a "loss of personality" on producers. This permits buyers to avoid loyalty or commitment to producers and puts producers into competition with one another. Moreover, because buyers expect immediate satisfaction, that competition turns on both price and rapidity of response. The corollary of this product quality situation is the standard contractual relationship in which the two parties are reduced to their objective interests, and each one is rational and opportunistic as these terms are normally used in economic theory. For this reason, we call this realm of action the Market World.

In the Market World, it is the producer who faces uncertainty, constructed as an inability to predict the immediate future in terms of price and quantity of demand for a standardized product. Each person involved in the collective action is considered by others to be there in the moment: their common context is precisely that producers are available to respond immediately to buyers' desires and that buyers assume this is just what producers are there to do. They share the rationality of spot market relations, and this underlies their competence as actors in the Market World.

The Interpersonal World. Uncertainty reaches its extreme when there is no pre-existing external point of reference for evaluating product quality, but it must be established concretely between the parties to a transaction. This is the practice of the Interpersonal World. Examples of its products include machines designed to fabricate specialized products, craft- and design-based products, certain frontier segments of the high technology enterprises, and those parts of personal and business services requiring a high degree of attention to particular customer needs.

In this situation of interpersonal action, knowledge and preferences cannot be expressed in terms of codified norms. Orthodox approaches assume that this gives rise to "adverse selection" (as in the example of "lemons" given by Akerlof,[18] since buyers do not know how to determine the product's quality. Adverse selection does not come about, however, when neither producer nor consumer attempts to evaluate the other according to a general class of equivalent objects or agents, but instead works through direct mutual understanding. (Adverse selection is found principally in the Industrial World, and secondarily in the Market World.)

Uncertainty with respect to other actors requires understanding the meaning of actions taken or needs expressed. This communicational need[19] is progressively relieved as individuals acquire, through experience, something like a "common language" that can be pressed into service to define products and describe the nature of the others' actions. This common language allows people to learn specialized skills,[20] but acquiring these skills and their meanings are matters internal to a limited community. Marshall provided a now classic example of this with respect to "hereditary skills":

> When an industry has thus chosen a locality for itself, it is likely to stay there long: so great are the advantages which people following the same skilled trade get from their neighborhood to one another. The mysteries of trade become no mysteries; but are as it were in the air, and children learn many of them unconsciously. Good work is rightly appreciated, inventions and improvements in machinery, in processes and the general organization of the business have their merits promptly discussed: if one man starts a new idea, it is taken up by others and combined with suggestions of their own; and thus it becomes the source of further new ideas. And presently subsidiary trades grow up in the neighborhood, supplying it with implements and materials, organizing its traffic, and in many ways conducing to the economy of its materials.[21]

In the Interpersonal World, individuals know each other, and their histories, both individual and collective, are constituted as tradition. This tradition makes possible seemingly "spontaneous" actions. In simplistic notions of tradition, such interpersonal action is credited to the long duration of such interrelations or transactions. In contrast, in our view transactions may be short-term; when they are not repeated, new transactions form on the basis of pre-existing community-wide points of reference, standards, understandings; that is, on the basis of a common language.

Note the contrast: in the Industrial World, heavy fixed investments encourage a certain stability of relations, through internal labor markets (seniority systems),[22] but at base this internal market consists of a juxtaposition of interchangeable individuals within a bureaucratic structure. This is a far cry from the content-rich relations between persons that typify the Interpersonal World.

The World of Intellectual Resources. Specialized intellectual activity is designed to change the qualities of existing objects or services, develop new ones, or find new properties and uses for existing ones. We call this the World of Intellectual Resources. Intellectual action proceeds in a context of uncertainty with respect to the future, since no one is assured that the development and deployment of specialized knowledge will actually result in a product or whether this product will meet demand.[23] In other possible worlds, the final product's destination is known from the beginning of collective action, even if nothing guarantees that it will be fully successful. The situation in the World of Intellectual Resources is fully uncertain from the beginning.

Intellectual workers, too, attempt to apply a convention of consolidation to demands. To this end, they develop knowledge with general applicability, not simply uncodifiable practical know-how specialized to a given product or a given client; this is what differentiates their knowledge from that of the Interpersonal World. In effect, they invent qualities which can later be recognized by, and, if recognized, ultimately codified and imitated by others. The knowledge is thus made public, and the products become generic. To produce a novelty that has general utility it is necessary to develop and follow a codified method, such as the rules of science and professional norms (for example, doctors, lawyers, other professions). Actors in this world develop protocols and rules rather than simply inheriting them from the past or having them handed down by tradition (as in the Interpersonal World). These methods are continuously verified and adjusted by the actors themselves, in light of their ongoing experience; they form a paradigm (in the sense defined by Kuhn) embraced by the group, and each individual acts by drawing on the methodological conventions that constitute the paradigm. Confidence with respect to others is an adaptive form of behavior here, much more so than in the Interpersonal World.[24]

Major corporate R&D projects fall within this world—not only particular establishments or firms, but also the departments of firms otherwise in the Industrial and Market Worlds devoted to the search for new generic product qualities. Parts of the high technology sectors, especially those which recombine new technology- or science-intensive components, or specialized knowledge, to larger, more generic technological outputs, are also found in the Intellectual World.

THE NATURE OF A PRODUCT

The commodity, as Marx noted, is the material result of an extraordinarily complex ensemble of social processes. Marx was primarily interested in unveiling the creation of value hidden behind the production of objects;

we are more interested in the product as a concrete outcome of a complex network of relations between persons, reflecting their frameworks of action.

The precondition of coordination is that participants agree as to the qualities of products bought or sold. In the absence of such an agreement, the exchange cannot take place. By "qualities" we do not mean "good" or "bad" quality, but the fact that any exchange presupposes an agreement about what the product is. For example, consider a buyer who wants a product that responds to very particular demands (such as a specially designed component incorporating an unusual raw material) and a producer who offers only mass products designed to satisfy generic demands. Such products are not substitutable. The buyer needs a personalized product and a personalized relationship with the producer; that is the buyer's framework of action. The seller's anonymous product, in contrast, is produced by way of a different action framework. In such a situation, in general, there is a fundamental incompatibility between demand and supply, and no price change will satisfy the buyer. Quality is a convention in the sense that it is a datum constructed by producers and consumers; it is then known, recognized, and incorporated into the expectations of both parties.

Even if we follow Marx and the other classical economists in defining the product as the material representation of exchange values and use values, its material character is not strictly physical. It retains something of the persons who made it and those who consume it, by virtue of the relations they establish in order to produce and consume. Since such relations vary greatly from product to product, so the nature and extent of a given product's "personality" vary according to its world of production. The less specialized and dedicated the product, the more anonymous and substitutable, the less important are the specific personal identities of supplier and demander. Such a product is evaluated by objective methods; it becomes a mere quantity in a nomenclature of abstract qualities. The more specialized and dedicated the product, the more it looks like a specific service rendered by person A to person B, and the value of that service is intimately linked to precisely how person A's action is identified as meeting the needs of B. The individuality of persons in the economy is expressed most strongly in the specialized-dedicated products of the Interpersonal World, a world in which we may truly say that objects have "souls."[25]

In the Market World, products reflect a conception of the individual as a set of tastes and preferences that must be immediately satisfied. Contemporary organizational innovations designed to reduce the time needed to respond to a demand (just-in-time, flex time, and so forth) are based on this convention of availability. By contrast, the products of the Industrial World deny individuals any personal identity; the character of the product is closely related to its abstraction from any particular personality and to its purely physical dimensions.

Broadening the notion of product in this way renders superfluous the traditional opposition between products (the materialization of productive labor) and services (so-called "non-productive" labor). All products incorporate services, in the sense of relations between persons. The relevant distinction between products is between the worlds of production according to which they are produced, not their material content. This is why we use the term "product" and not "good," to signal that the target of economic analysis is the culmination of different forms of coordination between actors.

Pragmatics: Four Elementary Action Frameworks

The four frameworks of action are combinations of basic actions in production. In this elementary form, they are mutually exclusive: either one attempts to consolidate (to classify all demands according to known criteria) and to standardize (to classify all acts of work in forms of known equivalence, which we use to evaluate our own actions); or one considers the work of another, or one's own demand, as essentially unique (so production and consumption require mutual comprehension). Why are there just four elementary action frameworks, and not a hundred? There are epistemological, practical, and empirical answers to this question.

Scientific method since the time of Hobbes, Boyle, and Newton (among others) has enjoyed success by combining falsification and cumulation of knowledge in experimental situations. Scientific optimists, of whom the best known is Popper, like to claim that hypothetico-deductive science—the progressive refinement of hypotheses through deduction and evidence from what is already known—is sufficient to ensure both the exclusion of non-knowledge and the accumulation of new knowledge. But this positivism has not met the tests of either philosophers or historians of science. The philosophers point out, quite simply, that deduction, no matter how well practiced or how long the evidentiary trail, provides no basis for claiming complete coverage of a subject. There is no way to know whether the path being followed is the right one or the only one; we can only show that it is the wrong one, and even by demonstrating a multitude of wrong ones it is never possible to prove positively that the remaining, unfalsified, pathways are correct or valid or complete. For their part, historians show how the paradigmatic trap (the "hermeneutic circle") has limited investigation to what were ultimately wrong pathways in even the "hardest" and most empirically based of the physical sciences. Thus we may ultimately be able to falsify the postulated existence of the four possible worlds of production, but there is no method inherently capable of showing that they cover the terrain completely. (This, however, puts our theoretical exercise in the company of all science.)

The question then becomes whether the initial categories are plausible relative to our goal and whether they are completely deployed. The goal of this book is to explain productive activity. In this process we are committed to using theoretical categories which, while serving as abstractions, remain as close as possible to the categories actually employed by the relevant actors; that is, we want to avoid highly transformative categories. Moreover, we hold that the principle of theoretical parsimony is a good one: where possible, theories should aim for fewer rather than more categories, to the extent that this is possible without severing a recognizable connection to perceived, lived reality.

Obviously it is easier to state these as principles than to determine what they mean in the practice of theorization. Still, the starting points for our exercise—that each actor both faces uncertainty and actively perceives a need to coordinate with other persons in productive activity, and that the lived goal of that activity is to make and sell an output, a product, defined by its end uses and its critical inputs—fit our methodological commitments. They do this better than, say, standard approaches which reduce the product to highly abstract functions such as quantity and utility on the demand side, or standard approaches to coordination which reduce it to the deployment of universal, interest-based rationality under differing material circumstances. We think our starting points, in short, are closer to actors' lived reality than the standard starting points.

THE BOUNDARIES BETWEEN WORLDS

There are two main coordination problems/dilemmas attached to the two main dimensions of what a product is: how to get from the producer to different kinds of end users, and how to get the critical inputs required for a given kind of product. The actor trying to meet a certain kind of end use faces a certain kind of fluctuation of demand, predictable or not, amenable to consolidation or not. The actor trying to economize in securing critical inputs can try to standardize or to specialize them, a choice that leads to a technological strategy in production. Notice that we build up to the abstractions "markets" and "technologies" from interaction dilemmas as they would present themselves to economic actors, and we show that the interactions have different possible turning points—that is, different possible conventions can arise at each of several junctures—but that each choice leads to a particular kind of product and implies other, consistent choices or evolutions. This is, we would argue, how groups of actors actually develop their outputs: they are not controlled from above by mega-structures, but instead they act, and routinize their actions, according to this series of practical choices. Insofar as the actors' basic choices take the form of tradeoffs between consolidation and non-consolidation, or between specialization and standardization, four elementary frameworks of action emerge—and there are only four pure-form combinations of these action rules.

Do actors reason or choose along these lines, and not according to a greater or lesser number of variants? Perhaps the best way to illustrate this is to think in terms of an analogy to linguistic action, the mental processes which lie beneath "speech acts."[26] It is impossible to imagine reasoning simultaneously in terms of both consolidation and non-consolidation of the same demand; the same is true of specialization and standardization. As linguistic constructs (and hence, as resources for reasoning and calculation) they present themselves in terms of difference or opposition, and, for the moment, allow no alternatives. Hence, the two pairs are mutually exclusive, and there can be only four combinations.

In empirical terms, the story is more complicated. Each category can, in practice, have very different boundaries. For example, the limits to scale economies for producers in one industry may be very different from those in another, with a given level considered high for one industry but inadequate for another. But the principle of economies of scale cannot be mistaken for that of variety. It is possible, of course, that the efficient combination of many products would provide scale economies for a given firm or industry, but this in no way reduces the distinction between the category of action "scale" and the category of action "variety." One might ask if combining the two does not put us in the situation of having gone beyond the four possible worlds. The answer is no, because the elementary framework of action is deployed for each product. In operational terms, the economies which flow from deploying that framework are simply strengthened by the combination of scale resulting from variety.

Concrete products are, of course, frequently made within an elaborate division of labor in the economy. Moreover, there are many intermediate situations between dedication to one single demand and the anonymous market. Concrete products are thus frequently the result of variable combinations, or syncretism, of different frameworks of action; either persons who use different frameworks to make a product are brought together through the division of labor, or one individual uses different frameworks while acting in different situations. Real products may also reflect unresolved tensions between action frameworks due to defective coordination (this can lead to defective products or to poor firm or sector performance). Still, from the point of view of coordination, the concrete variety of products may be traced back to the matrix of basic frameworks which define possible worlds of production.

At present, then, we can identify four basic frameworks of action. But nothing in this theoretical exercise claims that the number four is eternal or even universal. Advances in technological possibilities could, in principle, efface the tradeoff between variety and scale and make possible a completely novel category of action. Perhaps there are unimagined possibilities for dealing with market fluctuations, or kinds of products, as yet uninvented, that go beyond known categories. Our theorizing is more genealogical than predictive; its deductions are outcomes of its inductions. That in our view is the way a good economic theory should be.

Summary of the Theoretical Framework

The discussion may now be summarized in the following terms:

(1) Many possible worlds of production exist, each centered on a certain type of product.

(2) Each possible world appears as a form of coordination between persons mobilized to realize the product: those who make it (workers; management) and those who utilize it (consumers; demanders).

(3) Each possible world is a conventional world. To be efficient, the coordination of individual actions must be inseparable from the coordination of anticipations. Both depend on conventions shared by persons in the same world. A convention is a system of mutual expectations with respect to the competences and behaviors of others. Conventions concern both the activity of work (production) and that of exchange; different worlds of production have different conventions.

(4) Each possible world of production is a world of objects. Actors are surrounded by objects in production activities (equipment, raw material, products in process, written rules) and by exchange activities (the product

exchanged, written rules, and so forth). They rely on these objects in order to act; thus, the objects are both resources and constraints. Actors are also engaged in transforming these objects.

These objects have different roles, capacities, and significations according to the world of production in which they are inserted. A system of machines, for example, may be reorganized to increase flexibility when a new product is introduced. The significance of an object for given actors and the use they make of it will also depend on the particular situation.

(5) Each possible world of production is a world of persons. Appropriate action within the collective context involves different requirements for each world and its products in terms of the particular knowledge actors must have of other persons. For example, verifying the quality of a pair of blue jeans requires only an occasional ex post inspection, but a firm that produces high-fashion clothing must have knowledge of (or the ability to predict or anticipate) the particular client's desires in terms of "fantasy." Not only must such a firm be attentive to the client's individual needs and ready to respond rapidly, but the client must also be ready to define those needs precisely. In short, two entirely different systems of expectations, appropriate actions, and coordination are involved.

(6) Actors generate conventions in the situations in which they find themselves. The course of collective action specific to the production and exchange of a certain product develops according to a process of learning which progressively modifies actions and anticipations, and allows each person to form an idea of the conventions in use for the particular situation. When a situation recurs and the actors see this, learning is a matter of recognizing what conventions are in use.

We will now leave the theoretical definition of possible worlds of production and illustrate what this approach contributes to understanding the organization of the firm, the economics of profitability, the use of labor, and the production of innovations.

3

FIRMS, PROFITS, WORK, AND INNOVATION

Firms do not directly choose a process of production or a kind of market; they choose the products which they believe will yield profits. In so doing, the firm must develop a "representation"—an image or idea—of what it can feasibly do to meet the technological demands of production and the financial and profitability constraints associated with a given product. We call this the firm's "model" of production: the set of routines, organizational structures, and operational principles which guide the firm from day to day and year to year.

This model of production is analytically distinct from a world of production. The latter describes the action framework itself. In addition, each possible world of production is manifested in and made functional by practices such as firms' organizational routines, strategies of profitability, ways to organize work activity and interact with the labor market, and pathways of technological innovation. The important point is that these observable dimensions of productive activity belong to, and are outcomes of, action frameworks, without which they make no sense to the actors involved.

One consequence of this view is that, in contrast to traditional industrial economics, we consider it doubtful that the firm is the basic unit of theoretical analysis.[1] In practical terms, the firm's boundaries are determined by the collection of products it makes; thus one way to restate the problem of determining the firm's boundaries, its horizons of control, is to consider them in terms of the problem of managing the combinations of worlds of production necessary for particular product mixes. We know relatively little about which such combinations are feasible. Each firm also participates in (intra- and inter-industry) divisions of labor, and in the process of regrouping certain pieces of the division of labor the firm becomes the site at which these productive activities are coordinated. The feasible boundaries of the firm, then, are determined in part by which action frameworks can be incorporated successfully within a single organization.

Models of Production: The Firm's Routines

In each world of production, the structures of expectation and action are oriented toward particular forms of efficiency. One critical form of efficiency is the flexibility characteristic of production routines for each world, which must be consistent with the economic fluctuations faced by actors within that world. Figure 3.1 shows the different kinds of external (market) and internal (organization of production) flexibilities associated with each model. The distinction between predictable and uncertain markets (corresponding to that between generic and dedicated products) allows us to distinguish the types of *external* flexibility the firm requires.

In the predictable situation (risk), the principal external unknown has to do with the quantity of output that can be sold. Firms in the Industrial and Intellectual Worlds try to anticipate the market by planning (using statistical estimates of risk, planning surplus capacity, market studies, and so forth) while at the same time cushioning unanticipated fluctuations by using networks of external suppliers.[2] In the case of uncertainty, the external unknown has to do with non-price dimensions of the product. Firms in the Market and Interpersonal Worlds are not so much concerned with estimating the risk of unsold quantities as with being sure that products have the qualities clients really want. Ideally, their method would develop or absorb the information required to refine product quality continuously. This in turn requires enough flexibility in resource use to allow the firm to bring together or hive off necessary factors of production as demand evolves.

The distinction between specialized and standardized products corresponds to different forms of internal flexibility. For firms in the Interpersonal and Intellectual Worlds, internal flexibility means deploying highly specialized competences in a narrow, but ever-changing, range of tasks and outputs. If production technology is sufficiently divisible, modular, and polyvalent, the resulting economies of variety reduce the irreversibility of investments in fixed capital and labor skills.[3] This sort of dynamic flexibility seeks to maximize the learning capacities of actors in the firm; when this learning can be cumulative, it eliminates the distinction between short- and long-term planning horizons found with standardized prod-

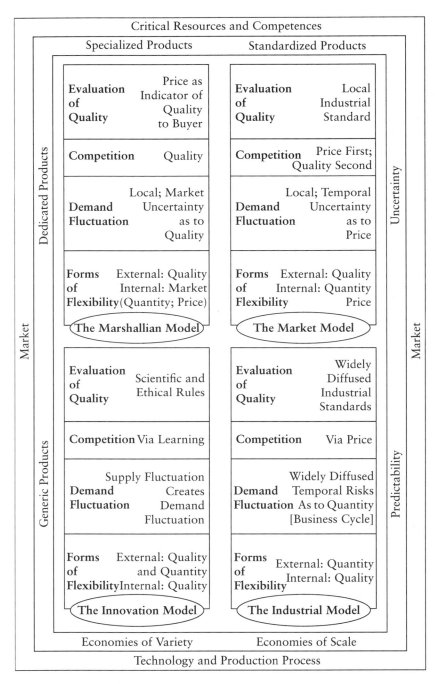

Figure 3.1 Models of production.

ucts.[4] Flexibility can take quantitative form as well, as the specialized firm or production unit tries to serve more and more extensive market territories, often through internationalization; however, this requires strong reputation effects to "attract" distant buyers.

In the Industrial and Market Worlds, with their standardized products, the firm is organized to adapt to active cost-price competition. Thus the most important conventions concern internal procedures for incorporating technological change, choosing external suppliers, and work rules to achieve economy of labor inputs. To achieve quantitative internal flexibility, the firm may also adopt a multi-product strategy and attempt to generate an ensemble of outputs with different, but complementary, market fluctuations.[5] It may also manage its relationship to the market by adjusting stocks.[6]

We now turn to a more detailed description of the basic routines corresponding to each world of production.

THE INDUSTRIAL MODEL

A standardized generic product has a wide, impersonal market governed by general industrial norms of quality; these norms are widely understood and apply to all products in a given category. Firms and production units look something like the firm-as-hierarchy (in contrast to the market) described by Coase.[7] Prices are rigid in the short term. In its formal planning process, the firm distinguishes between short- and long-term market fluctuations: such a distinction is a key convention of resource allocation in this model of production. Products are changed only over the long term; in the short term, the nature of the product is defined by the firm's heavy fixed investments in production technologies—in other words, a generic product is made with a dedicated, relatively inflexible, technology. Firms must make such irreversible investments in order to pursue economies of scale, because competition is centered on the prices of these substitutable products. This model of production corresponds closely to contemporary mass production.

THE MARKET MODEL

In the Market model the product is differentiated, but produced in series. Differentiation is a form of dedication to narrow market segments. Demand is limited in each segment to a certain number of clients—sometimes to a single client. The "local" nature of demand (that is, clients are known and specific, rather than anonymous) promotes incessant effort to follow the market very closely, yet, since key inputs are standardized, there is pressure to routinize production and competition tends to center on price. A tendency toward overproduction is enhanced by the use of scale economies to push costs down. To resolve these tensions, production units combine two very different forms of flexibility in resource use. Internal flexibility consists in fabricating a group of products that exploit (and are dedicated to) different market niches while planning for temporary capacity adjustments; units thus use somewhat oversized capital equipment. This is complemented by labor input flexibility (usually temporary workers and variable hours). In addition, capacity subcontracting permits firms to increase product differentiation, which in turn helps resolve the tensions between standardization and dedication.

Order-giving firms thus rely heavily on an input-output system consisting of many suppliers and subcontractors. The principal convention of this system is that each upstream firm must respond immediately to orders from downstream to allow for adjustments to demand without delay. Each agent adjusts to the impossibility of predicting the immediate future. We call this a market model because it involves relations which conform to the standard definition of the market: constant variations of prices and quantities. However, the situation lacks the principal characteristic of the neoclassical market: a large number of buyers and sellers. An input-output system based on anonymous inter-firm relations of that sort would be particularly subject to instability and to market failure in transactions, and in fact successful systems are often supported by non-market mechanisms, ties that bind the participants in input-output systems together more durably than pure spot market relations. They become *network markets*.[8]

THE MARSHALLIAN MARKET MODEL

In the Marshallian market model the firms or units engage in diversified quality production;[9] their specialized products serve individualized demands within families of products in volatile, variable markets. The problem facing the firm or production unit is to maintain contact with these particular client demands. Such firms try to develop routines to search for and find new clients; this is part of their external market flexibility. Once they make such contacts, however, uncertainty as to quality and price remains. Firms must therefore develop routines to communicate the qualities of their production to new clients. This means there is a need for a common language between producer and consumer, and a strong emphasis on cultivating relationships and maintaining loyalty. The common language may be based on strong community or kinship structures, which give "depth" to economic communication and allow for confidence in what is said. These non-market relations not only promote market contacts but also provide access to specialized inputs such as labor, in a context where high levels of turnover may be required.

These firms must also have a high degree of internal flexibility, to produce an extended family of products based on specialized technology and know-how, and adjust to a changing stream of outputs. Indeed, the high level of economies of variety impedes the development of economies of integration. Internal flexibility routines are extremely varied, but often include multi-skilling, polyvalence, fluid organizational structures, and the use of multi-purpose equipment and tools.

The appellation "Marshallian Market" for this model, which corresponds to the Interpersonal World, refers to the specialized, localized, and interpersonal relationships which are key to the transactions- and information-intensive characteristics of such production. Judgment of product quality in this model is reflected directly in the prices that products command, and firms often earn a sort of rent on their abilities. Different versions of this model may be found in flexibly specialized industrial districts in a number of regions in North America and Europe.[10]

THE INNOVATION MODEL

The unit or firm involved in making a specialized product intended for a generic market must cope with a special kind of uncertainty, one that concerns the design of the product itself as well as its eventual uses. Examples of such products include high technology outputs based on large investments in research and development: innovation presupposes the creation of new kinds of scientific and technical knowledge, yet activity must proceed in a reliable way. To this end, routines are based on rules of scientific method, which structure research and new product development, and define product quality. The knowledge created and mobilized in this model thus has less to do with secrets of fabrication (as in the Marshallian Market), and more to do with theories, concepts, and generalizable formal methods. These routines are used by intensive local interpersonal teams, by project-based organizations (within or between firms), and by far-flung professional-scientific "virtual communities." This model of innovation corresponds to the Intellectual World.

The precise ways in which such routines are organized have evolved rapidly in recent years. Whereas once the paradigmatic example of the

Innovation Model in the American economy would have been Bell Laboratories or the national laboratories, today it might be anything from Microsoft to the small entrepreneurial start-ups in high technology or biotechnology. In many ways, however, Microsoft now resembles Bell Laboratories in its bureaucratic mastery of the R&D-intensive product development and roll-out, though it operates under much more competitive conditions than Bell ever did it its heyday. Moreover, all the examples are organized to deploy scientific or theoretical knowledge to create generic-specialized outputs. What differs is how, over time and across different market segments, they are articulated with other parts of the firm and with the market, and the competitive selection effects thereof. Case studies of California and French high technology in Chapters 6 and 8 bring this out in more detail.

Note that the Marshallian and Innovation models of production depend to a greater extent on economies of variety than the Market and Industrial models, where economies of scale predominate. The Marshallian Market model includes both dynamic and static economies of variety, that is, at a given moment it has the capacity to produce a number of things using the same equipment; added together, they push the scale of production upward. In the Innovation model, by contrast, economies of variety are overwhelmingly dynamic, involving ongoing changeover of products, the fruit of a process of learning and innovation.[11]

Profitability in Each World

Under conditions of perfect competition, efficiency is the result of an economy of resource use achieved by minimizing costs, and the most efficient firm in this sense is the one that earns the highest revenue per unit of output. In reality, however, firms must navigate between multiple and sometimes conflicting influences to resolve the practical problems of production. As a result, cost minimization is not always the primary goal of all firms, even when "all other factors are considered equal."

Different product niches in the economy are connected to durable differences in profitability because firms pursue different forms of efficiency in response to different sets of possibilities and external constraints.[12] For example, firms that are highly involved in technological innovation seek quasi-rents rather than normal profits. From one product to another, qualitatively distinct resources are utilized in the search for efficiency (fixed capital, intermediate outputs, circulating capital such as stocks, commercial credits, labor of different qualities, and so forth). The importance of each type of resource varies according to the model of production adopted by the firm.

Firms have a wide latitude for "non-trivial" decisions with respect to their products and their investment strategies. But such decisions must be coherent and must pass a test of pragmatic realism within each world, in the sense that they compete with forms of economizing adopted by other firms making products with the same qualities. Both the logics of profitability and ways to pursue those logics differ for firms in different worlds. A low rate of profit (at least over the medium term) cannot be attributed to external causes beyond the firm's control (such as "worsening market conditions"), but rather reflects a faulty conceptualization of the firm's mission and unsatisfactory models of production. A lasting crisis in the rate of profit may mean that the firm is riven by tensions between different possible worlds.

DIFFERENT MODELS OF PROFITABILITY

Firms attempt to increase their profitability by selecting products with characteristics suited to two different "sites," the market and the production process. The market is where flows of short-term resources are optimized; the production process is where fixed assets are coordinated over the medium term. The two often tug in opposite directions. These are not simple "formal" quantitative forces; they are tensions that the firm actually encounters, and it must negotiate a satisfactory solution between them. The nature of that solution is particular to each model of production.[13]

In the Marshallian model, the need to economize on short-term capital commitments makes it difficult to increase capacity; producers must invest in specialized resources while maintaining a low capital-output ratio, and "cheap" increases in scope-variety are one way to do this. In the Industrial model, by contrast, the goal is to maximize capacity and its utilization, but this raises the cost of circulating capital, which can weigh down the profit rate. Firms therefore continually try to push down unit costs by means of standardization and scale, but this, too, is costly in terms of capital, which in turn causes firms to seek yet more standardization and greater scale economies. Use of low-cost capacity ("price squeeze") subcontracting may also figure prominently, if quality controls can be effective and transactions costs are manageable.

In the Market model, the capacity to respond rapidly to differentiated demands may carry a price premium, but insofar as uncertainty prevents full process standardization, labor costs occupy an important role in price. Moreover, since the product is standardized, competition on the supply side is stiff (generally, supply exceeds demand for intermediate outputs), and there is severe downward pressure on prices.

In the Innovation model, high value added and investment costs are likely to be reflected in high prices, but they also pull down per-unit margins. Labor and circulating capital costs are very high, as is the cost of specialized labor.

The two axes which define the models of production may be expressed in quantitative terms as variables which compose the rate of profit. Figure 3.2 offers two formulas for analyzing profitability: one in terms of the market, the other in terms of the production process. Both take as a starting point a rate of profitability defined in terms of gross profit as a percentage of both fixed and circulating capital.

The first way to analyze profitability emphasizes the market axis, that is, the choices made by firms guided by the market. If the market is relatively predictable, the firm's short-term management problem is to use product stocks and commercial debt to smooth fluctuations in demand around a central tendency. Management of stocks at different stages in the production process allows the firm to carry out long series production and thus benefit from scale economies. However, while long series production of generic products allows optimal capacity utilization, it also means low margins. If the market is relatively uncertain, by contrast, the firm must have the greatest possible short-term adjustment capacity, and this will tend to limit long-term financial commitments. The client demanding a service tailored to its needs—a dedicated product—tolerates the fact that the firm earns a higher margin, but the firm must learn to live with lower overall rates of capacity utilization.

The second formula analyzes profitability in terms of components of technology and the production process, that is, essentially in terms of choices of fixed capital and labor. Standardized products and economies of scale call for reducing unit costs; hence the firm's priorities are to reduce the share of labor costs in value-added, to substitute capital for labor, and to maximize labor productivity. With specialized products and economies of variety, in contrast, it is necessary to recognize the role of specialized labor and give priority to the use, development, and reproduction of various forms of know-how—labor is a specialized asset, sustained through investments in its quality. The share of labor costs is greater but, as a consequence, capital efficiency is higher than in the first case.

Figure 3.3 summarizes the interrelations of the different variables and their role in each model of production.

Maximization of the profit rate does not define a hierarchy of choices between models of production. Since all models are profitable if they are implemented in coherent fashion, profitability is not a positive guide to organizational choices or to movements from one world of production to another. However, a fall in profits is initially evaluated and interpreted for a given production unit (possibly for an entire firm) by the conventions of the world in which it is placed and not by those of other worlds.[14] In the Industrial World, for example, a fall in profits is "normally" dealt with by reducing labor costs, increasing the substitution of capital for labor, and trying to expand sales. These responses, internal to that world, should improve the profit rate, all other things being equal. But if competition has shifted to new product qualities, or to new technologies that depend on different principles of organization, work, and producer-buyer relations, this response will not succeed. In that situation, developing a new and efficient plan of action requires information about factors other than constituents of the rate of profit: external expertise, questioning accepted routines, using new kinds of material objects. It therefore requires employing different conventions. If these changes undermine the conventions of actors in the existing world, then incremental measures consistent with the internal logic of that world will not suffice to allow the firm to adapt to the new world where it must insert itself in order to survive. Thus the U.S. automobile industry long pursued adjustments within the Industrial World, yet saw profits and market share sink despite huge increases in hourly labor productivity. Not until they understood the need to upgrade product quality did the hemorrhaging stop. This change in product was not undertaken via the action framework of the Industrial World, but by drawing on the Market and Intellectual Worlds, an effort which met with huge resistance at all levels of the industry because it was inconsistent with the conventions in place. By the same token, typical policy incentives for industrial adaptation (such as small firm "modernization" programs) often fail to bring successful adjustment[15] because they cannot take the place of a substantive conception of the world into which the firm should go, nor show it how to get there.

Defining capital as including both fixed and circulating capital, the profitability of a firm may be shown as follows.

$$r = \frac{EBE}{K + AC + PC}$$

where:

EBE = total surplus or gross profit
K   = fixed capital
AC = active circulating capital
      (upstream, intermediate, and final stocks and short-term credit to clients)
PC = passive circulating capital (short-term credits from suppliers)

(1) One way to dissect profitability is in terms of the market, that is, the firm's choices of products and forms of organization are guided by market pressures.

$$r = \frac{EBE}{Q_v} \times \frac{\dfrac{Q_v}{Q_c}}{\dfrac{K}{Q_c} + \dfrac{AC - PC}{Q_v} \times \dfrac{Q_v}{Q_c}}$$

where:

Q_v = installed production capacity
Q_c = total sales

The ratios may be interpreted as follows:

$\dfrac{EBE}{Q_v}$ is the gross margin per unit sold;

$\dfrac{Q_v}{Q_c}$ is the rate of capacity utilization;

$\dfrac{K}{Q_c}$ is capital per unit of output;

$\dfrac{AC - PC}{Q_v}$ is the ratio of net circulating capital to sales.

The controlling variables are in this case gross margin per unit sold (EBE/Q_v); the rate of capacity utilization (Q_v/Q_c), as a measure of ability to adjust to short-term demand fluctuations; and the ratio of net circulating capital to sales ($AC - PC/Q_v$). Optimization in the market thus gives priority to flows, i.e., to management of the short-term.

Figure 3.2 Analysis of firm profitability and performance.

(2) A second set of formulas emphasizes the production process; in other words, it looks at profitability in terms of the optimal management of technology. In the first case, the firm chooses the productivity of labor as its measure of efficiency; in the second, it focuses on the efficiency of capital. Note that both forms of optimization place priority on stocks—on resources immobilized in equipment and labor force, that is, on the management of the medium-term.

The first formula is as follows:

$$(2a) \qquad r = \frac{\left(1 - \dfrac{LC}{VA}\right)\dfrac{VA}{N}}{\dfrac{K}{N} + \dfrac{AC - PC}{K}}$$

VA = value added
LC = labor costs (salaries and benefits)
N = number of workers

The firm using such a formulation will attempt to increase labor productivity (that is, value added per worker, VA/N) by substituting capital for labor (that is, increasing the K/N ratio) and by reducing labor costs per

The second formula is as follows:

$$(2b) \qquad r = \frac{\left(1 - \dfrac{LC}{VA}\right)\dfrac{VA}{K}}{1 + \dfrac{AC - PC}{K}}$$

Here, the firm's strategy is to maximize the efficiency of capital use, that is, to minimize the capital to output ratio. This implies production based on highly skilled labor—that is, investments in intangible resources destined to increase the quality and productivity of labor.

Figure 3.2   (continued)

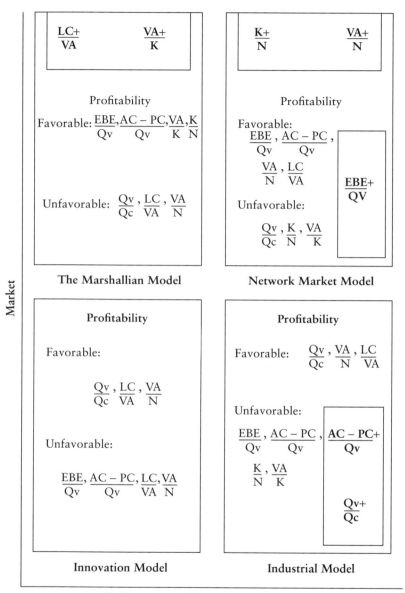

Figure 3.3 Economic ratios for each model, according to predicted influence on profitability. *Note:* Horizontal and vertical boxes indicate the relative values (plus or minus their mean) expected for economic ratios influencing profitability.

Labor Conventions: Productivity and Unemployment

The activity of work itself is filled with uncertainties similar to those attached to products in their markets. Each worker must cope with uncertainty in interpreting the acts of others. The particular uncertainty of interest here concerns the quality of work and level of effort of those others, which is the subject of an extensive literature.[16] This uncertainty appears because the worker is a person: Marshall, in 1890, identified this as the "singularity" of labor that distinguishes it from the other factors of production:

> . . . the fact that human agents of production are not bought and sold as machinery and other material agents of production are. The worker sells his work, but he himself remains his own property . . . When a person sells his services, he has to present himself where they are delivered. It matters nothing to the seller of bricks whether they are to be used in building a palace or a sewer: but it matters a great deal to the seller of labour, who undertakes to perform a task of given difficulty, whether or not the place in which it is to be done is a wholesome and pleasant place, and whether his associates will be such he cares to have. In those yearly hirings which still remain in some parts of England, the labourer inquires what sort of a temper his new employer has, quite as carefully as what rate of wages he pays.[17]

Put another way, every person is a human being with a biography which reflects context, idiosyncrasies, and distinct forms of knowledge. This means that every person's work actions are, to some degree, autonomous and unpredictable.[18] Since this inherent and pervasive uncertainty can only be resolved in productive activity by making a product, it follows that work activities are highly dependent on coordinated reciprocity.

Particular competences are necessary to identify the kind of reciprocity required in each world. Knight refers to several kinds of capacities which differentiate individuals at work, including the capacity to form correct judgments about the future course of events (an important element of which is being able to forecast the behavior of others); the ability to plan and make the adjustments required to stay ahead of an evolving situation; and having confidence in the judgment of certain persons and their ability to implement those judgments.[19]

The actual content of these particular competences varies according to the type of product at hand, but all are mobilized by the conventions of labor in each world. These allow the individuals involved in a given production context to form correct—not necessarily perfect—anticipations and enter into coordinated effort with fellow-workers. These conventions also constitute the basis for producing information and circulating it between persons in the work sector. Two key conventions of labor concern productivity levels and quantity of labor employed or unemployed.

The firm's model of production can only define an efficient action space if the workers' conventions of labor effectively lead to a sufficient level of productivity. A first labor convention, the *convention of productivity,* thus defines the worker's side of the bargain: in return for the assurance of being paid a wage, the worker will make concrete efforts to enable the product to succeed in market exchange. For workers, this convention resides in work routines, customs and traditions, the development of shared expectations, learning, and the transmission of skills; use of material objects (equipment, tools) and work rules contributes to the convention by encouraging and stabilizing certain behaviors.

Productivity standards are endogenous to possible worlds of production, so there are numerous conventions of productivity.[20] Yet there is no a priori certainty that such conventions will emerge; when distributional conflicts become prominent, as they did in the postwar United Kingdom, for example, no satisfactory convention may emerge and firms will suffer declining profitability—and, as a consequence, workers will suffer unemployment.[21]

The collective action process in production comes to an end only when the product is sold. Expectations held during fabrication are not met when no customers appear; firms have already paid out wages by that time, however. In the face of repeated unexpected external fluctuations, a second labor convention emerges, that of unemployment. This convention carries out ex post adjustments of expectations, modifying work time, the number of workers, and the total wage bill, without disrupting the convention of productivity for those who continue to work.

We now describe conventions of productivity and unemployment for four types of workers with very different identities owing to different action frameworks: the occupant of a work station in the Industrial World; the individual who is available to conform with the uncertain demands of the Market World; a member of a community of workers in the Interpersonal World; and the expert in the Intellectual World (see Figure 3.4).

	Interpersonal Labor	Intellectual Labor	Market Labor	Industrial Labor
Unknown Factor	Uncertainty as to Quality Demanded	Uncertainty as to the Future	Specific, Local Demand Uncertainty	Predictable Risk
Identity for Others	A Member of a Work Community	The Expert	Available, Autonomous Individual	Occupant of Work Station
Evaluation of Work Quality	Market Price of Product	Scientific and Ethical Standards	Availability	Job Description, Classification of Tasks
Wage	Individual, According to Output	Investment in Persons	By Task, By Time	Hourly Rates by Work Station
The Firm	Deliberate Grouping of Persons into Networks	Small Groups	Collection of Individual Agents	Internal Labor Market
Adjustment to Unknown Factors	Personal Responsibility	Development of Knowledge	Variability of Volume Work	Unemployment

Figure 3.4 Labor conventions of worlds of production.

Labor Conventions of the Industrial World

The Industrial World firm uses forecasts to interpret short-term economic fluctuations as deviations from a medium-term average and its trend line. Identifying such trends allows the firm to make irreversible investments in special-purpose equipment.

This strategy leads the firm to construct a convention of productivity which takes the form of a description of work tasks, based on objective rules external to, and independent of, persons working in the firm. The range of future events that can be dealt with efficiently in the course of production is circumscribed and routinized, and handled according to unvarying, hierarchical procedures. As in Taylorism, the description of work activities is intended to be exhaustive ("work analysis"): it enumerates elementary tasks, classifies them and places them in sequence, and identifies maximum times for their execution in order to receive a given salary. The firm's management identifies each individual employee as a "work station," a "job." The particular qualities of persons disappear, to be replaced by roles, tasks, and positions within a hierarchy.

In the Industrial World's firm, seniority is typically associated with internal promotion, and is an essential parameter for personnel management and salary policies. Entry into the firm is limited to those whose quality of work can be said to have an "industrial" aspect. In some places, this may involve diplomas and credentials,[22] but as the literature on labor "queues" has shown, it may also depend on the employer "reading" certain external characteristics on a preconceived list of "industrial" worker qualities (often involving race, gender, ethnicity, presumed level of education, presumed political attitudes).[23] In any event, the worker who wants to enter this world needs neither a particular history nor local roots, as is required for entrants into the Interpersonal World.[24]

The mass product associated with the conventions of industrial labor offers the firm the organizational capacity to predict its own economic fluctuations with some confidence. These fluctuations create a measurable risk for social policy, so the conventions of this possible world extend even to the notion of social rights designed to protect individuals against economic risk, such as unemployment insurance.[25] Modern unemployment insurance was initially designed to protect income, albeit only partially, against the effects of temporary and predictable economic fluctuations. For its part, the public sector limits its risk because it can model these fluctuations and hence adjust its needed inflows of funds.

Labor Conventions in the Market World

The Market World firm standardizes its critical inputs, but deals with each demand individually, in the moment. The range of products which have to be made without delay must be amenable to a particular form of standardization; for example, clothing producers have in place routinized procedures to meet the particular demands of department store buyers on short schedules. As Marglin suggests,[26] specialization by task, which is one way to save time, can be carried out in successive batches of production without requiring specialized workers themselves.[27] Thus the convention of standardization is implemented in a fashion very different from that found in the Industrial World.

Indeed, in this possible world, the producer is frequently a subcontractor responsible for a specific task, who must be available and must maintain sufficient capacity to respond rapidly to the buyer's requests. In this market relationship, individual producers are identified as having time available for a particular task.

Here, the convention of unemployment adjusts work income closely to market fluctuations. In a world of production dominated by standardized work tasks, creating islands of market relations would lead to, for example, irregular forms of employment (interim work, fixed-duration contracts, multiple-tier subcontracting, and so on). Total wage income reflects time worked, which is unpredictable under these arrangements. We thus approach a pure exchange of quantities: time for wages.

Labor Conventions of the Interpersonal World

Products in the Interpersonal World are specialized (based on a stock of know-how) and dedicated (adjusted to a demander's particular needs). Producers (and their tools) must be able to cope with a constantly changing variety of product qualities. With no consolidation or standardization, each producer considers the action of work or demand of another as specific, sui generis. Production is carried out by small numbers of individuals who assess others in the production system on the basis of their common history.

To enter this world an individual must have a past or common roots with those already in it, or must somehow join the system of existing community-based values and practices. This spirit of "community" (in a pejorative sense, the clannish spirit) is a convention of this world.

The convention of productivity rests on common knowledge that cannot be formalized. Wages, while regulated by custom, vary according to the quality the demander attributes to the product. The price of labor is attached to the product and attributed to the individual producers, not disaggregated into work time or hourly rates. The quality of work is directly assessed by the demander's satisfaction as reflected in the price paid for the product. An example of the most modest sort is the *tarif* negotiated by skilled French craft workers for a completed piece of work; at the high end, it is the specialized artisan's ability to enjoy quasi-rents on his labor. Though in one sense this may be called "market" labor, this market has no Walrasian features; products as well as labor[28] are personalized within a community of individuals.

Mobility, whether geographical (from one local labor market to another) or vertical (via learning) regulates the allocation of work. Nonetheless, individuals in this world are typically strongly attached to a network of persons. Interpersonal conventions are found in service industries, artisanal fabrication, and very small, highly specialized niche firms, but also in the typical large Japanese firm, as well as the core innovative communities of the high technology industries.[29] The influence of conventions of the Interpersonal World is amply, if implicitly, described in the literature on "networks of firms" and "industrial districts."[30]

Labor Conventions in the Intellectual World
Because the purpose of activity in the Intellectual World is precisely to create novelty, its conventions of labor are addressed to a unique form of uncertainty. Unlike the uncertainty facing actors in other worlds, this cannot be gauged in terms of risk, nor resolved through a simple information exchange, because the necessary information does not yet exist. Still, there must be some rules to the interactions that occur, and in the Intellectual World, scientific or professional praxes are applied to work activity as conventions which create confidence and give rise to procedural norms of productivity.

In this world, the quality of an individual's work cannot be directly measured in terms of the quality of the product or of consumer satisfaction. Rather, individuals are containers of intangible investments. Wages thus have the character of a medium- to long-term investment in the individual actor. The convention of unemployment here can take only one form: the holder of specialized knowledge engages in "mobility" between points where that knowledge can be applied, whether within the firm (between tasks and projects) or on the labor market.

Innovation in Worlds of Production

We now turn to the concrete problem of economic development today, identified in Chapter 1 as that of technological and organizational learning, or the invention and modification of products and processes. These rest on an extraordinarily complex variety of institutions, social habits, ideologies, and expectations, all of which also serve as underpinning to the structures of firm and market.

In recent years, much of the thinking about innovation has been inspired by the rise of Japan and Germany as economic powers, and the growing recognition that these nations (that is, their firms, labor processes, institutions, and cultures) differ in fundamental ways from their less successful competitors. To date, however, the discussion has been posed almost exclusively in terms of the differences between "national innovation systems,"[31] and, while such analysis is promising, it may be that the puzzle must be solved at other analytical levels. For one thing, innovation can probably not be analyzed exclusively at the level of sectors that involve a broad range of products; possible worlds are specific to products. Second, while formal national institutions undoubtedly influence the selection of innovative processes (the literature on national systems of innovation concentrates on scientific and engineering institutions), conventions and action frameworks have much to do with what specializations nations select, and their differential levels of success. Third, the conventions which underlie innovative performance and specialization are in some cases highly specific to discrete sub-national regions, places in which certain learning-based real worlds of production are concentrated, with associated action frameworks and conventions rooted in the regional population.

Innovation does not concern only some worlds and not others: asymmetric information is developed, absorbed, and deployed in each world of production, in a way that allows innovators to construct absolute advantages and earn quasi-rents. The "innovation problem" involves two essential constraints that innovators face: the material and market qualities of their products, and the profit constraints which follow from their particular mix of specialization-dedication-generality-standardization. Innovation must respond to both these needs simultaneously. Each world deals with such constraints in its own distinct way, through development of the organization of production and external relations. There are thus four different basic collective action processes of innovation.

THE QUALITIES OF INNOVATIVE PRODUCTS

In discussing innovative products, the term "qualities" refers to the particular kind of asymmetric information which constitutes an advantage over the average producer in the market at hand. For products of the Interpersonal World, for example, differentiated to particular uses or niches targeted by clients, innovation consists of inventing new dedicated qualities requiring specialized resources. At the heart of product-based technological advantage in this world are continuous refinement, modification, and mastery of materials and designs in ways that are not entirely codifiable (through formal labor or off-the-job scientific training) and not highly amenable to being incorporated or transferred by way of special purpose equipment. User-producer relations play an important role in the development of dedicated-specialized qualities with groups of "dedicated" demanders (users) and specialized producers engage in communications which underlie knowledge evolution.

For the Market World, with its differentiated series production of standardized products dedicated to a narrow band of tastes or uses, innovation consists of inventing new dedicated qualities amenable to standardization. Advantage comes from developing products that are standardized (that is, products that draw on codifiable combinations of forms of widely available standardized products), yet dedicated to particular uses (that is, highly differentiated and targeted combinations). The key to such advantage is thus the ability to respond to the market rapidly. Producers must either take new standardized-generic knowledge or product qualities and differentiate them more quickly and more broadly than other producers, which requires following consumer tastes more closely than competitors are doing, or they must take specialized, dedicated products and standardize them by innovating in the production process.

For the Industrial World, competition is focused on widely available standardized-generic products, broadly diffused quality standards and consumer expectations, and codifiable knowledge which can be incorporated in special purpose capital equipment. Innovation consists of inventing new generic product qualities that are amenable to standardization. This involves basic technological innovations, since it means standardizing generic product qualities: breaking them into constituent parts and tasks. In practice, new generic-specialized knowledge (coming from the World of Intellectual Resources) is made codifiable and widely reproducible (hence standardized). The first producers to do this will be able to drop their prices rapidly and will enjoy a (relatively short) period of quasi-rents before other producers imitate them or reverse-engineer their products, at which time they will need to repeat the process of standardizing new generic-specialized knowledge. Their advantage is always fragile.

For the Intellectual World, innovation consists of developing new generic qualities by exercising specialized capacities. New scientific and technical know-how must be widely usable, thus generic; but it cannot be produced by standardized methods. It is produced by a community of specialists which itself uses many interpersonal conventions to develop highly codified, hence impersonal, knowledge.

INNOVATION AND THE ORGANIZATION OF PRODUCTION

When product and process change interact, the technological pathway of a product, and thus of its world, tends to be cumulative and self-reinforcing. This is a fundamental insight of recent work in evolutionary economics. This self-reinforcing characteristic poses a central problem for firms wishing to remain innovative. To elucidate this problem, and how it frames the question of the organization of innovative production systems, we summarize in the following paragraphs the basic propositions of recent work in the economics of technological change from the evolutionary and neo-Austrian perspectives.[32]

Technological change is subject to increasing returns, not decreasing returns, so development and adoption tend to be characterized by positive feedback. One source of such feedback is learning-by-using, which diffuses and deepens the cognitive framework associated with a given product or process and makes it ever easier to use; another source is external economies of scale in use: the more independent users there are (in the sense of a network of users), the more difficult it is to change the basic nature of a product or process, for such a change can make worthless some users' physical capital as well as their experience in learning-by-using.

Technological complementarities between base technologies and diverse applications, and between linked applications, help "build in" external economies in use, as does increasing the scale of production. As a result, after a certain point in the history of a product or a process, its production and use tend to become increasingly locked in, that is, irreversible or at least relatively resistant to fundamental change. There is no way to tell at the outset which products or processes will be locked in, nor any way to claim that what does get locked in is the most efficient of all possible ex ante alternatives: efficiency is in large measure an endogenous property of adoption and use, and like lock-in, it is *path-dependent.*

Indeed, along the way relatively minor events, even accidents, may "select" the (medium- or long-run) path which is locked in, and thus the efficiency of the technology; this is the "first comer" effect. It does not imply that any random approach will suffice, but it does suggest that oftentimes multiple acceptably efficient paths are open and the choice among them is not preordained by any global rationality.

This reasoning holds both for hardware and for "soft" technologies and goods: with hardware, lock-in involves sunk capital; in the latter case, it has to do with reputation and brand name; but for both, intangible capital in the form of skills and knowledge is subject to strong external economies of scale.

Lock-in may provide cause for concern for the same reason that it may be beneficial to both producers and users: as external economies in production or use increase, it is not only more difficult to change from one path to another, but it may even become difficult to move further along a given, narrowly defined product path if production technologies become over-specific. Yet the logic of cost-minimization calls precisely for making resources increasingly specific and dedicated to the production of a given output, to lock in producers. This subjects them to competition from other cost-minimizers, or to the risk that producers who are not locked in will come along with better products or more efficient technologies, as apparently happened with the U.S. steel and automobile industries in the 1970s. Technological dynamism—*ceteris paribus*—thus involves compromise between the goals of minimizing costs in production and the need for some reversibility in production and product design: on one hand, to minimize lock-in to particular products while keeping production costs down; on the other, to maximize the possibility and minimize the cost of moving to new products and production technologies. In these circumstances a firm's innovativeness is a question of the degree to which it is organized to redefine continuously its technological trajectory through learning.[33]

EXTERNAL RELATIONS IN INNOVATIVE PRODUCTION SYSTEMS

We have suggested some general tendencies of innovative systems, but now we want to discriminate among organizational forms to see the ways in which these dynamics are played out in the contexts of different worlds of production. The key dimension here is external interconnections between firms and production units, that is, the transactional structure of the system.

Figure 3.5 depicts external relations for the different worlds of produc-

System Organization Technology District Industrial District	**System Organization** Diffused Industrialization
Product Innovation: Similar	**Product Innovation:** Complementary (Recombination)
Nature of Interdependencies: Traded + Untraded Territorial Proximity	**Nature of Interdependencies:** Traded + Untraded Territorial Proximity
Production Transactions: Non-Similar + Complementary	**Production Transactions:** Similar + Complementary (Capacity)
(**The Interpersonal World**)	(**The Market World**)
System Organization Technology District; Strategic Alliances	**System Organization** Technological Core + Spatial Division of Labor
Product Innovation: Similar	**Product Innovation:** Complementary
Nature of Interdependencies: Traded + Little Proximity	**Nature of Interdependencies:** Few; Traded
Production Transactions: Non-Similar + Complementary	**Production Transactions:** Similar + Complementary (Capacity)
(**The World of Intellectual Resources**)	(**The Industrial World**)

Left axis (top): Dedicated Products
Left axis (bottom): Generic Products
Right axis (top): Uncertainty
Right axis (bottom): Predictability

Economies of Variety   Economies of Scale

Figure 3.5   External relations in innovation in different worlds of production.

tion. The right-hand vertical axis reproduces Knight's distinction between uncertain and predictable (though fluctuating) markets. The capacity to plan and stabilize external transactions is more limited under conditions of true uncertainty than in systems where incidence and magnitude of fluctuations can be reliably estimated; hence producers of dedicated products tend to experience more variegated external transactions than producers of generic products. This analysis differs considerably from the view of transactions cost economics (see Chapter 13), which holds that the nature of productive assets determines the volume and nature of external transactions. For transactions cost economics, the distinction between standardized and specialized (or "specific") would govern transactional patterns. Standardized productive assets are available in large numbers and hence can be had through external-market transactions, while specialized assets tend to exist in small numbers, creating potential hostage problems for buyers and sellers, and hence lead toward internalization. Our explanation is different, and the predicted empirical outcomes are quite opposite. Mere quantity of external transactions is not related in straightforward fashion to the degree of uncertainty associated with them; rather, the nature of fluctuations determines much about the unit cost of transactions as well as the way the transaction is governed in contractual or non-contractual relationships.

The nature of the transaction depends on its substantive content. The horizontal axes of Figure 3.5 show the principle which shapes the division of labor in production for each product, and hence the kind of coordination required for each production system. This draws from Richardson's four-fold distinction between similar-nonsimilar and complementary-non-complementary phases of production.[34] External transactions involve two distinct issues often confused in the literature: transactions concerning the management of "normal" production activities, and transactions concerning asymmetric information, the development of which underlies product innovation, our subject here. The latter transactions may take both traded and untraded forms. Many are not input-output relations through buying and selling, contracting, and the like but are part of indirect interdependencies operating through spillovers between activities sharing similar or complementary base technologies; similar or complementary kinds of labor, deployed in different industries; or similar or complementary materials.

Specialized and standardized products have different divisions of labor in production as well as in innovation. For day-to-day production of specialized products, the division of labor centers on securing non-similar but complementary inputs, that is, a "vertical" division of labor. This is easily seen for certain products of the Interpersonal World, such as fashion- or design-intensive products, or for certain outputs of mechanical engineering industries, but a word of clarification is needed with respect to "production" and "innovation" in the World of Intellectual Resources. In this world, production involves applying specialized intellectual resources to the development of new, but generic, knowledge; so producers seek out other producers with non-similar but complementary forms of knowledge, which are then combined into a "whole" generic innovation. For example, in the electronics industry extremely specialized research teams (in different specialized firms or units) may come together to develop a new chip design, a material, or even a complete subassembly such as a peripheral or a software package. The dedicated-specialized elements of these generic innovations constitute this world's "innovative" activity, as does the work of those who experiment with software languages which are then combined into generic forms. These actors, the "basic" innovators upon whom the Intellectual World depends, are themselves in the Interpersonal World (in that part of the electronics industry which is in Silicon Valley, for example); their external relations in innovation are to other specialists who work on similar problems.

Thus both worlds of specialized products—the Market and Interpersonal Worlds—have external relations in production which are non-similar and complementary, and external relations in innovation with other specialists, whose knowledge frameworks are deepened within interpersonal communities. The World of Intellectual Resources, however, then recombines such interpersonal products into new generic forms, often through formal traded interdependencies with firms having complementary and non-similar talents, as in technology partnerships and strategic alliances between big technological firms. These transactions take place in predictable markets and involve personal relations less than do transactions of the Interpersonal World. However, in the most specialized-dedicated parts of the high technology industries, transactions are based on uncertain relations within communities of specialists, and between specialists and users. Hence, these relations tend to be untraded as well as traded and to rely on non-contractual as well as contractual forms of governance; and territorial proximity is frequently the basis of the cooperating specialists' common action frameworks. In other words, external transactions of the Intellectual World have a complex double pattern: in "production" they extend over long distances in predictable, formal, contractual governance regimes; in "innovation" they take place in the circumscribed "districts" of the Interpersonal World. Many high technology industries therefore have a locational pattern which looks like multinational "systems of districts"—that is, large firms which look upward and outward to other technology-based oligopolists, but usually have basic technological capabilities rooted in the Interpersonal Worlds of their home countries.

For standardized products the situation is quite different. In the day-to-day production activities of the Market World, producers use external relations within the division of labor to secure similar and complementary inputs, either horizontal or vertical, to smooth out market fluctuations by increasing capacity. In the Market World, we find Marshall's famous supply curve interdependencies. In the Industrial World, where market fluctuations are predictable, such uses of capacity tend to be the object of long-term contracts and spread over large geographical distances; this leads to the typical multiregional or multinational production system. In the Market World, where uncertainty is present, vertical and horizontal suppliers must be able to respond immediately, though they are promised little security about the future; the specialized production region with a large collection of firms typifies this system.

There are also marked differences in the ways external transactions are used for innovations of standardized products; in both the Market and Industrial Worlds, the need is to make up for lacks, not to deepen knowledge as in the specialist communities. In the Market World, product innovation involves the continuous rapid differentiation of standardized outputs, essentially through the rapid and expanding recombination of differentiated standardized inputs. Territorial proximity can be of help here, and both traded and untraded, contractual and hybrid interdependencies are likely to appear. In the Industrial World, producers of standardized-generic outputs innovate by finding new generic outputs which can be standardized. Firms may do this directly in Methods and Engineering Departments, through interconnected third-party innovators such as universities or government agencies, or—quite likely—through relationships with innovators of generic knowledge in the World of Intellectual Resources.

FOUR COLLECTIVE ACTION PROCESSES IN INNOVATION

Innovation is a collective action problem shaped by the specific kind of product at hand. Any innovation defines both constraints and opportunities in terms of product qualities, construction of the market (as a temporal structure of expectations), technological contours of the production process, and profitability. It is a collective action problem because particular kinds of persons with particular kinds of knowledge (that is, with their collective identities) must be mobilized to develop asymmetric information for each kind of product.

In the Interpersonal World, innovators attempt to increase the product's dedicated qualities by deepening the application of their specialized knowledge. This involves developing the communities of persons in which such knowledge is created, refined, and transferred. The economic problems that stem from low scale and high variety production, the need to offset high overhead costs, and the ongoing threat of "theft" of products by those from the Industrial or Market Worlds cannot be resolved by imitating those worlds because standardized products are no longer Interpersonal World products; their loss of "personality" condemns them to price competition. It is true that individual producers might solve some problems in the short run by standardizing their products, but such practices will ultimately undermine the Interpersonal World; at the extreme, it would lose its identity and become something else, and would have to face the competitive struggle in those other worlds.

The economic contradictions of the Interpersonal World have one overarching solution: major increases in the scope-variety of production to offset production costs and improve capacity utilization. This requires finding appropriate technologies and management techniques which can realize the benefits of scope-variety without destroying the community's interpersonal character. The danger is that increased scope-variety and larger production units imply greater internal hierarchy and increasingly formal external relations of production units, both of which tend to depersonalize the production system by substituting bureaucratic knowledge for personal knowledge. If this process destroys the ongoing deepening of knowledge and strengthening of frameworks, the problem returns: instead of making the Interpersonal World more viable, this effort replaces it with worlds based on standardization, and a new set of economic constraints replaces the old one.

Innovation in standardized-dedicated products of the Market World centers on the degree and pace of rededication of products. This includes developing new conceptual frameworks for dedication—closer ties to clients, faster changeovers, greater scope-variety to offset costs. The Japanese car industry, for example, replaced Fordism with Ohno-ism (or Toyotism), taking the essentially generic products of the American car industry and making them more dedicated. This involved a managerial and organizational revolution: specifically, Ohno rejected the idea of competition based solely on the long production run and its cost advantage, and added the complementary idea of extremely frequent model changeovers. To conform to this rapid pace of product redifferentiation, Toyota organized appropriate routines in the production system, for example, instituting shop-floor repairing and changeovers. In turn, the success of such routines was due to changes in expectations of actors, who accepted the principle of continuous adaptation in a context characterized by loyalty.

Other examples of Market World products include central city garment or furniture complexes in the United States. Here, competition is the neoclassical economist's dream, approaching spot market pricing with low levels of contracting and hierarchy. These complexes gain advantage by being able to respond rapidly to the market: subcontractors survive or die on this capability. Innovation lies largely outside the production system, in the communities of designers, themselves subject to extreme levels of uncertainty. The economic constraints noted above—the fact that downstream order-giving firms can place their suppliers into competition with each other because the inputs are based on standardized components or skills—make life extremely difficult for all concerned. The situation tends to create severe downward pressure on subcontractor and supplier prices (that is to say, on wages); and, in general, the problem facing product innovators is that they must either increase the generic quality of their products (the compromise found by Benetton) or become more specialized (moving toward the Interpersonal World). The pure "market" version of the Market World is a hard life for all concerned.

More stable and highly innovative versions of the Market World have apparently been organized by creating institutions which reshape economic coordination. The Japanese automobile industry again offers a good example. Japanese carmakers organized "upstream" institutional frameworks to make them consistent with the requirements of this form of innovation, notably the banking system, which provides patient capital with low financial rates of return, permitting frequent, intensive recapitalization of the production system without dragging down profit rates. They also organized "horizontally" in the form of the keiretsu, a resource-pooling and loyalty-inducing device that permits their well-known levels of flexibility without exit or opportunism. The mechanical engineering industries of southern Germany have also used institutions to reshape expectations, blending attentiveness to the market with the ability to mobilize long-term, expensive labor and capital resources usually not available in the Market World's characteristic conditions of uncertainty. Note that in both the German and Japanese cases, these efforts suggest the presence of a social "cement" which seems to have an interpersonal character: communities bound by the exercise of voice over time. In a sense, collective action leading to innovation in capital-intensive products in the Market World rests on a paradox: the need to underpin the market with forms of social commitment, not to indulge in pure Liberalism.

As noted above, with standardized-generic products, the problem of innovation involves using formal corporate R&D to invent new qualities compatible with standardization. Product innovation is a great deal more mysterious than process innovation in this world: in effect, it has little to do with rationalizing production processes; it is rather a form of intellectual work, applying standardization to new generic knowledge, crystallized in the product. It is now understood that this form of innovation is not endogenous to the Industrial World, but involves a host of extremely complex external relations to other worlds in the public and private R&D infrastructure. Moreover, the breaking-in stage for truly new standardized-generic products—the first few years when massive quasi-rents are earned, markets are shaped, brand-names created, and technological trajectories for the product set into motion—often requires high levels of territorial proximity, between producers, Intellectual World innovators, production engineers, customers, and service support agents. Later, increasing codification of these processes permits greater and greater territorial distance.

We know from hard experience over the past two decades that the Industrial World—once heralded by Chandler, Galbraith, and others as the most advanced form of innovative activity, because the big corporation could plan technology development programs—no longer allows high-wage, high-cost countries to get ahead. The failure of the Industrial World to earn innovative quasi-rents has spawned a voluminous literature on post-Fordism and production flexibility. It might be more insightful to note that the advantages once possessed by Industrial World firms have been chipped away on two sides: as Japanese and German versions of the Market World combine standardization and dedication with more rapid product changeovers, and as consumers turn toward products of the Interpersonal World. Moreover, Industrial World firms in the developed countries are imitated by, or move to, cheap Third World production zones.

The ground for economically viable innovation in the Industrial World is very narrow. The need to realize new standardized products means finding generic qualities which are unlikely to be subject to rapid imitation. It is also important to avoid confusing innovation in the Industrial World analytically with mere imitation of state-of-the-art products or production technologies: the very high capital costs of innovation and price competition will impede the flow of quasi-rents that accompany innovation, and will subject high-cost, developed country producers to competition from Third World or, worse, more flexible Market World producers. The example of General Motors, pitifully imitating every Japanese product and process innovation a few years after it appeared, comes to mind; clearly, they did not understand that the Japanese were operating in the Market World and not in the Industrial World.

All this suggests that the main hope for the Industrial World on the process side is in the Market World, and on the product side in the Intellectual World, but the latter requires deploying specialized resources—a very costly effort, especially with high levels of uncertainty. This uncertainty can only be overcome, paradoxically, by proceeding "as if" it did not exist, that is, by going forward with methodologically coherent R&D programs. Traded (usually contractual) interdependencies between groups of specialists, themselves organized along interpersonal lines, are a key strategy for combining resources, attenuating uncertainty, and sharing costs, and this has given rise to the well-known research partnerships and strategic alliances.[35]

Three main groups of actors are engaged in these interdependencies. First are the "internal" agents of a given firm, its scientific-engineering-conceptual workers. The firm must invest in them and give them appropriate incentives; society must create them and give them an appropriate identity. When these workers belong to large companies mainly acting in the Industrial World, they must find ways to absorb the culture needed to perform in the World of Intellectual Resources, where principles of identity and collective action are very different from those of the Industrial World. This is, indeed, one of the dramas that large, old firms—even those with powerful R&D bureaucracies, such as Bell Labs, General Motors, or IBM—have faced in recent years. Their problem has less to do with the operation of their innovation apparatuses per se than with their subjugation of these innovative capacities to the Industrial World. Institutional change was necessary for the parent firms of the R&D operations to allow the Intellectual World to "drive" their Industrial World operations, and not the other way around.

For any given firm, such workers are specialists, sometimes coming from specialized milieus, always dependent on interactions with specialists external to the firm. Communities of specialists have always, to some degree, operated on interpersonal ties: this is the second group of actors. They are frequently highly territorialized, which is why even the major firms acting as technological partners to multinational strategic alliances often "source" their inputs to those alliances from well-known technology districts in their own countries.[36]

When these workers, in turn, are inserted into alliances with their partners in other Intellectual World firms or units, they form the third group. These groups must relate to each other through formal, traded interdependencies. The thorny question of "terms of trade" arises: how to execute agreements with the correct ex ante incentives and ex post payoffs. Contracts executed in advance, in the presence of radical uncertainty, will tend to misallocate rewards because it is difficult to know in advance the value of what will be created. If such contracts are simply based on property rights, with ex post reward proportionate to ex ante investment, they will tend to provide too little incentive to realize innovation under conditions of uncertainty. There is no way around the need to create appropriate conventions to share rewards, that is, it is necessary to agree on what is fair, and it is doubtful that either contract law or formal management practice can resolve the question. How is it possible to engender such "virtuous" social conventions concerning the rewards to innovators?

This question might also apply to the frequently informal and territorialized technology-development relationships of the Interpersonal World as well. What sorts of conventions should be developed for communities of specialists, if contracts and property rights alone cannot do the job efficiently?

Innovation is, then, the outcome of a coherent framework of action, involving appropriate coordination among the principal economic agents necessary for a given type of product. Action frameworks have costs, and all forms of competition involve cost constraints. Product innovations, to remain within a given world, must deepen the essential qualities of those products; to introduce innovations that bear qualities of products of other worlds is to introduce their competitive constraints, which can become incompatible with some forms of collective action. Process innovations may be designed to escape each world's profitability constraints; some are compatible with the world's products but others undermine those product qualities, and thus reintroduce new and different economic constraints.

3.5 Conclusion

We have described some of the many dimensions of possible worlds of production—but possible worlds are merely elementary frameworks of action. We have said little so far about the passage to real production systems, a passage that is extremely complex and is the subject of a number of case studies in several countries in Part II of this book. But first we present evidence in Chapter 4 that firms do exist in different worlds of production as a way of showing that these worlds are empirically accessible. Moreover, by exploring a sample of firms in France in the 1980s we illustrate the diversity, unevenness, and heterogeneity in the contemporary process of industrial restructuring, even for firms with satisfactory profitability. Many worlds of production are coming into being, not a single model of growth.

4

SITUATING FIRMS IN
WORLDS OF PRODUCTION

In this chapter we take an empirical look at products and production systems as frameworks of action. First, to show that the theoretical concept of worlds of production is empirically tractable, we develop a quantitative approach to situating firms in those worlds. Second, we analyze a broad sample of firms in the French economy in the 1980s (empirical efforts in later chapters center on case studies). The sample indicates a general movement away from the Industrial World toward the Market and Intellectual Worlds, and to a lesser extent toward the Interpersonal World. Though the dominant pathway between worlds of production is bound to differ from one national economy to another, according to its product specialization and conventions, any advanced economy would likely show some of the dynamics seen in the French case. The data help us understand some of the complexity of economic adjustment; they show that the transition between worlds is a slow and tortuous process, involving experimentation, mixing of strategies, and frequent failure.

Background, Data, and Methods

For the reader not familiar with the French economy, some brief background material will help situate the analysis that follows. (A more detailed account of French economic policy and the key groups in it can be found in Chapter 11.) France is an advanced economy today, but was relatively late to industrialize compared with its neighbors Britain and Germany. The French economy was predominantly rural longer than in those nations, and the country's early manufactures were more concentrated in military industries and artisanal production. Throughout the nineteenth century, the map of France was dotted with an enormous array of complexes of artisanal producers, often making high-quality, specialized products. In most of these complexes, small workshops were linked to larger, leading, family-owned firms; these were often oriented as much toward amassing and conserving wealth over the long term—building the family patrimony—as toward maximizing short-term profit or even growth. Capital-market financing developed later and more weakly in France than in the Anglo-American world. Family-owned firms often developed hierarchical, paternalistic relationships with their workers and with certain other nearby firms, and exercised great local political influence. Alongside these firms, and frequently in concert with them, was a longstanding tradition, dating back to the times of Louis XIV (circa 1660), of State manufactures both for armaments and for certain forms of prestigious products.

In the period after World War II, the State involved itself in an ambitious economic modernization program through the national planning agency. "The Plan," as it was called, was committed to building large-scale, capital-intensive industries, then less common in France than in competitor nations, and emphasized industrial concentration for scale, in some cases through nationalization. Some traditional forms of family-based, quality-oriented, and regionally-based industries were broken apart by the Plan; others were absorbed into the modernization process and transformed through subsidy and State involvement in management. Over the years, the Plan's administrators—powerful technocrats in State agencies—have consistently exhibited a commitment to applying the most recent hardware and organizational methods to the widest number of sectors possible, persistently pushing an Industrial World vision of modernization and competitiveness.

Although economic planning has now gone out of fashion in France, many of the instrumentalities of State intervention remain in force, and with them the underlying notions of modernization as technical modernization, and of competitiveness as a matter of reducing costs with hardware and scale. In fact, the data analyzed here were gathered as part of one such modernization program. The Industrial Modernization Fund (FIM), operating under the aegis of the Ministry of Industry, provided low-interest loans for "modernization" investments with high "new technology" content to approximately 400 large and medium-sized firms in the 1980s. As part of its request for assistance, each firm had to submit an application including quantitative data (detailed balance sheets, both past and prospective) and qualitative information (products, markets, state of competition, technological choices, legal structures, organizational strategies). Using these data, and data obtained from agreements between firms and the National Employment Fund (*Fonds National de l'Emploi;* FNE) from 1982 to 1990,[1] we were able to trace the evolution of firms throughout the 1980s. To be eligible for support from this program, all the firms attempted to restructure their operations to encompass products and processes they perceived as being dynamic in international markets. The data are especially interesting in that they cover a period of high productive investment in France.[2] (See Illustration 4.1 at the end of this chapter.)

The horizontal and vertical axes of the models of production described in Chapter 3 were transformed into composite variables. Using data from the FIM and FNE, we classified the sampled firms in terms of their worlds of production in the early 1980s: 76 were located in the Industrial World, 58 in the Market World, 70 in the Interpersonal World, and 20 in the World of Intellectual Resources (see Table 4.1). Then, examining the difference between the firm's positions along the axes in 1980 and 1987, we detected movements of firms between worlds. Though many routes of change are apparent, a few were particularly important: from the Industrial World in the direction of the Market World (28 firms) or in the direction of the Interpersonal World (27 firms); from the Market World toward the Industrial World (21 firms) or the Intellectual World (20 firms); from the Interpersonal World toward the Industrial World (23 firms) and the Intellectual World (20 firms). In the following sections we analyze these principal trends in more detail.

The Difficulties of Firms in the Industrial World

The Industrial World lost more firms than any other in the sample: the majority of firms initially in this category moved away from it toward market or interpersonal products by 1987. Some firms did seem to be moving toward the Industrial World, but they did so hesitantly, as can be seen in the case of Firm A (Illustration 4.2).

The signs of difficulty of firms in the Industrial World are multiple and convergent. At the time they entered into an agreement with the FIM, these firms manifested the weakest profitability of all groups (mean of −0.45), the greatest recent employment losses (−0.20), and mediocre progress in total sales. (All figures in parentheses refer to the average deviation from the median value of the indicator for that industry.) Their financial rate of return (−0.31) is poor compared to that of firms in the

Table 4.1 Number of firms in FIM sample, classified according to their initial worlds and movement between worlds

Firm's world	Total at time of entry to FIM	Changes along organization-market axes between entry into FIM and 1987				Number of firms classified into each world	
		Toward Interpersonal	Toward Market	Toward Industrial	Toward Intellectual	In 1984	In 1987
Interpersonal	70	11	16	23	20	50	35
Market	58	6	11	21	20	35	24
Industrial	76	27	28	12	9	26	13
Intellectual	20	1	8	5	6	11	14
Total	224	45	63	61	55	122	86

Interpersonal World and the Market World, and most asked for FNE aid at least once, and many several times, between 1982 and 1988, indicating an ongoing process of workforce reductions.

Not surprisingly, the Industrial World has the highest proportion of large firms (34 out of the 76 have more than 2,000 employees); many belong to publicly and privately held multidivisional corporations (18 and 13 respectively), or are branches of foreign multinationals (11). These firms constituted an important foundation for postwar French economic growth, which was centered on basic industrial goods. In the 1980s, they invested heavily in capital-intensive forms of modernization, acting according to the central Industrial World logic of irreversible and special-purpose capital investments. As a corollary, their proportionate investments in intellectual or human resources were the lowest among the four groups. They now face greater market uncertainty than in the past, which is forcing them to seek rapid amortization of their expensive investments (less than two years) and higher price-cost margins.

Firms in the Industrial World divide into two groups: one moving toward the Market World, the other toward the Interpersonal World, with very different consequences.

SHIFTS TOWARD THE MARKET WORLD: DIFFERENTIATED STANDARDIZED PRODUCTS

Industrial World firms moving toward the Market World (28) seem to have had some success in terms of profitability. Yet their transitions were incomplete: they moved away from the Industrial World but did not completely enter the Market World. Thus, for example, the substitution of capital for labor remained high and increased more than average. At the time of entry into the FIM program, these firms were making basic goods, almost all standardized products, often involving initial processing of raw materials. Over the years, most of the firms attempted to create new products within their specialty, improve quality, and diversify into different market segments to raise the level of value added, and most abandoned or reduced their low-quality products. About half invest in research and development and hold patents. Many are involved in automating production and computerizing market relations, so as to respond more rapidly to orders. Most of these firms succeeded, over the period, in reducing employment, improving productivity, and thus reducing the share of labor costs. Circulating capital was also reduced, with the use of just-in-time systems and continuous operation of production lines.

The labor conventions of the Market World are quite different from those of the Industrial World, since they require independent reaction and individual adaptability instead of predetermined procedures. Thus new rules have been negotiated over work time, which push for compromise between maximizing capacity utilization (an industrial rule) and the need to respond without delay to unexpected orders (a market rule).[3]

This group of firms drew heavily on the National Employment Fund (with an average of 4.3 contracts per firm in seven years) for help in reducing and retraining their workforces. Retraining is often part of reorganization of work groups:[4] "the workers keep the habit, acquired during training, of posing lots of questions and supervisors no longer make all the technical decisions."[5] (See Illustration 4.4.)

The fact that 11 firms stayed within the Market World suggests that highly differentiated standardized products might be a possible sustainable pathway of development. For these firms, capital intensity increased and there were gains in labor productivity without reducing the efficiency of capital; they developed subcontracting relationships and reduced active circulating capital, and although per capita wage costs rose, overall wage share did not. Price-cost margins remained rather elevated; workforce reductions were relatively minor and slow; and costs were lowered through automation and increasing market volume. Movement from the Industrial World toward the Market World in the French context is seen particularly with producers of standardized products with high levels of differentiation in very large markets, for example, new food products (and their packaging), whose markets are growing with urbanization and new life-styles (one sampled firm was a leader in this field).

It does seem that an orientation toward the Market World is necessary to maintain profitability. Twenty of the 61 firms which, in a time of rapid growth, continued to bet on massive, "industrial" investments (see the column labeled "Toward Industrial" in the tables) experienced declining profitability. Most of these are producers of mass, standardized products facing large multinational competitors with neither the size (18 of the 20 have fewer than 2,000 workers) nor the financial strength to maintain their position. Firm A (see Illustration 4.2) is one such firm.

SHIFTS TOWARD THE INTERPERSONAL WORLD: THE DIFFICULT
MARRIAGE OF INDUSTRIAL COSTS AND PRODUCT QUALITY

Firms that moved toward the Interpersonal World make a wide variety of products; indeed, they have multiple families of outputs, sometimes quite different. They must cope, more than other firms in the sample, with qualitative changes in demand and rapidly increasing foreign competition. Since they can no longer win on the basis of price, they must attempt to break into products characterized by specialization and economies of variety. To escape their "industrial" difficulties, such firms abandon the industrial approach to product quality and redesign products jointly with their customers. In so doing, they incorporate specialized savoir-faire within a product initially conceived for mass production methods, and thereby dedicate the product to a particular client's demands. Corporation C provides an example (see Illustration 4.5).

A look at individual cases reveals numerous strategic difficulties in achieving a compromise between industrial costs and diversified quality. Firms often seem to remain too narrowly "industrial": they reduce costs, raise productivity, and automate, but do very little research and development, and little labor training. They do seek proximity to the market, usually with a flexible downstream sales strategy. This reliance on Industrial World logic, as we shall see, is a general tendency in France and one source of the country's present economic straits. Evidence of the industrial approach appears in the fact that per capita labor costs are lower for this group of firms than for those in the other worlds (-0.24), a sign of continuing "industrial" rationalization of work. As a result of these blockages, this sample of firms is less successful in terms of financial returns than the others (-0.23) (see Table 4.2).

To acquire new competences, these firms would have to transform the entire context of labor conventions toward much greater participation, including high doses of training, and mobilize specialized forms of knowledge.

Interpersonal and Intellectual Sources of Employment Growth

As Table 4.3 shows, only two groups of firms are well positioned for employment growth: those in the Interpersonal World attempting to "industrialize" their knowledge (line 1, column "Toward Industrial"), and those in the Market World drawing strongly from the Intellectual World (line 2, column "Toward Intellectual"). Both groups show strong growth in OECD export demand, and France is highly specialized in both.

FIRMS IN THE INTERPERSONAL WORLD

Most firms in the Interpersonal World are medium-sized (29 out of 40 have fewer than 500 employees) and family-owned (more than half; many others lost this status only recently). Their products come from know-how

Table 4.2 Rate of return of firms in 1987, with firms classified according to their initial worlds and movement between worlds

Firm's world	Total at time of entry to FIM	Changes along organization-market axes between entry into FIM and 1987			
		Toward Interpersonal	Toward Market	Toward Industrial	Toward Intellectual
Interpersonal	0.06	−0.09	−0.07	−0.09	0.40
Market	0.12	1.00	0.40	−0.26	0.05
Industrial	−0.01	−0.08	0.29	−0.40	−0.33
Intellectual	−0.40	−1.00	0.00	−0.67	−0.60
Total	—	0.05	0.16	−0.28	0.05

Note: To interpret Tables 4.2 and 4.3, which are expressed in deviations from median values, see text.

accumulated over many years, and often involve small production runs to order. They are frequently found in moderately industrialized small provincial cities. Their trademarks or at least their market images are well known, giving them a distinctive identity in the eyes of the national and international public.

The share of value added in these firms is fairly high, as is profitability (+0.15). Most did not reduce their workforce during the study period, and tend to be optimistic about the future (+0.30). Since they are less capital-intensive than the mean, labor costs account for an above average share of value added; but capital efficiency is high and per capita labor costs remain low (−0.36).

These firms came to the FIM to obtain capital in order to grow without losing financial control of the establishment. Some also sought assistance from the FNE, but considerably less often than firms in the other groups.

They follow three principal pathways. The first (20 firms) involves products with a strong intellectual component. The second inserts interpersonal resources into a market context (16 firms); one example is smaller firms bought by big industrial holding groups to make dedicated products which are to be integrated downstream with other products of the group. In these cases, FIM and FNE assistance was mostly used to reorganize the labor process so as to integrate elements of the Interpersonal World (component quality) with those of the Market World (response to downstream demand). Employment dropped considerably in this subgroup, especially direct production labor.[6] The third pathway (23 firms) involves the industrialization of specialized savoir-faire, which is discussed in the next section.

84

Table 4.3A Change in exports of firms toward OECD countries, in percentages, with firms classified according to their initial worlds and movement (1983–1987)[a]

Firm's world	Total at time of entry to FIM	Changes along organization-market axes between entry into FIM and 1987			
		Toward Interpersonal	Toward Market	Toward Industrial	Toward Intellectual
Interpersonal	−0.08	0.50	0.43	−0.22	−0.60
Market	0.19	—	−0.11	0.17	0.38
Industrial	−0.31	−0.36	0.29	0.11	−0.60
Intellectual	0.08	—	—	—	—
Total	—	0.00	0.19	0.19	−0.15

a. Exports calculated according to the 5-digit SITC classifications of firms.

Table 4.3B Overall specialization of French economy, 1983, in products of firms sampled, according to the initial worlds and movement between worlds of sampled firms

Firm's world	Total at time of entry to FIM	Changes along organization-market axes between entry into FIM and 1987			
		Toward Interpersonal	Toward Market	Toward Industrial	Toward Intellectual
Interpersonal	0.08	0.00	0.14	0.44	−0.33
Market	−0.03	—	−0.56	0.17	0.23
Industrial	−0.02	−0.09	0.00	−0.11	0.20
Intellectual	−0.38	—	—	—	—
Total	—	−0.05	0.00	−0.02	−0.02

Table 4.3C Import-export ratio of French economy, 1983, in products of sample firms sampled, according to the initial worlds and movements between worlds of sampled firms

Firm's world, 1984	Total at time of entry to FIM	Changes along organization-market axes between entry into FIM and 1987			
		Toward Interpersonal	Toward Market	Toward Industrial	Toward Intellectual
Interpersonal	0.17	0.00	−0.14	0.00	0.60
Market	−0.14	—	−0.56	−0.17	0.23
Industrial	0.02	−0.18	0.14	−0.33	0.60
Intellectual	−0.23	—	—	—	—
Total	—	−0.14	−0.09	−0.12	0.36

THE INDUSTRIALIZATION OF SPECIALIZED KNOW-HOW

The use of increasingly industrial methods of production should be seen in terms of a long-term context of growth: firms in this position project the same rate of growth in the future that they have experienced in the recent past. In general such growth does materialize as measured by sales (+0.65), but this has required the firms to invest heavily (+0.43)—a situation favorable to employment: the workforce, predicted to grow (+0.63), did in fact do so (+0.48), and wages per capita went up as well (+0.12). Technological modernization is the key to a certain upskilling, either because wage grades were renegotiated or because more skilled labor was hired for new production units. Few firms in this subgroup asked for help from the National Employment Fund (10 out of 23 firms, with only 2.9 contracts per firm over the period). One consequence of the push toward standardization and long production runs is that the share of value added drops, as does the price-cost margin. The financial rate of return also falls: it is very high in the beginning, making investments possible, but declines throughout the study period.

For these firms, "innovation" involves trying to maintain the traditional form of their products and a close relationship to clients' needs while modernizing production and widening markets. There is a subtle line beyond which compromise with the Industrial World pushes the firm into mass production and its corresponding difficulties. The chance of this happening depends on the technologies used and their capacity to coexist with the product's "personal" qualities (its identity and ability to adjust to client's desires). It also depends on maintaining innovative capabilities, which in turn are linked to the deployment of the conventions of the Interpersonal and Intellectual Worlds. Industrial rationalization thus has certain dangers: it can push other necessary conventions aside, and with them the firm's innovative capacities, as the case of Firm E shows (Illustration 4.6).

PRODUCTS WITH A STRONG INTELLECTUAL
CONTENT AND PUBLIC SECTOR MARKETS

France has a strong presence in high technology products as a result of publicly supported basic research and large, protected public markets, and our sample includes a number of firms specializing in these products. (See the column labeled "Toward Intellectual" in the tables.)

In all these examples of the Intellectual World, the assurance that adequate investments will continue over a long latency period is critical, but these guarantees are sought principally by protecting the national market: in spite of rather low levels of international specialization, there is generally a trade surplus for their products. These firms are strongly tied to the State's "technological" agencies (ministries of transportation, telecommunication, space, national defense, and so forth) in defining products and quality, standards, which gives them an edge on future orders (see Chapter 6). Some firms use this advantage to position themselves for new State-dominated products; profitability is thus high (+0.40). One such firm is examined in Illustration 4.7.

The principal challenge for these firms is gaining access to international markets, government or private. This is particularly true for firms on the border of the Market and Intellectual Worlds, because their modernization strategies can only succeed if they develop and commercialize new products, and that will require cost reductions and organizational flexibility. Since these are highly technical products, they also require ongoing R&D and training efforts; and flexibility depends both on specialized subcontracting networks at the local level and on development of international alliances. These firms did not succeed, by and large, in gaining access to international commercial markets; more recent evidence suggests little change, a worrisome situation for French high technology.

Multiple Pathways Away from the Industrial World

If we take improvement in the rate of return on capital as an indicator that a restructuring strategy has been successful, we can point to five strategies that showed such improvement. This supports our claim that diversity, unevenness, and heterogeneity are the order of the day, not a single model of industrial change. Having said that, the Industrial World is the big loser, and there is a general tendency, depicted in Figure 4.1, to move toward the Market and Intellectual Worlds simultaneously. This corresponds to the general refrain of the contemporary economic literature, which stresses the importance of intellectual resources and the ability to track the market closely.

For this axis to become a broader reality in France, it would be necessary to redeploy the resources of other existing worlds—the Interpersonal and the Industrial—in new ways. Thus the standardization, industrial rationalization, and unit cost reductions of the Industrial World and the specialized savoir-faire, traditions of quality, and decentralized networks of persons of the Interpersonal World would be applied to the production of industrial products much enriched in quality, in a context of continuous

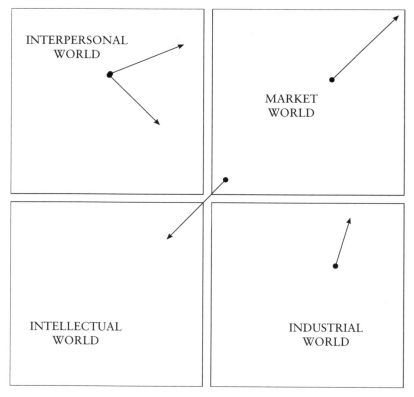

Figure 4.1   Movements between worlds of production for firms in sample that improved their profitability (between entry of firm and 1987).

innovation (thus joining them to the Intellectual World) and differentiated into services dedicated to consumers (the Market World). Taken together, these forces might be able to generate ongoing technological learning.

We expect that each nation has an analogous problem of refashioning existing resources into coherent worlds of production. In some cases, this could involve transforming the existing identities and forms of participation in the economy to clear the way for new action frameworks. In other cases, it involves strengthening and making more coherent what is already basically there. To see this in greater detail, we examine in the following chapters the strong points—innovative real worlds of production—in three nations, and try to unveil the conventions of identity and participation that have allowed them to excel in certain kinds of products in world trade, while at the same time excluding other possible worlds of production. This will permit us to consider the question of possible transition pathways in systematic fashion in Chapter 9.

Appendix: Case Studies of Firm Modernization in France
ILLUSTRATION 4.1 THE INDUSTRIAL MODERNIZATION
FUND AND THE NATIONAL EMPLOYMENT FUND

The 224 firms are a random sample of files evaluated by the ANVAR *(Agence Nationale pour la Valorisation de la Recherche)* for loans of more than 5 million francs approved by the FIM. They represent more than half the applications accepted between September 1983 and March 1986 (the program ended in August 1986). The FIM's stated goal was to "contribute to the financing of industrial firms which commit material and non-material investments toward modernization of processes of fabrication or for development of new products and processes." Well-funded, the FIM had two principal strategies: (1) to participate in making long- and medium-term loans at subsidized interest rates; (2) to ensure that their contribution was used in a way clearly oriented toward modernization, by calling on the technical and financial expertise associated with ANVAR or the General Directorate of Industry, in addition to financial advice from the Crédit National (a state bank whose initial mission was to aid small and medium-sized enterprises).

Files obtained from the National Employment Fund cover special agreements with these firms concerning early retirement and training and retraining of the workforce. Certain files contained detailed information on economic and social conditions underlying the request, including the firm's plan for softening the impact of employment reductions and, in some instances, a summary of consultation with the Enterprise Committee (see Chapter 11). In all, we examined 420 special allocation agreements (agreements which allow special funds to be disbursed to ease the pain of employment reduction, as in supplemental unemployment or layoff payments), 27 training agreements, and 41 restructuring contracts executed during the 1982–1990 period.

ILLUSTRATION 4.2 FIRM A: FROM THE
MARKET TO THE INDUSTRIAL WORLD

Firm A fabricates electronic components at its factory in a large provincial city, where it has been located for ten years, always with public financial assistance. The strategy of the firm, which is small by Japanese standards, is to serve highly technical markets with customized components using a highly diversified catalog of basic options. To operate in this difficult market, it must coordinate resources belonging to different worlds of production, make massive investments in materials and in R&D to keep unit costs down, and continuously transform the product technology. Production is in long runs but has to meet extremely precise specifications and quality standards, such as those of the "white room." Demand is strongly cyclical and in some ways uncertain. The firm fabricates; R&D is done upstream in large government laboratories. Hiring is not based on formal credentials, but rather on the results of tests of aptitude for adapting to change. Since production equipment changes every two years, skills have no lasting value and the firm has no interest in professional experience; the firm does on-the-job training and seeks a high level of flexibility: polyvalence, fluctuating hours, temporary work, and so on.

Both the product and labor conventions suggest that this is predominantly a "market" model, but it faces the constraints imposed by the need to draw resources from other worlds, especially the Industrial World: massive investments to keep prices down; low price-cost margins; industrial classification of work stations and imposition of rules from the branch level agreement. At the time of its agreement with the FIM, we classified this firm as close to the Market World. But by 1987, changes in the firm's coordinates led us to reclassify it as having moved "in the direction of" the Industrial World. This partial "return"—found for many other firms—is a sign of tensions inherent in the need to coordinate the resources of different worlds, tensions which have not been resolved satisfactorily by this firm: it had to request an employment restructuring plan from the State in 1987, because its employment growth was not consistent with its FIM projections. It has since become an affiliate held in equal parts by a French firm and a German firm and continues to specialize in high technology components, now oriented toward European markets.

ILLUSTRATION 4.3 CORPORATION B: BETWEEN THE MARKET AND INTERPERSONAL WORLDS

Corporation B is the European leader in knitted yarn, but this market is declining and the firm has lost 800 jobs in nine years. It is concentrating on two strategies: fabricating yarn with integrated automation in order to reduce costs; and commercialization through a system of exclusive franchises designed to sell a greater variety of finished, high value-added products, especially sweaters with a "handmade" look. Such a product requires, in contrast to yarn production, a flexible and decentralized network of subcontractors to which the group brings organizational skills.

Strong tensions exist between these two strategies: one looks toward the Market World (yarn production via flexible automation) and the other toward the Interpersonal World (sales of sweaters, pulled along by demand)—a tension enhanced by the difficulties of implementing either one separately.

ILLUSTRATION 4.4 INTERNAL WORKFORCE FLEXIBILITY

One firm in our sample proposed (unsuccessfully) in 1987 an agreement on reorganization of work time which called for possible part-time work, variable hours, staggered shifts, and consolidation of hours, and for polyvalence, as a criterion for advancement and wage level, defined as "the mastery of multiple techniques; assignment to a job, for a relatively long period of time, in which a complex series of tasks is fulfilled, within assigned time limits, and at required quality levels; acceptance of permanent mobility between work stations within the same establishment."

The agreement also proposed that there would be a waiting period so that consequences of such flexibility could be considered and negotiated at the local level. In the event where flexibility would lead to consolidation of multiple establishments and workforce reductions, it was proposed that there be centralized local negotiations over the consequences for the local labor market.

ILLUSTRATION 4.5 CORPORATION C: QUALITY AND PRICE

Corporation C, located in northern France, produces plumbing fixtures. In 1988, it made the following analysis in the course of a request for aid:

"Among exporting countries, we find first of all Germany, whose producers have a reputation for *technical quality and reliability;* Italy, whose producers have entered the French market rapidly through *price competition* (20–40% below price norms) linked to an aesthetic mastery of *forms and colors.*

"The market has changed dramatically from the early 1970s, when it was dominated by industrially-produced fixtures for new housing. Today's market is dominated by *renovations,* with 50% for single-family homes, and sales to individuals are growing relative to those to builders.

"This new clientele is much more attentive to the qualities of *functionality,* aesthetics, and *quality-price relationships,* and has engendered a major transformation of the distribution system (toward retail).

"The level of international prices is currently quite low, often 50% less than those which prevail in France. Under these conditions, only very high levels of productivity, via *long production runs* (as in Germany and the U.S.A.) or very high levels of *flexibility* (Italy) can permit a firm to remain in these competitive international markets."

ILLUSTRATION 4.6 FIRM E

Firm E, until recently controlled by a group of white-collar workers, brings together a number of activities involving optical lenses and contact lenses. It has a worldwide reputation in this field due to its ongoing research activity, which has provided the basis for several major innovations. One unit of the firm was targeted for modernization, but faced severe constraints: although it supplies a highly technical product designed for a particular client, it must rely on industrial methods for cost control. This unit fabricated semi-finished lenses and marked them with the information necessary for the retail outlet to finish according to a client's specifications. The firm's modernization plan consisted of automating the entire operation; this included installing several types of robots and training personnel to supervise them. Today, a robot with "vision" prepares and sorts orders, with feedback to the production line, but this system is backed up by a traditional workshop. In other words, the robot incorporates the necessary know-how, but requires skilled servers. In other operations, however, it remains impossible (or excessively expensive) to endow machines with the required savoir-faire. For example, when a mold is filled, air bubbles may form along its sides; these are incompatible with product quality standards, and operators make the bubbles rise by pressing repeatedly on the mold with their fingers. With the continuing importance of the firm's R&D activity, and its connections to basic research (in optics, physiology, and so forth), as well as its responsiveness to clients' needs (comfort, aesthetics), the firm thus operates between several models and is always in danger of losing the proper equilibrium.

ILLUSTRATION 4.7 FIRM G

Firm G, founded by a group of engineers, makes capital goods in electronics and telecommunications; it has an extremely diverse product portfolio that draws on different methods of fabrication and uses production runs of different lengths. Though the firm unquestionably possesses considerable savoir-faire, it does not give the impression of actively seeking to best employ it. Its rate of value added has diminished as a result of increasing externalization. The firm has a longstanding and fundamental reliance on State markets and only weak experience in commercial markets. Thus, even though it developed early prototypes of fax machines in response to a call for proposals from the PTT (the French postal and telephone monopoly), it never launched its product onto the market. Faced with the explosive growth of demand for fax equipment, it entered the market quite late by acquiring a license from a Japanese firm. It is currently involved in trying to absorb its excess production workers while at the same time hiring highly qualified engineers though without—apparently—any defined strategy for research and commercialization over the long run. Firm G has recently restructured around three poles—two in high technology destined for government purchases, one in high-technology automobile components and fax equipment. It has had some success in this latest restructuring.

II

WORLDS OF PRODUCTION
IN THREE COUNTRIES

5

IDENTIFYING REAL WORLDS OF PRODUCTION IN FRANCE, ITALY, AND THE UNITED STATES

From Possible To Real Worlds of Production

Nations and regions have distinctive economic identities, in the sense that their products are results of the conventions of their economic actors. There are two main sources of these economic identities. First, the frameworks of action through which productive activity is coordinated affect the qualities of their products. This is less simplistic than it may at first appear. A given material object can have very different significance in different contexts. This effect is ubiquitous, as any European can report with respect to consumer goods produced in different nations of the European Union: not only are there subtle differences between objects, but even apparently similar objects call forth images of each country's particular industrial system and its social relations. Nations and regions have reputations for certain kinds of products, we argue, because their action frameworks provide or deny access to making different products successfully.

A second source of economic identity hinges on which (if any) production systems are especially effective, that is, capable not only of making products, but of being innovative about them. Innovation involves going beyond average "imitative" efficiencies for a given product or process, by generating an original, dynamic pathway of development and coordinating the objects and actors necessary for introducing innovations. This particular type of coordination marks the successful, coherent use of elementary action frameworks in real production activity or, for short, a "real world of production."

The empirical indicator of a real world of production used in this book is the existence of export specialization. In the context of a world in which the number of increasingly specialized exchanges is expanding, real worlds of production are highly competitive. Competitiveness, we shall argue later, results from coherent action frameworks in a given productive activity.

Contrasting Specializations in Three Countries

Table 5.1 presents figures on trade composition and trade ratios for a set of industrialized countries, using the OECD's classification of industry groups. These categories overlap with possible worlds of production to some extent: scale-intensive industry with the Industrial World; supplier-dominated industry with the Interpersonal World; some specialized supplier industries with the Market World, others in the Interpersonal World; and a part of the Intellectual World with science-based industry. Note the extraordinary presence of the supplier-dominated industries in Italian exports, along with the near absence of science-based products and very high imports from scale-intensive sectors. In contrast, France is very strong in scale-related exports, and the United States very weak in exports from supplier-dominated industries, with the rest spread among the other three categories.

Table 5.2 shows the direction of change in export specializations over the 1970s and 1980s, albeit at a rather aggregated *filière* level, for four European countries. Note that while Italy has strongly reinforced its position in the supplier-dominated and specialized supplier industries, France has had neither dramatic successes nor dramatic reversals, holding steady in scale-related production, slipping somewhat in supplier-dominated and science-based products, and improving modestly in specialized supplier sectors (a result, almost exclusively, of the growth of the Airbus Industrie consortium, as reflected in the "transportation" category).

France: A Weakly Specialized Economy, Poorly Adapted to International Demand

To sharpen this analysis and provide a basis for comparing the specializations of France to those of the United States and Italy, we defined three groups of products in which competition is highly likely to be based on elements other than price,[1] that is, on technological mastery or product quality. The first group consists of a subset of the supplier-dominated industries, the design-intensive or craft-based (DIC) outputs, products based on fashion or luxury (such as clothing or personal accessories); competition is centered on creative skills or, for manufacturing, on arti-

Table 5.1 Trade composition and trade ratios for main industrialized countries by typology of industrial sectors (1990)

Industrial Sectors	Italy	France	West Germany	United Kingdom	United States	Japan
Exports (E) %						
Supplier-dominated	41.57	19.96	18.63	21.88	13.70	12.10
Scale-intensive	26.90	42.85	44.27	29.85	27.17	57.18
Specialized supplier	21.99	21.15	25.36	25.86	28.29	23.25
Science-based	8.54	16.04	11.74	22.40	30.29	7.47
Total	100.00	100.00	100.00	100.00	100.00	100.00
Imports (I) %						
Supplier-dominated	18.78	25.48	29.94	26.78	28.18	26.40
Scale-intensive	46.95	43.53	38.74	39.19	44.98	36.62
Specialized supplier	18.15	21.26	16.00	18.97	16.22	15.02
Science-based	16.12	9.73	15.31	15.05	10.61	21.96
Total	100.00	100.00	100.00	100.00	100.00	100.00
Trade ratios (E/I, $ value)						
Supplier-dominated	57.57	−6.23	3.56	−12.21	−39.82	33.91
Scale-intensive	−0.15	5.18	32.71	−15.64	−29.43	74.69
Specialized supplier	33.78	5.72	46.46	13.26	21.38	74.50
Science-based	−5.91	13.11	13.91	1.55	43.28	20.11

Source: OECD.

sanal methods. The production problems correspond closely to the Interpersonal World (though some, as we shall see, are found in the Market World). The second group is a subset of the science-based industries, the high technology products (HTI). These correspond mainly to the Intellectual World, although more standardized outputs are tied into the Market World and more dedicated products into the Interpersonal World. The third group, precision metalworking and machining products (PMM), consists of specialized and dedicated mechanical items, found across the economy. Their producers correspond strongly to the Interpersonal and Market Worlds and are commonly categorized as "specialized supplier" industries. Table 5.3 provides a compact summary picture of the situation in 1985.

France is specialized in the first (design-intensive, craft-based) group, with 6.7% of world exports in 1985 (as compared to its total share of world trade, 5.2%). Its strongest positions are in products for the home, textiles and personal accessories, which together account for 10% of French exports. This position remains strong and deep, but the country's share for several products declined in the 1980s. In the second group, high technology outputs, France has 6.4% of world exports, and the group

Table 5.2A Export specialization

Scale-intensive industries (Industrial)	(1970–1973)					(1984–1987)					Change				
	GER	FRA	UK	ITA	Total	GER	FRA	UK	ITA	Total	GER	FRA	UK	ITA	Total
Chemicals	124.70	120.40	112.00	98.30	113.90	122.50	150.00	140.80	90.60	126.00	−2.20	29.60	28.80	−7.70	12.10
Oil	50.70	54.60	66.30	145.40	79.30	40.40	50.30	86.20	72.80	62.40	−10.30	−4.30	19.90	−72.60	−16.90
Electrical machinery	145.20	114.90	109.70	140.50	127.60	123.40	110.50	99.40	104.60	109.50	−21.80	−4.40	−10.30	−35.90	−18.10
Motor vehicles	145.50	123.20	114.40	96.70	120.00	146.90	105.50	62.20	61.10	93.90	1.40	−17.70	−52.20	−35.60	−26.10
Total	116.50	103.30	100.60	120.20	110.20	108.30	104.10	97.15	82.30	97.90	−8.20	0.80	3.45	−37.90	−12.30

Supplier-dominated (Interpersonal/Market)	(1970–1973)					(1984–1987)					Change				
	GER	FRA	UK	ITA	Total	GER	FRA	UK	ITA	Total	GER	FRA	UK	ITA	Total
Textiles	70.80	114.70	80.60	209.10	118.80	60.90	74.10	58.70	219.10	103.20	−9.90	−40.60	−21.90	10.00	−15.60
Non-metallic minerals	115.50	132.90	105.30	210.50	141.10	107.60	138.50	91.50	244.40	145.50	−7.90	5.60	−13.80	33.90	4.45
Metal products	136.50	106.80	128.60	128.80	125.20	133.30	112.30	100.70	164.80	127.80	−3.20	5.50	−27.90	36.00	2.60
Total	107.60	118.10	104.80	182.80	128.40	100.60	108.30	83.63	209.40	125.50	−7.00	−9.80	−21.17	26.60	−2.90

Source: OECD.

Note: Figures represent ratio of exports to imports. Totals are for all industries measured.

Table 5.2B Export specialization

Specialized suppliers (Market/Interpersonal)	(1970–1973)					(1984–1987)					Change				
	GER	FRA	UK	ITA	Total	GER	FRA	UK	ITA	Total	GER	FRA	UK	ITA	Total
Mechanical engineering	188.10	84.70	143.80	136.60	138.30	168.20	76.20	118.00	168.20	132.70	−19.90	−8.50	−25.80	31.60	−5.60
Mechanical and thermomechanical equipment	149.40	105.40	117.90	134.80	126.90	147.80	108.60	127.90	155.40	134.90	−1.60	3.20	10.00	20.60	8.00
Other transportation	48.50	85.50	105.80	41.90	70.40	66.10	119.50	162.20	53.90	100.40	17.60	34.00	56.40	12.00	30.00
Total	128.70	91.87	122.50	104.40	111.90	127.40	101.40	136.00	125.80	122.70	−1.30	9.53	13.50	21.40	10.80

Science-based industries (Intellectual)	(1970–1973)					(1984–1987)					Change				
	GER	FRA	UK	ITA	Total	GER	FRA	UK	ITA	Total	GER	FRA	UK	ITA	Total
Office	111.30	101.40	129.80	109.80	113.10	67.40	80.30	150.40	62.30	90.10	−43.90	−21.10	20.60	−47.50	−23.00
Electronics	90.30	60.10	75.90	69.50	73.90	60.50	57.30	75.60	37.50	57.70	−29.80	−2.80	−0.30	−32.00	−16.20
Instruments	128.70	88.30	108.10	59.90	96.25	111.70	87.00	140.50	54.60	98.40	−17.00	−1.30	32.40	−5.30	2.15
Total	110.10	83.27	104.60	79.73	94.42	79.87	74.87	122.20	51.47	82.07	−30.23	−8.42	17.60	−28.30	−12.35
Scale	116.50	103.30	100.60	120.20	110.20	108.30	104.10	97.15	82.30	97.90	−8.20	0.80	−3.45	−37.90	−12.30
Rest	115.50	97.76	110.60	122.30	111.50	102.60	94.87	113.90	128.90	110.10	−12.80	−2.80	3.30	6.59	−1.47

Source: OECD.

Note: Figures represent ratio of exports to imports. Totals are for all industries measured.

Table 5.3 Degree of country specialization in high technology industry, design-intensive/craft-based industry, and precision machinery metalworking industries, 1985

Clusters	Countries		
	US	France	Italy
High technology industries			
Value of exports ($billion)	60.13	15.76	7.85
Value of imports ($billion)	57.17	13.61	9.83
Country's share of total world exports in cluster (%)	24.72%	6.48%	3.23%
Cluster's share of country's total exports (%)	28.21%	16.13%	9.94%
Design-intensive products industries			
Value of exports ($billion)	6.42	10.07	22.04
Value of imports ($billion)	41.66	10.50	6.00
Country's share of total world exports in cluster (%)	4.27%	6.69%	14.64%
Cluster's share of country's total exports (%)	3.01%	10.31%	27.92%
Precision machinery and metalworking industries			
Value of exports ($billion)	1.38	0.56	1.15
Value of imports ($billion)	3.31	0.69	0.40
Country's share of total world exports in cluster (%)	10.01%	4.02%	8.30%
Cluster's share of country's total exports (%)	0.65%	0.57%	1.46%

Source: UNIDO (United Nations Industrial Development Organization); our calculation.
Note: Cluster's definition based on SITCs. High technologies' SITCs = 524, 541, 713, 714, 718, 751, 752, 759, 761, 762, 763, 764, 772, 776, 792, 871, 872, 874. Design-intensive/craft-based industry items = 551, 553, 61, 65, 665, 666, 724, 82, 85, 883, 88, 897, 898. Precision machinery and metalworking = 696, 73.

accounts for 16% of the country's exports. This reflects French dominance in a number of areas, including radioactive elements, aircraft, reactors, and computer peripherals. France is not specialized in the third group as a whole, but does have certain strengths, in mechanical engineering, cutlery, instruments, and some types of industrial machinery. Taken together, the three groups examined here account for only about 30% of French exports. France performs moderately well in all three categories, but spectacularly in none. As Table 5.4 illustrates, the 50 leading French exports in 1985 accounted for only 22.5% of French exports; corresponding figures are 33.8% for the United States and 27.2% for Italy.

To deepen this picture, we separated products according to several broad classes of final demand, categorizing by final output, intermediate products and inputs, and the corresponding capital goods as a way to illuminate the groups of products tied together through user-producer relations. France is specialized in only a few clusters or sub-clusters of products: beverages and food products; inputs to the transportation industry (automobile components, tires, and so on); production of energy and turbines; health care (including pharmaceuticals).

Note that very few products on the list seem to be based on dynamic economies of variety and collective technological learning.[2] A relatively large number are very likely listed because of favorable cost structures or simple scale economies. For example, with the exception of wines (where France is absolutely dominant on world markets, more by reason of its savoir-faire than climate or cost advantages), most of the firms in the food and beverage group are large-scale food processing firms. In the transportation category, only aircraft engines and reaction engines, electrical traction vehicles (such as locomotives), and radar apparatus are obvious cases of specialization based on learning or economies of variety. By contrast, numerous specializations in the clothing-textile sector are probably linked to savoir-faire: fabrics, lace, women's dresses and clothing, woolen yarns, furs, weaving machinery. In energy production, a number of products have benefited from scale economies as a result of the State's modernization of the national electric system, including rapid nuclearization, and the corresponding scale effects on related capital-goods sectors (although some energy products are knowledge-intensive). State direction has also affected the electronics and telecommunications sectors, which require technological mastery for competition. Finally, in the "health care" group, some firms—although they are beneficiaries of purchases by the public health care system—export certain drugs developed on the basis of superior scientific knowledge.

In sum, only 17 of the top 50 specializations shown in Table 5.4A seem to be attributable to economies of variety or collective technological learning. Not only are French exports as a whole not very specialized, but when divided into the three principal causes of export positions—costs, economies of scale, economies of variety/learning—costs and scale, the least appealing in terms of developmental effects, carry the day. We must ask how France has come to disperse its energies so widely. How did the industrial action framework acquire such a presence in so many sectors? In order to understand the promising aspects of the French economy, we must find what lies behind the limited but strong forms of Intellectual and Interpersonal action found there.

Table 5.4A   The roots of export specialization: learning industries versus the rest, France

Scale or process-based technological advantages in scale or costs	Product-based technological learning: economies of variety
Xylenes, chemical pure	Distilled wine from grapes
Malt, including flower	Wine of fresh grapes
Polyamides	Radioactive elements
Other wheat, unmilled	Household, hotel glass
Wheat flour	Aircraft, N.E.C., over 15,000 KG
Chemical elements	Essences, oils
Poultry	Reaction engines
Copper scrap	Off-line DP equipment
Refined sugar	Yachts, sports vessels
Fresh apples	Light electric vehicles
Dry milk > 1.5% fat	Pile, cotton fabrics
Anti-knock preparations	Spectacle frames
Glass bottles	Mixed perfumes
New tires for cars	Medicaments, non-antibody
Combustible products	Perfumery and cosmetics
Residual of 224	Residual of women's outerwear
Refractory bricks	(non-knitted)
Tires for buses	Laces, ribbons, tulle
Chair components	
Central heating equipment	
Ind. furnaces, non-electric	
Parts for refrigerator equipment	
Electric accumulators	
Polystyrene, prim.	
Polyvinyl chloride feedstock	
Stainless steel plates	
Tinned plates, sheets	
Shovels, excavators	
Bovine meat with bone	
Insecticides, retail	
Iron and steel wire	
Railway vehicles and parts	
Butter	
N = 33	N = 17
Export Value: $12.1 billion	Export Value: $9.86 billion
Value: 55.1%	Value: 44.9%

Total: $21.96 billion

Source: UNIDO (United Nations Industrial Development Organization), World Trade Statistics.

Table 5.4B The roots of export specialization: learning industries versus the rest, United States

Scale or process-based technological advantages in scale or costs	Product-based technological learning: economies of variety
Cottonseed oil	Commercial aircraft/helicopters
Photo film	Aircraft engines and parts
Petroleum coke	Analog hybrid DP machines
Rough sawn, veneer logs	Aircraft gas turbine engines
Fertilizers	War firearms, ammunition
Beet pulp, bagasse	Measuring, drawing instruments
Unmilled maize	(parts)
Soya beans	Warships, boats
Unmilled sorghum	Measuring, drawing instruments
Coal, lignite, and peat	(complete)
Fresh fish	Piezoelectric crystals
Fats of bovine, sheep	Electromedical equipment
Nitrogen, phosphate fertilizer	Glycosides, glands, sera
Whey	Footwear with soles of cork
Clay	Rolling mills
Green groundnuts	Civil engineering equipment
Typewriters, checkwriters	Pharmaceuticals
Stripped tobacco	Aircraft engine and motor parts
Iron pyrites	Office, ADP machine parts,
Dissolving chemical wood pulp	accessories
Raw bovine, equine hides	Radioactive materials
Cyclic alcohols	Aircraft parts
Edible offal	
Track-laying tractors	
Fungicides, disinfectants	
Kraft liner	
Polyethylene in rods	
Polyvinyl chloride in rods	
Artificial fur products	
Motor vehicle chassis	
N = 30	N = 19
Export Value: $26.9 billion	Export Value: $45.0 billion
Value: 37.46%	Value: 62.54%

Total: $71.9 billion

Source: UNIDO (United Nations Industrial Development Organization), World Trade Statistics.

Table 5.4C   The roots of export specialization: learning industries versus the rest, Italy

Scale or process-based technological advantages in scale or costs	Product-based technological learning: economies of variety
Groats, meal, pellets	Aperitifs
Worked building stone	Glazed ceramic sets
Fresh stone fruit	Precious metal jewelry
Rubber and plastic footware	Fabrics of combed wool
Domestic washing machines	Sweaters of synthetic fibers
Steel high-pressure conduit	Handbags
Fresh grapes	Woolen sweaters
Domestic deep freezers	Leather footwear
Domestic refrigerators	Other woven textile fabric
Coke/semi-coke of lignite	Woven silk fabric
Unbleached sulfited woodpulp	Cement, artificial stone products
Olive oil	Chairs and other seats
Bulk antibodies	Textile clothing accessories
Domestic heating, cooking app.	Women's outerwear
Foliage, branches, plants	Wood furniture
Solid sodium hydroxide	Machine tools for wood, ceramics
Plastic coated textiles	Leather
	Other sweaters, pullovers
	Footwear components
	Furniture and parts
	Men's suits
	Spectacle frames
	Knitted clothing accessories
	Metal furniture
	Wine of fresh grapes
	Ceramic ornaments
	Nontextured yarn cont. polyamide
	Packaging and bottling machines
	Men's overcoats
	Sinks, washbasins, bidets
	Lamps, fittings of base metal
	Other textile, special leather machines
	Woven synthetic fiber fabric
N = 17	N = 33
Export Value: $3.8 billion	Export Value: $17.7 billion
Value: 17.71%	Value: 82.29%
Total: $21.5 billion	

Source: UNIDO (United Nations Industrial Development Organization), World Trade Statistics.

Table 5.4D   The roots of export specialization: learning industries versus the rest

Scale or process-based technological advantages in scale or costs	Product-based technological learning: economies of variety
N = 80 Export Value: $42.9 billion Value: 37.15%	N = 69 Export Value: $72.56 billion Value: 62.84%
Total for 149 sectors: $115.46 billion	

Source: UNIDO (United Nations Industrial Development Organization), World Trade Statistics.

The United States: The Importance of the Intellectual World

The picture in the United States contrasts significantly with that seen in France. The United States is quite specialized in high technology exports, with more than 25% of the world's total. Its share of PMMs does not qualify as a specialization, since it is just below the "cutoff," but it is respectably close, while the share of design-intensive products is less than half the country's overall share, thus falling far short of specialization. ("Cutoff" refers to the country's overall share of all world exports and imports, which was about 12% for the United States in 1985, 5.2% for France, and 4.6% for Italy.)

Among U.S. specializations in high technology industries are a number of extremely strong positions: aircraft and aircraft parts, gas turbines, measuring and drawing equipment, electro-medical equipment, ADP peripherals, and digital computers all account for at least three times the cutoff level. Among the top fifty American exports, as ranked by world market shares (see Table 5.4B), are semiconductors, instruments, computers, and aircraft; in terms of both dollar volume and share in total U.S. exports, the most important specializations are commercial aircraft and helicopters, computers, firearms and ammunition, aircraft parts, piezoelectric crystals, aircraft engines, and office machine and computer parts. U.S. performance is strong in other high technology areas, especially in technologies related to health care ranging from equipment to pharmaceuticals and related chemical products. While the U.S. position in PMM industries has fallen in recent years, it remains strong in steelmaking equipment, metalworking machinery, and certain equipment sectors linked to high technology, such as semiconductor manufacturing machinery. The United States had very few strong positions in the design-intensive industries, however. What is it that makes intellectual action so strong in the United States, and why is interpersonal action apparently so weak?

Italy: The Predominance of the Interpersonal World

Italy looks something like the inverse of the U.S. case, with an overwhelmingly strong position in design-intensive products (almost 15% of the world total, or three times the Italian cutoff level) and PMMs (with a share almost double the cutoff), but an unimpressive 3.2% of world high technology exports. Figure 5.1 shows how important high technology is to U.S. exports, and the analogous role played by DICs for Italy, with France having a certain balance between the two and a small role for PMMs.[3]

What is so striking about Italy's design-intensive exports is the sheer number of sectors in which it is dominant, and the very high shares of world exports that Italian firms hold in those product markets (in a dozen sectors Italy's shares exceed 25%, six times the cutoff). The Italian presence is particularly strong in textiles and apparel; household products such as furniture, lamps, glass, and ceramic tiles; personal products such as jewelry; and miscellaneous fashion items such as eyeglasses and toiletries. Other specializations include paper making, film and film processing, and automobile design. The Italian economy also stands out frequently for specializing in intermediate products or equipment associated with its final output specializations. Thus, the list includes textile machinery, marble cutting tools, kilns for tile making, and some metalworking and woodworking machinery. Why is interpersonal action so present in Italy, and why are other forms of action so conspicuously missing?

Real Worlds As Regional Worlds

The export specialization industries of the United States, France, and Italy are not distributed evenly across their national territories. Indeed, the geography of these industries conforms rather well to popular impressions about these nations' "dynamic" regions. Thus the U.S. high technology industries, centered on microelectronics (semiconductors and computers), are highly concentrated in Silicon Valley in northern California, Orange County-San Diego in southern California, and the Boston area, with lesser concentrations in Minneapolis-St. Paul (Minnesota), Dallas-Fort Worth, and the southern Atlantic coast of Florida. Aerospace has its primary concentration in the Los Angeles region, with other significant concentrations in Texas, New York, Connecticut-Massachusetts, and Washington

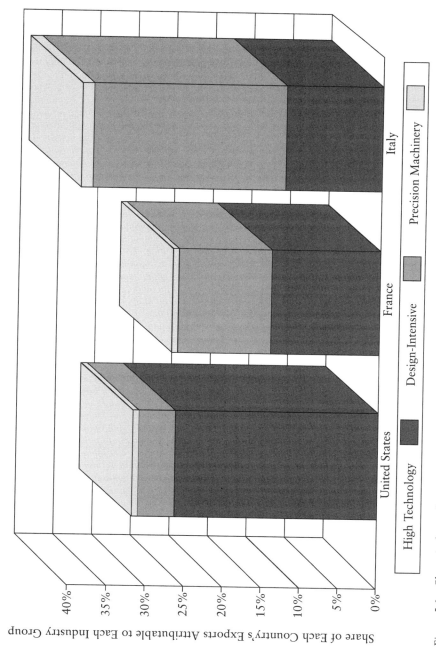

Figure 5.1 Cluster's share of country's exports.

state. (In technical terms, the sectors mentioned have location quotients in these places which are greater than 1.2, suggesting genuine (statistically significant) localizations (see Table 5.5).

In Italy, the export-oriented DICs and PMMs are highly concentrated in the northeastern regions of Lombardy (outside of Milan, for the most part), the Veneto, Trentino-Alto Adige, Friuli-Venezia-Giuilia (F-V-G), Emilia-Romagna, and Tuscany, with some extensions into the Marches

Table 5.5 Regional real worlds

Industry	Employment	Location quotients[a]
California		
Aerospace	229,124	3.02
Biologicals	5,255	2.08
Electronics and components	509,692	2.05
Precision instruments	40,913	1.59
Medical equipment	25,627	1.48
Massachusetts and Connecticut		
Aircraft and engines	17,918	7.78
Financial services	21,849	6.39
Aerospace and armaments	77,911	4.14
Precision instruments	36,042	2.81
Electronics and components	101,150	2.73
Radio, TV, and telecommunications	67,545	1.82
Research and development labs	12,272	1.80
Medical equipment	8,119	1.65
New York and New Jersey		
Pharmaceuticals and biologicals	47,599	2.41
Medical equipment	21,950	1.86
Banking and finance	319,952	1.51
Advanced services	504,500	1.50
Electronics and components	54,150	1.26
Texas		
Construction and engineering	677,463	1.73
Aircraft	29,374	1.57
Electronics	76,597	1.47
Ohio, Michigan, and Pennsylvania		
Instruments	31,816	1.40
Washington		
Aircraft	54,523	7.85
Electronics and components	3,809	2.62

a. Location quotient is the ratio of the percentage of output of industry x in economy y (the locality in question), to the percentage of output of industry x in the nation's economy as a whole.

and Umbria. And within these regions, particular provinces and communes are highly specialized: Udine (F-V-G) in chairs, Como (Lombardy) in silk fabrics, Sassuolo (Emilia-Romagna) in ceramic tiles and tile equipment, Poggibonsi (Tuscany) in wooden furniture, Bologna and Modena (Emilia-Romagna) in mechanical engineering, Santa Croce (Tuscany) in leather shoes, and so on. Thus, Italy shows not only extremely strong economic specializations, but a dramatically focused geography. (Sforzi has documented the existence of about one hundred "industrial districts" in the DIC and PMM industries.)[4] The action frameworks of these districts are studied in Chapter 7.

In trying to locate real worlds of production in France, it is helpful to note that several of the country's trade specializations are based on natural resources; others appear to be rooted in the economies of scale adroitly constructed in mass production sectors by the State's economic planning agency; and, finally, there is one group of industries qualifying as a trade specialization, very probably rooted in the existence of economies of variety or skill, the key corollaries of technological learning as defined here. These are the industries where the axis "Market World-Intellectual World" (Chapter 4) is in evidence. To select cases for study for this set of sectors, we measured the location quotients using a very strict cutoff (those with a quotient of at least two; see Table 5.6). This yielded the set of cases shown in Figure 5.2: regional real worlds of industries in which France is an international leader. A second set of cases involved a more inductive method: we identified certain industries in which it is widely assumed that international competition among high-wage countries is based on technological advantage—sectors such as microelectronics, precision machining, and certain fashion industries. We then established the location quotients for these industries and selected those regions with a quotient of at least two.

Several kinds of real worlds emerged from this procedure. The *Francilien* model, examined in detail in Chapter 6, is that of the high-technology and high-fashion industries in the Ile-de-France region. The prestige projects of both industries—what we call "economies of splendor"—are highly concentrated in and around Paris because of the particular way in which resources are mobilized and coordinated in networks of innovators in that region, in one case through the State, in another through a historically constituted community. These conventions of participation and identity of the skilled innovators in the Ile-de-France shape the particular nature of product qualities there, and form the regional basis for high-prestige products.[5]

Table 5.6 Percentage of French employment and location quotients by region for export specialized French industries in 1987

Regions except Corsica	Airplanes and Components	Semiconductors	Computers and Office Equipment	Plastic Products	Women's Clothing	Shoes	Precision Mechanics	Region's Share in Total Employment
Ile-de-France	37.10 (2.00)	41.70 (2.25)	47.10 (2.54)	9.40	14.10	1.10	21.10	18.54
Champagne-Ardennes	0.40	0.50	0.00	3.70	0.90	0.20	2.10	2.44
Picardie	0.00	0.60	0.10	7.50	3.50	0.00	1.00	3.20
Haute Normandie	4.70	4.00	2.10	0.00	2.90	1.90	2.00	3.06
Centre	4.10	6.60	4.70	7.30	8.20	1.70	6.60	4.20
Basse Normandie	1.20	3.20	0.00	1.30	3.30	0.60	0.80	2.48
Bourgogne	0.00	2.30	0.00	4.10	2.40	0.20	3.70	2.91
Nord-Pas de Calais	2.10	1.70	6.20	6.40	12.40	0.90	2.40	7.10
Lorraine	0.10	1.30	0.10	3.40	4.00	6.20	4.80	4.18
Alsace	0.60	2.90	0.70	4.90	3.00	7.30	7.40	2.89
Franche-Comté	0.10	1.30	8.80 (4.48)	4.50 (2.3)	1.80	0.00	19.30 (9.85)	1.96
Pays de la Loire	8.30	7.10	13.70 (2.51)	7.90	13.80 (2.53)	30.90 (5.66)	2.90	5.46

Table 5.6 (continued)

Regions except Corsica	Airplanes and Components	Semiconductors	Computers and Office Equipment	Plastic Products	Women's Clothing	Shoes	Precision Mechanics	Region's Share in Total Employment
Bretagne	1.80	6.50	2.10	1.50	3.00	3.50	0.40	5.00
Poitou-Charentes	3.20	1.20	0.00	1.10	3.50	6.30 (2.20)	0.60	2.86
Aquitaine	10.08 (2.19)	2.40	0.10	3.00	2.00	17.80 (3.60)	2.00	4.92
Midi-Pyrénées	10.10 (2.37)	3.20	1.70	1.30	5.20	0.60	0.60	4.26
Limousin	0.00	0.80	0.00	0.30	2.10	3.60	0.20	1.33
Rhône-Alpes	1.20	6.90	3.10	20.70 (2.22)	8.20	11.40	19.60 (2.20)	9.32
Auvergne	1.60	1.40	0.00	3.50	1.30	2.60	0.70	2.41
Languedoc-Roussillon	0.00	0.15	8.20	1.10	8.80 (2.40)	3.20	0.90	3.64
Provence-Alpes-Côte d'Azur	11.60	3.80	1.30	2.20	2.20	1.00	0.80	7.34

Source: SESSI.
Note: Figures in parentheses are location quotients for the region.

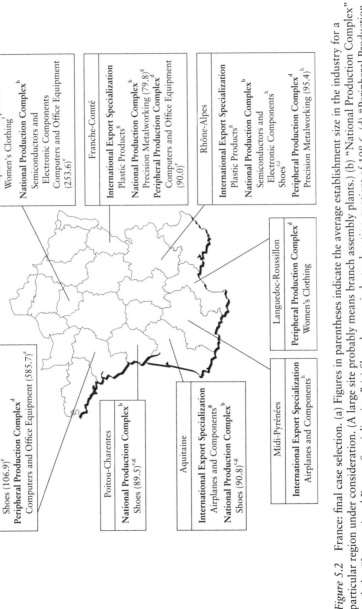

Pays de la Loire

National Production Complex [b]
Shoes (106.9)[c]

Peripheral Production Complex [d]
Computers and Office Equipment (585.7)[e]

Poitou-Charentes

National Production Complex [b]
Shoes (89.5)[c-g]

Aquitaine

International Export Specialization
Airplanes and Components[g]

National Production Complex [b]
Shoes (90.8)[c-g]

Midi-Pyrénées

International Export Specialization
Airplanes and Components[h]

Ile-de-France

International Export Specialization
Airplanes and Components
Women's Clothing[f]

National Production Complex [b]
Semiconductors and
Electronic Components
Computers and Office Equipment
(253.6)[e]

Franche-Comté

International Export Specialization
Plastic Products[g]

National Production Complex [b]
Precision Metalworking (79.8)[g]

Peripheral Production Complex [d]
Computers and Office Equipment
(90.0)[e]

Rhône-Alpes

International Export Specialization
Plastic Products[g]

National Production Complex [b]
Semiconductors and
Electronic Components[h]
Shoes[c,i]

Peripheral Production Complex [d]
Precision Metalworking (95.4)[h]

Languedoc-Roussillon

Peripheral Production Complex [d]
Women's Clothing

Figure 5.2   France: final case selection. (a) Figures in parentheses indicate the average establishment size in the industry for a particular region under consideration. (A large site probably means branch assembly plants.) (b) "National Production Complex" excludes "International Export Specialization." (c) Shoes have an industry location quotient of 108.6. (d) "Peripheral Production Complex" excludes both "International Export Specialization" and "National Production Complex." (e) Computers and Office Equipment have an industry location quotient of 284.9. (f) Though the location quotient is just below 2, all the case study evidence suggests an overwhelmingly high contribution to exports. (g) Not studied. (h) Studied, but case study reported only in the French language version of this book (Salais and Storper, 1993). (i) The shoe industry of Romans, in the Rhône-Alpes region, was added to our list of national production complexes because the case study literature suggests its importance and technological dynamism. We

Some of these territories with higher location quotients constitute a high proportion of the branch of activity under consideration for their respective countries, or at least its technological core. This is true of high technology (especially its military segment) in the Ile-de-France, certain industrial districts of Northeast-Central Italy, or the semiconductor industry in California's Silicon Valley. One must take care to identify the interrelations between national dynamics and regional dynamics in identifying action frameworks: in some cases, geographical proximity is key to the workings of the action framework, which is itself localized; in other cases, regional dynamics merely reflect conventions which exist at the national level as a whole. We shall explore these distinctions further in the cases that follow.

6

FRANCE:
INNOVATIVE REAL WORLDS OF
FASHION AND HIGH TECHNOLOGY

Interpersonal Worlds: Looking for Hierarchy or Market?

In this chapter we present a detailed examination of the real worlds of production of high technology and high fashion in France. This study reveals some of that country's secrets of economic development, its coordination of persons and resources, and the nature of its conventions.

In the fashion clothing industry of the Paris region, a large, innovative design and fashion community with a strong group identity has enabled development of new product qualities, from high fashion to ready-to-wear to youth mode clothing. A combination of Interpersonal and Market World action frameworks underlies this transformation, but the combination is far from perfectly coherent.

In high technology in the Ile-de-France, technocrats and managers in a tightly linked state-market nexus share a strong group identity, stemming from common schooling or social origins. Their extended interpersonal network is a "market" for technical ideas, but a very particular market which favors specialization in large-scale technological systems because they are amenable to bureaucratic production planning. Thus decision-making within the Interpersonal World is coupled to technological excellence from the Intellectual World, while much production takes place within the Industrial World. This case study illuminates one of the most interesting dimensions of the Intellectual World: the conditions under which it can flourish inside large bureaucracies, as opposed to a more entrepreneurial environment.

The Women's Clothing Industry:
In Search of a Viable Pathway to Modernization[1]

The clothing industry in France has not fared well as a whole in recent years: employment declined some 30% between the late 1970s and the late 1980s, from about 290,000 to under 200,000, while the ready-to-wear industry has seen its trade balance erode from a surplus of 1.5 billion francs per year to a current deficit. Beneath this generally dismal picture, however, is another story. Currently, women's ready-to-wear accounts for 63.2% of French clothing exports; men's clothing for only 22.5%; and the absolute value of the trade surplus has actually widened: most of the increase in women's clothing imports is concentrated in relatively cheap garments, so that France has become increasingly specialized in middle- to high-priced women's garments.

The French clothing industry differs markedly in organizational terms from its counterparts in other advanced countries.[2] Italy, the big recent success story in clothing, enjoys the advantages of modern technology and a bias toward products where design is key; close, though informal, coordination of the entire textile-clothing *filière* (commodity production chain) is achieved through designers, who pass information up the chain to clothmakers and down the chain to clothing producers. The U.S. clothing industry is directed toward mass production, with high levels of vertical integration of fabric and clothing production or, failing this, strong hierarchical coordination of subcontractors and short production deadlines.

Neither of these logics describes France, where textile and clothing industries have little vertical coordination, so that clothing producers must contend with longer delivery times and are less able than their competitors to squeeze subcontractors. Moreover, French mass production clothing firms were slower than American and German producers to develop such means of cost reduction as subcontracting to the Third World. In those sectors where France does not have an absolute design advantage, such as casual sportswear, that country has lost market share despite technological modernization and wages lower than those of many European competitors. The women's ready-to-wear industry is an exception, for here the role of design, and of French design in particular, is key.

Since the late 1970s, the French clothing industry's structure has changed markedly in favor of smaller firms. For example, between 1975 and 1985, the industry as a whole lost 16.8% of its establishments; the declines for establishments with more than 500 workers were on the order of 67%, while the declines were only 28% for those with 200–499 workers, 21.4% for those between 50–99, and those with 5–9 workers actually showed a gain of 6%. Total employment also declined most in the large firms, with employment either declining less or growing somewhat in the very smallest firms (Table 6.1).

Between 1979 and 1987, employment share increases in the textile-clothing *filière* were concentrated in two regions: the Ile-de-France, where employment share rose from 20.1% to 22.9% of the French total, and the Pays de la Loire (from 9.8% to 11.0%). Women's ready-to-wear is also concentrated in these regions: Paris is the design center for the entire French women's wear industry and for an important segment of production, while the Pays de la Loire, in particular that part known as the Choletais, enjoyed a boom in women's clothing production over the 1970s and part of the 1980s. Recent growth in the Paris region is all the more striking in light of the fact that its share of French clothing production had been declining since the war as factories relocated to areas with lower production costs—a consequence of both increasing vertical integration and French government policy. The changing fortunes of the Ile-de-France are also related to the return to smaller firms and units of production. It is very much a region of small plants, with almost 49% of national establishments (versus about 22% of employment) and a median employment establishment size of less than 9.8 employed compared to 57 for the Pays de la Loire.

The Paris clothing industry is markedly different in degree, if not in nature, from its counterparts in other major cities. For example, median establishment size is only one third the average of 29 workers in New York; more than 50% of the workers in Paris are employed in establishments with fewer than 20 persons, compared to 2% in New York.[3] Although very small establishments are found in London, that clothing industry has been declining in international position, unlike that of Paris.

The women's clothing industry of the Paris region includes three basic segments: true *haute couture*, where the product is made in batches of fewer than 10, and the production process is truly artisanal (St. Laurent has fewer than 50 in-house couturières); and two facets of the much larger ready-to-wear (*prêt-à-porter*) market: moderately expensive clothes produced in small- to medium-sized batches on a strictly seasonal basis by the former *maisons de haute couture*, and the less expensive, but still highly seasonal and fashionable, "knock-off" garments produced by small- and medium-sized firms for the new *système mode* or "young look" (youth and urban professionals) market. (See Figure 6.1.) The first two industries have

Table 6.1 French clothing industry, percentage change in employment by size of firms, 1975–1984

Size (number of workers)	Change in percentage employment
1–4	−12.08
5–9	8.25
10–19	−21.20
20–49	−12.05
50–99	−31.10
100–199	−27.50
200–499	−32.70
> 500	−75.50

Source: UNEDIC.

developed in close connection with each other over two centuries, with the design community of haute couture imparting important dimensions of its organizational structure and competitive advantage to "high" prêt-à-porter. High prêt-à-porter in turn provided the fashion authority and environment in which the new fashion system has recently developed.

The production communities of haute couture and high prêt-à-porter are interpersonal in nature. Indeed, the historical and contemporary relationship between these different segments, and the innovative (design) authority that underlies both, is what makes Paris an enduring world center of women's clothing production. The third, young look segment draws on the reputation and ideas of high ready-to-wear; it is almost entirely rooted in the Market World.

FROM ROYAL SPLENDOR TO HAUTE COUTURE: THE FORMATION
OF AN INTERPERSONAL MARKET

The *maisons de haute couture* date back to the early 1900s, when Paris took the lead in developing clothes for the woman liberated from the bourgeois dress of the nineteenth century. But this was really just the latest phase in the role of Paris as the capital of fashion and luxury products. Under Louis XIV, in the 1660s, Colbert had established various royal manufactories, at Sèvres (for porcelain and crystal) and at the Gobelins (for tapestries and rugs).[4] Establishing these systems of production centralized royal purchases and made it possible to enforce aristocratic standards

119

Price Range of Dress	Classical Production Cycle: Time: 6 to 20 weeks Series: 1,000 to 10,000 per model		Fashionable Production Cycle: Time: 3 to 40 days Series: 200 to 2,000 per model	
	Description	Examples of Firms	Description	Examples of Firms
$30 – $50	Several large European firms	Indreco Belleteste Steilman, RFA Large Importers from Hong Kong and India Interna dress, HK K Mohar, India	Numerous small specialized firms in the sentier	
$50 – $140	Several large and famous firms; long-distance subcontracting	Rodier Cacharel Max Mara, Italy Naf Naf	A few large firms' brand names, using local subcontractors in the sentier	Chevignon
$140+	A few large firms, using local subcontractors	G.F.T. Max, Mara, Italy	A few famous large firms	Tarlazzi St. Laurent Diffusion Rech

Figure 6.1 Competitive structure for women's dress industry. *Source:* Boston Consulting Group.

of quality. In other words, centralization provided resources, and made it possible to respond to shifts in orders according to the fashions of the royal bureaucracy.

Although clothing itself was not produced by a central royal manufactory, production was oriented toward a centralized market, the members of the Court. The first *modiste,* Rose Bertin, emerged at Versailles in the 1770s. By 1776, a new *corporation* (a royally chartered, guild-like structure), the *marchands de la mode,* was created and granted monopolies for designer labels. Even though the Revolution officially abolished the old artisanal corporations, new forms of exclusivity and new taste hierarchies arose. Under Napoleon I, Leroy became the official fashion supplier of the Imperial Court and hence enjoyed enormous market power. During the Second Empire, the designer Worth opened his workshop on the rue de la Paix in Paris; the Princess Pauline de Metternich became his client and started him on what was to be a brilliant career. Worth's clients chose from an album; there were no seasonal collections. Though the production system was highly fragmented and individualized—basic models were customized to order—there were already two elements of consolidation: a system of fashion stores that channeled orders, and a system of input manufactories—silk in Lyon, lace and bonnetterie in the North—well organized to produce in volume. Orders followed the rhythm of balls from Compiègne to Biarritz. The couturier's vocation as an exporter was effectively established during this period. Worth already had significant exports to the rest of Europe and the United States in the 1860s.

Paris was a center of clothing fashion in the nineteenth century because it was the home of Europe's most centralized court: men and women from England to the west and Poland and Russia to the east looked to Paris to know how to dress (but not the Italians, who had their own skills in this domain). The imperial couple in Paris had no competition as fashion leaders at the time: the Prussian court was austere, and in London there were few *mondanités* after the death of Victoria's husband, Prince Albert. Because of its commitment to luxury—not so far from the qualities demanded by Colbert's manufactories more than 150 years earlier—we might call this an economy of splendor; the whole system was propelled by the centralized fashion authority of the aristocratic hierarchy. The system grew progressively more splendid throughout the nineteenth century;[5] in the bourgeois-imperial society that succeeded the Revolution, the fetish of fashion grew, and clothing design was considered one of the *beaux arts.* Bourgeois men, too, engaged in dandyism in the nineteenth century.[6] For women, the situation was summed up in the slogan of the *Magasin des*

Modes (the most important of the fashion stores) that "boredom was born one day out of uniformity."[7] Fashion, with its obsession with change, was supposed to fight boredom.

Women's clothing was extremely complicated and cumbersome until 1885, when a major transformation began to take shape. Redfern, couturier to the Duchess of Wales, invented the modern women's outfit—a jacket and skirt in cloth, without the customary ornaments or constraints. In 1907, Poiret (who eliminated the corset) took advantage of the revolution in women's clothing to reshape the division of labor, designing the garment and turning it over to the *modeliste* to execute. The fashion authority of the designer was now effectively sundered from customized production, and made more independent of the client.

In the years after World War I, this separation was extended even further. Thus the opening of the first real *maison de haute couture* by Gabrielle Chanel, in 1924, did not at all represent the triumph of customization; rather, it marked an attempt to rationalize high fashion production under the authority of the couturiers, for Chanel abandoned continuous creation in favor of the system of two annual collections each with about 150 models, with two minor half-season collections in between. This enabled her to assemble a specialized staff for design, cutting, sewing, and completion. Patou, Lanvin, and Schiaparelli did the same in the 1920s, and all rose to become world-famous exporters before the beginning of the depression of 1929.

The Paris high fashion system continued its upward ascent in the middle of the twentieth century: the magazine *Marie Claire* appeared in 1937 as its mouthpiece, and other famous fashion houses, such as Balmain, Dior, Givenchy, and Cardin, opened immediately after World War II. The high fashion system was nourished by the continuing image of Paris as a world fashion capital. It is also important to realize that as late as 1955, haute couture served as much as 35% of the Parisian market, compared to less than 10% for U.S. buyers in 1940 or 20% for Germany. In the 1950s, a high fashion house might make 10,000 dresses per year (as compared to a few hundred today), and employ, full time, 350 models and several hundred production workers. With about twenty of these houses located in Paris, an important production complex was in place (see Table 6.2).

At its apogee, the *haute couture* industry of Paris shared many of the characteristics Marshall identified in describing nineteenth-century English industrial districts, in particular the tight linkages between producers, the circulation of specific information among them, and ongoing endogenous innovation within the district's product specialization. In this particular

Table 6.2   The French high fashion houses

House	Year founded
Pierre Balmain	1947
Pierre Cardin	1948
Carven	1937
Cacharel	1947
Christian Dior	1946
Louis Féraud	1953
Hubert de Givenchy	1947
Grès	1942
Lecoanet Hémant	1986
Christian Lacroix	1986
Jeanne Lanvin	1888
Ted Lapidus	1959
Guy Laroche	1856
Serge Lepage	—
Hanae Mori	—
Jean Patou	1919
Nina Ricci	1932
Yves Saint-Laurent	1962
Jean-Louis Scherrer	1971
Per Spook	—
Torrente	—
Emmanuel Ungaro	1965
Philippe Venet	—

version of the Interpersonal World, the reputation and authority of the couturiers, and their tight linkages with a restricted clientele, were the ties that bound the system together.

The modern high fashion system was, in many ways, the natural heir of the old royal system, with the designers dictating the norms of fashion; like their royal counterparts, they were the authority behind the convention of quality for fashion. As long as their ranks were stable, the structure of the production system could not be shaken because they controlled the brand name. This was a clearly identifiable Interpersonal world of production.

FROM HAUTE COUTURE TO PRÊT-À-PORTER:
THE WIDENING OF THE INTERPERSONAL WORLD

Ready-to-wear was, of course, not unknown in France in the nineteenth century. Indeed, the first garments "tout faits" are said to have been present in 1770. The sewing machine was invented in France by Thimonier in 1830; in the 1850s and 1860s, the department stores of Paris opened (Bon Marché: 1852; BHV: 1856, Printemps: 1865) and began to show their ready-to-wear collections. Still, both quantity and quality were limited; indeed, after its early advances, the French women's ready-to-wear industry went through a long period when it developed more slowly than its counterparts in other countries. French sizes, for example, were very approximate (hence unreliable) as late as 1952, which discouraged the bourgeoisie from buying ready-made clothes and encouraged them to remain as clients of the couturiers. Ready-made clothes did not gain their decisive advantage over haute couture for privileged French women until the second half of the 1950s.

With the creation of a middle-class consumption-oriented society in the 1950s came growing pressure for a fashionable alternative to haute couture. Part of this reflected the fact that the bourgeois woman was replaced as the fashion leader by other figures—actors, athletes, and others who had less traditional ideas about what constituted chic. Though this occurred much earlier and to a greater extent in, say, the United States, bourgeois culture remained important in France and strongly influenced the tastes of the emerging middle class society, as reflected in the widespread taste for very high quality, carefully fitted garments. This cultural mix created a very large niche for semi-customized or small-series production with a high artisanal content. When size standardization and longer series production did appear, they did so in a way that incorporated the basic notion of fashion *authority* inherited from the already-existing real world of production but gave it new, modern themes. One principal form of this development appeared in the 1950s when high fashion houses licensed designs for their now-expanded clientele to the department stores ("les producteurs associés"). However, the standards of the French consumer remained considerably different from those of the middle-class American, and these figured very prominently in the system that emerged, which is based on production of better fitting and more fashion-oriented garments via smaller production runs than are found elsewhere.

Another reason for the move toward ready-to-wear at this time was that haute couture's client base was being squeezed out of existence: the eastern European clientele, wiped out by the war and then the Soviet takeover in 1945–1946, had been replaced by newly rich South Americans, but by the end of the 1950s, the latter were already feeling the pinch of the pocketbook. As a result, the haute couture system could no longer serve as the basis of the Paris fashion industry, and a series of designers took initial steps directly into ready-to-wear: Cacharel and Hechter opened their own lines, independent of the department stores, in 1956 and 1957; and when Cardin launched his own prêt-à-porter boutique in 1962, it signaled the beginning of the end for true haute couture. There was effectively no longer any reason for most women to pay for true haute couture when it could be bought directly at one-tenth the price with the same label in the prêt-à-porter boutique.

The layered and differentiated prêt-à-porter system that has emerged includes a relatively high fashion component and a relatively popular component, both bearing the influence of the haute couture system. Haute couture exists today as a support for prêt-à-porter: it gives the latter a distinctive label identification, but is generally money-losing for the major fashion houses—at Dior, for example, it accounts for only 2% of the sales income. Haute couture exports have a value of 330 million francs, as opposed to several billion for ready-to-wear. Even at St. Laurent, the largest remaining haute couture house, only 17% of sales are in high fashion, and 81% of these are outside France.

In effect, "high" prêt-à-porter *broadened* the haute couture system without entirely replacing its conventions of participation and quality. Inter-producer relations, as well as producer-client relations, remain relatively personalized. Prêt-à-porter saved the values of the haute couture system by combining market frameworks of action with interpersonal principles of coordination. In other words, organizational learning, working through existing conventions of participation and identity, made it possible to extend the real world of high fashion into a real world of ready-to-wear. Innovations involved modifying the product's dedicated qualities by targeting wider groups, while successfully codifying part of the production process without losing the specialized character of design or, in some cases, production skills.

CONTEMPORARY PRÊT-À-PORTER: THE PROBLEM OF A
QUALITY-PRODUCTIVITY COMPROMISE

Contemporary high prêt-à-porter does not just reflect the special habits of French women. The French distribution system institutionalizes a more differentiated market than that seen in other countries. For example,

France today has 76,000 clothing stores, compared to 51,000 for (former West) Germany or 65,000 for Italy. The population per store is only 710, compared to 1200 in (West) Germany. In Paris, retail outlets *(détaillants)* are very small, with on average 120 square meters of sales space, even though by all estimates, 500 square meters is a reasonable break-even size, given overhead costs. This means that Parisian boutiques turn to high margin pricing to compensate for low volume, have small stocks, and make last-minute orders—all practices in accord with a Market World framework of action. Yet these boutiques accounted for two-thirds of total sales volume as late as 1987. Other stores may have scale economies and more flexible pricing policies, but they do not yet dominate the French market. This overall situation impedes standardization in production of ready-to-wear, while encouraging its widespread consumption.

There are 1,200 *salons* (fashion shows) for presentation of prêt-à-porter collections in Paris, highly concentrated in just a few central neighborhoods. The majority of the high women's prêt-à-porter is found in the second arrondissement with almost 10,000 workers, very high value added per worker, and almost a quarter of the city's garment employment. By contrast, very small, often clandestine, subcontracting firms whose main markets are in the cheaper, newer, more youth-oriented and young urban professional *mode* garments are concentrated in the 10th arrondissement (which adjoins the second arrondissement). This is the world-famous *sentier.* It is feeling some competition from new subcontracting firms in the 13th and 19th arrondissements, with their high numbers of Asian immigrants, but has more than held its own in recent years.

High prêt-à-porter can be said to operate halfway between high fashion and the competitive sweatshop system found in the United States. Its principal resource is design of the garment—that is, the trademark signifying quality, and this is still well guarded by the fashion houses, whose ranks remain rather closed. Since garments cannot be produced in-house if costs are to be controlled, producers use a classic putting out system for cutting and sewing tasks. The preponderance of these *façonniers* is in Paris, with fully 37% of the national total. Ethnic solidarity characterizes each level of the system: the design houses and distribution network of boutiques (French), the cutters (Middle-Eastern or Sephardic Jewish), and the sewers (Turkish, North African). The labor market for this industry is essentially a semi-closed network, organized by families or acquaintances for the highly skilled workers, such as cutters, who make their own work rules and whose labor processes are not rationalized or codified. The potential for vertical conflict between highly skilled workers and small subcontracting firms, or between subcontractors and design houses, is very strong. Price squeezing is not unknown, nor is illegal labor, but in general these behaviors are seen only in youth-fashion garments, one level lower in the system—that is, still fashionable but cheaper. The key to avoiding conflict seems to be that the whole industry enjoys considerable quasi-rents because of the garments' brand names and the closure of the ranks of the Paris boutique trade through interpersonal conventions. As a result, there is still a great deal of cost pass-through in the fashionable ready-to-wear market.

But the pass-through of costs which characterizes this form of coordination requires limits on price competitiveness. As a result, high prêt-à-porter is increasingly fabricated elsewhere. For women's garments, much of this occurs in the Choletais region of the Pays de la Loire. As Figure 6.2 shows for the case of Daniel Hechter, Paris remains the center in terms of conceiving designs, choosing fabrics, cutting (increasingly in suburban rather than central Paris), and sales; but sewing and other finishing activities are subcontracted to modern, capital-intensive firms in the Choletais and elsewhere. Even the high segments of the Paris fashion industry have increasingly adopted a geographical division of labor. All this is quite unlike equivalent production zones in Italy, which are situated for the most part outside the center city, with ample room for expansion and renewal of buildings and equipment. The situation in France also undoubtedly reflects the fact that no group of modernizing subcontractors was ready to provide the kind of cost-conscious production the fashion houses require. Many of the major houses now earn the great majority of their revenues from worldwide activity in licensing mass produced versions of their garments; for a long time, therefore, they were not committed to modernizing high prêt-à-porter in the *sentier* itself, being content with their economic rents. Their commitment to the Interpersonal World—even to a modernized version of it—has, in economic terms, been supported by other strategies of profitability at the firm level.

THE YOUTH-MODE INDUSTRY

The production system in Paris declined considerably during the 1960s and 1970s, as truly mass produced garment manufacture was moved either into the provinces or out of France altogether. These garments, with their industrial qualities, no longer needed the resources of the Parisian

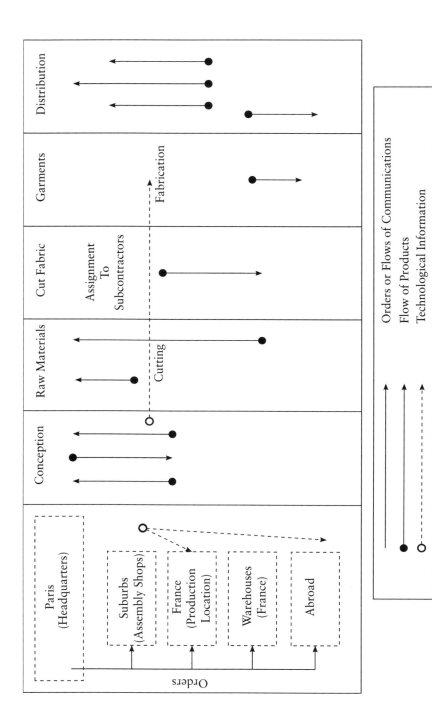

Figure 6.2　Geographical division of labor for high fashion ready-to-wear.

interpersonal world. But by the late 1970s, the position of Paris had not only stabilized, it had improved; in fact, it enjoyed a small increase in its share of the French women's clothing industry in the 1980s. At the same time, the industry maintained its position as a trade specialization of the French economy. Much of this is due to the latest phase in the industry's evolution in Paris, its spin-off of a segment producing fashionable but lower quality and cheaper garments, directed at the young urban professional classes and contemporary youth culture.

Consider a typical item of clothing in this segment: a jacket, a copy of haute couture, but usually less structured, simplified for the young clientele. It is produced in runs of 300. Fabric is bought the day before fabrication at a shop in the 3rd or the 10th arrondissement, cut at a small firm, and sewn by an immigrant, either in a workshop or at home. Walking the streets of these neighborhoods—the rue du Faubourg St. Denis or the rue du Faubourg St. Martin, for example—one is struck by the number of dark-skinned young men carrying bundles of garments to or from small trucks. A glance upward reveals workshops everywhere, including numerous operations that seem to involve whole families of Southeast Asians. There are also numerous, rapidly expanding, direct fashion outlets selling their own knock-off "brand" names. (Some production is illegal. The workers may be unregistered immigrants, paid less than the legal minimum with no protections. Or the firm itself may be attempting to avoid the value-added tax. With a combination of these, it can cut its costs by half for a shirt or a pair of pants, and about two-thirds for a dress. An influx of undocumented immigrants has modified access to possible worlds in the direction of the Market World, and this has permitted the innovation of products of the Interpersonal World by deepening qualities of standardization and rapidity of response to market fluctuations.)

This jacket, once fabricated, is sold in one of a number of ways. It may be sold in one of the innumerable boutiques that are continually opening and closing in the neighborhood. The clients may be individuals, or buyers from other stores in France or abroad. Frequently, the garments are illegally exported, in the trunk of a Mercedes to Germany or in the checked baggage of an American buyer.

This form of production is still clearly related to the presence of high prêt-à-porter in Paris, which is the source of free fashion information for the *système mode*. Indeed, this is what keeps the Market World segment in the city. If the only consideration were to lower labor costs, cheap rural (female) labor is available elsewhere in France. The paradox is that the high prêt-à-porter system is increasingly moving its production precisely to such rural zones, while the mode production is creating production employment in the *sentier* industrial district itself.

CONVENTIONS OF IDENTITY AND PARTICIPATION:
THE DESIGN AND FASHION APPARATUS OF PARIS

The dynamo of the high prêt-à-porter system is the fashion-design apparatus—the set of institutions and actors that constitutes the legitimate fashion authority in Paris—and it holds its position by controlling conventions of quality and the distribution network. This dynamism also explains the system's "technological conservatism": by preventing major new groups from entering at the design level, the system remains "royal," that is, hierarchical and closed. Restrictions imposed on the system by its conventions of participation also prevent the labor market from becoming entirely composed of sweatshops, by enabling the designers to pass through quasi-rents for these relatively expensive garments.

Renewing the fashion component—that is, injecting new asymmetric knowledge—does take place, but it is difficult, slow, and strongly filtered by those fashion authorities already in place. In the mode segment of the industry, sweatshop production has been growing precisely because, despite its reliance on the fashion authority of the high prêt-à-porter system, it is organizationally isolated and has historically been unable or unwilling to branch out into more flexible and more cost-competitive market segments. The nearly complete social and organizational separation of both those inside the legitimate prêt-à-porter system and those who copy it has historically prevented the mode system from being upgraded, even though the two segments are often literally on top of each other. Instead, the *maisons de haute couture* have increasingly contracted production to other regions of France, and some have become worldwide mass producers of brand-name garments; only the design function remains in Paris. Design remains part of an old Interpersonal World, while the new production activity is a low-wage, low-skill version of the Market World. It is noteworthy that those in haute couture have not chosen to widen the Interpersonal approach by modernizing production apparatus in the *sentier* or the Paris region itself, as has been done so brilliantly in Italy in recent decades. In other words, the industry has not found a viable way to combine its hierarchical and closed Interpersonal World with an industrialization strategy *in situ*. This is one reason the *sentier* has a somewhat incoherent character. This has not stopped it from growing, but it has prevented it from engaging in as much organizational learning as might be possible; in the end, it does not reap the full benefits of Paris's economies of splendor.

High Technology in the Ile-de-France: The Interpersonal World of the State[8]

FRENCH SPECIALIZATION IN HIGH TECHNOLOGY SYSTEMS ENGINEERING

France tends not to have strong trade or technology positions in the "base" or core high technologies, such as microelectronics, which are dominated by foreign companies. Instead, its high technology industries are specialized in systems engineering and construction of large-scale, applied technological systems such as military and civilian aircraft and space hardware, and large-scale electronics and communications systems.

Figure 6.3 shows French positions in various high technology *filières*, as well as their institutional structures. The country does well in all aerospace categories, but in electronics only military electronics and tele-communications switching systems are domains of French mastery, and both rely heavily on state purchases. France's specialization in software is also partly dependent on large systems bought by state military and civilian bureaucracies. The penetration of foreign capital by detailed industry within French electronics confirms these impressions. Computer industry employment is 51% foreign, and its value added is fully 71% of the total. Other sectors in which foreign presence is very high include medical equipment, industrial automation equipment, and semiconductors.

The sectors in which the French economy does well in trade correspond closely to the levels of French ownership. Pavitt and Patel, measuring the "revealed technological advantage" of French industry in the 1980s by examining patent activity, found that the prominent sectors were those noted above in which exports are strong and imports weak (with certain additions, notably in chemicals, medicines, and metalworking-machinery). They also observe, significantly, that there is no apparent correspondence, either within France or cross-nationally, between the level of concentration in a given industry in a region or a country, and the level of technological performance. French firms in high technology industries are equal to or greater in size than their foreign counterparts, without respect to performance.[9] Technological performance turns on factors other than the firm's size or budget. Pavitt and Patel comment:

> The French case presents the following characteristics: first of all, it confirms the . . . relative importance of "colbertist" industries, dominated by public orders and financing destined for technology-intensive activities. From 1981–86, three of the five premier sectors,

131

Item	Relative Position of French Industry	Public Research Laboratory	Government Department In Charge of Industrial Policy	Main Industry Firms	Main Projects	International Cooperation
Aircraft Engines	Good		Ministry of Defense: Délégation Générale pour l'Armement	SNECMA	ATAR CFM- 56	General Electric
Helicopters	Superior		Ministry of Defense: Délégation Générale pour l'Armement	SNIAS Turbomeca	Alouette Puma	
Space Launchers and Satellites	Good	CNES	Ministry of Industry: DIELI CNES	SNIAS MATRA Société Européenne de Propulsion	Ariane, Telecommunications and Television	Arianespace Germany
Aircraft Parts and Equipment	Superior		Ministry of Defense: Délégation Générale pour l'Armement Ministry of Transport: Direction Générale de l'Aviation Civile	SFENA-Crouzet Hispano-Suiza Intertechnique SFIM Messier Thomson-CSF		

Figure 6.3 French high technology industry. CNES = Centre Nationale d'Etudes Spatiales; DIELI = Direction des Industries Éléctrique et de l'Informatique; SNECMA = Société Nationale d'Etude et de Construction de Moteurs d'Aviation; SNIA = Société Nationale Industrielle Aérospatiale; ONERA = Office Nationale d'Etudes et de Recherches Aérodynamiques; CNET = Centre d'Etudes des Télécommunications; DIE = Direction des Industries Électrique; DGA = Délégation Générale pour l'Armement; INRIA = Institut National de Recherche en Informatique et Automatique; DIMME = Direction des Industries Métallurgiques, Mécaniques, et Électriques.

Item	Relative Position of French Industry	Public Research Laboratory	Government Department In Charge of Industrial Policy	Main Industry Firms	Main Projects	International Cooperation
Military Aircraft	Superior	ONERA	Ministry of Defense: Délégation Générale pour l'Armemt	Dassault-Berguet	Mirage Jaguar Ace	Jaguar (Germany) Ace
Missiles and Rockets	Superior	ONERA	Ministry of Defense: Délégation Générale pour l'Armemt	MATRA SNIAS	Exocet Roland	Germany
Civil Aircraft	Good	ONERA	Ministry of Defense: Délégation Générale pour l'Armemt	Dassault-Berguet SNIAS	Concorde (abandoned) Airbus	United Kingdom and Germany, among others
Leisure and Business Aircraft	Good					

Figure 6.3 (continued)   French high technology industry

Item	Relative Position of French Industry	Public Research Laboratory	Government Department In Charge of Industrial Policy	Main Industry Firms	International Cooperation
Electronic Components and Integrated Circuits	Average	CNET-CNS Commissariat à l'Energie Atomique-Leti	Ministry of Industry: DIELI Ministry of the Post-Office and of Telecommunications: DGT Ministry of Defense: DGT	Thomson-CSF MATRA	MATRA-Harris Eurotêchnique-NSM Thomson-Motorola
Military Electronics (Radiocommunications, Guidance Systems, Avionics)	Superior	Délégation Générale pour l'Armement	Ministry of Defense: DGA	Thomson-CSF MATRA ESD	
Telecommunications (Electronic Switching Systems)	Good	CNET	Ministry of the Post-Office and of Telecommunications: DGT	Thomson-CSF CIT-Alcatel CGCT	
Computers and Electronic Office Equipment	Average	CNET-CNS Commissariat à l'Energie Atomique-Leti	Ministry of Industry: DIELI Ministry of the Post-Office and of Telecommunications: DGT Ministry of Defense: DGT	Bull-CH MATRA Intertêchnique	Bull-Honeywell Bull-NEC Bull-Ridge MATRA-Norsk Data
Computer Software	Superior	INRIA	Ministry of the Post-Office and of Telecommunications: DGT Ministry of Industry: DIELI	CAP-Sogeti CISI, SG2 STERIA, GSI	
Industrial Electronics	Poor		Ministry of Industry: DIELI	MATRA, Renault CIT-Alcatel	
Consumer Electronics	Average		Ministry of Industry: DIELI		Thomson-JVC Thomson-Telefunken

Figure 6.3 (continued)   French high technology industry.

ranked in order of their relative technological advantage, were col-
bertist in France, including 6 of 11 most highly ranked: nuclear reactors, aeronautics, telecommunications, other forms of transformation, electrical engines and systems, and generating stations. In the
UK in the same period, the equivalent figures were two of six and
four of eleven: generating stations, aeronautics, mining equipment,
and telecommunications. In Germany, there was only one: nuclear
reactors.[10]

In other words, base technologies (frequently imported) are apparently recombined, adapted, and built into large-scale technological products with
great proficiency in France. These complex, costly, and often one-of-a-kind
products are frequently ordered by civilian or military bureaucracies and
involve large-scale coordination of human and physical resources—including those of the Intellectual and the Interpersonal Worlds.

The obverse of this success is weakness in base technologies and civilian
consumer products in the high technology industries. The Intellectual
World of French high technology does not have access to the Market
World as does its American counterpart. This is strongly suggested by the
structure of French imports in electronics and computers: import penetration is very high in consumer electronics (65.9%) and computer components (86.9%), and ranges around 35% for the rest of the electronics
branch; by contrast, imports have grown very slowly in electronics systems and aeronautics. Almost 70% of all electronics imports are components, or core technologies. Computer imports are almost entirely (85.8%)
finished products; those that are assembled in France rely almost completely on imported components. In electronics, the weakness in components but strength in large-scale systems is illustrated by the analysis in
Table 6.3, which shows how French positions in "electronique professionnelle" have improved in recent years.[11]

Much of the detailed analysis that follows will focus most closely on
electronic systems, which we take to be (along with aerospace) a key
domain of French technological excellence.

THE ILE-DE-FRANCE AS FRANCE'S TECHNOLOGY CORE

The Ile-de-France holds a commanding position in French high technology
in all respects, but especially in the areas of conception, design, and
high-level execution. In 1990, the Ile-de-France region had fully 57% of
national employment for the high technology industries as a whole, 47.5%
of production workers, and 68% of non-production workers. In the infor-

Table 6.3A French trade in electronic systems in 1976

| | Imports | | Exports | | Balance in millions of FF | Export-import ratio |
	Millions of FF	Percentage	Millions of FF	Percentage		
Japan	4.468	12.220	106.000	0.105	−4.362	.02
United States	13.027	35.630	1.646	7.180	−11.381	.13
United Kingdom	3.722	10.180	3.090	13.480	−0.632	.83
Italy	2.412	6.600	1.825	7.960	−0.587	.76
Germany	5.704	15.600	4.991	21.770	−0.713	.87
Netherlands	1.117	3.060	2.251	9.820	1.134	2.02
Belgium-Luxembourg	0.218	0.600	0.957	4.170	0.739	4.39
OECD	34.005	93.010	19.952	87.040	−14.053	.59
Developing Countries	1.556	4.260	2.325	10.140	0.769	1.49
EEC	14.921	40.810	15.400	67.180	0.479	1.03
World	36.562	100.000	22.924	100.000	−13.638	.63

Source: Customs Data, SESSI.

Table 6.3B French trade in electronic systems in 1985

| | Imports | | Exports | | Balance in millions of FF | Export-import ratio |
	Millions of FF	Percentage	Millions of FF	Percentage		
Japan	3.060	9.50	3.800	10.07	−0.740	1.24
United States	8.643	26.85	3.598	9.54	−5.045	.42
United Kingdom	2.257	7.01	2.828	7.50	0.571	1.25
Italy	1.710	5.31	2.994	7.94	1.284	1.75
Germany	7.062	21.94	5.874	15.57	−1.188	.83
Netherlands	1.048	3.26	1.103	2.92	0.055	1.05
Belgium-Luxembourg	0.993	3.09	1.098	2.91	0.105	1.11
OECD	27.753	86.22	21.626	57.34	−6.127	.78
Developing Countries	2.997	9.31	13.908	36.87	10.911	4.64
EEC	13.914	43.23	15.192	40.28	1.278	1.09
World	32.188	100.00	37.718	100.00	5.530	1.17

Source: Customs Data, SESSI.

mation technology sector as a whole, the Ile-de-France had 74% of national employment, and 69% for electronic capital goods.

For certain technologically advanced segments of the electronics industry, the Ile-de-France is the almost the only location in France; for example, 34 of the 43 firms designing ASIC circuits are located in the Ile-de-France and only 9 outside of it. Private sector electronics research is very highly concentrated as well, with more than 40% of all establishments conducting research situated in the Paris region (compared with only 15% of those engaged in fabrication). The Ile-de-France contains 81% of the managers in the French electronics industry and 62.5% of all technical and engineering managers, but only 6.5% of unskilled and 35% of semi-skilled workers. Despite this disproportion, the Ile-de-France is an important center of production in electronics with the lion's share of productive workers in the field, especially in the semi-skilled category, as well as conception and engineering/technical workers (some 35,000 production workers, compared to 17,000 in the rest of the country).[12]

Though high technology industries in France are overwhelmingly located in the Ile-de-France, they are not spread evenly throughout that region. Specifically, most of the region's activity in the electronics-based industries is concentrated in the western (the Yvelines and Hauts de Seine) and southern (the Essonne) parts of the Paris region, and their predominance has grown in recent years.[13] This locational pattern is consistent with the typical sub-regional geography of high technology industries: they tend to be found in or near comfortable suburbs populated by high proportions of educated people. Perhaps unique to Paris—not found among other major high technology centers—is the effective reconversion of the western part of the metropolis to high technology. Whereas the U.S. high technology areas of Silicon Valley or Orange County in California and Route 128 in Massachusetts were created *ex nihilo* by the innovators themselves, in the Paris region the social geography has been actively created through government effort, and by the conversion (and partial displacement) of an older industrial district to the new high technology economy. The French state has actively pursued a policy of building a "Scientific City" *(Cité Scientifique Sud)* southwest of Paris, which brings together numerous publicly funded research laboratories and agencies that develop high technology products.[14]

This localization provides clues to the particular form of organizational learning that typifies French high technology and the conventions which underlie it. An earlier phase of French high technology, the aircraft and parts industry, was born in the vicinity of the metalworking and machine tool industries: in the "red suburbs" (as areas controlled by the French Communist Party were called) of Paris, specifically the arc consisting of parts of the department of the Seine, from Bourget to Issy-les-Moulineaux, an area which became in the 1960s the département of Hauts de Seine. This world of production was linked to a very particular working-class culture centering on the skilled worker. The production system for SNECMA, which makes aircraft engines, has remained in this area, and some of the district's other former activities, essentially based on a high quality metalworking, have survived and have been incorporated within the emerging high technology industrial zone. To some extent this reflects the particular nature of production processes in aerospace. The fabrication of outputs such as jet engines is not well adapted to the deskilling of workers through routinization; the workforce required cannot be found in areas where there is no well-developed, skilled industrial tradition. The development of the "Scientific City," with its many electronics and computer firms, has created labor resources and potential interfirm linkages which are of use to the aircraft and parts producers. Military production facilities in the region, too, fall along the western arc: the departments of the Hauts de Seine, followed by the Yvelines and the Essonne, dominate in military employment. The locations of many of the major state agencies in charge of purchasing follow a locational pattern similar to that of private industry; the *Direction des Armements Terrestres,* for example, has its central administration at St. Cloud, and its major directorates are at Versailles and Issy-les-Moulineaux, employing nearly 3,000 people at these locations.

The state–private sector decisions which govern both the military and electronics sectors are negotiated in the Ile-de-France. The military-industrial complex accounts for a high proportion of the activities in the region, and is now the mainstay of its high technology specializations. The principal products of the business/professional electronics sector in France all have military uses as well: detection equipment, telecommunications, radio-television equipment.[15] In 1986, sales in the French electronics industry were divided as follows:

French armed forces (25%);
military equipment to other domestic clients, especially aerospace (7.2%);
subcontracting (3.26%);
exports, of which 75% are military, 46.35% (and hence France's trade specialization in this field).

In short, these figures show that the military-related share of the industry is 70–75%, and must be called its propulsive force. Military purchasing also has important spillover effects on other high technology industries; for example, about 14% of semiconductors in France are sold to the military, as opposed to a world average in this industry of about 10%. Moreover, the principal form of state support for high technology in the 1980s, the *Loi de Programmation,* directed much of its resources to military uses: 25% of the total went explicitly to electronics, of which the major share is, as we have seen, military; fully 35% went to aerospace, which is also dominated by military purchases; and 16% went directly to the Direction Générale d'Armements and another 11% to the Commission d'Etudes Atomiques, part of which is devoted to nuclear power generation, part to nuclear weapons.

Military production is extremely concentrated in France: five firms accounted for almost 80% of the sector's sales in 1986 (Thomson CSF, SINTRA [part of the Thomson group], Electronique Serge Dassault, TRT [Philips] and SFIM). Large French high technology firms devote very high percentages of their activity to the military.[16] As in the U.S. military industries, firms wishing to produce for the military must pass through a rating and licensing system in terms of their security and technical capabilities. Only eight firms have RAQ-1 status (the classification for firms permitted to work on the most technologically sensitive/secret projects).[17]

THE STATE CORPS OF ENGINEERS AND
DECISION-MAKING UNCERTAINTY

This highly regionalized world of production can only be understood in terms of the organization of French high technology as a whole. The extreme concentration of high-level conception and execution tasks in the southern and western parts of the Ile-de-France presents an analytical paradox. Most of this activity depends on direct state orders for military-related electronic or aerospace production, or on state-influenced orders to large, often nationalized, companies for large-scale electronic or aerospace systems; or on the administrative or production routines in activities of foreign multinationals (in computers and electronic components). These types of production do not respond to markets, but to purchasing priorities identified by state technocrats, and in postwar France, key priorities have been military independence and economic planning. Thus the high technology industries in the Ile-de-France are indeed more vertically integrated, more centered on large firms and less on innovative small- and medium-sized enterprises, than in other major high technology regions of the world: they look like the Industrial World, not like Silicon Valley. For example, the Syndicat National de la Sous-Traitance estimates that 15% of the total value of Ile-de-France electronics industry production is subcontracted, placing it well below the equivalent figures for U.S. high technology. Most of the French subcontractors are fairly small: only 15% have more than 100 workers; 8% have between 1 and 10 employees, 54% have 10–49, and 23% have 50–99. About 63% of their work involves direct fabrication, but most of it in activities that require relatively high degrees of skill: white collar employees and technicians constitute 28% of their workforce, skilled workers 42%.

Until recently, "innovative" small and medium-sized firms (SMEs) have been rare—there are no accounts in the Ile-de-France (and perhaps only one in France as a whole, that of the software firm Cap Gemini Sogeti) of successful SMEs developing into major high technology firms. Thus within French high technology there is a rough functional equivalent of the Intellectual World, the technocracy, which uses a production system that looks much like the Industrial World.

The Technocracy. This technocracy is a highly interpersonal network at the core of this world of production. Its bureaucratic and interpersonal nature means that the system is characterized by high levels of certainty; state-sponsored concentration and lack of domestic competition have led to productive integration. The interrelation of the state (that is, the military and the Plan and its aftermaths) with the productive apparatus has established a set of conventions of participation and resource mobilization that selects for the product qualities of systems engineering and against those of innovations in core technologies such as semiconductors or computers. However, while this participation in planning reduces some forms of technological uncertainty, encourages vertical integration, and discourages innovative SMEs, the interpersonal network creates other forms of uncertainty which account for the extreme geographical concentration of high technology and which lie at the heart of this regional world of production.

Just such a system was of concern to Tocqueville, who identified the ambiguous relationship of state and society in France two centuries ago. It inherited from Colbert the notion of the "state above society," a system of "rational" administration conducted by bureaucrats immune to influence from sectional or regional interests. Yet, said Tocqueville, French administration was riddled by "exceptionalism": there were rigid rules but lax enforcement, with exceptions made for many particular cases, according to their merits or to the influence of those requesting them. Students of French society have, since then, played on these themes: Skocpol, echoing Tocqueville, calls attention to the fact that the Revolution had relatively little effect on the notion of state above society as the idea was projected forward into post-revolutionary society quite intact;[18] Hall argues that exceptionalism actually became more common throughout the period after World War II, with the politicization of the Plan.[19] The combat between these two essential tendencies continues: technocrats retain very considerable powers to define the nature of innovations, and their participation and influence as agents of innovation are secured through their schooling-based socialization, through the fact that they staff the Plan and various ministries, and through the activities of those ministries, which play a major role in financing the high technology sector, private or nationalized.

High technologists and state and public decision-makers know each other because they attended the same *grandes écoles;* once graduated, they are organized into military-style groups of state functionaries *(grands corps d'Etat),* strongly interpersonal networks with high levels of internal solidarity.[20] They divide the state bureaucracies among themselves, each corps having its own points of strong influence. Thus graduates of three grandes écoles—Polytechnique (math and science), Sup. Aero (aerospace engineering), and Supelec (electrical engineering)—hold the majority of positions in the *Corps des Ingénieurs de l'Armement* (defense engineers), which, with 2,200 members, is the country's largest single Corps d'Etat. These technocrats, however, are not above society; there is a "revolving door" movement between large companies and the state which turns with increasing speed (known as *pantouflage*), so that the technological planning and decision-making process in the military electronic sector is essentially a "constant coming and going between industry and the agencies" based heavily on "social networks" between the two.[21] The directors and chief executives of virtually all the major military contractors (including Matra, SNECMA, Bull, SFENA, Dassault, and Aerospatiale) are members of this Corps.

Research and Development. R&D is, of course, one way technological knowledge is created and mobilized: it is a vector of participation. It is important to note that the grandes écoles, though created in France in the postwar period as elite training institutions, conduct relatively little research: professors are practitioners, and there are few permanent research structures or laboratories. The curriculum emphasizes rigorous theoretical training (for example, in mathematics, logic, philosophy) rather than applied science.

The Fifth Plan (1966–1970), recognizing the "intellectual deficit" of French industry, in particular identifying a problem of technological competition, laid great emphasis on technological catch-up and R&D, establishing the DGRST (Direction Générale de la Recherche en Science et Technologie) and launching a more active state role in R&D which endures to this day. The DGRST had much more responsibility than, for example, the U.S. President's Office of Science and Technology. It was charged with coordinating the research activities of state agencies, universities (France's university system is run by one central ministry), and the private sector. Graduates of the grandes écoles who staffed state agencies were directly responsible to the DGRST (and are to its successor bureaucracies). There was considerable growth in R&D funding during this period, especially on large-scale technological projects in such areas as aerospace (military and the Concorde), telecommunications, electronics, transportation (high-speed trains), nuclear power generation, and television (SECAM)—all research programs that emphasized pure technological sophistication, rather than appeal to individual consumers. These were in effect the *marchés régaliens* (royal markets): products were conceived by an elite to meet their performance standards and sophistication rather than to compete in consumer markets.

The state in France accounts for more than half of total R&D expenditure. Of the 1,500 largest private companies, only 130 carry out any research at all; of these only 100 had more than 50 researchers in 1985, and those 100 received more than 90% of the public support given to the private sector (or about 45% of the country's total research budget). The United States, with an economy about eight times as large as that of France, has fourteen times as many researchers in private industry. The result is a certain insensitivity of the R&D structure to the products of the Market World. In France, 72% of all industrial research is carried out in six industries (electronics, aerospace, automobiles, chemicals, energy, pharmaceuticals); these account for only one-third of industrial value added, but the state has disproportionate influence in these sectors.[22]

The basic organization and structure of R&D have not changed since the 1960s. The government of Giscard d'Estaing (1974–1981) was relatively unenthusiastic about state-funded R&D, especially in older industries, and adopted a kind of "sunrise" industry strategy *(politique des créneaux porteurs);* the Mitterand governments (1982–1995) dramatically increased R&D funding but explicitly based it on a Gaullist *politique de filière*—the idea that research and development cover the entire production chain, from basic research to the product at the point of sale—so the system has remained relatively insensitive to research for commercially viable products.

Curiously, this is not because the French research structure is isolated from industry: the two are probably more closely attached than in the United States, where the federal government restricts its support to basic research, or to applied research only in defense, space, agriculture, and health. Rather, it is because each part of the public sector research effort is directed by a separate ministry and its associated technocracy, and each in turn has its own client groups in the private sector. These vertical arrangements of separate horizontal groups—of technocrats, public and private sector researchers, and producers—are more successful where there is competition from private sector firms which are adept at continuous product modification (as in the Market World). French prowess in high-speed train technology, military and commercial aircraft and parts, nuclear energy, electronic banking, space hardware and missiles—all products where state purchases and Industrial World production methods are useful—exemplifies the convention of participation in R&D and the associated conventions of product quality. In other sectors, however, these conventions are incompatible with commercial success. A recent example of this is the Plan Calcul, a state-directed effort to develop an independent French semiconductor and computer industry, based on the *filière* concept. In such a case, where continuous technological innovation is necessary, the state's "royal" markets are not sufficient.

Production. The structure of production in French high technology is fairly straightforward: a state agency designates prime contractors *(maîtres d'oeuvre),* most of them aerospace firms such as SNIAS, Matra, ESD, or SNECMA. These firms then enter into production agreements with other major technology firms, such as Thomson or TRT, who become *co-traitants* (co-contractors). These in turn may rely on other major designers and fabricators of capital goods or components such as SFIM. Finally, for capacity subcontracting, there is a network of medium-sized enterprises. State order-giving agencies include the ministries, the Etat-Major, the DGA, the CEA (*Commission d'Energie Atomique*) and the DRET (*Direction d'Etudes et Techniques du Ministère de l'Armée*). Unlike the situation in the U.S. military-industrial complex, the state order-giving agency typically not only licenses firms eligible to participate in the production system but directly negotiates with co-contractors for each major project. Here again, the production structure is pushed to resemble a planned Industrial World, albeit one coordinated by interpersonal conventions.

Distributing state resources through networks based purely on acquaintance would not produce the excellence which French high technology has shown. Though decisions, once taken, are largely isolated from the ex post uncertainty of markets, the ex ante uncertainty of the political decision-making process is designed precisely to produce such technological excellence. The mechanisms of decision-making about technology-intensive projects are themselves highly politicized and *externalized* between ministries and the companies themselves. Conventions of participation place certain agents into an exclusive group, it is true, but they must then actively participate in the transactional "market" for ideas, influence, and state funding—for both civilian and military projects, and for research and development, both basic and applied. In essence, whereas large private high technology companies can internalize their decisions, but frequently externalize their production (that is, go into the Market World), in France large companies are forced to externalize their decisions but can, to a greater degree, internalize their production. The SMEs that benefit from this system are for the most part unlike their counterparts in Silicon Valley: they are either capacity contractors or protected technological partners, but rarely equivalent to innovative, rapidly growing SMEs.

The Plan and the Technocracy: The Interpersonal World of Technological Decision-making. The technocracy, through its involvement in R&D, has preserved the tradition of state above society; by contrast, the postwar history of French economic planning (and what remains of it) exemplifies the tradition of exceptionalism, of a state apparatus deeply involved with its clientele. As Hall points out: "The post war French state followed a practice of burdening firms with such a multitude of restrictive regulations that few could survive without selective exemptions that rendered them dependent on the good will of the industrial policy-makers."[23]

The original idea of the plan, at its inception in 1945, was to create a mechanism for making the process of economic growth not only rational, but also politically transparent by formalizing discussions between labor, capital, and the state. In the 1960s, however, planners learned that their strategies

> . . . required increasingly close cooperation with the managers who controlled the means of production in key sectors and firms. [This]

brought about important changes in the structure of relations between business and the state. This policy depended on the negotiation of bilateral agreements between the state and individual enterprises that could only be negotiated behind closed doors . . . while
the number of participants in the formal deliberations of the Plan
increased dramatically from 1946 to 1970, the locus of power within
the planning process shifted to a set of private discussions between
state officials and small groups of enterprise managers who bargained over an industrial strategy.[24]

Thus planning became a "rather clandestine affair," something like a
"conspiracy in the public interest between big business and big official-
dom."[25] The increase in *pantouflage* attests to this: while in 1954 only 4%
of the heads of private banks came from public service, in 1974 that
proportion was 30%. In 1973, 43% of the heads of France's 100 largest
corporations had at one time been civil servants; in 1985, this figure was
still 40%.[26] The overlap between the elite corps of technocrats coming out
of the grandes écoles, and the pinnacle of private sector power, has pro-
gressed to the point where they are effectively one group; and the Mitter-
and years did not substantially alter this trend.[27]

In this rather small world of the *corps d'Etat,* the technological ethos is
subject to a kind of internal competition, and the objects produced are
evaluated in terms of criteria defined by the state as contributing to the
national common good. All uncertainty is thus pushed upward to the
decision-making system, leaving those in the production system free to
rationalize production using principles of the Industrial World.

Conclusion. The high technology industries of the Ile-de-France are
organized by an elite which injects innovative and quasi-market impulses
into a strongly organized Industrial World. Products in which French high
technology has known international success are overwhelmingly those in
which state purchases are important, notably in aerospace and electronics—fields with only a few important systems integrators and components
producers—and telecommunications. It must also be noted that from the
1950s to the 1980s, French industrial planning was based on a technological concept—that of *filière*—not on market structures: the underlying idea
is that industrial competence starts with a final output and includes the
entire commodity chain.[28] Thus, when a prime contractor in France re-
ceives an order from a state agency for an existing or developing high
technology product, the agency is likely to accompany the order with
actions to support further development of the associated *filière.* (The most

recent examples of this are the Plan Calcul and another state-led but unsuccessful plan which was intended to revive the machine tool industry.) The basic problem here is that the more the products differ from outputs of the Industrial World or large-scale systems, the more likely this form of coordination is to fail. In contrast, the American practice is to give cost-plus contracts in the defense industries, leaving development of the *filière* (through subcontracting or creating new divisions) essentially to the prime contractors. The French convention of quality is *technological;* in the case of high technology, it permits the tradition of splendor to continue in the form of large-scale, ambitious technological-industrial projects. This method has had important successes.

Resources are mobilized in a very different way in the second tier, the network of input suppliers. Although both state and private employers in France have a centralizing tradition, the Paris region contains an extremely large and diversified economy; the opportunity grid is enormous, and the rate of new firm start-ups in high technology industries has been very high over the past decade—although no French start-up company has become a major high technology enterprise, like Apple in the United States in the 1970s, or Hewlett-Packard in the 1950s. This is because the system of purchasing, of access to markets, is also highly organized by the state and the large companies. Venture capital does not exist in any significant way (French firms desiring access to it must turn to the United States). The dominant expectations involve succeeding in the state's Interpersonal World.[29] Thus the presence of the dominant action framework—the Interpersonal World of the state—tends to block the creation of the Market World framework needed for a venture capital industry to exist.

The other side of the coin is that networks are more faithful: a subcontractor firm which curries the right relationships can enjoy a fair amount of stability.[30] Nonetheless, access is still determined to a fair degree by the type of qualifications held by the firm's principal: an engineer from a grande école has a much greater probability of receiving state or large-firm orders than someone who lacks this background.

To sum up: the rate of spin-off is lower in France than in the United States, but the inter-firm relations between these two levels of the production network are likely to be more loyal because of smaller numbers and social solidarity at both levels. The result is that when the dominant innovative corps of cadres makes good decisions, the Francilien—essentially "royal"—system succeeds, often splendidly. The price is that the system has not effected a satisfactory compromise between the World of Intellectual Resources and the Market World, that is, production of basic innovations and streams of commercially viable technology-intensive outputs.

Francilien Splendor

In the Francilien real worlds of production, we see a stop-and-go system of innovation in the high technology industries which remains very dependent on decisions of state-influenced technocracies—in essence, an attempt to create a World of Innovation fundamentally rooted in a state-organized Market World. In the *haute couture* industries of the same region, the couturiers are the equivalent of the state and their authority is equivalent to that of the technocracy; they can make and impose decisions about innovation. The fashion industry of Paris is an Interpersonal World in search of a viable strategy of industrialization. Both systems make products based on the notion of "splendor," where technological prowess or elegance take precedence over cost. These are truly "royal" products in that they draw on the nation's most exclusive, highly centralized, innovative resources and are designed explicitly to contribute to the nation's prestige.

The role of centralized or statist power in the development of certain products is particularly pronounced in France. The state has the means to create veritable real worlds of production around certain products: by creating supplies (making technological choices, directing research-development programs); by creating conventions which coordinate firms (setting production standards and management rules); by creating demands through state purchases.

Two real worlds, high fashion and high technology, are situated in the Ile-de-France in order to be close to centralized or statist power, but such power can provide a structure only for very particular kinds of products. Different as they are, both the high fashion and the high technology industries of the Ile-de-France derive their dynamism from the existence of steep organizational hierarchies and parallel elites with the power to create, define, and organize their markets for the production of prestigious outputs. This creates access to certain kinds of action frameworks and resources and blocks access to others. Paris's leading industries show off the capacities of the nation, and the limited coherence of compromises with the frameworks of action required for greater dynamism.

148

7

ITALY:
INTERPERSONAL ACTION
AND THE DIVISION OF LABOR

Northeast-central Italy:
Interpersonal Worlds of Learning and Competition

The story of industrial growth in northeast-central (NEC) Italy has been told often in recent years, and has sometimes been heralded as a new model for industrialization itself.[1] It has incited much scholarship and some polemic. Looking at this history in terms of worlds of production provides a fresh interpretation. We begin with a review of the basic facts.

Regions such as Emilia-Romagna, Tuscany, the Veneto, and parts of Lombardy, Trentino-Alto Adige, and Friuli-Venezia-Guilia, especially over the 1960s and 1970s, enjoyed a remarkable growth in employment and output in design-intensive or craft-based industries producing mostly fashion products—clothing, leather, fabrics, furniture, personal accessories— but frequently extending to the machinery sectors associated with these final outputs, and occasionally including other metalworking or mechanical industries, such as food processing or packaging machinery. In a number of sectors, these regions produce very high proportions of Italian exports; in a few, they are absolutely dominant in world markets. These areas are distinguished by dense clusters of very small firms—hundreds, even thousands of firms, averaging ten employees or fewer, depending on industry or locality. Other localized industrial areas in Italy share these characteristics and dense local concentration in narrow sectoral specializations, but per capita income grew more rapidly in NEC Italy than in other areas at a time of general growth. Numerous quantitative and qualitative analyses have shown that NEC firms partake of a local, vertical division of labor, whereas in other areas clusters of firms tend to be engaged in one activity;[2] further, the local system in NEC Italy is richly endowed with commercial agents who organize production activities and market local products as final outputs, with a local, independent brand name, whereas firms in other areas frequently act as subcontractors to larger, external firms (especially to Piemontese or Milanese firms), or sell intermediate inputs on open markets.[3]

NEC Italy attracted a great deal of attention because it is rare for a wealthy, developed country to specialize heavily in fashion-oriented and semi-customized industrial outputs, and to do so using production systems rooted overwhelmingly in small—often very small—firms. Even when developed economies do show similar trade specializations (such as Germany's textiles and textile machinery), the production systems tend to be more "normal," in the sense that they involve larger firms, more bureaucratic forms of work organization, and less geographical concentration than in NEC Italy. As a consequence, much of the vast literature on NEC Italy has focused on such properties of the region's systems as firm size, productivity, wages, prices, scale, and scope. In some studies, these systems' characteristics are said to define an ideal type of "flexible specialization," in others an ideal type of industrial backwardness and petty entrepreneurship.[4] Looking at the region in terms of a theory of worlds of production provides a more coherent interpretation than those advanced so far because it links these much-discussed structural characteristics to the underlying "glue" of the systems, their interpersonal framework of action. This understanding provides a better way to identify the problems, the degree of reproducibility, and the future possibilities of these production systems.

The Model of Production in NEC Italy[5]

To understand the sources of technological dynamism and the basic organizational specificities of production in NEC Italy, and place them in perspective, we must consider the region's product specializations. In many of the fashion products sectors, such as clothing, shoes, and jewelry, product differentiation means that producers face a very high level of uncertainty about the nature and volume of output that will be demanded. Vertical disintegration is always present in these industries as a way to cope with this uncertainty. In NEC Italy, producers occupy market niches defined by the reputation of their products. These brand-name or reputation-based products are specialized to fairly narrow uses and often dedicated to the needs of particular clients, and the production system functions via relations between producers regulated by reputation effects. The brand name is simultaneously attached to the product and to the region of production.

Two other possible pathways of development may help explain the specific characteristics of NEC Italy. In the first, firms also develop brand-name products, as a way to earn the quasi-rents or (at least) limit market competition, but the brand name is monopolized by a firm rather than a community of producers, and this firm often administers the division of labor in the form of subcontracting and creates a large-firm hierarchical network production system.[6] In this situation there is a very strong temptation to squeeze subcontractors, so that they become sweatshops. Subcontractors may remain capable of doing high quality work so long as their workforces and entrepreneurs are reinforced with infusions of outside resources (such as skilled immigrants), but frequently they lose their capacity to develop products, that is, lose their own identity, and then enter the Market World, not the Interpersonal World.

In the second possible pathway, producers counter market uncertainty by moving out of the most fashion-sensitive markets. In numerous cases, this has involved the one-time invention of new niches, which are more stable and amenable to longer production runs than are possible for fashion products. These producers then usually pursue more vertical integration, or more steady, hierarchical relations with cost-efficient suppliers; again, the Interpersonal World gives way to the Market or Industrial worlds. The problem here is that as assets become more dedicated, the system can lose its technological-product dynamism. Deft management may offer the possibility (especially with new technologies) of flexible high-volume production for low- to medium-priced, but fashionable items, but they are always subject to very strong price-cost competition.

A parallel set of options exists, in principle, for NEC Italy's other specialization, mechanical engineering. In one developmental pathway, firms put out relatively small batches, and rely for their innovative edge principally on knowledge of market niches, knowledge obtained from dense relations with the product's users. Knowledge in this case is rather "local"; while some producers may get ahead of others, innovation relies on inter-firm and producer-user flows of information to such a great extent that there is a continual reselection into dedicated-specialized outputs, that is, firms remain within the Interpersonal World. In some cases, however, where the commitment to produce dedicated-specialized products is not so strong, firms may attempt to formalize the process of machine design to some extent. Where it succeeds, this approach almost inevitably leads to greater monopolization of knowledge, and the product becomes closely identified with a company brand name. The division of labor thus becomes more hierarchical, and firms may come into being to serve the equipment or tooling needs of the principal firms which are then in the Intellectual World or, perhaps, in the Market World.

In NEC Italy, as noted above, brand-name systems were constructed to define the relationship to the market, with the brand name attached as much to the region as to any individual firm. In other words, the products are strongly associated with the particular communities of persons that make them. How have actors in these regions succeeded in making their products standard-setters in world markets? The answer can be found in interpersonalized market relations, regulated by reputation effects, within the local division of labor.

The discussion that follows draws empirical points of reference for the most part from Emilia-Romagna and Tuscany (although they themselves have important differences), with some examples from other regions. The very detailed literature makes it possible to identify, with considerable precision, the model of production, its associated labor conventions, routes to profitability, and processes of technological learning.

MARKETS[7]

Markets for the Italian trade specializations considered here—the design-intensive craft (DIC) and precision metalworking and machining (PMM) industries—underwent rapid domestic, and moderate international, expansion in the 1970s, the period of most rapid postwar growth in NEC Italy. In this period, NEC Italian producers captured increasing *shares* of both national and international markets in the sectors examined here; in other words, NEC Italy's growth was not a simply an effect of the general expansion of markets. Were this the case, it could be claimed that the region's highly fragmented, decentralized form of production was simply a temporary reaction to expanding demand (the "Smithian" division of labor effect) which, once stabilized, would settle into a more integrated structure (a "Stiglerian" consolidation effect).[8] Instead, the reverse appears to be true: the outputs of NEC production systems took greater market shares in Italy and in the rest of the world, especially continental Western Europe. Market growth, in other words, has been as much endogenous to the development process as an exogenous factor, and the sources of this market invasion deserve analytical attention.

FIRM CREATION, THE DIVISION OF LABOR, AND FLEXIBILITY[9]

In the 1970s, the number of Italian firms engaged in manufacturing grew very rapidly, generating a tendency for average firm size to decline in many sectors. In the country as a whole, the number of very small or "artisanal" firms (*artigiano* is a legal term referring to firms with fewer than 10 workers) grew by about 19%, while slightly larger firms with 10–19 workers increased by 62%, as compared to 20% growth in the number of all manufacturing firms. Value added in smaller firms generally kept pace with their proliferation, or better; smaller firms, for example, accounted for larger proportions of total value added in metallurgy, machinery, electronic materials, textiles, clothing/shoes, and furniture in 1985 than they had in 1973. This fragmentation of production was not simply an effect of expanding output: it accompanied a deepening division of labor in production, as suggested by the fact that the proportion of costs for subcontracting increased rapidly in the fashion industries.

Yet, though small firms and subcontracting have proliferated throughout Italy, there is still something distinctive about NEC Italy. Productive decentralization is qualitatively different here than it is elsewhere in the country, despite statistical similarities. At least five models of productive decentralization are found in Italy: (1) firms born out of industrial decline; (2) traditional, isolated artisans; (3) dependent subcontractors; (4) firms in the horizontally organized industrial district; and (5) new firms in the high technology industry. The first two are found disproportionately in southern Italy, although some examples appeared in the wake of the 1970s crisis in the Milan-Turin-Genoa triangle, and most new high technology start-ups are found in the triangle as well.[10] The third type, dependent subcontractors, includes satellites of large firms such as Fiat, Olivetti, or, in the fashion industry, Benetton.[11] Export specialization-oriented clusters of NEC Italy are characterized principally by the fourth type. As Del Monte puts it:

> The main feature of this model is the high degree of small firm specialization. Many small firms of this type manufacture for the domestic and/or world markets even though they have few employees. These firms perform very few tasks and purchase the rest from outside. Here there is a market for each stage of the manufacturing cycle, so that subcontractors may have a wide range of customers and are not dependent on a single large enterprise . . . The machinery in use in such firms is often highly sophisticated and the work undertaken by the subcontractor is of the highest quality. A distinctive feature of subcontractors is often their ability to find new, original solutions to problems provided by the customer. In the industrial district the birth of new firms is closely linked to a process of division

of labor of this kind, to the ability to detect market niches and consequently to boost output. In such conditions, the firm birth rate is found to proceed at the same pace as growth in employment.[12]

Turbulence has been notably lower in NEC Italy than elsewhere: firms are born at a very high rate in the industries in which these regions specialize, but the death rate is lower than in the more industrial north or the less developed south.[13] Numerous observers have suggested that the production systems of NEC Italy should be likened analytically more to externalized multi-product organizations—organized networks—than to mere collections of independent units or to arms-length inter-firm hierarchies.[14] In fact, these externalized multi-product organizations are the key to the product qualities and best practices of the NEC technology districts.

In the PMM industries of the region, the networks consist of durable (that is, consistently renewed) contacts between clients and specialized final output mechanical engineering firms, and between those firms and their suppliers. The actual number of basic kinds of products made by most engineering firms is quite low: their "mix" is not very high, and flexibility involves mostly variations on a theme (a basic kind of product), with the nature of the variations negotiated between the customer and the firm. This key linkage between customer and equipment maker explains the frequent association between final output specializations and equipment sectors in NEC Italy (textiles/textile machinery; tiles/tile machinery; and so on), but it does not impede these equipment makers from exporting considerable proportions of their output: on the contrary, it is the foundation of their export success. Their specializations last a long time; firms tend to stay with their domain of output and continue to perfect it for periods of 15–20 years.[15] The other key linkage within the "multi-product organization" is upstream of production: because a high proportion of output is to order, producers must be able to obtain key inputs, components, and piece work from other firms, to avoid stocking inputs and labor.[16] The system is almost completely oriented toward specialized supplier linkages between firms.

In the fashion industries, specialized final output firms generally have only indirect relationships to the market, through the intermediation of buyers (*impannatore*, for example). Even those designer-manufacturers who do have direct access turn immediately to specialized, middle-sized (30–50 workers) manufacturers who complete as much of the order as they can, generally the most fashion-sensitive aspects of the work. These firms, too, have low levels of internal "mix" flexibility at a given moment;

but they can switch rapidly from order to order. They, in turn, rely on the very smallest, artisanal firms for small orders. These *conto terzi* (dependent subcontractor) producers are usually extremely flexible and can switch their outputs several times in a day if necessary; they can also work extended hours to accommodate both capacity orders and very small scale, specialized demands. In some cases, they are helped by homeworkers, who mirror their activity but at a lower scale and usually with less sophisticated equipment.

LABOR CONVENTIONS: WORKERS AS ENTREPRENEURS[17]

Local labor markets of the industrial districts of NEC Italy have several distinctive features. First, neither "spot" markets nor internal labor markets are dominant. Spot markets refer to one-time, non-repeated exchanges, with terms and conditions negotiated on a case by case basis. In the local labor markets of such places as Prato or Modena, workers make and sever employment relations repeatedly, often with the same employers. Internal labor markets are present in only a small number of firms in these areas (the relative scarcity of firms employing more than 200 workers limits this possibility), yet the workforce bears many of the characteristics of workers in internal labor markets: they have high levels of acquired, very specific skills and high levels of commitment to the industry and even to particular firms. In effect, a "district labor market" exists which combines characteristics of spot markets (frequent exchanges) and internal labor markets (loyalty, skill acquisition, cooperation).[18] The result is that producers have access to high levels of quantity flexibility without losing skills that contribute to productivity. Thus, the labor conventions which define employment relations in these industrial districts are carved out of the principles of both the Market World and the Interpersonal World, weakening the usual distinctions among wage workers on one hand, and between those inside and outside the labor market on the other.

Note that this quantity flexibility is achieved in a way that cannot be captured statistically, because much "labor" is carried out by artisan-entrepreneurs (who are counted as such and not as workers) and their families. These non-worker workers constitute a significant proportion of the actual total "workforce" in some cases. This fluid border between the category of worker and employer is central to the way labor costs are adjusted to output levels.

This makes the task of wage accounting difficult as well. Hourly wages are clearly lower in the smallest firms, so wage flexibility can be relatively high, depending on which sort of firm is involved in a given production project. Small firms have an even greater gap with the medium and large firms in remuneration per capita than they do in productivity. In the 1980s the remuneration gap appeared to be closing, despite the fact that productivity was growing more rapidly in the medium and large enterprises. Apparently, the labor costs of the small firms increased relative to productivity, though the difference is still on the order of 20%.

A significant element of the "wage" package in these industrial complexes, however, is not reflected in wage statistics. In the same way that many workers are also entrepreneurs or non-employee family members, much compensation is taken in the form of profits rather than wages. And, as we shall see shortly, these small firms are, on average, the most profitable.

TECHNOLOGICAL INNOVATION AND LEARNING[19]

Small-firm systems in general, and traditional industries in particular, are widely considered to be technologically backward or sluggish; however, this is not the rule for the production systems of NEC Italy, although there are a great many technologically unsophisticated artisanal firms. Both the fashion sectors and the PMM industries of the region are characterized by considerable incremental modification of processes and products, and regular replacement of production equipment. Much of the equipment is itself produced in the region, or modified via negotiations between producers and users; regular changes and adaptations of final outputs take place in the fashion industries. This "diffused innovative capacity" [20] does not take the form of basic technological change, as in science-based industries (which depend on access to the Intellectual World), but is rather a matter of practical experimentation and development activity which is highly continuous with existing processes and broad product groups.

A recent technological survey of the Veneto, a region with industries resembling those we examine in Emilia and Tuscany, showed that the rates of product and non–high tech process innovation are indeed very high in the PMM industries.[21] A more limited survey of Emilia-Romagna (257 firms) revealed that 42% of firms carried out important product innovations, and 68% process innovations, between 1985 and 1987.[22] Engineering firms work on a set of semi-standardized product groups, and are arranged to modify or redesign particular products according to the nature of the order. Although these firms are major exporters, a high number of users (customers) of their outputs are situated in the locality, and there is dense information exchange leading to the production of a machine or machine system.[23] Almost 60% of innovations in these sectors are stimulated by customers.[24] While R&D and engineering are important, the absence of strong roles for foreign patenting and reverse engineering suggests that innovations are strongly rooted in these local user-producer relations.

The other salient dimension of innovation in the PMM industries is movement into new, but technologically cognate, product groups. This rarely involves existing firms; rather it is associated with new firm spin-offs by highly skilled workers. These spin-offs generally do not attempt to compete with existing local firms; instead, they try to find markets in related fields.[25]

In the fashion industries, the profile of technological learning is somewhat different. "Product innovations" per se are rarer (about half the rate seen in engineering industries), and tend to take the form of experimentation with new materials. Note that "fashion" is not counted as an innovation unless it involves a new *kind* of fashion. The principal stimulus of innovations in textiles is the customer, whereas for clothing and footwear the role of the entrepreneur is significant, and for clothing we may add the role of the engineer (for process innovations). In general, however, structured R&D and engineering, foreign patents, and reverse engineering—the textbook sources of innovation—play only a minor role.

People are very much aware of the importance of exports and, to this end, of the need to design products to sophisticated standards. The knowledge employed to achieve these responses to the market is essentially practical and customary, not theoretical or scientific (neither formal market research in the fashion industries, nor scientific design in the mechanical industries play important roles, although both exist). Indeed, by many standards, neither the new entrepreneurs nor their skilled workers are truly highly skilled, since their skills are qualitatively different and quite specific to the logic of these production systems. The strong point of the skilled workers and artisans lies in their ability to devise incremental resolutions of practical or aesthetic problems, and come up with well-designed products.

Fashion firms have a powerful economic incentive to engage in the sort of technological learning inscribed in the system of inter-firm relations that prevails in the region. When fashion firms prepare their sample books, prices are quoted on the basis of average costs because buyers have the power to prevent producers from bidding monopoly prices. But *if* the product is successful, a temporary monopoly does in fact exist, because the production run will be longer than that used to calculate average costs; so the price-cost margin widens, and the firm earns a rent, because the price is now fixed. The logic of discrepancy between average cost and price (and not marginal cost and price as in most standard models of monopoly) stimulates firms to innovate in order to enjoy this level of earnings again.[26]

ECONOMIC EFFICIENCY[27]

In the 1970s, it seemed as if the production systems of NEC Italy were overturning the rules of micro-economics. Analysis of a periodic detailed survey of the productive economy by Mediocredito (1987) revealed that, during that decade of rapid growth, hourly and per worker productivity in the small firms (those with between 11 and 50 employees) in the industrial districts of the regions considered, approximated, and in some cases surpassed, that of the largest firms. Profitability was superior in the smaller firms.[28] A series of other standard indicators also showed convergence: investment per employee in machinery and equipment, number of exporting firms, and value added per employee. These findings led a number of analysts to suggest that the district was something like a large firm turned inside out—without the managerial hierarchies and rigidities, but with the productive efficiency of the large firm.

Then, toward the end of the 1970s, the data began to show a weakening of the trend toward convergence, and the late 1980s saw the reappearance of micro-economic differences between the small-firm district-based production system and the larger firms. Value added per capita and output per capita, which grew much more rapidly in small firms in the 1970s, leveled off in the 1980s while big firms surged ahead. The Mediocredito GNP Survey revealed that mechanical engineering and textiles-clothing firms with fewer than 50 employees had significantly lower hourly productivity and lower hourly wages, but roughly equal gross output per employee when compared to larger firms; this means that the smaller producers realized a somewhat *higher* average profit share. In other words, in the short term the data suggest a cost structure whose viability depends not on high productivity, but on low wages and under- (or even de-) capitalization.[29]

A longer-term perspective suggests otherwise. In the 1970s, smaller firms enjoyed a smooth, upward expansion of output levels while big firms were cutting back on installed capacity. Per capita productivity, value added, and output levels should converge under these circumstances. In the 1980s, the roles were reversed: the restructured big firms had more modern installed capacity and much smaller workforces, while smaller units had not yet adjusted to flat markets. Thus large firms—whose value added and output per hour levels have always been greater than those of the smaller firms—took back a certain share of the market in the 1980s because they had a better aggregate productivity performance. This change in circumstances did not, however, alter the underlying logics of profitability of the small-firm segments of the production systems, nor their relative long-term viability; they were in the 1970s, and still are, organized around qualitatively different understandings about profitability and competitive strengths. In Chapter 2 we pointed out that, to be viable, production units in the Interpersonal World must be characterized by: (a) a high margin per unit output; (b) a high value added to capital ratio; (c) a low capital-output ratio; (d) high capacity utilization, in the sense of long working times for capital; in addition, they should be able to tolerate: (e) a high labor cost–value added ratio and (f) a relatively low level of direct labor productivity. These remain the bases of performance in the real worlds of production of DIC districts such as Prato.[30] The smaller firms are much more value added–intensive than the large firms, but they are also very high in labor costs (if not per hour, then in the aggregate). When times are good (as in 1982), their margins are greater than those of the big firms, because their price-cost margins are higher. In other words, the viability of the small-firm model is explicitly predicated on the margins that can open up between price and cost for products produced with relatively labor-intensive methods; profitability data suggest that these firms are viable even in hard times, such as the late 1980s. Their ability to expand production by time-stretching capacity utilization (which depends on the tradition of flexible working time for employees and family members) pushes total profit levels up in boom times when they build up the means to reinvest in the firm.

Two other attributes of the system are coupled to the qualitatively specific labor skills: (1) because the systems are keyed to rapid product change with stable personnel, productivity is moderate; in the fashion industries, it is higher than in sweatshop equivalents in other countries because more advanced production technologies are in use, but lower than mass production or flexible mass production; (2) the extraordinary internal flexibility of the labor process comes at the price of hourly productivity; in Tuscany one often sees wage laborers, independent skilled craftsmen, and entrepreneurs working alongside each other, resolving problems together and even carrying out standardized work tasks together in times of shortage.

The particular economic efficiency of smaller firms in NEC Italy has to do, fundamentally, with the specialized and idiosyncratic qualities of labor and its relationship to capital. While the average employee in the small-firm sector is paid less per hour than workers in bigger firms, it is important to recall the working context: not only are there many entrepreneurs not counted as workers who earn the high margins as profits, but workers themselves have innumerable opportunities to offset lower hourly wages through longer working time, thus giving them quite high levels of income. The figures on per capita income for the intensely developed industrial localities of NEC Italy illustrate this very clearly: places such as Prato and Modena are near the very top of the list.

Social Arrangements, Traditions, or Conventions?

A PATHWAY OF DEVELOPMENT[31]

Some of the controversy about Italian industrial performance, both in Italy and elsewhere in recent years, can be better interpreted by framing the NEC Italian experience in historical perspective. In the 1950s, the number of production units in most of the localities and industries discussed here began to increase rapidly, owing to the rapid appearance of entrepreneurs—workers laid off from shrinking factories or former peasants or members of their families. Yet in Italy as a whole, average firm size rose at that time, as the concentrated industries of the Industrial Triangle (Milan-Turin-Genoa) were growing rapidly.[32] The real question here is why in the 1950s Italy—which, like the other major European countries, had pent-up demand for all kinds of consumer and producer goods—followed the path it did: elsewhere in Europe, the mass production paradigm took hold much more strongly *in the same industries:* both DIC and PMM industries in France and Germany, for example, evolved toward industrial concentration, standardized outputs, and reduced product differentiation. A so-called difference in demand patterns alone is not sufficient to account for the different course taken by Italian industries. To give just one example: in the 1950s, clothing demand and distribution systems were at least as fragmented and differentiated in France as in Italy. Expansion of these same industries in both countries, as in the United States, involved concentration. Moreover, export performance of the Italian production systems considered here was already very strong in some cases by the mid-1950s, so they were not simply serving a unique local demand but were cutting into the shares of other Italian regions in the national market and steadily increasing their share of international markets—while holding their own against imports in the domestic market (unlike the French and British textile and clothing industries, which were already losing ground to imports in the late 1950s). Nor can the pathway be attributed to a simple shortage of production capacity, for existing factories were laying off workers and selling machinery at the same time that markets were expanding.[33]

The 1960s coincided with the second phase of development of the industrial districts of NEC Italy. The number of new firms entering the region increased, leading to rapid growth in employment and a downturn in average firm size. Aggregate statistics show Italian firm sizes leveling off, but this was essentially the composite effect of declining average size due to firms moving into export-oriented production systems, and layoffs in the big firms of the Industrial Triangle.

Italy's position in international markets for DICs and PMMs was analogous to Japan's in the same decade: it had a decisive cost advantage for relatively uncomplicated products as a result of low unit labor costs, helped along by a steady devaluation of the lira. At that time, NEC Italian firms also competed directly with domestic mass production firms in the fashion industries (although there were few of them) and performed much better than their French, British, or American counterparts in their home markets, because they could adjust capacity and outputs more rapidly and had lower production costs.

The third phase, from the early 1970s until 1985, is one of "regularization and modernization" of these production systems. Statistics show continued rapid entry and decline in average firm size, though many observers believe that entry was more apparent than real, principally an effect of regularizing the status of many existing firms and homeworkers. Hence their sudden appearance in employment and output statistics, combined with the now-famous decline in overall average firm size in Italy as major industrial enterprises with large factories laid off large numbers of workers.

Indeed, the simultaneous growth of decentralized production systems and the crisis of large firms in the Triangle led many commentators to assume the two were directly connected, a supposed geographical "trade-off" between Milan-Turin and the Third Italy. However, direct functional linkages between these phenomena were largely nonexistent (the only *indirect* linkage is that decentralized systems avoid labor troubles which affect larger firms). Growth was accompanied by two phenomena in this period. Like the Japanese, the Italian export-oriented systems upgraded their outputs, conquering markets on the basis of product quality and not simply low prices and quality. Unlike the Japanese, though, they did so without industrial concentration, by modernizing firms of the decentralized systems—leading to the statistical convergence noted above in levels of productive efficiency and wages between small and large production units by the end of the 1970s. At the same time, newer decentralized production systems appeared elsewhere on the Italian landscape, in places such as the Marches, and entered some of the export-oriented sectors, but generally with lower-quality products and on a basis of cost competition.

This "golden age" of the "flexible" Italian production system was not an automatic phenomenon. As the burst of postwar market growth slowed, the industries entered a critical stage which might very well have led them to consolidate around mass production of standardized products, that is, to construct an Industrial World—especially because in the late 1950s and early 1960s the fashion system had massive surplus capacity for production of standardized and relatively low-quality products. Instead, they solved the crisis by moving up-market into higher-quality products, and from national to international markets. How did this happen?

Certainly the growth of international luxury and semi-luxury markets from the early 1970s on encouraged existing artisans to allow newcomers in, and even to share technology with them. Buyers and commercial agents *(impannatore)*, sensing opportunity abroad, also turned to these firms as demand rose. Nonetheless, it is striking to note that in general existing artisans neither attempted horizontal expansion or vertical integration on their own, nor did they attempt to block commercial agents or buyers from extending relations with the new entrepreneurs. One can guess that this response was only possible because the local population system was relatively closed, so that dense information and reputation effects could flow freely between firms, not just in terms of evaluating skills, but to allow policing of the various producers' roles and business practices. Opportunistic behavior, or even the fear of it, would clearly have made it impossible to move from one system to another.

TRADITION VERSUS ACTION[34]

A long line of thought concerns the specificities of capitalist development in the Latin countries of southern Europe, which has taken fundamentally different lines from the Protestant, Anglo-Saxon capitalism of the Rhenish-

Lotharingian system. Barrington Moore formulated his well-known thesis of "conservative modernization," which preserves political stability at the price of more rapid growth and technological change, with respect to southern Europe.[35] Southern Europe is distinguished by the relative importance of its petite bourgeoisie (20–30% of total workforce, versus 8–12% in northern Europe); by political institutions rooted in clientelism (frequently church, class, and family-based, sometimes Mafia-based), where exchanges of favors secure political stability but also work to slow economic adjustments by impeding factor mobility; and by a conflictual and group-based form of democracy, where rights are secured through hard, active social conflict, in contrast to the individualistic notion of citizenship and the administered quality of northern European democracies.[36]

All this, of course, is part of the background of NEC Italian development, but it cannot help us understand why the NEC Italian experience differs so much from that of most similar areas in Italy, Spain, and France; why the systems of NEC Italy have not stagnated as in southern Italy; why the Interpersonal World has so much more force than in France.[37] In NEC Italy the traditional petite bourgeoisie has transformed itself into a rich and privileged entrepreneurial middle class; extremely rapid economic growth has now been joined to high levels of political stability; and clientelism seems to have assumed highly modern forms that do not—at least to the degree envisioned by Moore's theory—impede economic adjustments but instead channel them in qualitatively specific ways.

An alternative point of departure—the one taken by virtually all detailed studies of the NEC Italian production systems, by both admirers and detractors—is to see that the system's internal institutional arrangements are deeply inscribed in broader social arrangements, what economists might call the institutional "environment." Still another approach argues that the industrial practices visible in the postwar period were "traditions," but this does not hold up to scrutiny: traditions are longstanding, concrete routines and practices,[38] and NEC Italy's industrial practices were, for the most part, constructed in response to the 1950s. Conventions of participation, by contrast, are transitive rules, which provide actors access to certain forms of coordination and discourage others; hence they push for certain kinds of routines and not others—some of which may be stabilized in the form of tradition, while others may be changed as a result of the stresses and strains of the conventions of participation. Our analysis seeks a systematic understanding of these observed practices and routines by capturing them as results of conventions of economic participation which define individuals' action frameworks.

Conventions of Participation and Identity, Action Frameworks, and the Models of Production in NEC Italy[39]

Figure 7.1 presents a schematic view of the conventions of participation and identity in the Emilian and Tuscan real worlds of export specialized production systems. On the left are components of the model of production analyzed earlier in this chapter (markets, firms and the division of labor, labor, innovation, economic efficiency): these are *domains of economic action* and its results. On the right are the conventions of participation and identity mobilized by different groups, as well as the form they take. The middle column indicates the *conventions* of the action framework in production.

SELECTION AND ENTRY: RESOURCE MOBILIZATION AND IDENTITIES OF GROUPS[40]

Five basic communities have been mobilized to construct the production systems of NEC Italy: (1) buyers, designers, and innovators; (2) middle-class entrepreneurs; (3) new entrepreneur/artisans; (4) homeworkers; and (5) skilled workers. The conventions of identity of these groups are quite diverse, and the borders between some of them are quite fluid. For example, in the Tuscan fashion industries, there are special agents who almost always take care of buying products from producing firms, intermediating between the production system and the market; and there are designers who possess brand names or skills recognized directly in national and international markets. The ranks of these key agents are difficult to penetrate—there are skill and reputation barriers—but, surprisingly, there is considerable turnover. Thus, although designers are the modern heirs of aristocratic tastes (in Tuscany), their ranks were never fully closed as in the case of French *corporations*.[41] And in Emilia, product innovators rather frequently are former skilled workers who have attended technical schools, or have teamed up with scientists and technicians encountered through those schools. These production systems are thus strongly shaped by conventions of participation which allow entry into key technology-mastering groups.

Entrepreneurial activity in Emilia and Tuscany is mobilized by a series of push and pull factors which favor innovation. Middle-class entrepreneurs are usually first-generation inheritors of enterprises started by their parents; the stratified class barriers typical of the industrial north do not exist in the industrial economies of these regions. More recent firms are frequently of the smaller, artisanal (fewer than 10 workers) type. Here,

164

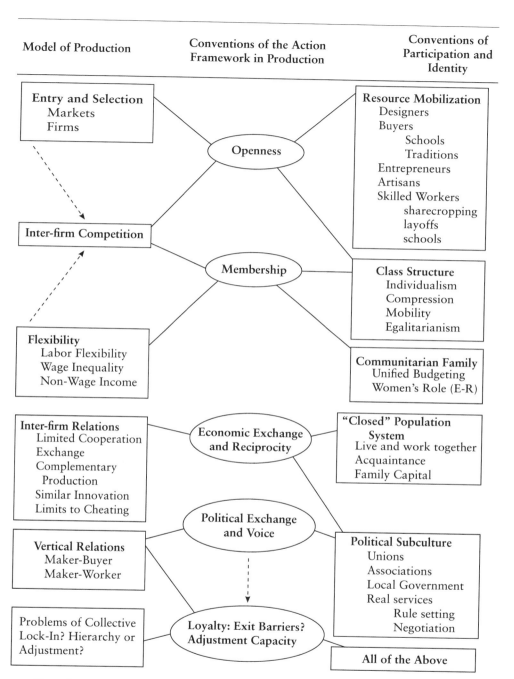

Figure 7.1 Conventions of identity and participation, action framework, and models of production.

entrepreneurs in the twentieth century have had three principal avenues of access to industrial activity. Many were released from agriculture, specifically from *mezzadria* (share-cropping), the dominant form of agricultural organization in both regions—indeed, share-cropping was dominant in NEC Italy only; historically it was fully dominant in *no* other European region.[42] This provided unusually strong experience in organizing independent, small-scale, family-based economic activity, and an extremely strong ideology of economic independence, or at least an unwillingness to work directly as a wage laborer. As late as 1950, 40% of the population of these regions was employed in agriculture; that figure had dropped to below 10% by the end of the 1970s.

A second source of entrepreneurs, principally in the metalworking sector of Emilia, is technical schools, which have a long history in the region. These schools combine theoretical and practical training, thus enabling innovative but applied activity, and because they were founded and operated in a region noted for its socialist orientation, they have been accessible to people from all classes.[43] Third, in the postwar period, both Emilia and Tuscany suffered massive layoffs of workers from large industrial plants, but those workers typically did not emigrate from the region, turning instead to entrepreneurial activity. Many were highly skilled workers provided with machines by former employers to start their own firms. One further asset is that many families who remained in agriculture, and some who turned to urban work, had at least one member available for industrial homework, including many women with skills in earlier specialties of these regions (weaving straw hats [*paglia*] in Emilia, for example, a predecessor of the knitwear industry). Women homeworkers in Emilia have been politically organized for many decades, able to formalize their work and institutionalize their position in the regional economy. In both these regions, but especially in Emilia-Romagna, the class structure is compressed: the structural differentiation typical of large-scale industrial centers has not been heavily in evidence in the twentieth century; rather, the region has manifested such qualities as a spirit of egalitarianism and there have been high levels of upward mobility from working to entrepreneurial class, and quantitatively a low level of income inequality when compared to the North or the South.[44]

These conventions of participation have had a clear functional effect: the rate of entry into entrepreneurial activity has been extraordinarily high. And that, in turn, has had distinct economic outcomes: namely, it tends to favor regional production activity directed at markets for products whose qualities are most amenable to a structure with low barriers to entry and resulting high levels of productive decentralization: the DIC and PMM industries.

FLEXIBILITY: RESOURCES, MEMBERSHIP, AND THE FAMILY[45]

NEC Italy is characterized by a family structure, the "communitarian family," almost unique in Europe: extended family households, in which parental (usually paternal) authority is secure, hierarchical, and multi-generational, coupled with a tradition of fully equal inheritance among siblings. The economic logic in this kind of situation very clearly calls for unified family budgeting, that is, families share income with a goal of maximizing the income of the whole rather than the individual parts. This is enforced by the authority wielded by the *capofamiglia*. The logic of individual labor is not predominant,[46] nor is the logic of individual survival, which makes economic fluctuations less traumatic for individuals.[47] Most students of NEC Italy insist that work, entrepreneurship, and participation in the region cannot be understood by looking at the individual in the labor market, but must be analyzed in terms of the individual within the family unit. This membership has many effects on the structure of the production system; for instance, as noted above, smaller firms generally are characterized by lower productivity and hourly wages than larger firms, but in this region, income redistribution within the communitarian family compensates for lower individual earnings as a rule in the short run; and in the long run this is achieved by accumulation of productive and real capital, which is then used to generate rents.

For both entrepreneurs and workers, profit is a source of income in boom times. Quasi-rents earned on some products made in the region come directly to entrepreneurs, who, in some cases, share them out with higher wages for loyal, skilled employees. This mechanism, combined with family income pooling, has allowed the extraordinary levels of capital accumulation and firm formation in the region. The principal way of raising incomes over the 1960s and 1970s was not, in any case, through productivity-led price reductions, but by moving up the price-performance curve to "better" goods, and by enlarging markets geographically (that is, by further internationalization).[48]

For entrepreneurs, then, the advantages are clear. But why are workers willing to tolerate wage inequalities vis-à-vis larger firms? To be sure, many have few formal skills and could not secure positions in larger "industrial" operations; this is certainly true of a significant number of workers in the smaller firms, and of homeworkers, who are frequently overworked and underpaid. On the other hand, interviews with workers in the small firms suggest that many hope to become entrepreneurs themselves and prefer smaller firms because of family and friendship connections, and because they can use their experience in these firms to learn about entrepreneurship.[49] Where extended family relations are involved, these workers will often be partially financed by their "employers" later on.[50] This is not an unusual trajectory: one recent survey found that 56% of workers had moved from firm to firm voluntarily at least three times, and 10% more than three times.[51] As a representative of the *Confederazione Generale Italiana del Lavoro* (Italian General Confederation of Labor) put it recently:

> The features of work in industrial districts are at the root of the difference between district workers and workers in traditional businesses. In districts, for example, work may be paid for by a combination of earnings and a share in company ownership. Those workers who possess the greatest professional skills are in a position to use this as a lever on the labor market and hence to move from one firm to the next until they are offered a real stake in the ownership of the firm for which they work.[52]

In short, membership has a redistributive, income-smoothing effect which provides firms with extraordinary labor flexibility while providing non-wage income for a large number of entrepreneurs, and training for a certain number of workers. The one group which is largely left out is the homeworkers.

These circumstances call attention to a critical dimension of the role of labor in the production system: the motivations of those who work—they ways they interpret their own circumstances—have to do with their wider network of social relations. Their interpretation of overall income and life-chance structures is as important in mobilizing them as a collective resource as their immediate hourly pay conditions and their formal status as wage-labor.[53]

INTER-FIRM COMPETITION: OPENNESS AND MEMBERSHIP[54]

In NEC Italy, ease and continuity of entry virtually guarantee high levels of inter-firm competition. Ideologies of economic independence, combined with a compressed class structure, make entrepreneurs equals among equals; there is little of the paternalism and local hierarchy—both of which limit the possibility of inter-firm competition—found in many systems for producing DIC products elsewhere in Europe. Inter-firm competition is assured, moreover, by the system of commercialization: buyers, designers, and final output manufacturers are all keenly aware of the prices and qualities that the area's best producers can offer, and enforce these standards on all firms to which they give orders.[55] Fierce, though bounded, local competition is the order of the day.

INTER-FIRM RELATIONS: RECIPROCITY AND SOCIAL CLOSURE[56]

At the same time, local populations of NEC Italy are characterized by high levels of closure, that is, high percentages of those living and working in the area were born there.[57] In strictly economic terms, this is reflected in the very low levels of internationalization of ownership and control of firms, and in very high levels of ownership and control by natives of the regions.[58] This does not imply the absence of capital and resources from outside the regions, or outside Italy—indeed, the levels of strategic alliances and external capital participation have tended to rise in recent years—but overall extra-regional and international participation remains strikingly low.

Here, economic reciprocity rests essentially on dense interpersonal ties between individuals and families who know each other for life. The most common form of cooperation between firms is work sharing: a firm with too much work may share it out with other firms, expecting a return when the shoe is on the other foot. At times, firms will even permit workers from another firm to use their equipment on their premises. There are also limits to cheating, which takes two principal forms in these contexts. In a fiercely competitive environment, when work loads are low, producers might bid below their average costs rather than have no work at all, in an effort to buttress their connections to the buyers. For their part, buyers might force down prices to untenable levels when their power is great. Both of these behaviors do occur, but they have been surprisingly rare, even in the very difficult 1980s. One can only assume that the circulation of information is such that the negative reputation effects outweigh, in most cases, the benefits of cheating.

Finally, as we noted earlier, dense connections between people promote complementary technological developments in both fashion and mechanical engineering sectors. In the latter, there are numerous documented instances of firms aiding skilled workers to set up their own firms, but in complementary or cognate, rather than directly competitive product lines. User-producer relations for complementary technological improvements and market-widening are thus the basis for economic reciprocity.[59]

VERTICAL RELATIONS: VOICE AND THE DEFINITION OF THE COMMON GOOD[60]

The regions of NEC Italy are characterized by distinctive political subcultures: both the communist ("red") areas of Emilia and Tuscany, and the Christian Democratic ("white") areas of the Veneto or Friuli-Venezia-Giulia, have distinctive, uncontested local political majorities. These unified political subcultures tend to aggregate fragmented demands and free the local political system from pressures of divided loyalties[61] (this did not change in the 1993 elections, where the PDS is well installed in Emilia, for example). Political stability also provides the opportunity to construct mechanisms for voice between the principal parties in the local economy, and thus to negotiate solutions to problems. Neither the "red" nor the "white" regimes are heavily associated with the ideologically motivated programs those labels normally suggest: both are fundamentally neo-localist, devoted to a local definition of the common good, although the organizations through which voice is exercised do have different ideological colors: in the red areas, unions and cooperatives, as well as artisanal associations and local government agencies; in the white areas, the local church, rural savings banks, charities, and agricultural organizations.

In Emilia, unions have been considerably more favorable to the system of decentralized production than in Tuscany, where they have opposed small firms as backward and contrary to the interests of the working class.[62] In both, only about one-third of the workers in the artisanal firms are organized, whereas more than 70% in firms employing over 100 workers in Emilia are in unions. In both regions, however, unions have been critical in securing district-wide agreements that protect wages even in the smallest, artisanal firms, even where—as in Tuscany—they refuse to participate actively and ideologically in political projects to "build" the decentralized production structure.[63] Other critical organizational bases of voice include the local branches of the *Confederazione Nazionale d'Artigianato* (CNA), which negotiate for the smallest firms, as well as industry associations of the kind found elsewhere. Thus, the local system is highly negotiated and inclusive, but in the form of a four-party local corporatism: artisans, unions, political party locals, and local-regional governments. The leadership of these groups is strongly interlocking in Emilia-Romagna and Tuscany; an unusually strong case of "tight" social networks is in evidence. In combination with the relatively low level of entry/exit in the regional population and the communitarian family system, the effect is a strong push for mutual acceptance of collective actors.

These conventions of participation have a strong effect on the nature of products which these regions select: their collective capacity to innovate is rooted in the very high motivation for problem-solving at the regional level and for avoiding deep distributional conflicts; both are consistent with gradual innovation rather than radical departures that could cause upheavals in roles and divisions of labor.

LABOR CONVENTIONS

One outcome of such problem-solving is "flexible rigidities."[64] Unions secure district-wide agreements on wages and working conditions. In the Prato woolen textiles district, for example, unions have negotiated an agreement on the production calendar covering hundreds of mills which share the same production cycles, agreeing to reduce the work week but allowing overtime (without wage premiums) when demand is high, with overtime hours banked against slack periods of the year. The agreement's preamble states that "both unions and industry recognize the need to find solutions to plant restructuring, above all regarding personnel redundancy." [65] This type of agreement is important for the mutual obligations it creates: unions support the modernization of firms, and do not take advantage of boom times to press for conditions which are untenable across the entire production cycle or across the booms and busts inherent to the fashion industries. Employers commit themselves to paying wages in the slack parts of the production cycle, and to avoiding redundancy when there are cyclical downturns. How important are these mechanisms? Perulli surveyed a large number of firms in Modena (Emilia-Romagna) and found that 20% of artisanal firms bargained with unions for flexible working arrangements, that 50% of all firms had temporary contracts for young workers, 50% incorporated internal mobility and flexible work organization in their contracts, and fully 60% had agreements for working time flexibility over the year.[66]

There are certain differences between the red and white areas in the ways these flexible rigidities are maintained—the former tend to have more, but less severe, labor conflicts than the latter—but in both cases, there are almost never strong, prolonged attempts by employers to deunionize or severely reduce worker protections in the district-wide agreements.[67] There are two weak points in employer-worker relations. First, homeworkers are rarely unionized, although they have secured legal protections through regional government actions in recent years (indeed, homework is highly regulated in Emilia and Tuscany); this gives homeworkers certain legal minima, but little collective bargaining power.[68] Second, a critical group of "employers," the buyers, operate largely outside the system of flexible rigidities. They remain extremely flexible with respect even to the established middle-sized firms in the fashion industries, and everybody else must absorb the effects of such flexibility. Buyers transmit the force of the market to the production system directly, and can create significant stress on firms and workers who are party to the kinds of flexibly rigid agreements described here.

A LOCAL DEFINITION OF THE COMMON GOOD

Local political solidarity in NEC Italy also takes the more traditional form of "sectionalism," that is, lobbying in the local interest with respect to the national government. This sectionalism can even involve strong vertical solidarities. Artisanal firms, for example, have been steadily institutionalized in the form of a series of national laws on financial assistance for machinery acquisition, R&D support, supporting cooperatives, and the basic artisanal statute, which deregulates labor markets for firms with fewer than 10 employees. The CNA, which has powerful branches throughout Italy, has been instrumental in securing such protections for small firms. Local governments in the red areas have helped passage of these laws by contributing to the national majorities, despite the fact that the national government was dominated by the Christian Democrats for most of the postwar period. This is another example of how solid local structures can exercise voice on behalf of particular strata in local production systems. While sectionalism on behalf of local firms is not unknown in other countries, vertical solidarity works to considerable effect in the presence of local voice systems such as those described here: national protections for homeworkers (largely unenforced elsewhere) were supported by the entire political spectrum in Emilia, including employers of all types.

Coherence: Pathways of Development

The strength of any successful real world of production is precisely the way in which it is chiseled out of conventions which function together coherently and are made possible by conventions of identity and participation; these elements cannot be mixed and matched à la carte.

The conventions of participation and identity in NEC Italy not only steer actors to particular, highly interrelated sets of conventions in production, they foreclose other possibilities. These sets constitute an action framework which is highly interpersonal but also marked by intensive market competition because of openness to entry, which in turn is bounded by interpersonal membership. Remove any major element in the action framework, and the production system would evolve very differently. Without openness, this world would become much like certain traditional industrial communities in France: prone to a static division of the market and, over time, to hierarchical relations inside the production community. Take away membership, and competitive pressures would be translated more directly into wage pressures, eliminating one major source of flexibility in the Italian Interpersonal Worlds. Withdraw economic exchange and reciprocity, and competitive pressures would likely turn into unbounded market competition. Without political voice and loyalty, virtuous circles of maker-buyer relations would very likely give way to more open purchasing patterns, with some improvement in cost efficiency but at the expense of backwardly-linked regional innovation patterns.

The precise outcomes of different combinations (and degrees) of changes in the action framework cannot be predicted with precision. But we can be confident that the Interpersonal World of production and its associated Marshallian Market model of production would be distinctly different, moving in the direction of a more technologically stagnant Interpersonal World (as in the French cases discussed in the previous chapter) or toward a straightforward Market World. The survival of these alternative worlds would depend on many factors: in a purer Market World, it is difficult to imagine survival without severe downward pressure on costs, accompanied by more hierarchical social and economic relations in the region (at present incompatible with conventions of participation and identity). The long-term result would probably be a greater industrialization and greater concentration of the production system. Local conventions of participation could evolve so as to make this option competitive and stable in the long run, but it could very well lead simply to failure. This is the point of understanding a successful real world of production as a complex, integrated action framework, leading to a coherent model of production, and underpinned by conventions of identity and participation. Changing any one element brings deep repercussions within and between all these levels. Worlds and their models of production have some indivisible properties, and their pathways tend to be irreversible. The role of seemingly "small" factors is often great when they are mediated through the systematic and interlocking character of conventions.

8

CALIFORNIA HIGH TECHNOLOGY: THE INTELLECTUAL WORLD IN A MARKET CONTEXT

As in the Italian case, there is no lack of published material about U.S. high technology; in this chapter, we present a brief resynthesis from the standpoint of worlds of production, arguing that its particular developmental trajectory has been produced by the joining of certain frameworks of action.

High technology and advanced services are just the latest in a series of innovative product specializations in which the United States has held a dominant position in world trade over much of the twentieth century; the logic of American industrial development in this period has been precisely to invent or—where it is not the first mover in purely scientific or inventive terms—to commercialize production and create mass markets for new types of products, based on utilization of new *generic* technologies.

We will now examine the real world of contemporary California high technology. Its members enjoy a high level of access to the Intellectual World, but join this to a framework of action based on the Market World, a conjunction with many strengths and certain weaknesses.

Technological Dynamism and American Economic Growth[1]

Economic historians have long inquired into the relationship between technological dynamism and American economic growth, debating the relative influence of demand conditions and factor supplies.[2] Both supply and demand influences have a deep and common set of roots, which provide clues to the conventions underlying America's technologically dynamic production complexes, but to see this, we have to modify a bit the definitions of supply and demand offered by most students of the subject.

It is a commonplace today to note that U.S. industries enjoy a natural advantage over competitors because of the country's huge and homogene-ous internal market. This demand-side explanation for industrial growth over the last century has serious lacunae, however, for in purely quantita-tive terms the internal U.S. market was not huge at the time the country's industrial takeoff began. Rather, the *qualities* of demand seem to have been instrumental in the mid-nineteenth century. The notion that the United States has presented a special, perhaps unique, set of demand conditions for goods has been central to the analyses of Fishlow, Rosen-berg, and others.[3] The spread of population across a largely empty conti-nent generated a demand for goods that were "light, fast, and cheap," rather than durable, steady, precise, or heavily ornamented: that is to say, for goods with generic qualities amenable to standardization. In virtually all intermediate or producer goods sectors (guns, locomotives,[4] industrial machinery, bicycles, agricultural equipment), U.S. industry produced ver-sions with these three characteristics to reach more widespread markets than their European counterparts, who concentrated on manufacturing products destined for economic elites. Thus the creation of large internal markets in the United States was based on qualities of demand defined by a technological configuration of daily life which included capital intensive-ness (household consumer durables), large personal spaces (hence the need for many personal products), and a high degree of spatial separation (cars, airplanes, telephones). This technological package could be produced in large volume to meet the needs of a large and expanding country, and thus the conditions existed not only for breakthroughs into production of new sorts of products, but also the means necessary to commercialize those products through standardization and mass production.

Qualities of demand alone, however, do not suffice to account for the sources of American specializations. The mobilization of resources—of the supply of human and physical capital—is conventional in nature, and underlies the resulting developmental trajectory of these complexes. This trajectory may be schematized as follows:

(a) The United States is the pioneer of the basic product group.
(b) Territorially-focused technology districts develop rapidly through the proliferation of independent firms, spin-offs by new groups of entrepreneurs that create identity and draw lo-cal participation.
(c) Entrepreneurs typically sell their firms at a certain point to larger companies, which concentrate production.
(d) Taylorization and high average productivity are attained

through product standardization, which in turn enlarges markets; international market penetration, principally through foreign direct investment, adds to this effect; routinized manufacturing is often located outside the product-pioneering agglomeration so that its share of employment declines, but growth of the industry and the American position within it allows absolute growth to continue in the agglomeration.

(e) The U.S. share of global production begins to decline, either because other nations can now produce standardized products of identical quality and lower price, or because they can now compete on technological grounds, that is, make superior products, whether through basic innovations or incremental alterations; in the latter case, U.S. companies lose market share because they are unable to switch to meet such competition in what is considered a "mature" sector. Employment in both core production areas and in the country as a whole now declines in both relative and absolute terms in this sector. Policy does not generally resist this transition, because it is conventionally considered to be part of a necessary "structural adaptation" of the economy to rapidly growing sectors. What is lost through "maturation" is supposed to be replaced through *sectoral succession* into another product-pioneering industry.

This list of stylized facts about U.S. industrialization may be recognized as the sequence of events recounted in much economic development theory, particularly the product life cycle theory. But we argue that this sequence of events, and the system's particular way of operating at each stage, is not a universal logic of industrialization, but in many respects a particularly American one, with deep and coherent causes in the set of conventions we shall now investigate with respect to American high technology.

In France, we observed a clear vertical structure with respect to the important collective actors in the industrial system, with well-defined groups and a tendency toward conflict; we showed that specializations tend to arise when one group is capable of overcoming the conflict and in addition has a talent it can exercise in the market. In Italy we observed high levels of horizontal inflow and a tendency for the system to adjust relations between different groups to attain new cooperative "equilibria" at the level of the regional production system as a whole, by actively searching out new markets to accommodate the new actors, and using producers' organizational capabilities to achieve the new balance. In the United States, we shall again observe high levels of horizontal inflow into new activities and new markets, but we shall see that the principal action frameworks underpinning long-term adjustment involve a kind of abstract logic of industrial organization, characteristic of the Industrial and Market Worlds, leading to *exit* of capital and labor resources when the frameworks no longer work rather than a search for other action frameworks in existing sectors. We can call the American pathway to development "Innovation, Maturity, and Succession." In effect, both of the traditionally acknowledged strong points of American industrial practice—science (Intellectual World) and the capacity for mass production and highly professionalized mass marketing and services (Industrial World)—give way to the deepest convention of American economic life, that of the Market World. This is the way in which the American search for a "commercial republic" is carried out.[5] The dominant action framework is thus rooted in abstract, depersonalized knowledge and organizational styles, and depends on high levels of factor mobility. What follows is a stylized analysis of the conventions of participation of a contemporary and localized version of this trajectory, drawn from our understanding of California high technology districts in electronics and aerospace.

The Mobilization of Resources: Identity and Participation[6]

The United States system of mass higher education has created a large class of technologists; it has also extended principles of abstract but practical reasoning, and the accompanying socialization, to a higher proportion of the population than any other country. This dominant intellectual-social paradigm, crystallized in the early maturation of quantitative social science, public administration, and management science, represents social life as a series of lawful interactions between individuals caught up in complex systems. It rests, at one and the same time, on highly idealized abstractions such as those of the French tradition, as well as on Germanic historicism. As a meta-framework for the society's elites, this paradigm arrived earlier and spread more widely in the United States than anywhere else. Much literature concentrates on the supposed absence of class ideology and the "belief" in the market in the United States. More to the point, in our view, is the fact that educational institutions actually produce actors, in both consuming and producing roles, who are capable of realizing forms of economic and societal organization that follow from the ways economy and society are represented to them. They are equipped with the cognitive tools, in other words, that enable them to act as if society really were a machine, and resources really were abstract and depersonalized in nature and hence mobile. As these tools have become more and more widely diffused, they have become the basis for coordination between actors— keys to identity and participation. They have defeated, rapidly and thoroughly, other ways of representing resources and other ways of coordinating with others in purposive social action: traditional, localist, class-based, personalized, or "non-cosmopolitan" forms of coordination.

These "positive" representations of resources and coordination fit well with the notions of individual mobility, formally equal chances, and unequal fates which are the normatively justified rules of action for the American in a way that is inconceivable in the other countries we have examined.[7] The positive and the normative converge and strengthen each other as real resources in action, as starting points for coordinating with other actors. In any given historical period of development, this rationality is embodied by a key resource mobilizing group: if in the early nineteenth century it was the frontier settler, and from the mid-nineteenth to the mid-twentieth century the industrial capitalist, it is certainly now the entrepreneur/ professional, especially the engineer/scientist-turned-entrepreneur. Each of these groups, while sharing the basic faith in individual achievement, has been constituted by a distinctive set of conventions of work and identity, and each has ultimately come to be identified with a particular wave of industrialization and its core regions.

In the 1930s, 1940s, and 1950s, the initial resource mobilizers in what were to become the California high technology industries were entrepreneurs, their identities defined by membership in a scientific-professional culture. As in France, formal knowledge and training were key elements to admission; unlike the engineers and scientists who graduate from the *Ecole de Mines* or the *Ecole Polytechnique,* however, the American scientist-engineer frequently applies formal knowledge to entrepreneurial activity, not to directing large, technologically important bureaucracies (notable examples include Fred Terman, the "grandfather of Silicon Valley," Donald Douglas, who founded Douglas Aircraft in Santa Monica, and Simon Ramo, who started up TRW; Steve Jobs, founder of Apple Computers, Bill Gates of Microsoft, and even William Hewlett and David Packard in the 1950s).[8] Thus where professionalism means insertion into a prestigious hierarchy in France, in the United States it is a means to break away. The professional-scientific culture of the United States is not like *métier* in France or artisanship in Italy, either, since their notion of mastery involves solidarity and creativity "within the rules," not innovation in the sense of technological experimentation designed to break away from the existing, "normal" path of technological adaptation to develop new generic knowledge.[9] Each person attempts to realize his or her potential as an individual in this way, in a system which is collectively thought of as a vast abstract action matrix, that is, an "opportunity" economy founded on mobility and commercialization. It should be remembered that the founding entrepreneurs of high technology did have particular, prior industrial or institutional experience. In the microelectronics industry, the scientists and engineers who were eventually to become the key figures in Silicon Valley were originally associated with either university research programs or defense-oriented research laboratories. In the aircraft industry, the founders of what were to become the important firms were initially associated with one or another kind of machine-building industry in the eastern United States. In aerospace as well, many of today's important companies were started by individuals with experience in a related sector. Some had these formative experiences in the very locality which would ultimately come to dominate the new industry (Silicon Valley); just as often, they did not (Los Angeles aerospace founders came from the East Coast). But all acquired an intimate knowledge of the existing trajectory of technological development, against which they could identify the possibilities for change. Thus, the convention of quality which underlies the innovative small firm in the United States is clearly the combination (difficult to attain) of adherence to a scientific rule while coming up with a novelty. This may involve the new application of existing knowledge, or research and development "prospecting," which is equivalent to *planning* research and development to serve a market that has yet to appear. One can find this same phenomenon in the early history of the aircraft industry, the microelectronics industry in Silicon Valley, and in the defense-related equipment sector.[10]

Other routes depart from this purely entrepreneurial model. A number of the most important high technology specializations in the United States today were, for considerable periods of their history, supported initially by military procurement or by regulated oligopolistic markets (as in the civilian aircraft industry in the 1950s and 1960s, where the large regulated airlines supported much of Boeing's research and development and product planning). In any event, our purpose here is not to resolve the debate over the sources of technological innovation in American industry but rather to argue that all the high technology industries, even those in which the early stages of development did depend on regulation or on the military, had their origins in technological experimentation and entrepreneurship, even if they were later subsidized or regulated. The record is clear on this point in the case of the aircraft industry and the microelectronics industry;[11] and it is certainly being repeated today in biotechnology and medical instruments.[12] The innovative scientist-entrepreneur plays a critical role in this process.

Market Conventions of Participation: Solidarity Based on Exit[13]

To use Hirschman's terminology, participation in contemporary California high technology communities involves a paradoxical sort of solidarity, since it is formed around a consensus about the rationality and disciplining force of exit (mobility). The Market World conventions of exit and resource mobility help explain several phenomena: the geography of new complexes, spin-off of new firms, and the selling out of firms to the Industrial World. In the industrial communities of NEC Italy, by contrast, entry is not difficult but is accompanied by loyalty and voice, and there are barriers to exit; in the Francilien system, the barriers to entry are extremely high, and the system is governed by hierarchy combined with loyalty. Let us look at the phenomena that characterize the U.S. experience.

SPIN-OFF AND AGGLOMERATION

Once new families of products emerge, and an entity such as the "semiconductor industry" or the "aircraft industry" becomes known, the process of new firm formation takes on a regular pattern, that of "spin-off."[14] Spin-off essentially consists of a process whereby *key personnel* separate themselves from existing companies in the now-established industry and set up their own firms. The fact that key personnel have such a strong impulse to move on in this fashion is evidence of the deep, underlying rationality of factor mobility, in this case entrepreneurialism, the Market World, in the United States. This career path is much less common for engineers of similar competence in France, for example, where loyalty to prestigious large companies is the rule. The standard interpretation of rates of entrepreneurship refers to the incentives given to agents, where it is pointed out that the United States imposes relatively few costs on a new firm while heavy fixed costs and numerous regulations in European countries discourage firm formation. The evidence does not support this interpretation, since there are high rates of start-up in certain high-cost European countries (such as NEC Italy)—but not in these high technology sectors. Thus the conventions of participation and identity of technologists in the United

States are responsible for this situation, not merely the costs of doing business, just as the conventions of participation and identity of small-firm entrepreneurs in Italy are responsible for high rates of start-up in the fashion industries there.

With spin-off, a more complex division of labor in the industry begins: the proliferation of companies pioneering new products and of specialized input-suppliers is manifest in the growth of the industrial complex and a tendency for average firm size to decline in early years, as in the semiconductor industry in Silicon Valley, the aerospace industry in Los Angeles, electronics in Orange County, and, now, in the medical instruments industry of Orange County, just south of Los Angeles.[15]

Key personnel in the new establishments are no longer the same genre of entrepreneurs involved in start-up of the industry, although the same basic professional-scientific culture and conventions of quality guide their technical performance. The difference is that they have been formed within an industry which is already institutionalized: not only is its basic technological scope now defined, but the professional culture is now considerably more specialized. The existence of this industry-specific and highly specialized "human capital"—that is, of knowledge, conventions of quality and labor, and conventions of participation and identity—is an important basis both for regulating inter-firm relations and for their geographical configuration. New firm founders do seem to be linked by their strong professional culture, which defines the rules of the game, and is reinforced by relatively small numbers and personal reputation effects. A framework of interpersonal action is established, a convention of identity in this now clearly demarcated industry, where at the outset only individual inventors existed.

Interviews with the founders of the military equipment industry and the semiconductor industry confirm that these two mechanisms—the tendency of key personnel to break away and the strong industry-specific professional culture—give a powerful order and coordination to transactional relations.[16] At the same time, the very fluidity of those relations encourages producers to group themselves together in geographical space to minimize the costs of contracting and recontracting, and maximize the probability of successful market search, where formal contracts do not govern transactional relationships. This helps explain the "paradox" of agglomeration in the United States, where the extraordinary geographical mobility of resources, and the highly developed system of transport and absence of customs barriers, might be thought to encourage dispersed production systems.

As the industry develops, several different production complexes may come into existence (as with Dallas, Boston, and Minneapolis in the microelectronics and computer industries, in addition to Silicon Valley). Then, although a high proportion of inter-firm transactions may remain local, certain highly specialized inputs may only be available from outside. It is nonetheless striking that most specialized production continues to occur in a small number of highly concentrated local production complexes rather than taking on a generally dispersed pattern. It appears that new specialized producers are overwhelmingly located in the existing agglomerations, for the key personnel who spin off these firms need to keep their privileged access to their Interpersonal Worlds: they are highly dependent on their existing networks of contacts for information crucial to the development and marketing of technologically advanced products.[17]

SOLIDARITY BASED ON EXIT[18]

Product-pioneering industries in the United States are not only typically agglomerated, but these agglomerations are typically located outside zones of traditional industrialization. In the case of high technology, most of the important agglomerations are not only outside the northeastern and midwestern industrial regions, they are also located outside of existing metropolitan regions—whether in relatively new regions, like California, or in old ones like Route 128, which is outside of Boston. While there is some parallel to the situation in France (with nascent high technology complexes in Grenoble or Toulouse, and the fact that the Cité Scientifique Sud is outside of Paris proper), the differences are more striking: in the new industrial spaces of the United States, there is no well-defined local elite that organizes the new system of social relations and mediates between interests; new industrial elites are generally formed and absorbed by the already existing structure of landowning elites (who profit from the rapid rise in land prices that follows local industrialization).[19] In the high technology complexes of the Toulouse or Grenoble regions in France, by contrast, old local elites accommodate and mediate the role of the young professional workers, in some cases through local political contestation (Grenoble) and in other cases through political continuity.[20] In France, the professionals appear as agents of modernization with respect to the existing elites, who continue to act as hierarchical integrators of the local community. In the U.S. cases, the professional-entrepreneurs are elements of the new elite business class.

American historians once took it for granted that the U.S. population's high level of geographical mobility had a destabilizing and radicalizing influence on American political life.[21] But this was the mobility of the nineteenth and early twentieth centuries, when the working class would circulate among large cities, often amassing in large numbers to face unstable employment.[22] What is striking about the more recent development of industrial spaces in the United States is the reversal of this logic: these areas are resolutely conservative in outlook, in spite of high rates of in- and out-migration. One reason is undoubtedly that the migrants are very different from those studied in the past: whereas in the late nineteenth and early twentieth centuries, radicalism was prevalent among migrants born in the United States and among certain European immigrants, the working forces of today's new industrial spaces are women and migrants from southeast Asia and Latin America, all of them politically marginalized in the labor market.

But this alone does not explain their conservatism. Both the migrant working classes and the professional-entrepreneurs share an ideology of individual accomplishment and social mobility, and social mobility is held to be encouraged by geographical and sectoral mobility. Thus the economic actors tend to conform to the conventions of identity (historically constructed and regularly repeated) of American individualism. We have noted that the professional-entrepreneurial in-migrants become the local elites, but this is not the only reason for their conservatism: professional culture in the United States is not a matter of solidarity among the existing concrete members of the group, as in the *grands corps* in France; rather, it is adherence to a set of conventions of identity, one of which is mastery of scientific or technical knowledge, another individual achievement through the use of that knowledge. The deeply rooted themes of American rationality are strongly present in the resulting conventions of participation: equal chances via professionalism or training; unequal fates via differences in level of intelligence, hard work, or luck.[23]

FROM SPIN-OFF TO SELL-OUT[24]

Inter-firm relations in the context of vertically disintegrated production systems have been the object of considerable study in the United States, especially in light of the apparently very different Japanese and German systems for coordinating these relations.[25] In the highly regulated military-oriented industries, the problem of inter-firm coordination is resolved by establishing a hierarchical system directed by the prime contractors. But this is a special case. In other sectors, many observers have noted the relative absence of strong associational ties at the industry level, and a resistance to government regulation.[26] Market relations and "arms-length" contracting appear to dominate.[27]

Once a product pioneering industry grows to the point where reputation effects weaken, that is, when entrepreneurs are linked by their technical-professional culture but not by personal knowledge of each other, a qualitative change in inter-firm relations appears. Start-up firms feel enormous pressures from their lenders (whether private lenders or capital markets, especially with "impatient" venture capital), and they sense the need to race to the market because others are doing what they are doing. Such a sentiment is generated by the pressure of immediate performance required by the market environment, the same environment that was initially an important source of their support.[28] Unlike the entrepreneur in NEC Italy, these firms have few resources outside the money economy, and they generally require significant quantities of capital, for which they receive little or no direct public assistance. Under these conditions, the temptation to engage in opportunistic behavior grows—and with it the possibility of business failure. The large final output firm may be the victim (when it cannot secure sufficient loyalty from its input suppliers), or the perpetrator (when it uses its superior market or legal power to unload risk on suppliers).

A high percentage of those firms which do not rapidly grow beyond a certain threshold of size and product diversity, and do not die in their first few years, are sold to larger companies by their founders. This high rate of "sell-out" of even successful small- and medium-sized firms is a rational response to the system of inter-firm relations. These entrepreneurs are very clear about their motivations: as successful innovators faced with the hazardous transactional environment of American industry, and the vastly superior financial resources of large firms, they decide to capitalize a portion of their possible stream of innovative quasi-rents by selling out.[29] This is action in accord with a convention of avoiding risk and liquidating assets to redeploy them elsewhere, a convention which is itself largely created by the transactional environment, that is, by the entrepreneurs' expectations of other individual and collective actors. This environment of creating and then avoiding "moral hazards" is conventional: the product of an ideology and practice of creating and taking risks that is deeply ingrained in the key actors' culture and experiences. The result is not simply a process of development characterized by high rates of spin-off, but—via sell-out—a generally high rate of turbulence.[30]

Much of this is well predicted by transactions cost theory, for what we observe is, indeed, a series of *market failures* followed by a tendency toward vertical integration. Some of these are classical external diseconomies of scale and scope: they represent the difficulty of coordinating large numbers of interdependent actors without hierarchy. Our point, however, is that this market "failure" is in fact built in to the construction of the market itself in California worlds of high technology. The markets are ordered by conventions in such a way that they "fail." The sell-out process is a consequence of powerful positive motivations, deeply rooted in the conventions that lead actors to create markets in the first place and then to interact in particular ways. (Transactions cost analyses of these phenomena are discussed fully in Chapter 13.)

SELECTING INNOVATION

The idea of *craft*—a long-term commitment to incremental improvement frequently found in the Interpersonal World (or even in the Industrial and Market Worlds)—is largely absent from the notion of *innovation* in the sense of new generic knowledge described above. It has been carefully documented that American industries lead either in very new, "breakthrough" technologies, or in applying breakthroughs from elsewhere directly in routinized production processes.[31] Japanese industries, by contrast, appear to be much better at implementing continuous innovations through learning-by-doing at either factory level or production level, where the key to both is close transactional coordination.[32] In the United States, the way in which the intellectual action framework is combined with market and interpersonal principles of action in the activity of invention and early commercialization tends to select for radical innovations and against incremental ones.

FROM BREAKTHROUGH TO MATURITY

We have tried to show why U.S. industry can be characterized simultaneously by great ability in product-pioneering and strong tendencies toward standardization and Taylorization. Innovation is not followed by an external environment in which resources are available to firms in durable and stable fashion; this transactional "failure" ultimately encourages vertical integration. Lazonick[33] presents a model of this pathway of development, noting that in the late nineteenth century American firms were forced to internalize resources to a much greater extent than their British counterparts. This adaptation took place through very high firm-specific investments (the "high fixed-cost" strategy), whereas British firms, in a dependable external environment of suppliers and services, could avoid such investments. Necessity proved to be the mother of invention for American firms: they offset their high fixed costs through organizational efficiencies and long-series production, whereas the British firms' low fixed costs left them less efficient in the long run. To this day, managerial practices in large American firms are consistently more oriented toward imposing rigid and hierarchical role distinctions and limiting information feedbacks than are Japanese or German large firms (but the American firms are similar to the French large firm in this regard, albeit in a less formally regulated way).[34]

The Industrial World efficiencies of American firms are more than just a response to failures of their external environment, however; they are also arguably central strengths of the framework of action in which labor and capital are constructed and identified as possessing abstract and deperson-alized qualities. Hence, they are well adapted to large organizations which function according to bureaucratic rules. In other words, this abstract quality of resources permits the industrial form of coordination to excel in the American environment and makes other forms of coordination appear less efficient because their profit content is, by definition, radically differ-ent from that of the Industrial World, with its low price-cost ratio, long runs, and low unit margins, but high scale. American firms are well known for their ability to extend the reliability, interchangeability, and replicable qualities of Industrial World action even to sales and consumer services.

Under these circumstances, it is perfectly logical that American large firms will do better in manufacturing standardized products (as opposed to those requiring either incremental improvement or coordination of many components) than will competitors who are better at coordinating trans-actional systems, whether external or internal. This helps explain why American product-pioneering industries enjoy a period of very high pro-ductivity ("maturity") after they cease to be pioneering. This trajectory is defined by a series of coordination "failures," which are themselves out-comes of the dominant model of production and its underlying action frameworks. The strong points of coordination in American manufactur-ing are made possible by the same conventions that generate these failures.

Industrial maturity in innovative American industries is thus not an outcome that indicates the leveling of technological innovation in produc-tion processes; the production processes are themselves logical *outcomes* of a system of conventions and rationalities that privileges product-pio-neering innovations but, through the sell-out or exit process, discourages certain forms of incremental innovation. The exit practiced by the principal actors of these worlds clears the way for new actors, who carry with them the action framework of the Industrial World.

The California real worlds of production thus involve a triple foundation: resources are well mobilized in the Intellectual World where early key personnel, acting according to the Market World's rationality of liquidating resources and making them mobile for other purposes, sell out and give way to the Industrial World, where the size of the American market and its relative homogeneity permit the effective construction of industrial resources; but the same Market World principle of exit which dominates the first transition also ultimately undercuts the Industrial World.

Sectoral Succession: The Importance of Exit in a "Commercial Republic"

Mass production methods, with their declining capital-output ratios, are incompatible with sufficient employment growth in a country with increasing population. The U.S. economy has, for a considerable time, coped with such "technological unemployment" through *sectoral succession:* replacing mature sectors with product pioneers. It is no accident that the product cycle is an invention of American intellectuals, for it describes rather well the particular histories of a number of American innovative industries, although the theory incorrectly elevates this description to a general theory of industrialization.[35] The latest versions of sectoral succession, according to many analysts, are the development of the biotechnology and medical equipment industries in manufacturing, and of producer and financial services industries. In both cases, the sequence elaborated above appears to have commenced.

The loss of market share in many high technology industries, such as semiconductors, consumer electronics, and, possibly, civil aviation, has led many observers to claim that U.S. industry excels at basic technological innovations ("breakthroughs") but does less well at commercializing innovations and maintaining market shares over the long run ("follow-through").[36] Some have gone even further and claimed that the U.S. system of breakthroughs, in other words the effectiveness of its Intellectual World, is breaking down.[37] Yet the account given here shows that follow-through is not absent in the American system; it exists in the particular form of the Industrial World. When we observe advanced high-wage economies such as that of Germany, where the share of manufacturing employment is very high and stable, we can see that the pattern of succession is not at all automatic, but it is governed in the United States by the great importance placed on conventions of participation which provide access to Market World action. Will the United States continue to have the sort of success with product pioneering industries that it has enjoyed in the past? Only when we know the answer to that will we be able to answer two vital underlying questions: just how relevant is the opposition between fundamental and incremental innovations? and how sustainable is the Market World role in relation to the Intellectual World in global competition?

If this opposition turns out to be a stark one, and sectoral succession can no longer compensate for maturity and decline, then the United States will face a large-scale problem requiring collective action: how to reform conventions of participation and identity, and the accompanying action frameworks of the Industrial World, to better accommodate incremental innovations. This effort would be directed at creating a more stable underpinning of Industrial World action with interpersonal ties, and so tempering the radical effect of Market World principles of exit.

Once again, there are tradeoffs between coherent real worlds of action because of their broadly indivisible nature. The American system of combining the Industrial World with exit depends on conventions of participation and identity which both accept the costs of such factor mobility and offer real compensation for those costs by making it possible for actors to enter into new productive situations. This is why, for example, France and Italy would have difficulty in borrowing U.S.-style entry and exit dynamics "à la carte." As the high rates of long-term unemployment in France suggest, exit is not followed by reentry there, for reentry depends on the strong presence of conventions of identity and participation providing access to the Market World. By the same token, for the United States to emulate German incremental innovations in manufacturing would require broad action frameworks that cannot be picked out of a management textbook, but must be built up through precedent, by reforming expectations and competences, and this would require different sets of conventions and the frameworks of action which they make available to actors.

9

SELECTION, STABILITY, AND TRANSFORMATION OF REAL WORLDS OF PRODUCTION

Conventions of Identity and Participation Compared

We want now to close the circle of the empirical and theoretical arguments presented thus far. Each country discussed—France, Italy, and the United States—has real worlds of production, for the most part in different industries. Even where there are certain overlaps (high technology in the United States and France, precision mechanical engineering in France and Italy), these real worlds are significantly different. An examination of their economic identities reveals great diversity, unevenness, and heterogeneity, owing to the ways groups of actors select themselves into different kinds of markets, production technologies, and forms of coordination. In this chapter we propose a model of how conventions of identity and participation select for different possible worlds; we then discuss the possible pathways of evolution between worlds, the limits to such evolution, and the coordination of multiple action frameworks—possible worlds—in real worlds.

A MODEL OF CONVENTIONS OF IDENTITY AND PARTICIPATION

Figure 9.1 shows, in a highly schematic way, the conventions of identity and participation of real worlds of production. The horizontal axis describes participation: it can be organized through a "membership" system, in which a member, once admitted, enjoys rights, expects reciprocity, and has duties—if so, we expect the process of substituting new members for old ones to be complex, slow, and hence limited. Or participation can be through a non-membership system, where belonging confers no particular security. Participation can be distinguished by the process of entry: is access relatively open, or is it quite difficult because of formal barriers or because those who are in customarily close ranks? Even when a member-

189

ship system is relatively easy to enter, the significance of membership may lie in interaction with others once an actor is admitted. Conversely, those in a non-membership system may still find it difficult to obtain the access needed to participate in productive activity. Only those non-membership systems with open ports of entry are equivalent to full markets; those with limited entry blend principles of competition (through non-membership) with a limited supply of competitors.

The vertical axis of Figure 9.1 captures identities. Those at the top are constructed on the basis of the personalized, concrete qualities of economic actors; in practice, this generally means that identities are constructed around acquaintance or reputation; small-scale interactions between agents are most important. In the bottom part of the figure, identities are constructed according to abstract categories, usually based on certain kinds of formal knowledge or skills attributed to the persons involved, often incorporated into formal devices such as diplomas or degrees. Since the agent's personal qualities are not part of the requirement, these identities are abstract and anonymous, that is, not dependent on individual characteristics: individuals can be replaced by others from within a more or less expandable pool (depending on the amount of skill which makes up the identity). The law of large numbers governs relations between agents.

Both personalized identities and abstract identities may be more or less permeable or rigid; the firmness of their borders varies. With personalized but rigid identities, it is difficult to establish personal recognition; conversely, permeable personalized identities exist when recognition by others is relatively easy to obtain. Abstract identities that are rigid involve high levels of formal qualification, where means of entry (such as schooling, professional credentials, or formal status) are scarce or highly specific to the designated economic role to be played—for example, education targeted to precise jobs or roles in bureaucracies. Permeable abstract identities may be just as demanding in terms of formal qualifications; they are permeable because the supply flow is large, or because formal qualifications are general in nature and can be deployed in any number of specific economic roles (as individuals with a certain kind of formal education can follow many different job pathways).

Conventions of identity can be observed most clearly with respect to key participants in the real worlds of production we have studied. In NEC Italy, the artisans' *Confederazione nazionale d'artigianato* (CNA) is organized into regional groups. A visit to the CNA in Bologna, for example, is very impressive. A 23-story office tower on the outskirts of town is entirely

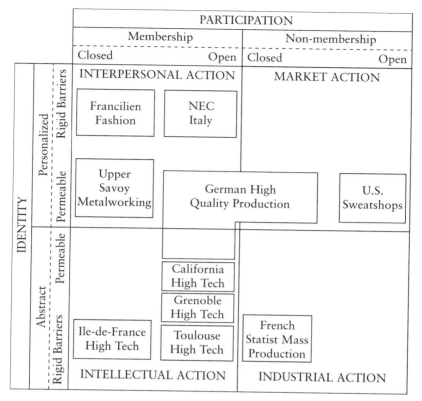

Figure 9.1 Identity, participation, and innovation compared. Abstract = categories which are abstracted from personal traits, usually involving large numbers and formal credentials. Personalized = specialization of persons, small numbers, acquaintance, reputation.

occupied by the regional CNA. It offers programs for small entrepreneurs ranging from research, training, and finance to instructions on how to conduct forceful local political interventions (through political parties as well as through direct relations with elected officials) to ensure that the entrepreneurial environment is highly regulated and supported by regional government. The principle of membership is personal; the CNA takes responsibility for integrating new members and stabilizing identities under conditions of entry. In France, organization at each horizontal level of the system is very strong: as noted, Francilien technocrats have narrow class origins and have shared the rigors of the grandes écoles, to the point where they have recently been dubbed "la noblesse d'état" ("the aristocracy of the State").[1] Identities are abstract, and highly rigid membership conditions link schooling to very specific economic roles. Thus the *sentier,* the tightly linked fashion-design community, on the one hand, and the ethnically solidaristic manufacturing community, on the other, hold key skills. Here identities are interpersonal and highly rigid. In the United States, the scientific-professional culture is strongly imparted by the university training system and its counterpart, formal credentialing. Yet these abstract qualities are generated "upstream" of actual economic roles, so that the agent must determine which of the many possible uses of the high levels of abstract and formal human capital apply in specific economic situations. Abstraction and permeability thus combine nicely.

In all these cases, key resources are mobilized by a group constituted by a convention of identity, a set of shared behaviors which underlie their ability to mobilize production skills and competences. These mobilizers do not exist in isolation, of course, and their patterns of participation with respect to other groups in the production system, and in the regional and national society, are crucial to whether their competences are used to promote learning and technological dynamism.

WORLDS OF PERSONALIZED IDENTITIES

The upper two cells of Figure 9.1 depict systems in which personalized identities are dominant. We expect that learning in these systems will be incremental and continuous, drawing heavily upon the Interpersonal World (for specialized know-how, customary familiarity with objects of work, and the like). But the interpersonal action framework is only fully dominant when personalized identities combine with membership participation; when personalized identities combine with non-membership conventions of participation, the market action framework is present.

The Interpersonal World. In a membership participation convention, key collective actors, when they exercise production competences, must respect the concrete identities of other participants. This imparts a strong gradualist character to innovation. Indeed, where membership is closed, the tendency is toward extreme technological conservatism, even stagnation; where it is more open, selection pressures exist and these tend to bring greater product quality, which confers a certain underlying inventiveness and dynamism on the system.

In our case studies, the NEC Italian DIC and PMM production complexes are characterized by open but strong membership of the key technology-mastering group, the artisan-entrepreneurs or worker-entrepreneurs. This fluid participation is made possible by very strong integrative, identity-creating processes at the regional level, so that Interpersonal World actors are continually created. At the local level, hegemonic agents in the community enjoy sufficient support both to mobilize resources which sustain in-migration to dominant groups and to establish—via formal means or informal pressures—the rules governing new entrants. A number of forms described in Chapter 7—compressed class structure, the communitarian family, closed population structure, strong local political subcultures—not only create propitious conditions for voice and political exchange, they also discourage exit from the region in general and from the production system in particular.[2] The high degree of loyalty to the local economic and social systems creates strong exit barriers. The effects of such barriers are not fully understood, nor are they easy to formalize or quantify. However, virtually all close analysts of the NEC Italian production system agree that they create pressures toward innovation, adjustment, and, perhaps, stagnation of the local systems that are manifestly different from those found in, say, U.S. production regions with their high levels of labor entry and exit.[3]

Note that the conventions of participation combine voice and *community* loyalty. Existing entrepreneur-artisans are heavily supported not only by the CNA and local governments, but also by their moral "first comer" rights inside the production system. Yet they do not oppose entry of new entrepreneurs, because they often know, or identify with, the newcomers. Their action is thus inscribed in a market framework: they recognize that the newly arrived have the right to participate. Their action is also in accord with the communitarian spirit of the Interpersonal World, however, as they allow entry into products in ways which avoid direct competition with existing producers—products new to the regional system or complementary to existing outputs, within the same general type of activity. In this case, the existence of exit barriers creates strong pressure for periodic adjustments of the precise field of production and for learning, as local supply outstrips demand or as extra-regional competitors enter.[4]

In Bologna, Modena, and Prato, this pressure has pushed producers up the price-performance curve into increasingly high quality products. Such attempts take many different forms: Carpi's knitwear producers moved into "fantasy" fabrics; Prato's mills went from industrial quality carded wools to high quality combed wools, and are now attempting to move into other markets; Bologna's machinery industries have continually branched out into new, closely related outputs, and have worked to improve the quality of existing models. As long as ever-increasing product quality is possible, then people can "work to quality," and horizontal entry without vertical conflict is possible. The model is self-selecting for technological dynamism through steady improvement or adaptation of product qualities via an ongoing and variable fusion, mostly successful, of the Interpersonal World with market frameworks of action.

The Market World. Where conventions of participation do not confer membership, the exercise of skills is not so constrained by rights or responsibilities toward others in the system. This does not mean that actors are free to be opportunistic; rather, though personal recognition is key to being a competitor, it confers in and of itself no presumption of remaining in the game. Participation can be regulated through very different conditions of entry: where entry is easy, liberal market interactions will tend to develop as a result of open supply conditions; where the flow is relatively controlled, the barrier to entry tends to be a personalized reputation effect. Once in, however, performance is continually verified and tested; there is no presumption of great loyalty, beyond the right to be considered for the quality test, as a participant in a closed non-membership system.

Our detailed case studies include no examples in which the Market World action framework is fully dominant. We can cite, however, many production systems in southern Germany (Baden-Wurttemburg and Bavaria)[5] where access to employer and worker groups is relatively difficult, because communities of skilled workers are knit together by occupational consciousness and training requirements, and the employer class is relatively immutable. The traditional family structure of these regions adds to the importance of reputation effects, aids skill transmission among workers, and reinforces certain entry barriers. Yet there is constant quality testing and relationships can be broken, permanently if necessary. This results in *de facto* compromises in the workplace and in the production system: labor is highly skilled, there is some movement from firm to firm, and workers' reputation effects are strongly in evidence throughout. In southern Germany, with large firms and a developed formal innovation system, we see the formalized German version of the local-inclusive system. Group loyalty and hierarchy are concretized through explicit, institutionalized neo-corporatist "voice" mechanisms—forms which normally attach to the Industrial World. These groups are less based on membership than in NEC Italy precisely because of this institutionalization of change. As a result, there is a mixture: market action is dominant, underpinned by a strong interpersonal fabric and strong formal institutions. This southern German system therefore differs radically from pure versions of the Market World, such as those found in sweatshop industries in U.S. cities.

WORLDS OF ABSTRACT IDENTITIES

In the cases filling the bottom two cells of Figure 9.1, interactions must respect the abstract categories to which identities are attached and resources are amassed according to the codified rights and duties of each group of resource holders. Abstract identity principles, permeable or rigid, are the result of formal skilling. Conventions of participation influence the way these identity characteristics are deployed in economic action. This tends to create innovation processes that are either planned (where a convention of non-membership is in place) or radical (where there is a convention of membership).

The Intellectual World. A convention of membership includes rights and responsibilities for those who belong, notably attention to and respect for scientific and professional ethics or norms. Such conduct generally confers a certain belonging to the population of possible agents. But entry to such a community can also be limited by other entry barriers, such as qualifying for military-industrial contracting, or belonging to a network not just of educated engineers but of graduates from a particular grande école (where there is no difference in technical capability between engineers from different schools). Such membership could also be relatively open, requiring little more than the appropriate identity. Where membership is closed, the exercise of competences derived from abstract skills is likely to be displaced upstream, into projects defined (often hierarchically) by the skill-holding group itself, as in the case of French technocrats. In the open membership situation, there will be a tendency toward a competitive free-for-all between products generated by such competences. Both situations generate radical technological innovations but of very different sorts, as our comparison of the French and American worlds of high technology has shown.

Innovation in large-scale technological systems, as seen in Francilien high technology, rests on the command over key technological or knowledge resources by groups with membership that is highly restricted but also highly abstract. Although there is severe competition to get in, starting with the grandes écoles, the leading group has little competition on the day-to-day level: its members are linked to the state; all are guided by principles of technological excellence and centralized planning of economico-technical relations. There is a high level of latent conflict in the system, however, among unions, with their anarcho-syndicalist tradition; private capital, which is at the same time dependent on state purchases in high technology but hostile to direct state management; and technocrats, who see themselves as an independent force but are in fact divided between engineers (usually *polytechniciens*) and high-level administrators (usually graduates of the *Ecole Nationale d'Administration*). Under the circumstances, it can be very difficult to implement learning. Technological learning for commercial high technology products is difficult in this setting, because state technocrats hold tenaciously to their existing identities. Even when the technocracy is highly mobilized, as with the *plan calcul*, their action routines—technological plans and subsidies—are incompatible with the kind of learning needed for products with different, commercial, qualities. The technocracy does succeed in situations involving direct state orders for major technological systems, as with aerospace, telecommunications equipment, and certain types of computers, because in these cases technological planning can be directly implemented all the way down the production chain.

Radical commercial innovation is found in contemporary Californian high technology industries, where professional technologist-entrepreneurs, who hold key skills, form a group on the basis of a large, impersonal national resource pool. Many observers hold that U.S. high technology should be viewed as an extremely hierarchical system with giant order-giving companies and dependent subcontractors.[6] But entry of new firms continues to be important, and these smaller firms are neither technologically backward nor, usually, dependent on one or even a small number of clients. The institutional structures are, in fact, quite porous. One reason for the relative ease of entry (and occasional rise to importance of new participants) is that university scientific-engineering faculties, large high technology firms, and the Pentagon do not exercise the kind of direct control of inter-firm relations characteristically exerted over French companies by their allies in the ministries; nor do universities and professional associations in the United States provide the kind of group consensus offered by the grandes écoles in France. Even the Pentagon's military contracting has considerably less influence on the form of the production system than its French equivalent: in the United States, control is indirect and relies on contracting; in France, it rests on planning for the entire *filière*. In a system where participation is structured in this manner, learning tends to take place through technological breakthrough and competitive shake-outs, among a wide diversity of choices, leading to high rates of success and failure (statistical turbulence in the firm population) and eventual consolidation.

Finally, where these abstract identities apply and conventions of participation do not involve membership, Industrial World action becomes dominant. The only way to remain a participant is to deploy the skill of rendering resources abstract, over and over again in productive activity, where they are subject to the market-cost test and to the possibility of being replaced by other, similar generic-standardized products. Yet even here, again, participation can be more or less difficult. True, mass production is characterized by interchangeability of actors—hence easy participation—even when there are traditional scale or capital-related barriers to entry. And in terms of access to the identities (cognitive frameworks, skills) needed to produce these products, entry barriers are extremely low in the contemporary advanced economies, and this explains why these industries are subject to such fierce competition. But there can be other kinds of barriers, conventional in nature, having to do with participation: strong barriers to getting one's skills verified in the first place, when the search (for workers, subcontractors, or partner firms) of existing firms is highly restricted. Such search behavior is probably chosen where the exigencies of coordination between intermediate inputs are particularly great, and interchangeability is limited; high quality but high volume industrial production, for example, requires a more intricate form of coordination than traditional mass production.

Possible Development Pathways

Worlds of production as frameworks of action, like their underlying production systems, do not stand still. Production systems are subject to competition and technological change; conventions are like hypotheses, subject to continuous verification, which may keep up with changing circumstances or impede them. Which patterns of evolution are more likely than others? The theory of worlds of production is founded on the substantive notion that production is the result of a large margin of action that is not predetermined—a space of doubt, unpredictability with respect to behavior, due to the existence of each actor's subjectivity. Thus the theory can make no claims to predictability or determinacy. However, some pathways of development are more likely than others, and some are quite unlikely. The problem of possible developmental pathways has three dimensions:

The first is in terms of product qualities: as outcomes of conventions for dealing with uncertainty and models of production, certain pathways can be envisaged and others excluded for the four basic kinds of products.

Second, some pathways of evolution can be imagined from actors' existing political and institutional conditions of existence, what we have called conventions of identity and participation.

The third is more ambiguous in logical terms but empirically very rich. Real worlds, as we have shown, often involve major and minor keys: dominant elementary action frameworks, blending or coordinated with other action frameworks. Fusions of such frameworks may be quite complex in real worlds. Yet even here the possibilities are not limitless: some are more likely to succeed than others; and some are more likely to evolve in movement from one world to another. There are general aspects of the art of economic syncretism which can be identified.

EVOLUTION, RUPTURE, COORDINATION: A THEORETICAL PROPOSITION

We have considered the question of evolution in economics extensively with respect to technology, by using the metaphor of technological trajectory. In addition to the properties of irreversibility and path-dependency (discussed in Chapter 1), the possible pathway of a technology at any given moment in time is defined by a sort of "envelope" of possibilities. For technology, the determinants of the envelope generally involve complementarities, similarities of technologies and deepening of their existing qualities. A similar logic applies to elementary action frameworks: at any given moment, there is an envelope of probabilities and, all other things being equal, an improbability space lying outside this envelope.

Evolution is more probable between the horizontal pairs of worlds of production in Figure 9.1 than between vertical pairs; evolution along diagonals is least likely. In other words, the evolutionary pathways between the Interpersonal and Market Worlds and between the Intellectual and Industrial Worlds are wide and deep; weaker channels of evolution exist between the Interpersonal and Intellectual Worlds and the Market and Industrial Worlds; and it is highly improbable that the Market World could be transformed into the Intellectual World (or vice versa) or that the Industrial World and the Interpersonal World could change places.

The horizontal pathways involve changes in certain key inputs (specialized versus standardized inputs) and technologies (scale versus variety). These are significant transformations, as recent management literature has amply illustrated, but they do not involve fundamental changes in the convention of identity: key actors retain their personalized or abstract identities and continue to understand them as basic principles of their existence in and relationship to the world. They can therefore remain as they are while effecting changes in product qualities or the technological structure of the production process.

It is thus quite easy to imagine NEC Italian Interpersonal Worlds of production evolving in the direction of the Market World, where greater exit would be permitted, thus weakening the membership system. Increased standardization of inputs would make the end of the membership system technically possible, while the interpersonal action framework would continue tying producers to each other and to buyers.

It is equally possible to imagine the Francilien fashion industry evolving toward the Interpersonal World by opening its membership system or even becoming a non-membership system. Either would increase the incentives for commercialization within the system, the former for specialized products, the latter with more radical change toward more standardized products. In neither would the convention of identity undergo a fundamental change.

It is possible as well to conceive of the Californian Intellectual Worlds evolving in the direction of greater Industrial World activity, something that has actually been happening on an ongoing basis in many of its product segments, as we noted in analyzing industrial "maturity" in the United States. Full transformation of such intellectual action into that of the Interpersonal World, however, would imply that the key innovators had abandoned their abstract identity.

Changing participation patterns, while obviously extremely difficult, is superficial when compared to changing identities. Vertical development pathways, because they involve switching from one form of uncertainty to another (from predictable risk to true uncertainty or vice versa), entail a change in identity: such switching requires key actors to interact with the world according to principles of existence which are radically different from those with which they identify themselves and others.

This difficulty of changing identities makes evolution between interpersonal and intellectual products, and between market and industrial products, much more problematic than horizontal shifts. Nonetheless, competitive pressures often "call for" these vertical developmental pathways. For example, the Japanese reinvented the car industry even though personnel in large Japanese firms are chosen in part on the basis of abstract, formal qualifications (particularly the schooling system), and there is fierce competition between firms in different *keiretsu*. However, once they are accepted membership is closed, and there is a strong personalized element in interactions. Japanese subcontractors straddle the Market and Industrial Worlds. Thus the system as a whole, while it benefits from the industrial action framework, draws resources from the Market and Interpersonal Worlds. U.S. competitors in the car industry have apparently been unable to do this—though literature directed at management is full of recipes for such transformations, while the literature on industrial and economic institutions suggests they would be difficult if not impossible, as does our reasoning here.

In the absence of changes in identity, the most likely way to alter a real world along the vertical axis may be communication between worlds. Thus it is quite possible to imagine NEC Italian producers recognizing a need for more formal innovation inputs, and to that end establishing durable, effective coordination with Intellectual World actors. In the opposite direction (in Figure 9.1), our case studies of Intellectual Worlds showed that the core technology-inventing community was strongly tied through interpersonal bonds: those of the grandes écoles and the state in the Ile-de-France, those of regional innovative networks in California. These are not transformations, but coordinated combinations.

Where such communication is not possible, organizational ruptures often appear within an industry, as a new competitor reinvents the product in the vertically-proximate action framework and takes the market by doing so. This is not evolution, but replacement—and could be the long-term outcome of Japanese-American-European competition in automobiles, if Western producers continue to lose world market share while the Japanese continue to gain.

In short, vertical evolution is not impossible, but it would seem to be a much longer-term process than transforming patterns of participation. Over the long run, if NEC Italian producers develop a formal innovation system, they could enter the Intellectual World, but the chances of their doing so, as such, are quite low in the short run. Over the long run, U.S. managers might realize that they need to act within the Market World to compete with the Japanese. One generation has not brought about this transformation: although they have introduced limited measures toward coordination with Market World firms (in their subcontracting practices), it is safe to say that these managers retain industrial action as their frame of reference. Finally, it is difficult to understand why the Silicon Valley technologists would want to enter the Market World fully and abandon the abstract identities which are key to their technological capabilities. Vertical pathways exist, but in some cases have only limited attraction, while in other cases they would involve long-term reconstruction of existing conventions of identity.

Diagonal transformations bring us to the realm of impossibility, since they would mean complete rupture of a framework of action and its model of production. Key inputs, the nature of uncertainty, conventions of identity, patterns of participation would all have to change. For an Interpersonal World to become an Industrial World, for example, the conventions of specialization and unpredictable markets would have to become conventions of standardization and predictable risk; technology would switch from economies of variety to those of scale; identities from personalized to abstract; participation from membership to non-membership. There are no channels of reflective action, interaction, and precedent that would allow a given set of actors to transform one such action framework into the other. The same logic applies to putative transformations from market to intellectual action.

Yet collaboration and coordination of elementary action frameworks across the diagonal of our model are eminently attractive in an economic sense, precisely because the diagonally opposed model contains all—in its search for profitability—that the other lacks. What Interpersonal World producer would not want to enjoy the advantages of industrialization? And what high technologist does not dream of the suppleness of the Market World while tasting the fruits of intellectual action? The problem is that contact between these diagonally opposed worlds of production frequently generates pervasive coordination problems, precisely because their differences are so deep and broad. California's real worlds of high technology do in fact combine intellectual and market action. But this leads to coordination problems (the "created market failures" alluded to in Chapter 8), which are resolved by falling back on the Industrial World. A more coherent approach would be to couple the Market World to the Intellectual World through interpersonal action, but this is contrary to the deep-set identities of American actors. This same problem is now very apparent in France: the dominant axis of restructuring, as observed in Chapter 4, links the Market and the Intellectual Worlds and is extremely promising in economic terms, but has not yet been achieved for lack of ability to coordinate these opposed action frameworks. Whether it can be achieved remains to be seen; if not, the question is whether the French economy will seek more attainable compromises or evolutionary pathways than this one.

COORDINATING ELEMENTARY ACTION FRAMEWORKS IN REAL WORLDS

Our case-study real worlds are all, in fact, blends of elementary action frameworks. Each has a dominant framework, but all have certain minor themes which help explain their particularities and distinguish them from other real worlds with the same framework. Concrete products mix forms of labor and demand from different possible worlds of production, a mix that varies from product to product and may change over time even for a given product as it is transformed through technological and organizational learning.

In many cases, the viability of a real world of production depends on the capacities of persons involved: first, their capacity to act by drawing on different possible worlds; second, their capacity to accept the presence of persons acting according to their own possible worlds and effectively coordinate activities with these persons.

The capacity to act according to multiple worlds requires *translating*[7] one world in terms of another. For example, a particular demand may be defined along the lines of the possible Industrial World and nonetheless work in the Market World: a carmaker frequently buys "industrial" components and assembles them into different models with a "market" character. In addition to conventions and know-how, such translation depends on tools and objects, that is, on technologies (flexible assembly is radically different from classical assembly).

The limits of real worlds of production are defined by the people that participate in them, since populations possess the ability to act in certain ways and not others. A real world that is closed off (and products of that world) will develop differently from a real world that is open to other possible worlds simply by virtue of the competences brought in with changes in the participating population. This is easily seen in the different evolutionary pathways of the Interpersonal World of Francilien fashion and the Interpersonal World of NEC Italy: the latter's openness in participation and somewhat permeable identities infuse it with Market World dynamics. The *impannatore* serves to link Market World actors (with their international orientation) and Interpersonal World actors (with their local orientation).

The stability or development of a real world of production also depends on its degree of closure, or its ability to consolidate around secure identities of its actors. Under stable or closed conditions, conventions of identity define roles within social and technical divisions of labor. Conflicts of interpretation of conventions, when certain actors find that their expectations are at variance with responses of other agents, often result in "going back" to the initial conditions (especially in the law), to try to reconstruct what is no longer in active memory. In these cases, both the propensity to engage in conflict and the way in which it is resolved depend on the rigidity and permeability of identities.

Closure and stability have to do with material objects as well as behaviors. Objects—especially fixed capital and technology—play a strong role in stabilizing trajectories of development because they underpin coordination (not because of their costs, as claimed in most economic theory). Each world of production has different kinds of objects; their differences are due in part to the ways actors define their roles—their identities—in the situations of action particular to these worlds. In a viable real world of production, there must be a certain congruence between the actors and the objects at hand, in the sense that the actors must be able to recognize the character of the objects and to use them appropriately and in a coordinated fashion. Investment in new objects, as for technological "modernization," may call into question the existence of a real world of production if these objects cannot be efficiently utilized without actions from possible worlds other than those already in use by actors. For example, in their early attempts to use flexible, computerized production technology, many manufacturing firms did not see a need to revise work practices. Only when productivity gains failed to appear did they understand that objects can require new forms of work coordination. In turn, there is the possibility of struggle over these forms, because they involve changes in worker and manager identities. Innovation within a real world may, as we saw above, require objects from more than one possible world, as well as effective translation between the terms of these different possible worlds and re-skilling—in terms of frameworks of action and not merely of "skills" in the normal sense of the term—of the persons involved.

Industrial adaptation and the development of real worlds thus do not merely involve developing the right rules of interaction between groups; it is a question of whether those groups have identities consistent with the patterns of participation we attribute or would like to attribute to them.

III

INSTITUTIONS, STATES, AND THE COORDINATION OF REAL WORLDS

10

STATES AND INSTITUTIONS
AS CONVENTIONS

Institutions and the Coordination of Worlds of Production

If all individuals acted purely according to one possible world of production, the production systems would require no institutions (although coordination between them might): persons, conventions, and objects would work together efficiently, and a real world would flow naturally from the possible world. In a pure Interpersonal World, for example, familiarity with objects and persons would lead to spontaneous, and largely implicit, coordination; in a pure real Industrial World, the articulation and circulation of objects would coordinate the persons in contact with them.

In real worlds, however, individuals act by drawing on more than one possible world of production, or do not act strictly according to one given possible world, and thus there is a constant threat of *coordination failures*. Institutions take shape through efforts to protect the real world against this threat. There is nothing functionalist about such efforts. Institutions do not eliminate coordination failures, but rather attempt to establish the terms of a solution which, if successful, can be employed by the actors involved. In other words, successful institutions establish conventions for the populations they are intended to affect.

In an institution, coordination is explicit for those involved; this is not the case for coordination by conventions, objects, and identities—although ironically, institutions operate through benefits and mechanisms that create new sets of expectations among those affected; once formed, these function like conventions.

Institutions potentiate and constrain each real world actor's "access" to possible worlds (and particular combinations thereof) just as conventions of participation and identity, and objects, do. For example, a binding industry-wide labor contract which establishes standard job qualifications, lists of tasks, skill levels, and so on, will push firms in the industry toward possible worlds compatible with such a contract: in this case, toward actions with a strong "industrial" flavor and products coherent with them. Or consider another example: legislation on competition which bans certain forms of "collusion" or cooperation might make some types of "interpersonal" action difficult and hinder the development of real worlds based on that possible world. Institutional constraints are not absolute and rigid, but rather are the effects of orientation, partial selection, tensions that must be bypassed. And some differential barriers are necessary to the existence of real worlds of production; when institutions become conventions between actors, they have the same effects of positive selection and orientation.

The Specificity of State Institutions

There is a critical difference between institutions established in an autonomous fashion by persons involved in a given activity and those embodied within the State. The State, like other institutions, is essentially a convention between persons, but unlike other institutions, all State conventions must define the way the "common good" is constructed for the society. Whereas non-State institutions and conventions may be constructed by actors in pursuit of their particular common interests, that is, as part of efforts to resolve particular problems of coordination, the State is formally assigned the role of creating the conditions that maximize the possibility of attaining a general common good. One problem here is that there are so many possible definitions of the common good in a democracy. For example, we may ask: is egalitarianism a result or part of a process? If the latter, how does democracy deal with the fact of diverse means and endowments? All such debates center on the tension between the nature and degree of autonomy allowed to actors, individual and collective—so they can express and realize their particular character—and the nature and degree of universality of actions required of them. There are many different substantive conceptions of autonomy and universality, their interrelationship, and how they should be pursued. Some conceptions simply collapse the two into one, as does "libertarianism," whose notion of the common good holds that the only possible universalizing vocation of social institutions is to maximize individuals' autonomy to pursue their particular interests. But that is a caricatural extreme: most debates over the question are far more complex and nuanced.

These issues are widely discussed in political philosophy; since we are not professional philosophers, we shall limit ourselves to the different conventions of the State deployed by economic actors and their connections to possible and real worlds of production.

In all contemporary advanced economies, the State is highly present in situations of action involving production. But the effects of this presence are not straightforward; they are mediated by the conventions of the State around which actors organize their expectations of both the State and other actors. Such conventions, in turn, shape what the State is actually able to do in pursuit of the common good. Conventions of the State are mobilized, like other conventions, in situations of economic action. This definition does not require us to hypostatize the State, but to consider how states are developed and how they affect unfolding situations. In this chapter, therefore, we "reimagine" the State's intervention from the standpoint of the economic actor, engaged in coordination with other actors in light of his or her expectations about the State. This conventionalist approach shows that there are many possible types of states with respect to their response to many forms of action: the liberal U.S. state, for example, or the interventionist French state. Such a reading allows us to go beyond the tired "states versus markets" paradigm to suggest that the considerable variety and diversity of frameworks of collective action should be at the center of philosophical as well as analytical debates about how states function in the economy.

Our position is quite different from that of contemporary institutionalism, which tends to attribute to institutions themselves a role in coordination failures, to the extent that institutions do not mimic the market and promote the exercise of individual rationality. The economist who invokes such optima in the name of efficiency, hence necessity, remains the counselor of the prince. We have attempted to see things from the standpoint of the economic actors themselves, in the midst of different active situations.

In this chapter and the two that follow, we extend this analysis in two ways. First, we offer a detailed critique of state intervention in the economy in France, illustrating the pitfalls of a state which is not sufficiently situated in viable real worlds of production. Then we compare this analysis with contemporary debates about competitiveness, which allows us to define policy problems facing each of the three countries at hand in terms of how state institutions can assist in the coordination and evolution of real worlds of production.

The Various Conventions of the State:
External, Absent, Situated

In some societies, each person expects the State to intervene in the economy from a position outside and above the situation of action—this is the convention of the "external state" which is particularly strong in France. In other societies, each person expects the State to be absent from situations of economic action, and for individuals to work out coordination among themselves—this convention of the "absent state" is particularly marked in the United States. A third possibility is that the persons involved in economic action (including representatives of the State) operate on the premise that the State participates in economic coordination but as an equal, neither superior nor absent. We call this the convention of the "situated state," adapting slightly the concept from contemporary political philosophy, which terms this the "subsidiary state."[1]

THE OBJECTIVE COMMON GOOD OF THE EXTERNAL STATE

In France, postwar economic planning in particular and economic interventionism in general have been rooted in a widespread expectation that the State will insert itself from outside and above society to supply elements of coordination assumed to be essential to meeting common goals of national independence and full employment. The State is not defined in opposition to the popular will, as in Anglo-American liberalism, but as the embodiment of it. This convention between actors allows the State to intervene in the economy, applying monetary, fiscal, budgetary, industrial, and employment and training policies, to maximize the common good.

Our purpose is not to judge the veracity of this idea of the State as external to economy and society, but to emphasize the powerful real effects this notion can have when it operates as a convention between persons. According to this convention, the State is the flux that allows the solder to hold; it covers the gaps and eliminates failures in the coordination of economic activity. Each person thus is aware of, and anticipates, gaps in coordination (for example, a shortage of necessary resources) or failures (for example, to meet commitments); and each person thus expects that the State representatives authorized to intervene in the particular situation at hand will take corrective or complementary action. Most important, each person defines his or her action on the basis of this premise and thus holds back to some extent from fulfilling commitments to action or mobilizing resources. As a result, the convention becomes part of a self-fulfilling prophecy: in the final analysis, the State appears to be truly necessary to economic efficiency.

This convention of the State-as-external is only efficient for certain worlds of production. Situations of action must be objectively definable, so that State intervention can appear impartial and able to balance differing relevant interests. This can only occur if the intervention is amenable to measurement, that is, where criteria, methods, and results can be verified "objectively." Thus the common good is defined in terms of such quantitative measures as number of jobs, rate of growth, size of deficits, and so on, the stock in trade of standard economic indicators. In production itself, this tendency measures the presence of (and often promotes the use of) standardized-generic objects ("technology") whose performance can be objectively assessed. This convention tends to stymie those kinds of collective action that cannot be represented by objective, universal indicators. In France, as we have seen, the notion of a rationalizing and organizing State-from-above plays an important part in the identity of the corps of engineers who manage the State's technical agencies and administrations; this identity in turn forms a key part of the expectations of other actors in the French economy. That this dynamic strongly influences the orientation of State products toward the Industrial World should not be surprising.

THE CONVENTION OF THE ABSENT STATE: "STATES VERSUS MARKETS"

The convention of the absent state takes the form of opposing the "state" to the "market." In the United States, for example, the common good is defined, first and foremost, as a structure of opportunities which maximizes for each person the chance to pursue his or her particular interests; this is assumed to act as a powerful incentive which leads to the greatest possible economic growth and full employment, and thereby reproduces the structure by allowing a great number of people (according to their different and unequal efforts and talents, of course) to enjoy upward social and economic mobility. The general common good, then, is defined as the result of maximizing the interests of particular persons: this is the Market World action framework. External (interventionist) action is criticized by those within this framework on the grounds of its supposed *effects*: by hindering market action, it blocks actors from realizing their individual potential and hence works against the common good. The convention holds that the State, and all forms of non-market coordination, are inherently worse than the market because they inhibit human agency and limit the supposed diversity of choices that individuals could make in the absence of a state.

This argument is blind to its central paradox: a direct effect of the convention is that for the State to be really absent from each situation of action, the State itself must *enforce* this particular conception of the common good. The State thus becomes an activist in the name of continually "effacing" barriers to the market, including itself. In so doing it must reduce access to possible frameworks of collective action and principles of coordination other than those of the market.[2] It becomes the policeman protecting the market against other forms of collective action: an odd role for an institution identified in terms of its absence. Here, the economist is no longer counselor to the prince, as in the external state; rather, the economist becomes the high priest.

In the external-and-absent "Anglo-American" state, then, each person expects the State to impede collective action, save that which follows market principles; this pushes actors to expect that other actors will conduct themselves according to market principles. Actors then deploy strategies to protect themselves from the "moral hazards" of the market (cheating, opportunism, universal self-interest) while profiting from its transitory opportunities. This is the universe described by, and normatively defended in, the theories of contemporary institutionalism (see Chapter 13). In our view, the appropriate way to define the State's role is not in terms of state versus market, but in terms of the variety of conventions of the State and the variety of paths to economic efficiency.

SITUATED STATES

The notion of a "situated" state is entirely different from the concepts of external and absent states.[3] It views the general common good as a situation in which actors have autonomy to develop whatever worlds of production they find compatible with their frameworks of action. Autonomy is defined, in other words, not exclusively with respect to the individual's procedural rights, as in liberal-contractual theory, but (in addition to those rights) with respect to collective action and the right of groups to deploy different action frameworks in coordination with each other. The State's role is to ensure that these frameworks of action and practices of coordination are treated with respect. If, as we have shown, economies are built on a diverse mix of potential efficient frameworks of action and coordination, then a "democratic" State will respect and support the autonomy of actors, individually and collectively, to draw on such frameworks. The general common good, in other words, is directly linked to the extent to which the State and its policies grant actors the freedom and resources needed to draw on diverse possible frameworks of efficient economic action.

Central to the notion of situatedness is a rejection of holist or essentialist conceptions of society which define the common good through recourse to a self-referential doctrine that offers descriptions of the society as objective realities. These holisms include despotism, elitism, socialism, and liberalism: all define the common good by reference to a doctrine external to the society itself.[4] To the extent that the virtues of such principles are considered to be beyond debate—as the inherent content of or exclusive means to the common good—they may be legitimately imposed onto the actions of members of the society; diversity of ends and means is not considered central to the definition of the common good. Note that not all these holisms oppose forms of individual autonomy (for example, citizenship rights and representative democracy may be assured); they simply negate any possibility that many forms of autonomy may contribute to the common good: they delegitimate other principles of collective action.

Clearly, we are bringing up the classical distinction between universality of rights and universality of outcomes. Holistic conceptions of society lead to a priori definitions of the common good and are used to legitimate external states, which are then charged with universalizing the outcome defined as the common good. Even the liberal conception of society leads to this precisely by claiming, in holistic and a priori fashion, that democratic citizenship rights are the only outcome worth using state effort to preserve—and counterposing any other role for the State as a threat to those rights; though it uses the language of liberty, this doctrine is often used to enforce the universality of its chosen outcome and block the existence of others.

By contrast, in all conventions of the situated state, the common good is not susceptible to an external, a priori definition. As a result, situations of collective action and individual acts can only be judged according to an ongoing, contextualized evaluation of the public good. In this situation, individual acts have a certain irreducible "mystery." This is the notion that all attempts to describe, classify, and homogenize resources and actions—while often necessary—inevitably render some more legitimate than others; this is an intimate part of what Foucault calls the "micro-physics of power."[5] So any such forms of classification and equivalence should be viewed with great caution, as should their enforcement in an absolute way;

if not, the values of equality in consideration and responsibility are likely to be strongly compromised.

Thus the common good[6] can only be defined in relationship to concrete situations of collective action, in the course of this action, and by the actors themselves (an exception, the liberal version of the situated state, is discussed below). The autonomy of both individual and collective actors must be respected through the presumption that their resources and, most important, their frameworks of action all deserve *equality of consideration*,[7] and are not excluded a priori by abstract criteria governing either means or the ends of action in the economy. Each actor brings to a potential collective action resources or qualities that he or she believes, after analyzing the situation, are necessary to realize the collective goal; if all resources or qualities are considered equal, this removes obstacles to collective action by allowing other actors to consider how they might best complete the first actor's offerings with respect to the product at hand. Only by assuring equality of consideration can a state compensate, in real terms, for individual or collective failures of coordination. Since equality of consideration applies also to the State's representatives, they must participate on the same footing as all others, and not from the position of overseer.

For such recognition of the common good to emerge, however, each person in each concrete situation (representatives of the State included) must have substantial confidence in the capacities of others with whom the situation is necessarily shared. Confidence is, of course, something of a gamble, a decision to proceed in the face of uncertainty. Coordination is, therefore, a critical moment (in the sense of "crisis") which stems from the existence of autonomy. The convention of an external state is appealing in certain political contexts precisely because it offers a way around this uncertainty and the need to bet on other actors. In other words, the external state can ensure against the fundamental uncertainty of economic interaction, but at the heavy price of sacrificing collective autonomy and access to a diversity of action frameworks.

In sum, in conventions of situated states, each person acts to the best of his or her ability, and the State fills in as a last resort. In the convention of the external state, each person acts in his or her best interests, counting on the State to fill in coordination gaps; in the convention of the absent state, each person looks to the State to remove any public presence from the situation and to block the formation of any type of collective action that does not obey principles of the market. In the situated state, the State is a present, involved actor, but one that is kept somewhat in abeyance and acts as a last resort, not as a primary participant. The external state regards actors from above, and acts in accord with generalizable, abstract principles. The absent state enforces policies designed to assure that there will be no autonomous collective action.

The particular mix of real worlds of production found in each country, and constituting its economic identity, is related to each country's dominant conventions of the State. Conventions of the external and absent states favor, albeit in different ways, access to the possible worlds of Industry and the Market and tend to discourage the Interpersonal and Intellectual Worlds. Only the conventions of situated states allow sufficient access to all four possible worlds, because they are inherently favorable to the possibility of multiple frameworks of action.

Formation of Capacities for Action in Situated States

The effects of state presence on the capacities of actors have been a central axis of the political debate of the twentieth century. As we shall see in Chapter 13, social science is slowly moving on (even if political discussion often is not) from simple state-versus-market distinctions to more subtle theories about how different "incentive and disincentive" systems affect the nature and volume of actors' efforts in different institutional circumstances. We suggest that some of the controversy over questions of "agency" and "incentive design" can be recast in terms of the distinction between different conventions of the State, and the different capacities for action they mobilize or exclude.

Coordination between actors is only possible when actors recognize the capacities of other actors and allow them to be deployed;[8] this is effectuated by what we have called conventions of identity and participation. But what are these capacities? This question provides a point of departure for considering the conventions of the situated state.

CAPACITY BASED ON PROXIMITY

For Tocqueville,[9] capacity based on proximity is eminently tied to a concrete situation, or several similar situations, through accumulated learning. This capacity is rooted in an intrinsic knowledge of one's own, close needs, in a talent for organizing the quotidian. It requires intimate familiarity with a given situation, its objects, its actors—which in turn requires close association with others. Of course, Tocqueville's reflections on modernization contain a central ambiguity. As an admirer of the *ancien régime*

215

and a close observer of post-revolutionary America and France, he re-affirmed his belief in a natural hierarchy in human society. But he also held that all underlying, indelible differences between persons merited respect and a *place* in the resulting social order. Differences between persons, he argued, flow deeply from their concrete capacities, one result of the great diversity of roles to be played in any social structure. These different talents must be given equal consideration in the course of collective action. According to this analysis, the State, as protector of the social order, supplies missing capacities, but does this according to particular demonstrated needs rather than to fulfill universal criteria about what is to be supplied, what "must" be missing.

Bringing Tocqueville into the present (and putting aside his belief in natural hierarchy) leads to the notion of a state that refuses to run the affairs of individuals, but limits itself to governing their particularities. This is a situated state, then, which assists in the development of interpersonal action. Consider Interpersonal Worlds of production whose products penetrate national and international markets (without the aid of protectionism); local, regional, and national situated states would help actors fill in missing coordination capacities on a case-by-case basis, according to local concrete needs. NEC Italian regional governments come forcefully to mind here. By contrast, State intervention based on strongly objectivized universal criteria is likely to threaten such real worlds of production. One example is twentieth-century European industrial and social policy, which classified many artisanal or traditional production systems as "non-modern" or "backward" because they did not perform according to the universal criteria of "modern." Such policies led to the destruction of many such systems.

Proximity can also lead to a distortion of capacity. This takes the forms of localism or nativism, which are species of collective autonomy and coordination that exclude the possibility of universality of any kind. This defensive border between insiders and outsiders is not a capacity at all, but a way to stave off recognizing one's own weaknesses and thus avoid building real capacities. The Poujadist movement in France in the 1950s, or campaigns to "buy American" in the United States, are examples of this distortion.

CAPACITY BASED ON PARTICULARITY AND UNIVERSALITY

For Hegel, capacity to act depends on recognizing the universal vocation of the particular situation at hand. Hegel's point of reference, it should be remembered, was the debate over the nature of the German "nation" in the early nineteenth century. In view of nation-building processes elsewhere—which were centered around positive, universalistic conceptions of identity and the common good, notably those inspired by Enlightenment values—Hegel lamented the German community's localistic and naturalistic character. More generally, individuals who do not recognize their positive bonds remain stuck in a kind of mutual aid or self-help syndrome, usually quite particularist in character (in the economy, for example, between practitioners of a single craft or neighbors). Though such action is often highly satisfying to actors and gives them the impression of having "control" or "sovereignty" over their lives, it is usually no match for the actions of communities with more universal, broadly applicable, and positive principles of coordination. Collective autonomy is legitimate, but it is not sufficient when defined particularistically. For Hegel, the State's role is to help actors get beyond particularism by bringing out the universality within the particularity of each situation of action; particularity can in this way be voided of particularism.

In our terms, the situated state encourages the building of capacities that support real worlds of production in which products with a strongly specialized character are made widely accessible by endowing them with generic characteristics, as in the outputs of intellectual action. In such a state, communities of mutually dependent persons establish freely available *principles* of interaction which, while not excluding interpersonal bonds, provide a language for constructing relationships with a much wider reach than the strictly interpersonal. We might also think of products with potentially broad applications, where specialized skills become intimately linked into the value chains of many kinds of final outputs and hence require actors to coordinate with other communities of producers. The specialized metalworking firms of the Upper Savoy in France today, for example, make parts for the world automobile industry and often suggest to the big automakers better design or production techniques, or ways to integrate new materials.

There are also deformed versions of the claim to universality. This would include exclusionist communitarian sentiment, based not necessarily on proximity but on a subjectivist definition of supposedly common identities which are then held to be universally important (and cited as grounds for excluding or oppressing those outside the community). These identities are subjectivist when they do not provide the basis for real processes of coordination. They are imitations of solidarity, juxtapositions of individuals who seem to be similar, but that similarity is not realized in the form of conventional coordination. In economic policy, one example of such a deformed universality is support for "small- and medium-sized firms" (SMEs). SMEs are not a category of collective action; they have superficial resemblances to one another, and these can be defined in opposition to the equally superficial resemblances among large firms. As an analytic category, "small versus large firms" is overly abstract, and appropriate to external states; it has no functional relation to real processes of economic coordination. It is based on the false appearance of similarity, and often leads analysts to assume homogeneity and imagine a common economic purpose which does not exist.

CAPACITY BASED ON INDIVIDUAL SOVEREIGNTY

For liberals, the capacity for action is based on individual sovereignty. The individual is not seen as the bearer of universal values or principles; moreover, only the individual can judge his or her own particularity, because the individual's preferences and utilities are sovereign. Each person expects that the other will recognize that sovereignty; each person's capacities are defined by this expectation. Liberalism transforms the sovereign utility of the individual into a goal, and state authority is used to protect individual sovereignty.

This form of coordination depends on an *equality of particularities*. Equality is assured by a contract between two free agents with respect to a specific, precise, and time-limited goal. The common good is defined as the outcome of the *process* itself, whatever that happens to be—the result of the fleeting and renewed encounters between free agents.

In this convention of the situated state, each individual expects the State to remove obstacles to the full deployment of individual sovereignty in the exercise of free will. This effectively leads to an insistence on competition because each person, believing himself or herself sovereign, looks to the State to suppress what others might do to block the exercise of that sovereignty. This convention of the situated state supports real worlds of production based on market principles.

Here we should recall a distinction, easily forgotten, between the situated liberal state and the external liberal state. The convention of the situated liberal state rests on a clear paradox with respect to the pure theory of liberalism: it is constructed collectively by autonomous groups of persons to apply to themselves and not to all other actors; the situated liberal state is neither a crusader for nor a policeman of the market. The convention of the external liberal state rests on another paradox: liberalism is enforced on all persons; it impedes the construction of "non-market" groups and attempts to prevent the exercise of other collective principles of action. It extends its liberty and sovereignty only to individuals—indeed, other collective action principles are cast as opposing the mere possibility of individual freedom. In short, externally imposed liberalism denies the liberty of other forms of collective autonomy to exist.

CAPACITY BASED IN DIGNITY

We have come full circle. If a situated state would admit the legitimacy of a number of different capacities for action, what would allow them to flourish together? The notion of equal consideration can only survive if actors have certain capacities. The question of what sort of framework would allow true diversity of action to flourish is raised, implicitly, in many well-known contemporary debates about diversity and justice in democratic societies. These can be reinterpreted in light of the notion of situated states.

It might be thought that the notion of an external state, one that is "above society," refers to a Kantian ethics, but this is not the case. Kant's ethical formula consisted, first, of the notion that any individual should choose actions so they might serve as a general rule and, second, that humanity is an end in and of itself, never only a means to another end:[10] "In other words, one should follow a consistent, generalizable ethic regardless of the specific circumstances; that ethic requires always putting oneself in the place of the other; and its basis is a view of people as sharing a common humanity within a social network."[11] Rawls has extended these notions by arguing that Kant's categorical imperative would be freely chosen by people in the "original position" and hence, that it is fair.[12] Simmel argues that the imperative includes equality, and that such equality is a freely chosen ideal state.[13] Kant, Rawls, and Simmel, in other words, would propose something like a universal but situated ethics, one that is not external at all.

The problem is that the ability to make "free" choices implies people existing outside all material and cultural constraints and all material and cultural differences. Kantian ethics runs into the actuality that there are real-world backgrounds for the choices that Kant (or Rawls or Simmel) supposes free agents would make. This is what Marx reacted to so strongly in rejecting the possibility of an ethics grounded in rational necessity or universal obligations—by arguing that it idealizes the historical process and thus fails to provide any real guidance about realistic ways to reach just outcomes. For Marx's followers, only an ethics grounded in historical materialism is viable, and this would mean identifying the universal interests of humanity with those of the proletariat, the only real moral community that matters. Thus, Marxists react to the extreme avoidance of material and historical conditions in the Kantian approach, but replace it with one so radically historicist that it delegitimates action frameworks that are not considered proletarian.

Still, both Kant and Marx would acknowledge the fundamental importance of a moral community of interrelated individuals who would choose some kind of ethics. The notion of a situated state that allows equal consideration of different action frameworks is the same as the notion of allowing that different moral communities—in our terms, different legitimate action frameworks—can exist within a society. Mannheim suggested this when he argued for the "acquisition of perspective," so as to overcome "talking past one another."

> Mannheim . . . argues that concepts cannot be abstracted from their historical situatedness even while not foregoing the possibility of a transcendent ethic. At the same time he is calling for demystification and empathy, thereby assuming that this ethic will be reshaped and reinterpreted within differing historical realities. . . . Within Mannheim's conceptualisation we can continue to hold up fairness as the key to social justice while developing its content differently depending on our standpoint and historical location. Such an activity requires both self-criticism and criticism of the other. In particular, there is no "other," whether high or low on the social hierarchy, so privileged as to be immunized from outside criticism.[14]

Shifts in the connotations of fairness and freedom are measured by reciprocity, communication, and mutual acceptance of obligation. These notions are contained, albeit implicitly, in a number of brands of social thought. For example, the inheritors of the European tradition of "social Catholicism" see capacities as rooted in recognition of equal dignity of persons. Versions of this notion may be found as well in the contemporary traditions of North American "liberal Protestantism" and in the non-religious reasoning employed by a variety of contemporary social theorists, known as the "communitarian" movement in the United States.[15] Going farther afield, echoes of this notion may be found in certain contemporary philosophers who celebrate the idea of a truly pluralistic "postmodern" politics but reject its radical moral relativism and epistemological subjectivism.[16] It also appears in some contemporary social movements, and even in certain "neo-Marxist" reflections on contemporary democracy.[17] In these conceptions, there is a certain wariness of abstractions derived from social theory or measurement, such as categories or classes, and of categorical rights. Such abstractions, while often used to protect certain kinds of people, also can be used to construct hierarchies of the good, and thus to give greater consideration to some categories than others. This approach is incompatible with the ontological proposition that all persons, including all economic persons, are equally human. The equal humanness of all persons, not their particular categorical qualities or performance attributes, is the starting point for any approach which truly respects diversity, and sees this respect as key to fairness. As a starting point, this view holds that one thing is universal—equal humanness requires that we treat the needs and capacities of all persons as if they merited equal dignity or consideration. This does not mean that, in the end, we find in fact that all persons' expressed needs and desires merit equality of consideration or dignity; rather, it is a beginning, a sort of rebuttable presumption.

This presumption leads obviously to complex debates in political philosophy. Let us concentrate on what it means with respect to economic persons, by making several observations.

First, the convention of situatedness based on equal dignity is not so much related to a specific possible world of production as to the general circumstance of the many possible worlds, elementary frameworks of action, and real worlds as complex fusions of them. Indeed, recognizing the existence of different frameworks of action suggests measured optimism with respect to the human capacity to develop coordination around a notion of the common good. We explicitly reject both the pessimism of holistic conceptions of society—from totalitarian to liberal—and the liberal faith in the individual as a substitute for society. Put simply, optimism evoked by the existence of multiple ways of coordinating is just as merited as pessimism in response to multiple ways of tricking, excluding, and violating the dignity of others (see Chapter 13).

Second, equality in dignity is a form of universality needed to preserve the range of products of economies characterized by complex divisions of labor. An ever-present danger in an increasingly international economy is competition between particular*isms* (not to be confused with particulari*ties*): different national systems, internally practicing particularism without universality (Hegel's fear), and attempting to make other economies dependent through competition. But (and here another paradox emerges) it is not possible to define an international regime of particularity without particularism exclusively in terms of general and abstract rights. These rights may be necessary, but they are unlikely to be sufficient, for the same reason that mere market rules, say a pure laissez-faire international trade agreement or a simplistic "commerce clause," are not adequate for economic governance at the national level.

Third, and this is the greatest challenge, to realize the developmental possibilities linked to the many possible worlds of production, it is necessary to allow the maximum possible expression of resources available in different worlds in each situation of economic action. The only route to this is equal consideration in substantive dignity—not in any formalistic senses such as the notion of procedural "rights" in Anglo-Saxon jurisprudence—in each situation where individuals and groups mobilize their resources. The common good may be debated on the basis of this premise. The convention is that the State, fully involved, helps actors (collective and individual) to coordinate on the basis of equality in consideration, and intervenes to prevent abuse of the dignity of others.

Finally, experience has shown that even in modern democracies there is an asymmetry between rationality and power, favoring the latter. That is, except in the most stable and highly structured situations (and often even then), power tends to win out over opposing arguments, where those exercising rationality are not the powerful. Without a presumption of respect for the autonomy of different forms of collective action through equal consideration (again, within the limits imposed by formal, universal citizenship rights), power, in the form of universality of effects desired by the powerful, will tend to win out. Equal consideration—dignity in substance—is such a criterion.[18]

This is not a plea for relativism or subjectivism; on the contrary, it is a realistic recognition of the limitations of administrative rationality as a way to categorize and classify economic resources. Equality of consideration requires that State and non-State actors carefully consider the resources and competences of actors at hand, lest administrative categories be created which, by virtue of their abstraction, freeze those competences and block the evolutionary processes at the heart of economic innovation. Where pragmatism bounds administrative rigidity and infuses it with information about the real abilities, desires, and expectations of collective actors, policy becomes the place of incessant compromise, of continuing institutional reorganization. Pragmatism also accepts the fundamental condition of all collective economic activity as defined in this book: the uncertainty which underlies economic coordination and, paradoxically, leads actors to construct conventions and institutions in the first place.

Corporatism is a caricatural version of this conception. Corporatist organizations, sheltered by law, tend to use the State to defend categorical interests, confusing monopolistic practices with the common good.

The notion of equal dignity should not be confused with superficially similar movements. Contemporary democracies face powerful claims from groups defined by strong identities who want to redress their economic problems by turning to the notion of formal citizenship rights (claims about economic "discrimination," for example). While these claims are important, they are not the same as the notion of capacity based in dignity, for these groups couch their claims in terms of discrimination from a norm of equal treatment defined in terms of the formal, universal citizenship rights of modern democracies. Ultimately, their project has to do with the perfection of universal citizenship rights—in many ways similar to the liberal project of individual sovereignty—not to the construction of situated states based on collective equal dignity. Economic claims expressed in the language of formal citizenship rights are not capable of substituting for economic coordination. In many cases, the language of citizenship rights (especially in its liberal version) is incommensurable with the ties of reciprocity which bind many economic groupings together.[19] Such claims are particular to the Market World, not general to contemporary capitalism.

11

STATE INTERVENTION:
A CRITIQUE OF THE FRENCH CASE

The Economic Common Good

In this chapter we examine conventions of the external state in France, showing how they affect economic intervention, especially the relation between the State and economic actors. We argue that a situated state would be preferable. We also study the emergence and renegotiation of conventions at critical moments, showing how economic practices defy theories that reduce them to the mere results of tradition or to perfectly rational interest-seeking.

In France, the accepted definition of the economic common good includes three elements: first, social mobility is founded on equal access to education and then to employment; second, State intervention must be defended on the basis of objective, universal criteria; but, third, historically established groups, and not merely individuals, can figure as legitimate subjects of these criteria. These are all the marks of an external state.

These elements pervade the State's intervention in the economy in twentieth-century France. In the 1980s, there were numerous attempts to reform State intervention, but none went so far as to change this conception of the common good. Instead, they shifted it onto political institutions at lower levels than the central State. The firm, through its "enterprise committee," a legally mandated body including representatives of both workers and employers and of regional and local governments, is now charged with involving social groups in pursuit of the common good. But because these institutions continue to operate according to the same principles as the central State, the dominance of the Industrial World has not been challenged. As a result, France continues to experience increasing tension between its goal of full employment and the reality of steadily increasing unemployment.

The State, Economic Participation, and Economic Identity in France

To begin, it will be helpful to review the general background to the French state's interventions in establishing conventions of participation and identity in the economy. Three institutionally recognized collective agents, known as the "social partners," operate in the French economy: employers or the *patronat;* the State; and workers. As elsewhere, the constitution of these groups as concrete social agents is the result of the way qualitatively specific economic resources are mobilized.

The French working population has been constructed, over a period of two centuries, as a series of subgroups, each with its own official status, privileges (however minimal), and customs. Before the French Revolution, important segments of the industrial working population, then heavily artisanal, were organized into *corporations,* organizations which conferred monopoly rights on groups of skilled artisans. Members of these guild-like organizations *(compagnons)* enjoyed significant control over their tasks and—most important to the "employer" class—systematically refused to be attached to any given firm. Artisans generally insisted on their own mobility and, through their formal monopolies on specific skills, were in a position to enforce their job choices, work rhythms, and geographical preferences. With the Revolution, a struggle against artisanal monopolies began (the Le Chapelier Laws), but rather than simply breaking up the corporations, it reconstituted the increasingly industrial working population (and the remaining artisanal segments) into other regulated organizational forms, thereby continuing the already existing tradition of state intervention.[1] The history of these developments is too complex to recount here in detail, but we can briefly point to four features relevant to the way French workers are constituted today in strongly defined fragments and subgroups, through legal, organizational, and cultural processes.

First, the post-Revolutionary reconstitution involved the State codifying the rights and privileges of skilled workers or occupationally defined groups in much greater detail than in most other countries.[2] For a large percentage of occupations *(professions),* there are meticulously defined courses, diplomas, and entrance tests an individual must pass to be admitted, whether it be a manual, technical, professional, industrial, commercial, or service occupation. These tests are standardized and regulated at the national level by the State, and the practice of all but the most menial jobs is limited to those who possess a credential. Nevertheless, a high proportion of the training needed to perform tasks within large industrial firms still takes place on the job, through internal labor markets,[3] because the credentialing process bears little relationship to the continuously evolving structure of jobs. This is why credentials do not promote labor mobility within an occupation, but instead function to define positions and privileges for those who possess them.

Second, in virtually every important part of the economy, an industry-wide collective labor agreement sets out wage, salary, and qualification minima for that branch at the national or regional level. Although there is frequently little correspondence between these minima and actual conditions, especially with respect to wages, a high proportion of the agreements do refer to the credentials required to work, and spell out the limits and responsibilities of firms and workers in great detail. Even certain categories of the self-employed and artisans are covered by such agreements. It is the State that identifies the parties who will negotiate each agreement, which then affects all firms and unions in the branch, regardless of whether they participated in negotiations or signed the agreement. Such agreements became widespread after 1936 (see the following section). As Paxton put it, the French employer class accepted this form of corporatism because it permitted them to escape their two principal torments in capitalism: class struggle and competition.[4] The regulation, codification, and division of the French working class have vastly expanded the firms' power to negotiate anything beyond the legal minima for the branch and occupation, and thus have consistently impeded union plans to reunite the working class in a modern form, as the corporations did for artisans before the Revolution.

Yet, and this is the third point, statism has not wiped out occupational consciousness or resistance to employers' rules: in certain industries, including many modern, technologically advanced sectors, the notion of craft or *métier* is very powerful in terms of behavior on the job.[5] That is, there exist very strong conventions of workers' rights and responsibilities in each concrete profession, and employers cannot easily abrogate these rights and responsibilities. In certain industries and occupations, working culture is so powerfully rooted in the notion of "honorable" work that it is the worker, not the organization (the employer), who defines the way a job is to be performed (this is probably least true in certain phases of mass production). The diplomas and branch agreements, which were in many ways intended by their authors to reduce class cohesion, fit well with the remaining "corporatist" mentalities. Competitive unionism, branch agreements, the cult of diplomas, and the surviving customary element of craft consciousness all combine to constitute workers as small groups with very strong awareness of rights and responsibilities, of membership and the borders of membership. Labor markets and inter-occupational mobility in France, while statistically similar to those in other large advanced economies, are underpinned by qualitatively different conventions; underlying expectations and tactical space are also different for the actors involved.

Fourth, and finally, France is a country of weak union density. Its unions enjoy surprisingly few rights under the law, even by comparison to countries such as the United States: unions frequently do not participate in contract negotiations, cannot obligate their members to follow a strike order, and are often compelled to follow industry-wide wage and working condition agreements *(conventions collectives)* to which they are not signatories. In large firms, there are frequently several competing unions within a single production unit, in part because the unions are affiliated with different political parties. This, combined with the impediments of the legal structure, has historically directed unions toward political and symbolic action—that is, toward the State—rather than toward concerted workplace or firm-level negotiations as their main vehicles of progress.

French capitalists, too, are constituted as a series of distinct subgroups whose logic is based as much on defending accumulated privileges and positions as it is on attempting to maximize revenues or expand markets. It is important to remember that France is only now developing a capital market-based system of finance, having in the past relied on a highly controlled system of credit-based finance dominated by the State,[6] which served as the main instrumentality of French industrial policy and of the postwar economic Plan. Moreover, private savings in France have traditionally been highly oriented toward real property rather than productive investment; where this was not the case, savings were taken in by the State, which in turn pushed them through its credit-based system of finance. Some of the specificities of the "French model" have thus resided in its distinctive capitalist behaviors. In the nineteenth century, when England was filled with competitive Marshallian industrial districts, France was characterized by paternalistic family-based firms, surrounded by captive and dependent subcontractors. This idea of the "enlarged family circle," that is, of the firm as patrimony,[7] is to this day an important reference point for large numbers of French entrepreneurs and managers.

The development of the "big firm à la française," when it came, did not mark the advent of Anglo-American style competition, because French firms continued to use the State to intervene in their markets. The relationship between the State and both large and family-owned firms in France has often been characterized as a war, yet from the Vichy period on, many firms have permitted themselves to be transformed into large, modern enterprises with State aid in return for protection from competition. As Saglio puts it, in France "competition is just one rule of the game among many."[8] Indeed, the struggle for the assured revenues that come with monopolizing particular market niches, controlled prices, and barriers to entry has been critical in many sectors, often justified as the only way to maintain the country's industrial patrimony.

The State has played an important role in many areas of the French economy, especially in the postwar period. It has served as the key intermediary, defining some subgroups as insiders and others as outsiders. The State as modernizer has not typically intervened to promote market dynamics: rather, it has projected the will of key groups of technocrats and private interests, and worked to preserve industrial patrimony and employment by installing modern technologies.

We shall now illustrate some of the ways these deep-seated patterns are rooted in conventions of the external state, and how they push the French economy toward the Industrial World by shaping the action frameworks of those involved in myriad ways.

The State's Logic of the Branch of Production versus Real Worlds of Production

To understand why there is such a propensity in France to provide access to the Industrial World and impede access to other worlds of production, it is helpful to examine one of that country's "peculiar institutions," the collective labor agreement *(convention collective du travail)* at the branch level. "Branch" in economic nomenclature is something like the notion of "industry," but with certain important differences, as will become clear. The definition of a branch of production is especially important in France because it determines the population of firms or establishments that are subject to collective labor agreements and other policies. The State has not defined branches coherently with respect to worlds of production; indeed, through the collective labor agreements, it has reinforced patterns of participation and identity that often do not work. We are especially interested in two critical periods when collective branch-level labor agreements were structured, 1936 and 1946–1950.

THE COLLECTIVE LABOR AGREEMENT OF 1936: MIXING THE INTERPERSONAL AND INDUSTRIAL WORLDS

The collective labor agreement in France is something less than a contract between employers and unions of a branch of production. It defines certain working conditions and establishes skill and occupational categories, as well as certain wage levels, usually in terms of minima which must be observed by any firm in that branch. The agreement must be concluded between the organizations that the State recognizes as "representative" of the branch at the national level. In practice, this means major national organizations, three on the employers' side and five on the side of the workers. Collective labor agreements have very broad effects: for example, parties to any labor contract (worker and employer) are necessarily guided by the agreement since all such contracts within the branch must be consistent with it. (As a high-level contract concluded for the "welfare" of the workforce, the collective labor agreement is legally superior to individual contracts.)[9] It also has an *erga omnes* effect: it applies to all workers in all firms within the designated field whether or not they are unionized.

The collective agreement now in use was born in 1936 in the context of an interpersonal real world of production: that of the highly skilled workers of the metallurgy and mechanical engineering industries in the Paris region *(les "métallos")*.[10] For these workers and their leading union (the CGTU—*Confédération Générale du Travail Unifié*—dominated by activists linked to the Communist Party), the model was the "old" craft workers' contract, an agreement between the craft group and the local employers group to set piece work rates *(tarifs)*. Prices were established for each piece of work completed by the worker meeting customary standards. Organization of the work depended on specialized, nonstandardized know-how in an essentially unmechanized production process, and product quality depended entirely on the craftsman, who was fully responsible for his output. These written agreements contained a list of products with their associated *tarifs;*[11] the total wage was closely associated with the price of the product. In the 1930s, then, the workers were tied in solidaristic relations among themselves and with the urban fabric, consisting of community-based lines of apprenticeship and knowledge transmission as well as occupational mobility among the metalworkers. Thus there was a high degree of coherence among the product, the place of work, the branch of production, and its firms—a common context typical of a viable, real Interpersonal World of production.[12]

The State had a strong interest in "industrial" rationalization of these industries to raise quality, output, and speed, all of which were becoming critical in the second half of the 1930s in the face of rising German military power. The State was the principal customer for these firms' military-industrial outputs.

In 1936, following a major strike during which plants in Paris were occupied, the metalworkers and employers signed an agreement under the tutelage of the Popular Front government, known as the Matignon Accords of June 7. The collective agreement itself was signed five days later, and the law making it final was enacted on June 24, 1936.[13] This agreement served as a model for the text of collective agreements negotiated in other regions and branches in 1936 and 1937[14] and thus was critical to the institutionalization of labor conventions in French industry in the mid-twentieth century.

The Matignon Accords mixed elements of the Interpersonal and Industrial Worlds. The Interpersonal is reflected in that the wage is linked to the price of the product, fabricated by a person who has mastered the needed skills thanks to specialized knowledge derived from a community of fellow workers. The Industrial is reflected in the setting of a normative time for a task, and minimum hourly productivity rewarded by a minimum hourly wage, both closely tied to industrial rationalization, itself a project of engineers, who were to play increasingly important roles in those industries where State ownership was growing. Retière[15] shows that many of these engineers—known as *Ingénieurs des Tabacs,* graduates of the highly prestigious Ecole Polytechnique—regard the production unit in state-owned industry as a kind of sub-directorate of the Ministry of Industry, making the directorate itself the branch of production. The Ministry forecasts production, plans orders by product, and allocates resources to establishments according to their specializations; in these industries, all procedures are written and codified in great detail for the personnel. Thus we see two strongly opposed conceptions of the firm, the branch, and the collective agreement: on one side are autonomous communities of individuals; on the other, structures of tasks rationally organized and incorporated within the apparatus of the State.

Yet the Matignon Accords mixed the two by combining customary status and rights for the *métallos* with increasingly hierarchical and normative organization of the production process in conformity with the State engineers project. First, the Matignon Accords reinforced belief in the efficiency of centralized, hierarchical economic coordination. Salary classifications and job descriptions in the collective agreements brought diverse criteria into one linear scale for each industry: prescribing standards for initiation and individual advancement in a community of equals; ranking tasks according to technical complexity; establishing seniority in terms of length of service. Hierarchy was, in all the collective agreements, based on the procedure of classifying all jobs according to a consistent nomenclature, and assigning them a minimum wage.

Second, these industrial job/wage classifications, once established, were nonetheless imbued with a craft spirit as part of the 1936 compromise between the *métallos* in their Interpersonal World and a rationalizing State. This "spirit" was channeled into corporatist forms, such as a generalized notion of employment security and minimal, but guaranteed, "social rights" attached to and administered to particular socio-occupational groups in the economy. Inside the labor process, this corporatist culture means that it is the worker—not the organization nor the employer—who defines the way in which work is carried out. Most important for our analysis, this system perpetuates relatively small groups, conscious of their rights and responsibilities, knowing where they do and do not fit, and giving them a certain plasticity in their means of organization: this small-group culture is known as the "sheltered autonomy" of the labor process. Such groups may be constituted by roots in a particular place, by long experience within one firm, by craft skills, or even by membership in a wage category, independent of skills. But—and this is both its weakness and its strength—this group culture has been prolonged and institutionalized by the State's postwar system of employment, income security, and collective labor agreements.

The hierarchical system of training and credentialing extends into the public educational system, through a series of criteria linking training and qualification with a given type of employment.[16] This system is closely related to product standardization in that it codifies new forms of employment and the means of access to them as they appear in the economy. There is a broad consensus in French society with respect to this system, which amounts, in effect, to a convention of participation (though it still excludes workers in so-called "unskilled" positions).

The system issues credentials for occupation-specific skills rather than firm-specific positions, so an important share of learning must take place on the job through the internal labor market.[17] Indeed, the links between firms and the training system have been progressively distorted by reforms that seek to incorporate labor in the general, abstract model of education at the national level. As a result, in the 1980s, young workers faced a high barrier to entry because their training did not correspond to the needs of firms. This barrier depressed employment levels generally, since employers—especially the biggest and most capital-intensive—prefer to invest in technology and hire a minimum of very highly trained workers. (This strategy is also favored as a way to get around the inertia of existing corporatist groups within the firm.) The result is a permanent tension between enterprises favoring technological rationalization and workers depending on recourse to the State; what emerges is an unsatisfactory compromise between homogenizing rationalization and small group politics.

Finally, the collective agreement of the 1930s also institutionalized the notion of "status" or "category" for public employees, with a job-based system of salary grades linked to security of employment and seniority, covering all jobs and all steps in the career. Every possible circumstance is described in written form, its consequences defined in detail, including procedures for contesting decisions. The underlying principle again mixes industrial rationality and workers' status. The demand for regulation of civil servants came from both workers and the State, but for different reasons: the State hierarchy sought more control of personnel; the civil servants themselves wanted to limit the power of the hierarchy and enjoy guarantees in the areas of hiring, promotion, sanctions, health care, and retirement. This agreement was endorsed by the CGT before it joined with the organization of public servants *(Fédération des Fonctionnaires),* as well as by the Socialist Party elements most favorable to economic planning.[18] The civil service reflects the ongoing tension between Industrial World rationalization and corporatist culture more than any other facet of the French economy.

THE STATE'S DEFINITION OF THE BRANCH OF PRODUCTION:
ADMINISTRATIVE RATIONALITY VERSUS REAL WORLDS

The compulsory application of collective labor agreements to a branch makes them an extremely important strategic terrain for management, unions, and employers' organizations. The agreement strongly affects conventions of productivity, since it covers job and salary classifications, salary minima, credentialing or apprenticeship requirements for "skilled" posts, and internal promotion rules. It also heavily influences links between the firm and the external labor market, that is, conventions of unemployment, especially by defining layoff and unemployment payments.

Establishments are classified into branches according to the parent firm's products. There is a close link between the firm's legal classification and the particular collective labor agreement that applies to its workers. As the State's economic agenda has changed, so has its system of classification. The most important change came in 1949, with a new nomenclature designed to create categories appropriate to the planning of the economy[19] ("the Plan"). A distinction was made between the branch-as-activity, that is, the statistical aggregate of the parts of firms devoted to similar activities, and the branch-as-sector, groups of firms in which the principal activities are similar. Over time, the sectoral conception became increasingly central to national economic accounting, to the detriment of the branch-as-activity.[20]

There is significant tension between the two conceptions. Empirically, the more distant the two conceptions of the branch are from each other, the more the planned economy has tended to deny the existence of real worlds of production as they are constituted by economic actors around their products (and not the State's classifications of them). Thus, in 1949, the State tried to impose another layer of Industrial World logic on the economy—essentially an attempt to create Industrial Worlds where they did not exist. It succeeded in certain respects, but the collective labor agreements which were to be applied to these statistical-policy units were themselves far from consistent with the optimal performance of Industrial World production systems. The result was the further propagation of incoherent frameworks of action in many sectors and the effective denial of certain real worlds, which did not correspond to the definition of sector adopted in 1949.

The External State and the Industrial World
A CRITIQUE OF ECONOMIC COORDINATION VIA THE PLAN

In France, the economic *plan* is the way in which coordination is conceived and organized among economic actors; in the postwar period, the *Commissariat Général du Plan* formulated plans containing detailed macroeconomic and sectoral goals for the French economy on a five-year basis.

The notion of a Plan in capitalism can be traced back to Keynes's pessimism with respect to coordinating individuals in the financial market.[21] Keynes thought that individuals, finding themselves faced with absolute uncertainty and having to rely on conjectures of little validity, behaved by convention in financial markets. But this is the result of a sort of circularity. Keynes showed that economic agents tend to engage in counter-final rounds of imitation—where, for example, if one investor sells, so will another, such that the collective result is a self-fulfilling prophecy which is not desired by any individual—generating economic recessions involving durable unemployment.[22] The only way out of this vicious circle would be to predict the combined result of the agents' buying and selling operations—but the problem here, says Keynes, is like picking the winner of a beauty pageant where the question is not who we find most beautiful but guessing the average ranking of the official judges, a task that would require the infinite predictive capacities of an oracle. Rather, economic agents know that their assumption that things will continue as before is improbable. They can only resolve these uncertainties by entering into coordinated effort with other actors, but they avoid this, choosing instead to maintain their resources in a perfectly liquid state.

It thus falls to the State to implement macroeconomic policies that permit coordination, and hence bring about full employment. The Plan depends on an objectivizing description of present and future reality; it defines goals, means, and their mutual coherence, as well as the hierarchy of levels of intervention (national, sectoral, regional, and so forth) and the commitments (goals and means) of the different "partners" to each type of policy. The State is the involved but external party, the guardian of higher interests: as each interest group acting alone is incapable of realizing the common good, only the State can bring all together to attain it. The Plan defines the gap between reality and the common good, in terms such as employment levels, and implements corrective policies. In this closed circle, the Plan defines the collective identities each group uses to interact with the others (in the firm, in the market, and so on), with each group having recourse to the supposedly universal basis of its claims as defined by the Plan.

Keynes maintained a kind of skepticism with respect to the planned economy; for him, the expectations of agents remained decisive. He sensed that what we call an external state might not be consistent with the capacities needed for economic development because state intervention is subject to the same counterfinality as any financial market.[23] This is certainly evident in France.

In practice, commitments made to the *plan* are often simply not respected (recall Tocqueville's statement about French "exceptionalism" within administrative rigidity).[24] Yet the failure to respect commitments is not necessarily a sign of duplicity. They are not intended to be upheld; they are made to stimulate collective action and drive it in particular directions: those where identities linked to belonging to certain groups are represented as universal interests in France. In these circumstances, each interest in effect isolates itself from the possibility of having its legitimacy contested, precisely because legitimacy is constructed in a circular fashion and supported by the State. Because these interests cannot be questioned, actors have enormous freedom not to uphold commitments and to let the State step in to resolve the resulting failures of coordination.

In the face of this contradictory and pessimistic Keynesian situation, the problem becomes one of coordinating activities where there is a freedom *not* to keep commitments, to carve out exceptions and derogations to any rule. This can only be the case in the Industrial World, where freedom is, effectively, circumvented by technique.

RELIANCE ON THE INDUSTRIAL WORLD TO CIRCUMVENT FAULTY CONVENTIONS

In the French context, the organizational structure of the large, multidivisional industrial corporation (known as *groupe* in French) has emerged as the most capable of coping with the difficulties of coordinating corporatist closed groups, and circumventing the exceptionalism of the Plan, but at the price of specializing in "industrial" products. Table 11.1 shows that these groups are systematically more capital-intensive, produce less value-added per capita, and have higher direct labor productivity than the other firms in their sectors. Their products lend themselves well to the ensemble of stabilizing routines that make up the industrial model of production: economic forecasting, task rationalization, the objective force of "technical progress," management techniques that are independent of unpredictable market fluctuations, and employment security backed by social security and unemployment funds. Endowed with formal structures of management and decision-making, drawing its managers from the grandes écoles or even the grands corps,[25] the group is ideal for producing Industrial World outputs, with their planned, hierarchically organized production systems; it works well, too, with an interventionist industrial policy in the domains of financing, employment, training, and research/development. Thus these multidivisional firms are the biggest recipients of public resources in France. In this "mixed economy" these firms, whether public or privately owned, have come to be regarded as part of the national patrimony for which the State is responsible.[26]

The principle of a planned economy is inadequate for the realization of Interpersonal World products, where the key processes are cooperation and building a community of specialists: these elements can only be defined in relation to a given situation of action in relation to particular groups of persons. For an interpersonal product to succeed, each person must be committed to the collective effort. The relative weakness of metalworking and of precision mechanical engineering in France may be attributable to the failure to maintain interpersonal conventions in those

Table 11.1 Characteristics of sectors, France (1974–1989)

Code	Growth in value added in 1989 FF	Percentage change in number of workers	Growth in capital stock	Change in output/capital ratio	Percentage employment in large firms	Capital intensity	Direct labor productivity	Efficiency of capital
01	2.75	−38.6	5.50	−18.6	13.8	114.6	126.1	110.1
02	5.08	11.0	4.03	13.5	46.9	148.8	119.7	80.4
03	3.70	−7.4	4.28	−6.7	47.6	195.7	168.6	86.1
04	0.95	−68.2	7.32	−59.2	99.8	—	—	—
05	4.20	−17.0	4.80	5.6	96.5	140.4	113.3	80.1
06	7.00	26.7	3.92	40.0	97.7	297.6	196.2	67.2
07	1.91	−53.3	4.79	−14.4	89.8	216.6	98.8	45.8
08	4.35	−16.7	13.39	−6.1	87.9	462.1	133.6	29.0
09	3.34	−39.2	5.85	−6.1	46.6	215.7	156.3	72.5
10	3.71	−26.4	5.01	3.5	76.3	202.8	138.7	68.5
11	2.70	−26.5	4.82	−23.6	83.0	109.2	99.4	91.1
13	3.47	−26.3	5.92	−20.4	27.5	176.5	113.0	64.0
21	3.15	−28.9	8.51	−47.9	55.0	201.2	137.5	68.3
23	4.18	−12.9	4.44	8.0	56.5	148.8	119.4	80.2
14	3.66	−29.1	6.43	−18.1	38.8	182.9	120.5	65.9
15A	4.58	−11.9	7.29	−34.1	75.1	220.2	140.5	63.9
17	4.26	−18.3	6.12	−14.9	88.1	251.2	148.4	59.1
15B	2.14	−43.9	7.50	−49.0	—	—	—	—
16	4.91	−30.5	7.38	−4.3	86.7	290.7	139.5	47.8
12	5.02	−3.4	5.95	−11.8	69.8	160.9	117.6	73.1
18	2.83	−47.8	5.73	−5.5	27.6	180.8	123.4	68.3

Table 11.1 (continued)

19	2.68	−43.6	5.23	−9.1	31.3	176.0	113.5	64.5
20	2.96	−20.3	5.71	−34.9	18.1	187.5	123.2	65.7
22	4.94	5.3	4.87	−3.7	28.9	149.5	136.0	91.0
24	3.36	−23.1	5.09	−14.0	27.8	103.5	108.2	104.5
25–28	4.61	6.2	5.10	−15.0	—	—	—	—
31	4.16	10.8	4.00	−6.4	60.4	215.9	126.8	58.8
32	7.26	21.1	6.63	−9.3	(100.0)	—	—	—
29	5.76	3.1	5.17	7.9	10.2	231.2	143.3	62.0
30	7.27	33.7	4.87	11.6	26.7	63.6	94.0	147.8
33	7.19	76.7	3.57	13.9	34.7	175.1	118.3	67.5
34	6.84	48.0	5.14	−10.2	23.8	119.6	124.5	104.1
35	6.30	—		−15.4	—	—	—	—
36	4.35	33.3	—		83.9	—	—	—
37	5.37	21.3	—		92.2	—	—	—
38	5.58	31.6	—		47.7	—	—	—
Total	4.72	1.4	—		43.7	—	—	—

Source: INSEE (French national statistics agency), our calculations.

01 = Agriculture, forestry, fishing; 02 = Meat and dairy products; 03 = Other food products; 04 = Combustible solid minerals; 05 = Refined and crude oil; 06 = Electricity, gas, and water; 07 = Ferrous metals and minerals; 08 = Non-ferrous metals and minerals; 09 = Construction materials; 10 = Glasses; 11 = Chemicals and synthetic fibers; 12 = Pharmaceuticals; 13 = Foundries and metal working; 14 = Mechanical engineering; 15a = Electrical and electronic materials; 15b = Household appliances; 16 = Transport (except aviation and maritime); 17 = Shipping, aerospace and armaments; 18 = Textiles and clothing; 19 = Leather and shoes; 20 = Wood, furniture, and associated; 21 = Paper, cardboard; 22 = Publishing; 23 = Rubber and plastics; 24 = Construction and public works; 25–28 = Wholesale and related trade; 29 = Auto, sales, and repair; 30 = Hotels, cafes, and restaurants; 31 = Public transportation; 32 = Telecommunication; 33 = Sales to firms; 34 = Retail sales; 35 = Real estate rentals; 36 = Insurance; 37 = Financial services; 38 = Non-market services.

activities. Now "industrial" rationality, based on the roles of the engineer and the bureaucratic State, has pushed them aside. Resources for interpersonal activities exist, but they are inaccessible and unidentifiable, with only rare exceptions, given the way group identities are structured and resources appropriated. Successful Intellectual World products of the French economy are those which come closest to the Industrial World—hierarchically organized by the State in the context of large public works systems; other forms of the Intellectual World have been handicapped. The Market World has been left in a subordinate position around the margins of the favored Industrial World, where its more advanced visions are hampered by the nature of State decision-making on one hand and by elements of corporatism on the other.

The Failed Reforms of the 1980s

Recognizing some of the difficulties outlined above, France has been engaged for almost fifteen years in a process of "democratizing" its economic planning institutions and weakening them. Much of this effort has taken the form of attempts to bring more actors into the planning process, in particular firms and local and regional government agencies, as opposed to the State and its "branch of production." But this has done relatively little good in terms of reversing the phenomena described above; indeed, in many ways these efforts have strengthened the hand of the external State. We will examine three attempts to reform conventions in France: the role of the Enterprise Committee and the definition of the firm; the role of the Plan as the normative basis of the chief executive's power in private sector decision-making; and the increase in local economic intervention following the decentralization law of 1982.

INVOLVEMENT: THE ENTERPRISE COMMITTEE IN THE 1980S

With the election of a Socialist government in 1981, the philosophy of extending workers' rights and encouraging greater union participation in the industrial system gained renewed currency in France. Yet the Socialists had no clear conception of the worlds of production which were to be built by their policies or by the collective actors themselves; many of the reforms intended to create greater participation did not do so, while many of those intended to inject "market" forces in a staid industrial system ended up reinforcing the already existing dominance of the Industrial World.

In 1982, the government modified one phrase in the French Labor Code which defined the prerogatives of the Enterprise Committee (EC). This is the legally recognized negotiating body at the firm level, elected by the firm's personnel to represent them to management. As a way to institutionalize voice for workers and ensure ongoing adjustment of the firm, the government made annual negotiations between employers and Enterprise Committees obligatory. Moreover, the EC was essentially redefined. In 1945 it was where "workers *cooperate* with the employer in order to better work and employment conditions" as well as the conditions of *"life"* of the "ensemble of *members* of the firm."[27] In 1982, the EC was to negotiate to "insure the *collective voice of the workers,* allowing their *interests* to be taken into account on a *permanent* basis with respect to decisions as to the *management* and the economic and financial *development* of the firm, the organization of the labor process, and production techniques."[28] Note that these two versions of the law are based on two very different theories: the first is an Interpersonal World where collective "members"[29] "cooperate" in a firm which is intertwined with the population of its immediate surroundings (the conditions of "life"). The second reflects a theory of the Market World: collective action brings together a group of persons (the "workers") who act according to explicit rules (their "interests"), in light of a given economic environment and who, by implementing their intersecting interpretations ("collective voice"), will become involved in the optimization of an outcome ("management"). In short, these are two opposed conceptions of the enterprise and its underlying conventions.

Today, the EC must be consulted on workforce reductions or "restructuring plans" (mandated by the Law of January 1985 on the support of firms in difficulty), or on social issues such as early retirement (the *Fonds National de l'Emploi*): since the EC's primary mission is to protect employment, its right to approve such plans is justified on the grounds that it ensures employment benefits for the greatest number. Generally, this means that the survival of the distressed firm becomes more important than saving any particular jobs—it is argued that at times some jobs must be shed to save the rest of the jobs. Unlike the situation in a fully Liberal policy environment, however, priority is placed on saving the firm to save these other jobs. The firm is thus regarded as a patrimony of assets to be preserved.[30] (Paradoxically, given the intent of the law, obligatory EC-employer negotiations now usually lead to agreements on traditional productivity issues, especially on reorganizing the labor process to improve utilization of equipment. These agreements frequently contain special

dispensations or derogations, some verging on illegality, but all justified, jointly by ECs and employers, as required by the goal of saving
firms–cum–saving jobs.)

For a firm to receive State funds, restructuring agreements must be
signed by at least one union at the national level, in part because unions
which received more than half the votes in the last representation elections
can oppose implementation of such an agreement.[31] This is merely a
gesture of democratic control, however, given the overall architecture of
collective bargaining in France. In the United States, a union signs a
contract in the name of its members and only its members (or, at the limit,
for the workers in a closed shop), and generally only one union may
represent the workers of either a whole firm (industrial unionism) or a
given occupational group (craft unionism). In France, by contrast, a given
firm workforce or occupational group may be represented by a number of
different unions, and there is no requirement that a majority of the total
workforce be represented by any or all of these unions. Moreover, the
agreement signed by a single "representative" union, even when it represents a minority of the firm's workers, applies to all workers within the
firm and to all labor contracts. A union could, for example, sign a contract
granting a firm special dispensation for night work by unskilled women
workers only (whether or not they are members of the union); those
workers would then be obliged to do night work unless they were willing
to quit the firm (or be fired for refusing to work).[32] This gives unions a
"veritable regulatory power whose source cannot be attributed to any
particular mandate and has no particular guarantee."[33] In effect, the union
decides in the name of the supposed common interests of all involved
parties; this is another example of State-sanctioned corporatist institutions
in the economy.

One perverse outcome of the 1982 laws has been a notable increase in
the normative rights exercised by chief executives of firms. Management
has assumed an increased role as the maker of rules. In virtually all areas
of mandatory negotiation (for example, work rules, or hiring and firing),
when workers and management fail to reach agreement, the disagreement
is made official in a hearing, where management reveals the measures it
intends to apply unilaterally (article L 132-29, Labor Code). These measures then become the central point of reference for an administrative law
judge, who evaluates them for consistency with the State's overall goals,
especially employment. In the course of the 1980s, judges interpreted such
management proposals increasingly as commitments on the employers'
part, effectively taking the place of collective labor agreements. Manage-

ment's edicts thus became incorporated in publicly sanctioned administrative rules (article L 122-33 et seq., Labor Code); in effect, the State has invested the employer with regulatory powers.

The conventions of actors in France, as described above, mean that persons within a firm "in difficulty" expect the State, as an institution, to ensure their future, or at the very least protect them from their failures of coordination. This has come to mean: (1) that the employment level must be protected in the name of the common good by (2) an "external" intervention acting in "objective" fashion to save the maximum number of jobs possible and (3) in a way that treats as equals all legitimate "interests" present. All the collective actors in the situation share these expectations, including representatives of workers and firms and agents of the State charged with designing the external intervention. In other words, all parties have come to define the firm as an individual property which is part of a collective interest in employment, and therefore part of a national patrimony to be preserved in the name of this collective interest.

The outcomes, however, have not been consistent with the stated policy objectives: employment levels have fallen at a particularly striking rate in France over the last fifteen years, particularly in the capital-intensive sectors and in very large firms, with the most dramatic losses in major public and private industrial firms. Table 11.1 shows that the more a sector is composed of such groups, the greater the substitution of capital for labor and the higher the level of layoffs between 1974 and 1989; this is precisely the universe of firms in the Industrial World, closest to the State in France. To be sure, there were also high employment losses in certain other sectors where large firms do not dominate: foundries and metalworking, mechanical engineering, textiles and clothing, leather and shoes, wood and furniture, construction materials, and building and public works. In these cases the culprit seems to be a vicious circle of weak demand and premature responses by increasing capital intensity. Qualitative transformation of products (increasing quality, finding differentiated niches) becomes increasingly infeasible in these sectors once the "industrial" route is chosen. And the State did nothing to push these firms out of the Industrial World: indeed, the FIM encouraged them to use capital intensity as a way to raise static factor productivity (see Chapter 4).

Although this situation cannot be blamed entirely on the State, our analysis in terms of possible worlds of production suggests that the conventions within which State representatives are acting—conventions they reinforce in other actors by reducing the uncertainty those actors face—play an important role. In making available financial, technological, and organizational resources for "modernization" in "defense of employment," the State reinforces the patrimonial conception of the firm and draws other collective agents into the patrimonial project. Thus there exists a strong, self-reproducing convergence between the instrumentalities of the State and the structures of large industrial corporations in their orientation toward products of the Industrial World.

TERRITORIAL AND ADMINISTRATIVE DECENTRALIZATION: THE PERILS OF LOCAL ECONOMIC INTERVENTION

In 1982, the Socialist government enacted a series of laws calling for significant territorial decentralization of economic decision-making in France. Nearly a decade and a half into the process, it looks as if elected officials, once accused of exercising a kind of "measured Jacobinism"[34] (centralized control), have substituted a "republic of fiefdoms." Throughout all this, though, there has been one constant: the reshuffling of competences between territorial levels of government has not weakened the convention of the external State.

The very notion of territorial "level" is an essential dimension of the organization of the external State, which intervenes on a hierarchy of levels: national (or global), regional, followed by local or sectoral, and finally at the level of the firm. The lower the level, the narrower is the legitimacy of the actors and the narrower the scope of administrative power; the lower the level of action, the less general importance is attached to it: in this conception, an action at the local level is an action with only local validity. The central State in France is strongly represented at the local level (through the prefectural administration, and other representatives of national agencies), and these representatives transmit local needs upward through the hierarchy. One effect of this is to convince local actors (who in general need little convincing) that the importance and validity of their actions are directly proportional to their positions within the hierarchy. Thus, macroeconomic policy has a "greater" effect than sectoral or local policy. Before 1982, the role of local governments in the economy was limited (under the guise of preventing local particularism)[35] from substituting itself for the national, supposedly "general" interest. Local economic development was defined top-down by the DATAR, the State's territorial planning agency, "as a means to implement large-scale national choices via specific, well-adapted local policies."[36]

The industrial crisis of the 1970s and 1980s, and the concern with maintaining local employment levels, brought a profusion of local policy initiatives; the laws of the 1980s were mostly attempts to inject legal coherence and order into an existing reality. This movement implicitly challenged the notion of the external, hierarchical State. The old division of roles, with the central State and its large firms on one side and local elected officials charged with helping their small- and medium-sized firms (in an interpersonal context) on the other, has changed in the face of conflicts over employment policy. There has been a considerable awakening to the possibilities of creating real worlds of production at the local level by drawing on resources, business networks, and spatial proximity between economic actors. The traditional role of the prefect as coordinator of national macroeconomic and sectoral policies and distributor of financial incentives has been diminished significantly, and local elected officials have become aware of their role as creators of public policies; in a certain sense, they have begun to go beyond their traditional status as merely "local" actors.

At the same time, those whose identity is rooted in the convention of the external State and draw their legitimacy from its definition of their "objectivity" and from the resources they control—the many corps of civil servants—have appropriated the decentralization laws to reinforce their own action and power. A new dynamic of competition between territorial levels has been created, with the central State now acting as arbiter.[37] Fierce bidding wars between communities to attract firms tend to generate de facto inequalities between them in place of the traditional system of reciprocity based on clientelism.[38] Often, such conflicts can only be resolved by the emergence of local notables, who accumulate electoral mandates at several levels (in France, it is legal to be elected to many offices at the same time, even from different territorial jurisdictions).[39] These notables rule their fiefdoms from above and dispense State power according to a logic which is not all that different from the way territories were transformed into fiefdoms under the *ancien régime*.[40] The multiple positions and roles of these electoral "big shots" (who accumulate not only offices but non-elective roles in local chambers of commerce, public-private firms, state concessions, and so on) create a sort of oligarchy, quite independent of political persuasion. The notable, accompanied by his cohort of minor elected officials and his "clientele," helps channel national political favors to the fiefdom where his power is concentrated. Economic issues then tend to be subsumed to the political needs of the notables, who may take on either an identity of being "against" the State and defending the fiefdom against outside interference, or an identity of being "for" the State and well connected so as to reap multiple subsidies for the local clientele. This localism with a corporatist flavor is apparently one of the key ways in which the convention of the external State is being sustained in France in the face of current attempts at reform. It clearly impedes the emergence of development processes based on horizontal connections between actors (as opposed to the vertical, hierarchical architecture of the State and of the system of notables).

Nevertheless, these local experiences may also be read as a process of learning autonomy. A sort of "territorialization" of policy has accompanied the development of certain localized real worlds of production in the regions: this can be seen in the Vallée de l'Arve in the Upper Savoy in relation to the Interpersonal World of precision metalworking there; around St. Etienne in relation to a variety of light manufacturing industries which combine Market and Interpersonal World principles of action; in the high technology complexes of Toulouse and Grenoble, where local Intellectual Worlds are in the making; or in the clothing and shoe industries of the Choletais in the Vendée. The economic expertise necessary to such worlds of production is different from that mobilized by national administrative agencies, and these worlds are growing with assistance from new forms of inter-city and inter-regional cooperation which differ radically from the hierarchical administrative structure of the French state. Local and regional public officials, for example, develop situated, rather than objectivizing and external, forms of knowledge and information. They elaborate policies for themselves in ways that reject standard administrative rationality. There is a highly variable architecture of intervention and cooperation between many different kinds of agents in a highly context-specific way. Capacities based on proximity, dignity, and an awareness of potential universality are making their appearance and serving as resources in some cases. Whether these developments can gain strength and transform the centralized external state in France remains to be seen.

The principle of situatedness is not the same as the principle of "subsidiarity" adopted in the U.S. constitution or the European Union. Subsidiarity reflects Montesquieu's (and Jefferson's) general distrust of state interventionism; it is merely a negative version of the hierarchy of levels of the external state.[41] The principle of a situated state is not about higher or lower levels, but about coherent matches between collective actors in real action situations and the State at all territorial levels.

Conclusion

This analysis of the French state in terms of worlds of production is offered as an example; critiques of the American or Italian cases examined elsewhere in this book could show the extent to which the forms of intervention or non-intervention adopted by those states are coherent in terms of the action frameworks which underlie successful productive activity.

This critique of the French case is not an appeal against interventionist states per se. Rather, it targets the substantive rationality of interventionism as practiced by the state in contemporary France, a rationality based principally, even if unintentionally, on Industrial World objects and on categories which are frequently insensitive to the diverse real identities of actors, real patterns of participation, and real capacities for action. The continuing struggle between these groups of actors and the external interventionist state has resulted frequently in incoherent outcomes.

The task for every state is to find ways to situate itself coherently with respect to existing real action capacities in its society, and to help actors develop new capacities. This task assumes very different concrete forms in each society, according to existing conventions of identity and participation, and according to potential real worlds of production for each economy.

12

COMPETITIVENESS, SITUATED STATES, AND REAL WORLDS IN THREE COUNTRIES

Theories of Competitiveness and Conventions of the State

The approach to competitiveness implied by the analysis of worlds of production is very different from that found in the contemporary literature on the topic. Competitiveness theories all imply particular conventions of the state and particular capacities of actors in four broad approaches which we characterize as deregulationist, macroeconomic, neo-laborite, and neo-institutionalist.

For deregulationists, competitiveness problems can be resolved by removing the state and liberating the economy to find its optimal combination of specializations and techniques. Although the fact is rarely remarked, this theory is totally untested since no nation uses it as a policy guide: all nations intervene heavily to reinforce the strengths and protect the weaknesses of their economies. Economic history is cited as the primary source of intellectual justification for deregulationist reasoning, especially the story of modern economic development, which is recounted as involving the advent and perfection of markets in those places that develop best and most quickly. Such interpretations are heavily contested, of course, both by historians who claim the market was not the primary vector of modern development, and by those who claim that markets take a great diversity of forms and were themselves constructed by non-market mechanisms.[1]

In any case, the deregulationists view the composition and structure of an economy as a gigantic Market World, where price-cost changes induce efficient substitutions of activities and techniques. The theory thus ignores such realities of interdependence as scale economies, asset specificities and complementarities, circular and cumulative productivity, and learning dynamics. Critical among these interdependencies, we have argued, are action frameworks and their conventions, and these are not instantaneously created and abolished by responses to market forces. Even if there were a widely held convention of the absent state that corresponded to deregulationists' notion of competitiveness, their view would work only for those very limited segments of the economy amenable to its representation of the economic process—pure Market Worlds of production. Moreover, it would lead to destruction of other frameworks of action and the worlds to which they provide access.[2]

For macroeconomic managers, competitiveness in the new international environment essentially involves making judicious calculations about interest rates, exchange rates, and public spending; the conservative branch of this is monetarism, the liberal branch an updated Keynesianism. No one would deny that macroeconomic management, the science and art of which have increased significantly since the 1930s in all the developed economies, is a necessary element in maintaining competitiveness and sustaining growth. Few, however, would claim that such management—even if handled well—is sufficient to ensure competitiveness. Monetarists, as well as advocates of competitive deflation through currency overvaluation and high interest rates, believe that "stress" in capital markets is the key to competitiveness. The theory is that making capital relatively scarce and products relatively expensive in international markets keeps up pressure to use capital efficiently and, more important, applies extreme pressure to increase labor productivity—which is seen as an especially severe problem in the heavily institutionalized European economies. All in all, the monetarist vision is one of replacing labor with capital, essentially a preference for the Industrial World as the key to competitiveness. This Industrial World is to be produced by extreme monetary stability in the macroeconomic environment. The Keynesian version obviously emphasizes demand, but Keynesianism is strongly out of favor, especially after the failure of the French experiment in the early 1980s revealed that it is impossible to have Keynesianism in one country in an international environment which is not Keynesian. Less commonly understood is the fact that Keynesians hold to a vision of competitiveness rooted in the Industrial World, just like their monetarist foes. Efforts to stabilize demand are intended to shore up the market conditions required by the Industrial World. Keynesianism has essentially nothing to say about other possible worlds of production, nor about the conventions of the state and capacities for action needed to make them realities.

For the neo-laborites and "information age" economists, competitiveness turns on investments in high-level human capital; high-value-added, high-wage activity can be attracted and retained with an edge in rarefied forms of human capital. Robert Reich, Secretary of Labor in the Clinton administration, has repeatedly invoked the phrase "high wage, high skill" economy, and stresses two related themes: labor-management cooperation and work force quality.

The first of these draws on the model of European co-determination schemes, where unions do not concentrate solely on distributional issues, but also on productivity and competitiveness. There is good reason to think the labor relations system plays a role in firms' adjustment capacities and their levels of efficiency; in Germany the system permits firms considerable internal flexibility in the deployment of labor, which raises efficiency, whereas in France internal rigidity creates drags on productivity in a situation of fluctuating markets. Also in Germany training systems upgrade both firm- and industry-specific skills, which enhances efforts at technological learning and reduces potential resistance to product and process innovation.

This is, nonetheless, a strictly Industrial World vision of the economy: formalized participation relations between parties with highly institutionalized and stable identities bring about ongoing adjustment of products and processes. It is a formula that works when an economy specializes in better quality Industrial World products, or for certain Market World products underpinned by a stable institutional environment, as found in Japan and Germany. The neo-laborites, however, are naive to presume that a formal obligation to negotiate, coupled with strong and centralized bargaining units for both employers and workers, suffices to bring about the observed result. The French experience in the 1980s, as we saw in the previous chapter, falsifies this notion. The appearance and efficacy of such neo-corporatist comprehensive bargaining structures are more a result of conventions—including those of the state at hand—that link the parties in a coherent project of industrial adjustment, than of any law or particular institutional architecture. In Germany, the existence of capacities of action based on both proximity and universality distinguishes participants from, say, unions and employers in France who tried to imitate the Germans in the 1980s by copying the architecture of their bargaining process and training institutions. As those institutions and skills are put to totally different uses in France, they confine actors to a blocked version of the Industrial World because their conventions—precedent and expectations—

are completely different when they go into the negotiating process. We suspect that neo-laborite policies would suffer the same fate in the United States or Britain that befell them in France.

The second major element of the neo-laborite analysis stresses workforce quality as the principal anchor for and attraction to high-wage, high-value-added activities. Reich argues that the "work of nations" is no longer associated with nationally based firms, but with those activities that occur in a national territory; activities in the economy are composed in ways that respond to the factors of production present. Human capital can steer the economy toward high wages and high-skill labor demand by changing the sectoral and occupational composition of investments in the national territory.

But this view of the high-technology-as-high-skill economy ignores production system interdependencies other than those between the firm and the labor market. Production systems are made up of ensembles of technological interdependencies and conventional interdependencies; they are not simple, off-the-shelf responses to a given, single factor of production. In this light, the neo-laborite "training" theory of competitiveness is merely a minor amendment to a standard neoclassical theory of comparative advantage, one which remains securely rooted in the Market World, but now holds out a role for the state to push the mix of activities in a favorable direction by providing more and better training. Although there is much that is convincing about long-run growth theories based in knowledge accumulation (see, for example, Romer),[3] this neo-laborite theory of competitiveness does not correspond to such theories because it ignores the ways in which skilled workers are embedded in interdependent productive systems; they are not merely individual units of human capital.

Finally, there are many branches of neo-institutionalist competitiveness theories. Among these are Porter's[4] "diamond," which advances a common-sense formula that calls for high levels of domestic competitiveness, tight upstream-downstream linkages, regional concentration, and complementary spillovers. MIT's *Made in America* report, and its cousin, *Made in France*,[5] argue for new management methods involving attention to quality and technological learning, backed by institutional reforms in financial and labor markets, the educational system, and a host of governmental agencies. The "systems of innovation" literature focuses on institutions that generate scientific and engineering-based knowledge and on the commercialization of that knowledge in the economy.

Underlying all these theories is, again, the notion of significant techno-

logical spillovers in the economy: knowing how to do one thing is conse-
quent on knowing how to do another, or key to doing yet other things.
This draws from the work of Schumpeter or François Perroux, who noted
that economies consist of "spaces" or fields of endeavor. That idea, updated by new research on the dynamics of technological change, suggests
that technological excellence comes in packages or ensembles. Since this
sort of excellence relies frequently on knowledge and practices that cannot
be fully codified, the particular groups of firms which master a specific
kind of knowledge do so through networks, including formal exchanges
with other firms as well as untraded interdependencies: labor markets,
public institutions, local or national customs, conventions, and understandings which enable the effective transmission of information and interpretation of knowledge. Moreover, technologies do not stand still: they
evolve along trajectories shaped and propelled as the result of actions
taken by firms that use them and other agents. In analytical terms, evolutionary theories of technological change through spillover acknowledge
that externalities are pervasive in the process of technological learning; it
has an inexorably social and embedded character. Thus the production
functions of firms in the same technological spaces tend to be interdependent, and decisions in any one firm are highly dependent on decisions made
in other firms.

Since all these neo-institutionalist theories explicitly recognize the interdependent and institutionalized nature of production systems, they appear
to be not inconsistent with the notion of multiple worlds of production,
and the need for situated states to assist in building the capacities associated with them. As formulated, however, each theory tends toward an
essentialist definition of the problem, which is said to apply to all products. Porter's diamond is advocated as a solution for all sectors and
products; *Made in America* and *Made in France* position themselves at the
level of institutional and management reforms said to apply to all sectors
and activities; literature on national systems of innovation sees the production and commercialization of science and engineering knowledge as coex-
tensive with all processes of innovation and learning, even though only
Intellectual World products fit their logic. In short, all such theories are
insufficiently "close" to products and production systems.

What is more serious, none of these approaches gets beyond institutional architecture into processes of coordination, or frameworks of action. All mention "culture" as somehow important, but none incorporates
its notion of culture directly into its analysis of competitiveness and recom-

mendations for an alternative. Rather, institutions as vehicles of policy are to replace culture. But this is, in our view, the wrong approach. Institutions are conventions, like the other conventions that make up action frameworks. Positing a separation between institutions and culture simply begs the question of action and coordination.

Our analysis reformulates the question in an entirely different manner. Any given economy must create products and processes that can give those products a viable presence in global markets. The particularity of its products is the vehicle of this global presence, an exogenous test. At the same time, actors within the economy must produce efficiently enough to generate levels of social surplus consistent with the distributional conventions of that society: this is an endogenous test. These tests are both met when people develop the competences required to fashion real worlds of production compatible with these tests.

Obviously, establishing real worlds of production for these two purposes is not simply a question of adopting exogenously determined "best practices," technologies or methods. The development and use of technologies and methods depend on the frameworks of action within which they are deployed, and those frameworks of action are theoretically above the question of formal institutions, for institutions are themselves just stabilized sets of social practices. Competitiveness policies must use and reflect frameworks of action, in all their diversity and complexity.

Conventions and frameworks of action may face a crisis when existing routines no longer meet exogenous and endogenous tests. Transition to new, coherent worlds of production is by no means automatic: virtually all the real worlds examined in this book are today facing serious challenges to their competitiveness; this was also true of a large number of the firms studied in Chapter 4. All these cases show a multiplicity of problems: the need to identify new resources and to legitimate and train new economic agents—what we have called capacities—as carriers of these resources; to transform and reconvert existing resources; to shift toward products for which demand is growing—products that are often new for existing worlds and their firms, so this shift implies coordinated learning of unaccustomed conventions of quality and labor. It is in these terms that the practical dimensions of economic, industrial, and labor policy should be posed. They are ambitious terms. We shall try to open them up here, by asking whether the production systems presented in previous chapters are poised to learn the conventions which will enable them to survive and prosper, or whether they will find themselves locked into conventions which could prove inadequate in the face of changing circumstances. In each case we ask what forms of autonomous collective action and situated policy are called for.

Italy: Combining Interpersonal Coordination with Scale

Three phases of development for the NEC Italian industries were discussed in Chapter 7, all characterized by growth. However, a fourth phase, which began in the mid-1980s, brought stagnation and, in some cases, declines in both employment and numbers of firms. From 1986 to the recession year of 1992, for example, employment in the Prato textile district fell by 9% and the number of firms by 14%. Other changes under way include increasing numbers of plants locating outside the region and growing import penetration. Although there have been other periodic crises in these complexes, the crisis of the 1980s was particularly severe.

European competitors have targeted NEC Italy's markets, using sophisticated flexible production technologies on one hand and larger firms on the other, so that some of the "medium-high" fashion markets (not Milanese high fashion, however) are increasingly difficult to retain. The design-intensive industries of NEC Italy, having long set the standard for successfully turning Interpersonal World possibilities into reality, face challenges with respect to two major elements of the collective action problem in innovation associated with the products identified in Chapter 3: the economic constraints which attach to specialized-dedicated products of this sort, and the need to continue deepening and perfecting the asymmetric knowledge which permits innovation and product qualities in this world to develop in a way compatible with those constraints.

"Best practice," as developed in the real worlds of Italian design-intensive industries, has been a local response to the global menu of possibilities and limitations through ongoing redefinition of products and production methods. A number of factors—the exhaustion of traditional sources of entrepreneurial resources (agriculture, layoffs); the slow but steady weakening of postwar local political subcultures; young people's desire to abandon direct production activity (in some cases to enter professions, though others prefer to follow their parents quite directly, for example in Prato); and the slight but consistent growth in rates of inter-regional mobility, opening local population systems—make it possible to ask whether the advantages of membership, reciprocity, and loyalty, which have proved so instrumental to the region's development patterns, can be preserved and used to shape effective new responses to changing competitive conditions.

Those small firms that do make large investments in new, more efficient equipment actually make themselves more vulnerable, because they raise their overhead costs (of debt servicing and increased minimum run size), yet the *impannatore* system of buyers cannot reliably provide them with the length of production runs they require. As a result, when downturns occur, the least modern firms, those in which the least investment has been made recently, tend to survive, while the more modern small- and medium-sized firms are driven deeply into debt and, often, into failure. A negative selection process may be at work which favors the low-technology, very small firms.[6] Should the crisis continue, the more modern small firms may disappear, while competitors—whether domestic large firms, or more modern foreign (especially German) firms—may take the market, either through import penetration or by merging with and acquiring existing production capacity. Thus, in some ways, it is precisely the strength of producer identities that appears to impede certain forms of modernization.

Attempts to cope with this situation have also revealed problems in the existing system of coordination of the production system. The buyers in Prato, for example, have their own short-term interests to look after: they are interested in the right product at a competitive price. They are faced with stiff competition in the export sector, and are not in a position to coordinate the system so that it will have a more efficient long-run configuration. The problem is not one of market failure, but of a locked-in system that works very well at coordinating independent producers. In other words, firms in the Interpersonal World are having difficulty coordinating their supply curves in the face of stagnant markets and competition from larger firms in the Market World, which can now combine dedication and standardization with higher levels of direct labor productivity and—this is critical—more direct and favorable access to international distribution, so they can coordinate the outputs of standardized-dedicated products with large-scale distribution.

Recent evidence on changes in the Italian districts is too new to indicate any definitive developmental trends. Throughout the 1980s in Italy, shares of employment held by large firms continued to decline and large production units continued to cut back on their employment, while employment shares in small firms held steady. International capital has entered into key Italian production systems, but in quite a minor way: the degree of internationalization in mechanical engineering is only 13%, in textiles 2%, and in clothing, *less than one percent;* internationalization is most elevated in the mass production sectors which are not Italian export specializations.[7] In terms of regions, the vast majority of foreign investment is in Lombardy and Piedmont; it has hardly touched Emilia, Tuscany, and the Veneto. Moreover, while the growth of employment in firms controlled from outside has been quite high in Emilia (+50%), it has been negative in Tuscany, and quite moderate (less than 15% in 1985–1990) in the Veneto, Lombardy, and Piedmont; most important, absolute levels remain very low in all these cases: 5% in Emilia, 2.5% in Tuscany, 3.1% in the Veneto. Finally, there is no coherent pattern of change in overall firm size distributions that would indicate a tendency toward vertical integration in the industries and regions discussed.

But if the crisis has not spelled the end of decentralized production in the form of vertical integration, it has not yet revealed a successful structure for survival either. The positive development in some places is that product mixes are changing; in Prato, for example, the proportion of output in the declining woolen textile sector has steadily dropped since 1985, and synthetics, cottons, and non-woven fabrics—all growing markets world-wide—now account for more than a third of output.[8]

It is possible that a new phase in the development of these areas thus may be taking shape. In analytical terms, it will later be recognized that these production systems suffered collective lock-in and decline, takeover and integration, or structural transformation *through* their conventions of participation. Such transformations would necessarily involve more organized production networks with greater capabilities in product-planning and marketing than currently exist, so they could combine more of the advantages of internal scale economies with existing static and dynamic economies of scope. The industrial complexes as a whole will most likely have to undertake long-term strategic planning for horizontal expansion of their existing specialties, that is, expansion into clusters of technologically cognate products and processes. This will probably require replacing existing firms or, where children are not present to assume succession in family-owned firms, transferring them into the hands of a new brand of entrepreneur ready to assume new forms of coordination, beyond those afforded by the existing system of buyers (in the fashion industries). In other words, conventions of identity and participation will change, and with them certain conventions of product quality, productivity, and labor.

In a hierarchical resolution, these systems will become "network firms," with critical product planning and marketing functions internalized within a central firm, and other firms acting as specialty and capacity subcontractors, as in the Benetton model; in a non- (or less) hierarchical solution, they could become federated networks or "planned constellations" with emphasis on planning and marketing to reap advantages of scale, but with those functions not internalized in a central firm. In the fashion industries, elements of both solutions will likely be combined with a certain degree of localized production in cheap labor areas outside the core regions; in the precision metalworking and machining (PMM) industries, they will combine with direct foreign investment in certain key markets.[9]

Note that both these alternatives imply situated involvement of the Italian state. Existing capacities of actors and the state, founded on proximity, will have to be expanded. The need, once again, is to build on particularity without particularism. The absence of strong specialization in products of the Industrial and Market Worlds in Italy (with the exception of three or four big firms, such as Fiat, Olivetti, and Benetton) is consistent with the fact that the Italian state cannot mobilize the concentrated industrial resources necessary to these worlds; indeed, Italian experiments with nationalization have not generally produced the successes of their French counterparts, and Italy is withdrawing from nationalization even more rapidly than France. It is no longer a question of Italy attempting to imitate the postwar French pathway to the Industrial World via the planned economy, but a matter of using public policy at all levels to broaden existing strengths in the products of the Interpersonal World. Interpersonal communities of actors could successfully pursue standardization or generic qualities to stabilize their firms' positions without wrecking the coordination which currently underpins their production systems. In this regard, a new law allowing Italian regions to conduct industrial policy activities hitherto reserved for the national state is promising. The law permits local intervention in an officially designated "industrial district."[10]

NEC Italy already sets the world standard for a situated form of industrial policy adapted to Marshallian markets: local and regional governments, in concert with the CNA, have attempted to encourage technological conversion by establishing a very sophisticated network of service centers, which offer technological counseling, market research, and product design assistance. In some cases these service centers even assist firms in obtaining financing for modernization—what the Italians call *servizi reali*, services tailored to the support of existing activities at a regional level, and their collective adaptation to new markets through incremental learning and improvement in both product quality and the efficiency of production processes.[11]

This is probably the leading example in the world today of the convention of a situated state promoting capacities based on proximity. Can the situated state, through service centers and related policies, introduce longer-term planning horizons into these very decentralized industrial systems without destroying their flexible structures? Ultimately, the question is whether the social structure of these areas is capable of generating the conditions of "economic citizenship" needed for successful industrial adaptation, or whether those conditions themselves are destined to give way to entirely new participatory structures incompatible with existing domains of specialization and success[12] in the face of the global competition and integration of the late twentieth century. The answer will depend on the extent to which the collective actors in these regions are able to combine the best of their existing capacities for particularity through proximity, with a widening of those capacities in a way that allows products with greater generic or standardized content and thus avoids particularism.

France: Joining the Market and Intellectual Worlds via Interpersonal Networks

In the 1980s, the number of French specializations in international trade declined. This was cause for alarm, since despite the country's strong economic planning apparatus and a nationalistic ideology of industrial self-sufficiency, the opening up of European markets has made a number of existing French industries vulnerable to invasion.

Today, in high technology, there are incipient blockages even in the most successful subsectors. Although the Airbus Industrie consortium (of which Aerospatiale is the key firm) has been commercially successful in recent years, it is now facing both market slowdown and increasing pressures for cuts in public support. Both civilian and military aviation have recently entered into a period of deep cutbacks, with permanent job losses of at least 30% predicted by the end of the 1990s. France's other high technology industries are highly dependent on orders directly from the state, and with the drying up of its traditional weapons markets in former African colonies and the Middle East, as well as budgetary pressures at home, France will likely reap fewer benefits from military high technology in the near future. Moreover, with the firm European Community commitment to open markets, it is very possible that other large, state-dependent high technology markets, especially in telecommunications, will be subject to increasing competition from outside. These are the classical problems of French high technology: unsatisfactory relations between the Industrial, Market, and Intellectual frameworks of action.

The French fashion industries are also facing difficulties: though still dynamic in intellectual terms, that is, in creating fashion, in recent years they have been notably less competitive than other countries in commercialization (compared, for example, to Italian successes such as Benetton and Stefanel) or cost competition (compared to Germany). This competitive weakness is a source of concern for many other complexes of high quality, design-intensive products in France, such as precision metalworking in the Haute Savoie or shoes in the Choletais—complexes that we studied in great detail but could not include in this book. In all these cases—from high tech to high fashion to design-intensity—strong interpersonal communities exist but they lack strong coordination with either Market or Intellectual World forms of action.

As we noted earlier, the only groups of firms in France that have been able to use the resources of the State and the *grands corps* of technocrats ("Francilien" resources) are those in high technology production, especially those producing large-scale systems mostly for State markets. Public and private resources in France appear to be well adapted to these real worlds of production, particularly where the managers of large industrial groups have conventions of identity coherent with, and sometimes identical to, those of State technocrats. These groups are particularly active in the (limited) successes of French high technology, yet it is doubtful that they will be able to construct the forms of coordination required to succeed in the emerging world economy without significant changes in their conventions of identity and participation, and in the action frameworks to which they provide access. It is instructive to consider some of the obstacles with respect to the identity and participation of groups linked to the traditional *Etat Planificateur* (the State engaged in economic planning).

Virtually all the important collective actors in the French economy (management, workers, State representatives) continue to define modernization in a highly "objectivizing" fashion. It is widely believed that transformation of labor conventions and products depends simply on transforming technical objects and equipment, or on changes to "objective" organizational rules: investment in new, costly, capital-intensive technologies; use of experts; adjustment of demand to supply ("redundancy" policies), and so on. The conventions of identity that construct membership in social groups, and corresponding conventions of participation, are not open to question except in marginal ways. They are fixed by State practices and rules, largely unchanged since World War II; all major social actors expect this State—standing outside and above civil society—to correct coordination gaps and failures.

Another major impediment is the weak coherence of branches of production and the minor role accorded them as spaces in which autonomous coordination of the involved collective actors could emerge. In Chapter 11 we noted that, in spite of certain modifications introduced in the 1980s, the State has continually broadened the space for firm-level negotiations (sometimes through exceptions to common law) rather than favoring collective autonomy. But, given the tendencies toward "intellectual" or "market" products (noted in Chapter 4), coordination cannot successfully be carried out by State-mobilized branch-level resources and collective labor agreements. A third impediment is that French economic actors have only weak access to non-bureaucratic, non-statist versions of the Interpersonal World. Products based on economies of variety and specialization, where quality depends on hard-to-copy savoir-faire, are among the dynamic points of contemporary international production and trade, but—except for certain luxury or fashion products—France is relatively weak in these areas, including metalworking and precision mechanical engineering. A relatively small proportion of French exports competes on a non-price basis. Of the firms studied in Chapter 4, almost all of those closest to the Interpersonal World were small or medium-sized, in rural or small-town settings, and paying relatively low wages. These firms do not emphasize the quality of their workforce as a fundamental principle. Their price-cost margins are low and have not recently improved, which suggests that they hold a subordinate position in inter-firm relations. These are manifestations of weakness in the Interpersonal World (that is, outside the circuits of "royal" production, whether currently statist as in high technology, or formerly statist as in high fashion) in French economic conventions.

The 1982 laws seeking "democratization of the firm," as described in Chapter 11, have engendered a number of unresolved conflicts in interpretation.[13] The history of the Enterprise Committees shows that management continues to expect adherence to the objectives it defines from above, while workers wish to be treated as partners, whose ideas and needs are taken into account. Legislators, for their part, want the spirit of the Enlightenment to shine on the firm, in a modern-day version of undistorted communication between social partners, but the conventions of identity and participation of these "partners" are incompatible with such a vision. Both owners and State representatives do share the notion of the firm-as-patrimony, but it is used to shape and co-opt labor.

Taken together, these factors make it extremely difficult to construct organizational structures capable of increasing personal and collective responsibility in the labor process with the productivity of the Industrial World. Only in this way could the mass market products representing an important share of national output be upgraded.

The last barrier, but not the least, concerns conflicts between those conventions that hold the State above and external to civil society and particular action situations, and those conventions more closely adapted to such situations. We noted this in discussing the form of the economic *plan* in France. Neo-liberal thinking would simply ascribe these dilemmas to the inherent inferiority of states as compared to markets; if this is the case, it follows that the French high technology industries must simply abandon their reliance on the elite technocracy and open themselves up to "market forces" and "entrepreneurship." Yet, as the analysis in Chapter 6 suggests, this recipe is poorly adapted to the problem. There is the danger that nothing could function as well as the highly competent existing technocracy, and that France would find itself in the position of Italy with respect to high technology. The alternative now being pursued is the aggressive internationalization of French high technology firms, through acquisitions on their part. The risk here is that French companies—to the extent that they become successful in commercial high technology markets—will in effect be dominated by the management they acquire, not the other way around: ownership would be French, but the companies would no longer have key French personnel nor therefore access to the vast, key technological resources of the Francilien technocracy. An even more grim scenario is that in acquiring these companies, the French management will reduce its commercial viability, which seems to be the case with Bull in recent years. In short, the participation problem is not simply one of "opening up" or de-statizing the ranks of technological specialists.

The problem facing French high technology today is how to transform the skill base into one that is less hierarchically administered and organization-specific (in the sense of the State), without losing the technological excellence these organizations have been able to generate in the past, and without losing the identities of organizations and actors. This would require a subtle and ongoing reorientation of the technocracy, at three sites: in the schooling/training system; in the State institutions themselves; and in major private and mixed firms.

The goal can be restated in terms of deepening innovative product qualities. French high technology is overwhelmingly centered on specialized-dedicated outputs coordinated in a state-dominated Interpersonal World at the national level. But these outputs are quite unlike those of, say, U.S. high technology complexes, as in Silicon Valley where products are mostly basic, intermediate inputs subsequently recombined (via the Intellectual World) into generic forms and then subjected to standardization in the Market or Industrial Worlds. In France, the technology planning system combined with the importance of the State orders leads to production of large-scale dedicated-specialized technological systems. There is no way to link them to generic or standardized products because of their very design from the outset.

This specialty of French high technology must be expanded into other domains. This would include conceiving systems that are ultimately amenable to "standardization" in order to give them commercial appeal. The first major potential example is the TGV rapid train system, now being sold in packages to other countries at a profit. Expansion would also require that specialized-dedicated outputs become intermediate and recombinable products, themselves amenable to standardization and commercialization; and that firms produce more medium-scale final outputs with greater generic qualities. This last goal will clearly require effective incentives to attract private sector partners of the State along with a somewhat more extensive decentralization of responsibility for the production system itself: less total *filière* planning and more contracts calling for private sector generic adaptation of public sector dedicated intermediate-basic outputs. This would create a virtuous circle between public sector specialized-dedicated projects and private or mixed sector specialized-generic or standardized-dedicated products.

The action frameworks of those in the existing real world of Interpersonal-State technocracy will also need to change—and this includes changing the way actors are mobilized, their identities in the grandes écoles, and the ways they participate in State and private bureaucracies. This is not a call for privatization, but for reorganization of State bureaucracies and their closely linked private sector partners, toward a coherent set of new identities and patterns of participation which adapts the industrial structure without destroying its considerable strong points. Likewise, convincing large segments of the labor force to abandon the (increasingly meager) benefits of corporatism for something else will depend on experiments in coordination that demonstrate the possibility of real respect for the identities of workers. This may prove to be the most difficult and elusive goal of all, for the "royal" identities of key private or public actors are strongly forged in France.

The United States: Creating Room for Collective Interpersonal and Intellectual Action

The real worlds of specialist American production systems have a central developmental logic of mobilizing Intellectual and Industrial World resources within a Market World framework. Although they excel in basic innovations, they tend to lose markets where incremental change is at a premium; for standardized products, though they enjoy very high productivity levels, they also suffer the instability that accompanies the need for high capacity utilization in the face of ongoing price competition. The underlying Market World orientation of American economic actors has also affected conditions for doing business there generally, in both positive and negative ways. For high technology, it mobilizes venture capital, but also encourages early exit of human and financial capital, and subjects firms to excessively difficult tests of short-term market performance which are fundamentally incompatible with the long time horizons of the intellectual action framework. This orientation seems to inhibit deployment of American advances in basic technologies into what could be more lucrative market segments—specialized-dedicated products, for example—in which production is closer to the Interpersonal World than to the Industrial.

These dynamics of U.S. high technology industries together result in losing markets in which incremental change in products is the dominant form of learning. This in turn frequently leads to recommendations that Americans must learn to correct their transactional failures through more deliberate systems of coordination, purportedly used in certain European regions and in Japan.[14] The skeptical response to this is that the U.S. economy should not, and cannot, be coordinated as are the economies of other countries: this would not be consistent with American conventions of identity and participation, which privilege abstraction of resource qualities and their mobility; indeed, it would be incompatible with the major strength of the American production system—the ability to produce and rapidly commercialize new breakthrough technologies, and to generate extraordinarily professionalized manufacturing and customer service organizations.

The problem of failure to compete in the Interpersonal (and even, paradoxically, in the Market) World is itself not serious, as long as the U.S. industrial economy can enjoy the other developmental mechanisms upon which it has depended for so long. Yet American superiority in static productive efficiency through Taylorization and mass production has been greatly reduced (if not entirely effaced) in sector after sector precisely by the fact that industries have been "de-matured" (that is, de-standardized and de-Taylorized) by competitors who are expert in incremental innovation and combine that with very high levels of static efficiency. At the same time, American reliance on decentralized, "spontaneous" emergence of industries based on major new technologies is being supplanted by efforts on the part of the European countries and Japan to pioneer in a systematic manner in such sectors as high definition television, aircraft, communications systems, computers, and biotechnology. Neither America's domestic demand structure nor its research-industrial structure appears inherently superior in this domain any longer, especially in view of the way that the growing importance of finance capital in the American economy increasingly applies Market World principles of immediate returns to public and private investments.

The conclusion that American production complexes must address the problems of liberal versions of the Market World, then, is not rooted in a desire to imitate European industrial stability, but in historical necessity.[15] The phenomenon of start-up and spin-off has remained remarkably strong in such places as Silicon Valley and Orange County in recent years, but the increasing perfection of functional equivalents elsewhere makes it very unlikely that this will continue to have the developmental effects it once had. The collective action problem is not, as many analyses have claimed, within America's R&D establishment, nor narrowly within its highly productive mass production economy. The American capacity to mobilize the resources of the Intellectual and Industrial Worlds is highly developed. The problem is rather that the entire American economy, whatever the particular product and world of production, is underpinned by such a strong principle of resource mobility, and by the Market World principles of immediate availability and convertibility, that other possible worlds cannot find and keep the resources they need for other sorts of compromises.

The conventional and policy problem thus presents itself as follows: is it possible to compensate for the inevitably declining overall shares of breakthroughs and follow-throughs (high productivity, high volume production) by increasing the ability to hold onto post-breakthrough production by mastering incremental innovations? Transactional failure—both in the negative form of opportunism and in the positive form of the urge to sell out—must be addressed. Dealing effectively with this challenge would require changes in the convention of participation to fix in place some of the professional-entrepreneurial resources which are presently subject to such high turbulence in dynamic industries.

Resolving the collective action problem consists in providing the means for frameworks of action and coordination between persons, other than those of the pure Market World, to exist in the innovative sectors of the American economy. This would mean allowing actors in the high technology complexes making specialized-dedicated outputs to preserve and strengthen the Interpersonal bases of their scientific cultures, by holding them together as innovators and product improvers after early superprofits are gone. There is a need for frameworks of action based on renewed versions of the sense of pride and craft in these scientific and industrial communities—and for the society to recognize this identity. This is likely to involve direct changes in the identities of key actors, but probably changes in the systems of financial incentives and in the availability and stability of labor resources as well. In other words, a move toward disincentives to labor turnover may be called for—a "European" move. The problem here is not the logic of such a policy, which can easily be demonstrated, but the violence it does to the "cosmopolitan" (abstraction, mobility) identities of U.S. managers and technologists and to the conventions of intellectual labor to which technologists are wedded.

On the other side of the American success, it is clear that there is a need to cut back on the "rush to Taylorize" which occurs after large firms swallow up smaller ones along with their patents and show one-period productivity so high as to eliminate potentially more dynamically productive but usually smaller competitors. This would mean that large firms would have to go through a rather comprehensive redefinition of their now narrowly "industrial" convention of productivity. Such a redefinition would require profound changes in these firms' legal and financial structures as well as in the identities and conventions of their managers and workers. Our model of profitability demonstrated that many different productivity formulas can lead to profits because the price-cost margin varies between models of production. Many studies document American management's attachment to the standard textbook definition of productivity as minimizing unit costs of production, notably MIT's *Made in America,* and the same university's World Automobile Study.[16] This phenomenon is related strongly to the particular industrial history of the United States, where massive scale economies and early standardization of tastes paid high dividends for a long time,[17] and is reinforced by incentives in the American corporate finance system. But one suspects that its roots lie as well in the models of production "seen" by the American manager and retailer, and the ways they coordinate with each other and with consumers. Their expectations that scale is the only route to success are deeply ingrained. It will be necessary to provide access to other frameworks of action.

How might producers in the Industrial World better harness the talents of the Intellectual and Interpersonal Worlds—that is, continue to benefit from their specialized-dedicated and specialized-generic outputs, without buying them up, installing hierarchical control, and often destroying interpersonal communities? The key problem for innovation in the Industrial World involves "terms of trade" between different possible worlds: no exogenous decision rule resolves all problems of such exchanges and provides determinate institutional arrangements for them in a context of "repeated improvements." Actors must learn to recognize the action frameworks necessary to their activity, and to respect the action frameworks of those upon whom they must depend in the social division of labor in innovation, and the terms of trade must be constructed around the recognition of those identities and respect for their autonomy. That this has not yet occurred in American high technology is evident from the fact that essentially liberal principles dominate the discourse, and other voices are weak. The debate has been falsely posed as a simple choice between markets and coordination, not between forms of coordination. In this light, it can be seen that the currently fashionable (among American liberals, at least) policy solution for American high technology, coordinated research consortia such as SEMATECH, offers no solution to the real problem of these terms of trade. American high technology producers do not have problems with scale as smaller European companies do; they *do* have a problem in defining terms of trade between science and engineering, on one hand, and production, on the other. SEMATECH is a highly formalized, external activity of major companies—it neither builds a real interpersonal basis for science and technology activity, nor does it propose a clear set of cooperative decision rules for transferring technology from R&D to production. Until the government develops institutional proposals that pose these questions clearly, industry itself is likely to regard government institutions as sideshows, and the only currently viable form of government intervention—protection of property rights—will remain the baseline position, however inadequate it is to the problems facing the American economy.

American government institutions figure importantly here. They have consistently and increasingly structured the rules of the game (through regulation of financial markets, policies on competition, taxation, and the labor market) around the principles of Market action, which do not respect the autonomy of groups of actors in other worlds of action; indeed, they have constructed Market action as a way to impede the existence of other frameworks of action. One example of this (among many) is the mounting evidence that the financial system stacks the deck in favor of short-term decision-making (essentially a Market World choice) and against developing production based on other forms of coordination and principles of action.[18]

When the State actually intervenes, in the United States, it is as an external state, whose regulations almost always raise costs of production for firms whose products are in the Market and Industrial Worlds. The ferocious resistance to the State in the United States is not just the result of liberal ideology; it is also rooted in the particular product mix and action frameworks employed widely in the American economy. The "external" character of the intervention—that is, the form of universally decreed rules and requirements with little subtlety of application or flexibility in implementation—is appropriate to an Industrial World conception of objects and actions, widely diffused in the American economy. Firms resist because enforcement takes a "market" form with extremely high transaction costs and a presumption that State and industry have conflicts of interest. Thus, it has a perverse effect of reinforcing anti-statism, in the form of a hard, universalizing liberal ideology.

The policy debates are often fruitless because the actors are talking past each other, unable to clarify the action frameworks they are using. Conservatives attempt to deal with the question of the State by trying to get rid of it, assuming that a pure Market World action framework and Industrial World objects alone suffice for economic coordination. Liberals argue that the State is needed to deal with the failures of the market, but do not acknowledge that an external interventionist state often cannot resolve these failures for two reasons. The first is that the administrative form of an external state uses excessively abstract and therefore very costly criteria of intervention; the second reason is that market failures often cannot be corrected without introducing action frameworks other than that of the market, notably the intellectual and interpersonal. In these cases, the question concerns different industrial strategies (products and action frameworks); these problems have little to do with the liberal program of regulating markets, and nothing to do with a conservative program of constructing a convention of an absent state.

IV

CONVENTIONS, ECONOMIC ACTION, AND INSTITUTIONS

13

A CRITIQUE OF CONTEMPORARY INSTITUTIONALISM

Moral Hazard versus Collective Action

To the limited extent that contemporary social science deals with the theoretical problem of action in the economy at all, it is in terms of the question of "institutions." Some of this work, known as the New Institutional Economics, concentrates on the relationship of rules, institutions, and practices to economic efficiency and performance and, more generally, theorizes on how the "economic institutions of capitalism"[1] are shaped. Other work, which we may call the New Institutional Analysis, looks at how groups of actors form rules and institutions in real economic history, at their springboards of action, and how they shape economic development. Institutions are also, of course, a major concern for sociologists, but sociological approaches rarely claim to analyze institutions on the economist's grounds of allocational efficiency or long-run development. We want to show, with an extended critique of the New Institutional Analysis and New Institutional Economics, that in fact the economist's problems require a richer approach to action than is found in most contemporary institutionalism.

Both the New Institutional Economics and the New Institutional Analysis offer positive models of how collectivities of actors construct economic institutions, yet both restrict the individual actions considered relevant to social life to two basic cases. In the New Institutional Economics, the basic situation is contained in the external objects (assets) to which one applies one's efforts, and which define the conditions of interaction with others in an all-encompassing, fully reliable way; the New Institutional Economics is a theory of the Industrial World. There is a determinate relationship between persons and productive objects; objects give rise to institutions, at least when behaviors and markets are functioning correctly, so institutions are important, but not economic action per se. For the New Institutional Economics, all persons have bounded rationality and tend to engage in opportunistic behavior; the contours of this behavior are shaped by the productive assets at hand. This creates endemic moral hazards in collective economic life. The problem of "credibility" is pervasive for the New Institutional Economics, whereas for the social science of conventions it is strictly associated with the Market World and its objects. For Williamson, this problem of lack of credibility and the existence of moral hazards creates the need for institutions, but also their fundamental dilemma, for they are imperfectible: all complex contracts are incomplete. The best we can do is continually *adapt* our actions and our institutional arrangements, on an ongoing basis, to limit moral hazards. Adaptive universal-rational economizing is the essence of action.

In the New Institutional Analysis, individuals act within "institutional environments" which determine the potential for constructing better or worse economic systems. Groups are the outcome of individual (rational or boundedly rational) choice and self-interest; methodological individualism is used to explain group structure. Institutions are something like markets for interests, and so the New Institutional Analysis is essentially a theory of the Market World. For the New Institutional Analysis, the objective constraints on interaction are not material objects, but the structures of groups themselves. Their starting point is the way actors define interests. Depending on the configuration of interests, different specific dilemmas of moral hazard arise, leading to a variety of institutional responses, some successful in terms of economic efficiency, others not.

To simplify, we may say that the New Institutional Economics and New Institutional Analysis work on similar equations: for the former, motivations and behaviors are the constant; objects/assets and institutional environments (background conditions such as laws, cultures, and so forth) are independent variables; and institutional arrangements (these are described in terms of three types: hierarchy, market, or hybrid—that is, contractual arrangements in production) are the phenomena to be explained. For the New Institutional Analysis, motivations and behaviors are again constant, and the structures of interests are the independent variable; the evolution of long-term institutional environments is the phenomenon to be explained. Both of these schools of thought build a vision of "state versus market" from overly restricted analytical and empirical starting points, which leads them to defend the superiority of the market over the state in normative terms.

This restricted definition of the "individual" and the "collective" domains appears over and over again in contemporary institutionalism. The "collective" is the residuum of the industrial and market frameworks of action, that is, everything that cannot be defined by objects or organized by the pursuit of interests. Collectivities and institutions thus become a deep, unresolvable analytical problem because they must somehow be explained as deviations from the industrial or market frameworks of action. This interpretation excludes the possibility of other frameworks of action, such as the interpersonal or the intellectual, as well as the possibility that even markets and industrial action systems are conventionally and collectively constituted, and themselves exhibit great diversity not only in empirical forms but in their makeup and operating principles owing to substantively different action frameworks.

Nonetheless, the main concerns of contemporary institutionalism—in both New Institutional Economics and New Institutional Analysis forms— are similar to those of the social science of conventions: the fundamental uncertainty of understanding and deciding in the context of interdependent action; and the diverse ways this uncertainty is resolved through regularizing interaction between persons. Williamson provides a good illustration of how a diversity of objects is a key determinant of economic life.[2] Each kind of asset (object) creates a particular set of problems of action, specific forms of market failure and moral hazard, distinct possibilities for opportunism, and particular means of adapting institutions so as to resolve the dilemmas of human failure. As shown in our analysis of worlds of production based on the forms of uncertainty associated with different kinds of products, all collective action is not alike, and the objects of the economy are a key way of understanding the diversity of forms such action must take. Yet the similarity ends there.

Work within these schools opens up extremely important questions and generates major insights into the nature and properties of institutions and markets, but falls short inasmuch as it fails to appreciate the diversity of frameworks of action that can underlie efficient production. As a result, its claim that only institutions which mimic the market—essentially a situation of minimal State intervention combined with a contractual legal framework—can possibly lead to economic growth is highly questionable. In contrast, in Chapter 14 we will outline a research program based on recognizing a diversity of frameworks of action.

Objects as Determinant: The New Institutional Economics

THE BASIC HYPOTHESIS OF OBJECTS AND TRANSACTIONS COSTS

The New Institutional Economics proposes a strong solution to the problem of economic institutions, holding that for a given set of economic objects there is a deterministic relationship to efficient forms of economic organization, which it terms "governance structures." It makes this argument by showing that objects, or assets, have intrinsic attributes which generate transactions costs, and these act as a signaling device to decisionmakers. Hence, the appellation "transactions cost economics": "Transactions costs are economized by assigning transactions (which differ in their attributes) to governance structures (the adaptive capacities and associated costs of which differ) in a discriminating way."[3]

This approach recognizes a good deal of complexity in determining transactions costs. Physical-technical determinants are most important: the specificity of assets and their degree of technological divisibility define a general range of possible economies or diseconomies of scope (range of activities) for the firm. These factors give rise to transactions costs which are determined, in turn, by the information or knowledge dimensions of transactions: directly, through the codifiability, tacitness, ease or difficulty of transmission or diffusion of information; and indirectly, through the influence of these characteristics on the possible frequency, regularity, and complexity of asset deployment, purchase, or use and hence the role of markets in guiding the behavior of asset deployers.[4] Thus, the intrinsic characteristics of these objects-assets are decisive in defining the respective roles of markets, contracts, and hierarchies to guide the actions of individuals who deploy them.

Market governance involves the highest potential transactions costs, and is selected "when the specific identity of parties is of negligible importance, substantive content is determined by reference to the formal terms of the contract, and legal rules apply."[5] When assets are of low specificity, supply will be abundant and information will flow freely, hence real unit transactions costs will be low. But transactions cost economics shows that conditions for efficient market relationships in asset deployment do not exist in a wide variety of circumstances, especially those involving small numbers, where there are no substitutable resources ("rival" goods) and ex ante or ex post uncertainty is high, or where buyers or suppliers could have different quantities or qualities of information from one another. These market failures require other forms of organization.

When agents avoid the market through internalization, the result is a hierarchical form of governance known as the firm. Hierarchy is chosen as a way to avoid excessive transactions costs arising from asset specificity, the difficulties of monitoring suppliers and codifying information, and the high risks the buyer faces in these circumstances because he could be held "hostage" by an opportunistic supplier. The "governance costs" assumed by the firm, and the costs of capacity associated with a high scope and scale of activities, must be less than the transactions costs which are avoided. Intermediate solutions consist of "relational" transacting, especially via contracts, which is chosen when asset specificity is significant, but not so high as to provide benefits to the buying firm (through quasi-rents or avoided transactions costs) that would offset the costs of governance were integration to be chosen.

Governance regimes are ordered by transactions cost economics in such a way that there is a univocal correspondence between the degree of asset specificity of transactions and the level of transactions costs.

The discriminating way by which transactions are assigned to different governance structures is thus conceivable as an adaptive process. Searching for minimizing the sum of costs of production and transactions, parties managing production processes and trade relations learn by experience, scan the relevant opportunities, and choose the right amount of asset specificity according to an established contractual regime. Or, more frequently, having to cope with given asset specificity changes, the parties choose to adapt accordingly the contractual regimes.[6]

The tight correspondence between asset specificity of transactions (physical-technical attributes) and the complexity of governance (information-knowledge attributes) means that institutional arrangements must change in response to one principal variable, the degree of asset specificity. And indeed, this variable is said to explain governance through the mechanism of transactions costs. Economies or diseconomies of scope are, respectively, the effects of efficient hierarchy or efficient markets/relational contracts.

Transactions cost economics is much richer than standard neoclassical economics in treating the firm as a governance structure rather than an individual agent, and in opening up the problem of collective action for the firm. But its analytic model reduces the endless variety, heterogeneity, and diversity of economic objects which constitute its starting point to a general, abstract description of those objects, with the single dimension of degree of asset specificity. Having applied an "industrial" logic to objects, the actions to which those objects are supposedly linked are now amenable to "market" rationality, whether in a pure form or in efficient functional equivalents which transactions cost economics calls "institutions."

Following its intellectual roots in the work of Coase, transactions cost economics intends to show that markets generally work, but that specific instances in which they fail lead to efficient internalization or contracting. Non-market collective action processes are not assigned a fundamental role in the operation of the economy. Institutions are reduced to forms that protect individuals against other individuals where perfect objective market conditions (objects) are not in evidence. The New Institutional Economics can therefore be considered an "industrial" reading of the Market World.

THE CAUSES OF INTERNALIZATION

Transactions cost economics offers a very selective reading of the forces which generate economic organization. Many other plausible explanations exist for the degree of internalization or externalization of production, some of which are summarized in Figure 13.1.

We begin on the ground of the transactions cost economics theory itself, that is, with an asset-driven explanation for the organization of production. In the face of uncertainty and technological change—precisely the conditions we place at the center of economic development and coordination—the comparative statics of transactions cost economics theory do not work. As Seravalli[7] shows, acting to minimize transaction costs, both before (ex ante) and after (ex post) making the organizational decision (that is, whether to internalize, externalize, or engage in relational contracting) does not always lead buyers to provide suppliers with the right incentives to invest (create and maintain assets). In particular, when there are significant uncertainties attached to the possibility of improving the supplier's performance (and hence, improving the supplier's contribution to the buyer's performance), the buyer, by minimizing ex ante transactions costs as a way to ensure maximum monitoring of the supplier,[8] will often fail to provide the supplier with sufficient investment incentives to survive and thus contribute to the buyer's performance over the long term. In other words, a strict approach using ex ante contracts to cut down on ex post risks and costs will often push firms into underpaying suppliers, with

	Goal	
	Economizing	Maximizing
Asset/Investment/Information-Driven Explanations	TCE (Coase, 1937; Williamson, 1985)	Property Rights: Multiperiod incentives to deploy/agency (Seravalli, 1992; Grossman and Hart, 1986)
Production/Substantive Explanations	Complementary vs. Similar Tasks (Richardson, 1972)	Technology: Converging or Diverging (Influences complementarity/similarity + appropriability, path dependency) (Dosi and Salvatore, 1992; Foray, 1990)
	Entry Barriers, Scale (Caves and Porter, 1979; Jacquemin, 1985)	
	Learning reduces TCs (Langlois, 1991)	Conceptual Frameworks: Substantive Content of Work-growth regime (Piore, 1992)
	Growth (Stigler, 1951)[a] (Chicago Classical Revival)	

Figure 13.1 Explanations of efficient institutional arrangements in production. (a) Cf. Romer, 1986; Bellandi, 1988.

the result that suppliers will not have the resources they need to contribute fully to the buyer's performance at a later time.[9]

Another perspective, the "property rights approach," goes entirely in the other direction, stressing the investment incentives needed to motivate optimal performance.[10] The "general principle determining allocation of ownership is that the greater a party's inclination to affect the mean income an asset can generate, the greater is the share of the residual that party assumes . . . If the party that will be more inclined to affect the outcome by varying the level of an attribute is put in control of that attribute, becoming therefore the residual claimant, misallocation will be minimized."[11] But this principle cannot be realized in many cases, for example when there are fixed costs irrespective of the result—costs which affect the mean income but cannot be varied. Organizational choices, in other words, are determined by much more than each party's role in making variable investments and their payoffs from those investments; the value of the results net of the other party's (buyer's or supplier's) fixed cost, and the probability of repeated incremental improvement, must be considered. The property rights approach, in other words, is not a simple replacement for transactions costs' concern with ex ante versus ex post costs under uncertainty. Both are deficient, it seems, in dealing with uncertain repeated improvements where there are investment and effort interdependencies between buyers and suppliers.

The transactions cost economics approach, because of its "distrust" factor, would tend to encourage buyers to underpay suppliers ex ante in certain situations; the property rights approach would tend to require suppliers making big initial fixed investments to take a big share of gains, irrespective of the repeated gains. The transactions cost economics school does admit that assuming there will be no "ex post surprises" could present a problem, and that it is extremely difficult to develop a cost-sharing rule which provides, simultaneously, incentive for the agent to be productive and pays the premium to compensate for added risk. To its credit, transactions cost economics does not propose the artificial device of complete complex contracts (for example, permitting ex post adjustment of appropriation of rents), but admits such contracts do not exist: so we are in the realm of real risks and real uncertainties. Instead, it proposes to divide the coordination problem into an ex ante stage (a "first order economizing problem") consisting of aligning transactions in terms of governance, and a "second order refinement" consisting of adjustment to efficient risk bearing.

Thus, the New Institutional Economics simply shifts the consequences of the uncertainty associated with changes in technology, organization, and products to a later time period. Neither the transactions cost approach nor the property rights approach offers a way for actors to move from ex ante "signals" to the best possible ex post institutional arrangements in the discriminating way claimed by the authors of these theories. Economizing on transactions costs ex ante, as we have seen, does not suffice; the arrangements must be adapted ex post, and there is nothing in ex ante economizing that ensures either the best possible innovative dynamic or the best possible ex post institutional arrangements. The central theoretical claim of the New Institutional Economics, that of a monotonic and determinate relationship between transactions costs and governance structures, falls apart in the face of uncertainty, the basic condition of all economic life.

THE SUBSTANTIVE CONTENT OF PRODUCTION

There are reasons other than dynamic uncertainties that should lead us to be skeptical about notions of optimal determinate institutional arrangements. Transactions cost economics sets out to reject the technological determinism of neoclassical approaches to the firm, which hold that technological configurations and price theory generate the contours of economic organization. Yet, in stressing the unique relevance of adaptive transactions cost economizing, this approach loses focus on the substantive content of production projects (except in their abstract form as combinations of assets). Our epistemological point of departure in pragmatics leads to the view that production systems are organized as distinct ensembles of objects, routines, and conventions. These ensembles are largely indivisible, in the sense that the parts of the ensemble are highly interdependent in both physical and cognitive terms. The assets of each such ensemble have strongly created histories and specificities, and thus give substantive content to the possible forms of production.[12]

Some production-based accounts of economic organization appropriately return our attention to the twin questions of the qualities of productive resources ("assets") and the origins of these qualities. In a seminal article, Richardson[13] considers the division of labor from a non-Coasian perspective, arguing that tasks and their associated technologies may be seen in light of their substantive characteristics. He explains strong linkage relationships in the economy as the consequence of two basic kinds of attraction: "similar" activities require the same core knowledge and skills, or may draw on the same kinds of tools (capital goods), and give rise to economies of scope (and, usually, scale) inside the firm or establishment; "complementary" activities are necessary to a given type of product, but may not be within the capabilities of the buying firm, and hence will be relegated to other firms or establishments. The two must then be coordinated; they show up statistically as dense input-output coefficients. Note that similarity and complementarity, as defined, will not have a straightforward relationship to the degree of asset specificity: similarity may be the result of knowledge spillovers which are not necessarily highly specific in nature; and complementarity might involve dedicated (in this case, specific) assets which are more optimally combined with other activities than with the activities of the buying firm.[14]

The question then becomes: what generates the qualities of those assets? The answer requires a positive conceptualization of industrial specialization and interconnection, showing how a variety of processual forces redefine the terms of similarity and complementarity, and the terrain of risk, over time. The boundaries of firms, for example, may be thought of as driven by the rate of change in product and process technologies, the direction of that change (convergence versus divergence), and the extent to which benefits from emergent capabilities can be appropriated.[15] As we discussed above, some institutional arrangements could allow the possibility of net gains from repeated improvements; this implies that the arrangements themselves may shape some of the innovation behavior and, hence, the evolution of similarities, complementarities, and appropriabilities.[16] Nor are similarities and complementarities, moreover, limited merely to the characteristics of assets; they also enter into the cognitive dimensions of production. This was the message of Arrow's[17] seminal treatment of the subject. The "horizons of control" do not necessarily correspond to the degree of asset specificity, because the so-called informational attributes of transactions do not follow the same lines as the cognitive-informational dimensions of production. The *pragmatic substance* of a world of production dominates its transactional dimensions in militating for a particular form of production organization.

Similarities and complementarities also depend on other paths: all input-output systems are user-producer systems, where the practices of one set of technology producers may importantly limit, foreclose, or otherwise influence the choices of users, and vice versa. Allyn Young[18] attempted to capture this by suggesting the cumulative and self-propelling nature of technological change and the division of labor in the modern economy, leading to what Kaldor, interpreting Young more than forty years later, called the "irrelevance of equilibrium."[19] Young suggested that the external interdependencies of users and producers (inter-firm trade) are intimately related to the internal boundaries of the firm. Changes in what is available outside the firm can generate efficient changes in its internal economies of scope, and such change has a cumulative and path-dependent character.[20] It is possible that such changes could be attributed to the overall scale of the economy, but the divisibility of activities also depends on what Piore[21] calls the "substantive" organizational content of any growth process: the fact that it is built on real, endogenously produced objects, themselves intimately tied into the conceptual frameworks used to approach products and productive activity. Foray and Garrouste push this conception further, arguing that production processes cannot be collapsed into the traditional production function, for they consist of multiple autonomous systems including basic product design, service characteristics of the product (evolution of uses), and the production technique (mechanizability, potential economies of scale).[22] Each is, to some extent, the result of outside determinants; the emergent effects of those determinants in the three spheres must then be brought together in a coherent manner. There is a constrained endogeneity of institutional arrangements; for the organizers of production, these arrangements are the result of a field of tactics, strategies, and emergent significations of their goals (much as was captured by the now-unfashionable modern organizational theory).[23]

All of this suggests that the notion, dear to transactions cost economics analysis, that institutional arrangements can be explained primarily as outcomes of "adaptive economizing" of both ex ante and ex post costs is highly doubtful. The configuration of products and productive assets responds to forces more powerful than transactions costs themselves.

THE SUBSTANTIVE CONTENT OF COORDINATION

The substantive content of coordination is not revealed through the New Institutional Economics' notion of governance as degree of internalization.[24] Figure 13.2 suggests that the degree of internalization of production is not straightforwardly related to the degree of market or degree of hierarchy.[25] The degree of internalization, shown on the vertical axis, refers to the extent to which a firm owns and controls a set of activities and/or the assets involved through transactions with other firms. In internal transactions, the firm has majority ownership and direct control; in external transactions, it has little ownership and direct control; in intermediate transactions, it has some degree of influence short of majority ownership and strong direct control.

Our analysis is that coordination of production is a complex, multifaceted form of collective action going far beyond what the governance literature analyzes. But let us assume, for the purpose of argument, that governance boils down to the nature and degree of power, as the governance literature claims. There are three basic kinds of governance as power. Market governance involves significant use of price or other quantitative equivalence measures; impersonality and lack of engagement are the rule. Hierarchical governance involves transactions mediated by authority or power (for example, contracts), whether through explicit and formalized rules, or through informal and personalized arrangements (for example, charisma). Relational governance involves relatively durable linkages with mutual dependencies, often through complex, non-monetary exchanges; it also tends to involve greater mutual knowledge and smaller numbers than market relations.

As Figure 13.2 suggests, different modes of governance can occur inside and outside the firm, and therefore the degree of internalization of transactions does not correspond neatly to a particular mode of governance. Apparently similar institutional forms may also be manifestations of different governance structures. Moreover, the benefits of economies of scale and scope may be realized through various combinations of the mode of governance and level of internalization. Thus, movements from market to relational to hierarchical governance do not, in any case, reveal the substantive content of the coordination of productive activity, nor necessarily show what kinds of incentives or administrative controls are used, or the form of contract law which underlies enforcement, or even the process of adaptation to change—all of which transactions cost economics claims as "discriminant" features of market, hybrid, and hierarchical governance regimes. For example, a firm might externalize through strong or weak relational subcontracting (supposed to reflect the difference between quasi-firm and quasi-disintegration). Likewise, within the firm, there can be vastly different regimes of attachment of workers to the organization, as in the American internal labor market and the Japanese lifetime employment system. These differences cannot be explained away with notions of numbers and specificities for the very reason that they seem to be largely outcomes of institutional and conventional arrangements.[26]

Governance and internalization, even taken together, thus do not explain the deeper problem of coordination of real worlds of production.

MODE OF GOVERNANCE

	Market	Relational	Hierarchical
Internal	Multi-Divisional Firms and Internal Labor Markets Market Industrial Interpersonal	Lifetime Employment: Basic Research and Development Interpersonal Intellectual Industrial	Unitary Firms: Labor Unions Industrial Market Interpersonal
Intermediate	Diversification Mergers Industrial Market Intellectual	Joint Ventures Business Groups Interpersonal	Horizontal Mergers Industrial Interpersonal
External	Exporting: Purchasing Standard Parts Market Industrial	Relational Subcontracting: Industry Associations Interpersonal	Cartel's Licensing: Government Mediation Interpersonal/Market Industrial/Intellectual

Figure 13.2   Coordination, governance, and internalization.

Figure 13.2 suggests that the forms of governance-internalization described in the cells may be underpinned by different possible worlds and hence held together by substantively different forms of coordination. Membership of any particular production system in these three dimensions is something like a fuzzy set: consider the different arrangements in the Japanese "J-form" external-relational firm in the automobile industry and the U.S. "M-form" internal-hierarchical firm, or the differences between Germany's relatively intermediate-relational mechanical engineering industry and the Italian external-relational,[27] or between the French aerospace industry's internal and external hierarchical governance and its American counterpart's internal and external market governance.[28] These are not mere differences in degree of internalization or externalization or in mode of governance, but substantively different forms of coordination, in different real worlds of production, held together by the different action frameworks of the participants.

PROCESS AND BEHAVIOR IN INSTITUTIONAL EVOLUTION

What could give rise to such differences? Even if actors were simply interest-seeking, maximizing, and opportunistic, markets alone would not generate institutional arrangements because, as we have seen, there are no unique ex ante efficient institutional solutions for a given set of assets, and because assets themselves are chosen and developed by actors in the context of technological change and other forms of true uncertainty.

The response from the New Institutional Economics is twofold. First, it relegates such differences to the exogenous "institutional environment." Transactions cost economics says little about the genesis of such environments; it merely analyzes their efficiency properties. Second, transactions cost economics claims that, in the absence of environmental impediments, the two-step adjustment process referred to earlier—first-order (ex ante) transactions costs economizing and second order (ex post) adaptation to efficient risk bearing—will bring institutional reality which corresponds to predictions of its model. To do this, the New Institutional Economics makes choices something like a proxy for the Market World: reversible, substitutable, adjustable.[29] But if this is the argument, it comes at the price of explaining real rules and institutions, and the New Institutional Economics becomes a sophisticated solipsism within the domain of the orthodox paradigm.

To construct a more effective theory, at least two major elements would have to be included: a realistic view of motivations, and a means to analyze behavioral interdependencies as a constructed social force that plays an independent role in economic evolution. Thus far we have been silent on behavioral issues, attempting only to show why, in economic terms, a deterministic link between objects and production organization does not exist. But claims about the institutional shape of production eventually rest, as do all economic theories, on conceptions of human behavior. The New Institutional Economics has been aptly labeled the "new Hobbesianism"[30] and the "economics of suspicion"[31] because of its emphasis on moral hazards and opportunism, and the notion that governance is essentially about protecting oneself from such risks. Orthodox economics has been roundly criticized for the narrowness of its theory of motivations by many and sundry scholars,[32] and these critiques surely apply to the New Institutional Economics.

The debate is not resolved simply by asserting that humans might have differentiated motivations, stemming from the socialized character of human existence. This would reduce all outcomes to the effects of actors' motivations and intentions,[33] and it is difficult to imagine finding any regularity or coherence in institutional arrangements if they were simply a matter of differentiated "internal" motivations. The question as embodied in the theory of possible and real worlds is how some motivations and principles become embedded in mutual engagement, in pragmatic contexts which involve material as well as social factors.[34] Such engagements come to have irreversibilities and limited substitutability because they constitute systems of external interdependencies among actors.[35]

The New Institutional Analysis:
The Microfoundations of Collective Failure

In recent years, the New Institutional Analysis has devoted a great deal of attention to two closely related problems: the generation of institutional environments (in the sense of rules, collective behavior, practices) in the economy, and their effects on economic performance.[36] Collective behavior is seen to be analytically problematic, in that it assumes a wide variety of observable forms, with widely varying impacts on economic development.

Since at least the mid-nineteenth century, social science—in concert with the rise of liberalism and bourgeois society—has been preoccupied with establishing a foundation for social order based on the pursuit of self-interest.[37] As a theory of human behavior, however, self-interest has always contained a set of unresolvable tensions:

> Its psychology is too anemic and its sociology too muscular. Lacking a developed analysis of motivation, it has been constantly forced to oscillate between a narrow and superficial utilitarianism that sees men as impelled by rational calculation of their consciously recognized personal advantage and a broader but no less superficial historicism that speaks with a studied vagueness of men's ideas as somehow "reflecting," "expressing," "emerging from," "conditioned by" their social commitments.[38]

As a result, mainstream social science has attempted to soften the rational choice version of interest-based theory with such notions as culture, norms, and traditions to explain coordination (and, for that matter, conflict). Marxist and other brands of "critical" social science have attempted to resolve the (so-called) contradiction of elite rationality but popular domination by considering culture and norms as forms of ideology and supports for the hegemony of the elites.

Both these theoretical positions have, in turn, created additional problems. They are not very helpful in explaining a changing landscape of institutional design in such spheres as labor markets, firms, and family structure. Norms, ideologies, and cultures do not seem to shift in concert with changes in detailed collective practices. Early attempts to deal with this empirical mismatch pointed to "lags" and "gaps" between motivation and practice; they also implied that the different motivations were really not very important at all, since everyone would sooner or later take the same basic developmental pathway. The turn to massive empiricism in mainstream social science followed on this, with attempts to discover complex determinants of practices (multifactorial analysis in sociology, for example). Much of this work proved descriptively interesting but unable to explain or predict patterns of change.[39]

Marxist/critical theories attempted to deal with change through the notion of conflict, but in so doing often collapsed all conflict into the notion of interest- (class-)based struggle. Moreover, they never succeeded in reconciling this with their notion of domination, or in identifying why and when "truth" and "struggle" take over from domination.[40] Mainstream theories, meanwhile, engaged in an ad hoc search for breakdowns in norms, transformation rules, and so on to explain conflict. All these perspectives, in effect, generally exaggerated, hypostatized, or internalized the sources of social order in the presence of a schizophrenic split between order and breakdown.[41] Notions of order and its disruption are also present in economics, of course, where order is a growth model and crisis the rupture of the model or structure of growth.

The New Institutional Analysis emerged in this theoretical context of post-1960s social science, with its home in political science, economics, and law. It purports to rescue the interest-based theory of human behavior and social order by showing that the observed diversity of relations between individual choices and collective outcomes is due to a series of micro-coordination problems. The New Institutional Analysis thus breaks with macrohistorical and structural approaches to coordination and substitutes methodological individualism; internalized norms, ideologies, even collective self-interest are replaced by a focus on interactions among actors pursuing their interests. The New Institutional Analysis represents a dramatic turn in the analysis of institutions, and its work has been conducted with a huge and powerful arsenal of micro-analytical models and tools, most notably those connected with game theory.

It is telling that most New Institutional Analysis is not only interest-based, but for the most part rooted in rational choice. Three "parables" underpin rational choice analysis: (1) individual, egotistical action can give rise to social organization of maximum benefit to all individual members of society, when markets operate freely; (2) the consequences of making rational choices generally allow the intentions governing those choices to be realized; (3) collective action is a form of social behavior found only in exceptional circumstances, since it is rational for the self-interested individual to opt out of collective actions. Note that the "market" definition of collective action prevails in these parables.[42] The New Institutional Analysis centers on four common circumstances which, if present, block collective action: (a) divergent or partially divergent interests;[43] (b) bounded rationality or information, or important transactions costs, or hierarchical structures;[44] (c) differences between payoffs to coalitions (concertation), groups, and individuals (distributional problems);[45] and (d) uncertainty about or difficulty in predicting the future.[46]

Putting these together, the New Institutional Analysis concludes that there are three dimensions of attempts to act collectively: (a) it is difficult to establish coordination (the problem of *concertation* among agents);[47] (b) it is difficult to sustain existing forms of coordination (the problem of *instability* of coalitions, and principal-agent relations);[48] and (c) it is difficult to undo existing forms, even where they are not efficient (institutional *sclerosis*).[49]

These kinds of unfavorable real outcomes, which block the potential efficiencies of actors' rational (or boundedly rational) choices, have to do mostly with inappropriate institutional environments. To deal with this, not surprisingly, most of the New Institutional Analysis devotes its attention to institutional "solutions" that involve efficiency-based contract and property rights law.

OLSON'S PESSIMISM

Mancur Olson's seminal work in the New Institutional Analysis[50] holds that free rider behavior, resulting from uncooperative (prisoner's dilemma) interactions, is the norm in social life. The basic tendency in a group is for some people to take advantage of others, and thus to destabilize social collectivities. As a result, society must provide the basis for continuous purging of free rider behavior; it does this by letting markets and contracts operate freely, supported by the meta-institution of stable, codifiable, and transactable property rights. Olson embraces property-based contracts because of his pessimism about institutionalized social order.

Olson's work appears to be based on a very selective reading of the circumstances in which action unfolds. On one hand, there are circumstances in which the free rider problem does not seem dominant; on the other, the envisioned pure world of property- and interest-based contracts is itself subject to serious breakdowns, suggesting that underlying even contractual relationships are forms of social coordination not considered by the New Institutional Analysis.[51] Let us look at these two issues.

Olson's pessimism about the possibility of rational, interest-based coordination among actors needs to be tempered, following Williamson, by considering the *transactions costs* involved in interaction. Where such costs are low, free rider effects can be controlled; consider the case of small, internally coherent groups, where effective monitoring is possible, and where the spread of capabilities is quite narrow, so that payoffs are proportionate to effort. In such situations, a high degree of solidarity is sustainable. In smaller countries, for example, coalitions formed in the face of foreign trade have at times overcome class antagonisms through wage solidarity and welfare state policies.[52] In addition, there has also been, historically, a high level of localist "voluntarism" in the United States, a large, heterogeneous country. But Olson's vision limits interpersonal relations to a question of ongoing individualist calculus in small groups, and does not admit the possibility that such interactions might have some recursive identity-forming effect.

Olson also overestimates the applicability of contracts. Some frameworks of action are not based on underlying premises of contractual interactions. The idea of trading the particularities of individuals (specialized know-how or idiosyncratic assets) in the form of exchangeable property is consistent with the Market World, where the individual is sovereign with respect to the domain of action and the contract is an exchange of particularities. Using tradable rights, other sovereign individuals can acquire competences or assets and use them as they wish. By contrast, for individuals inscribed in the Interpersonal World (for different products, of course), particularities are decisive for the outcome. The efficiency of the overall effort depends on the degree of "personality" (not the same thing as what contract theories reduce to "idiosyncrasy") of persons and other productive assets (what we called "substantive content" above), and not on the form of transactions applied to them. Contracts cannot cover the contingent claims arising from such complex interdependencies, and hierarchies are unlikely to motivate actors in this way.

THE ABSOLUTISM OF PUBLIC CHOICE
THEORY'S CONTRACTUAL WORLD

Another branch of the New Institutional Analysis, public choice theory, goes even further in transforming the three parables of rational choice theory into a normative vision of the economy. Public choice theory comes out of Chicago and follows Coase, and its key assumption sets it apart from Olson: transactions costs are assumed in general to be low. The costs of coming together, dissolving relationships, and recontracting are insignificant; this promotes institutional fluidity. Agents resemble perfectly substitutable "inputs" to collective action: they come together via contracts (formal or implicit) in relationships that look something like spot markets. As long as the bundling together of actors and their redivision is perfectly elastic, there are no free rider problems.[53] Likewise, there are no principal-agent[54] problems because all institutions are immediate and perfectly reversible combinations of the principals' interests. The coordination that emerges is thus a perfect representation of interests, and institutional equilibria are the outcome of the "marketplace" for representation and coordination. Public choice theory is ultimately an institution-free theory of social life, where the very need for coordination is eliminated by axiom.[55]

Public choice theory likens the large numbers of actors who flow into and out of alliances to perfect markets: high levels of turnover of individual buyers of standardized interchangeable "products" give stability to the structure of the market. The important insight is that interest-based behavior does not lead to cheating or opportunism in the presence of perfect information, reversibility, and large numbers: human nature is not pleasant, but it is kept in check by competition. It is up to organizations to compete for the attention of participants and resources in such projects.

The assumption underlying this analysis sees complete equivalence between individuals who "consume" institutional services. When their individual particularities are taken into account, the idea of large numbers—and hence of choice—collapses. If there are specialized, specific, idiosyncratic institutional resources in the economy, which must be produced with long latency periods and in small numbers, the solution is, naturally, contracts. The problem here is that such thorny issues as asymmetries of resources (leading to imperfect competition among groups vying for the "attention" of principals), imperfect information, bounded rationality (due to transactions costs, ideology, identity, history) are not considered as possible dimensions of the contracting process. It is difficult to imagine how contracts alone would coordinate actors so as to produce the results described by the three parables.

In any case, public choice theory offers no mechanisms that provide the stability needed to carry out some of these relationships, especially those not amenable to full contracting. The only possible solution is recourse to higher or hierarchical forms of coordination, that is, certain "social contracts" that regulate lower-level contracts. But here the problem of tyranny of majorities sets in: the rules established at one level could impede "exchanges" at lower levels, notably those of different possible worlds.[56] Public choice, in other words, depends on a constitutional order that promotes perfect competition and exchange, but says nothing about the potentially contradictory nature of an order that would crush all other orders in the name of perfect liberty of exchange (the contradiction of a "liberal state as policeman" noted in Chapter 10).

Public choice theory in institutional analysis puts us back at the elementary starting point of the New Institutional Economics, that is, the need to confront the widespread existence of market failure, the barriers to full contracting, and the non-contractual supports of contingent claims contracts.[57]

THE AUTONOMOUS FORMATION OF GROUPS AND INSTITUTIONS: PRINCIPALS AND AGENTS

In reaction to the institution-free theories reviewed above, another line of inquiry has drawn on Kenneth Arrow's social choice work on the instabilities and paradoxes of majority rule.[58] It recognizes the pervasive stability of political institutions, and the continuity of many other forms of institutions and practices, and credits these qualities to the fact that institutional rules eliminate much instability by systematically constraining the alternatives available to actors and decision-makers. The "positive theory of institutions" is an effort to provide a theoretical foundation for understanding why and how this occurs and with what consequences for collective choice.[59]

The positive theory of institutions centers on the "principal-agent" problem: holding that interest groups and formal institutions (which are agents) function to bundle and represent the interests of their members (who are principals).[60] They do so imperfectly because they must have rules for reaching decisions in the absence of perfect consensus and often in the presence of very important transactions costs. Groups bundle interests which may overlap only partially, and their members may have other allegiances as well (they may belong to other bundles, so groups as a whole may have only a rough correspondence to their principals' preference structures); the cohesion of the bundles may be more or less intense, as a result of differences in group size, levels of acquaintance, and reputation (and there will be different transactions costs associated with these). Agents who come out of these different internal structures and represent them must then interact with the agents of other groups, in situations which range from highly formalized and rule-bound to extremely informal.[61] All of this means that institutions and collective practices channel the expression of even rationally calculated interests. It also means that outcomes can be relatively insensitive to shifting patterns of basic interests, even those interests explicitly recognized by principals. The particular institutional location of interest-bundled groups, the ways in which they mobilize resources, the ways in which critical rules in a hierarchy of rules are manipulated or implemented, and so on, will determine the relationship among interests, choices, and outcomes (as manifested in qualities and quantities of cooperation or conflict).

This is a universe radically different from the perfect markets of public choice theory. Obviously, this vein of theorizing has a greater grasp on the variety of dimensions of collective order and their relationship to coordination than does the simple theory of rational, interest-based choice. The individual is no longer the same figure: still pursuing his or her interests, but in the principal-agent framework, and so recognizing that at least some particularities are shared by others. The complete separation between fixed individual interests and common goals disappears insofar as individuals must aggregate like interests in order to pursue their own. Our theory of possible worlds shares this concern with the ways individuals belong to groups and participate in coordination.

The sensitivity to principals-agents and the relationship of interests to institutional order are taken in a number of different directions in the New Institutional Analysis literature, each insisting on different dimensions of the problem of coordination. The first approach, inspired by Olson,[62] reveals the potency of small group cohesion due to low free rider effects and transactions costs. As we noted above, small cohesive groups have a disproportionate influence on decision-making because they make relatively few internal compromises (the bundling of principals and agents is "clean"). Only in small, homogeneous societies can coalitions be expected to bundle and represent adequately the interests of the society as a whole (as in the encompassing inter-class coalitions in small countries mentioned earlier).[63] In big, diverse societies, coalitions will be partial and hence ultimately ineffectual: over time they either become unstable because they are so internally compromised that they cannot pursue any set of goals with clarity and force, or they become more extreme in order to play to especially cohesive interests. This suggests a critical problem for democratic order: the possibility that either elites or extremist interest groups will have inordinate influence, and that it will be difficult to form and maintain broad-based ("encompassing") coalitions of any sort (including political parties, diffuse economic or social coalitions, and so on). The results are not consistent with respect to the initial distribution of interests and desires of wide majorities.[64] It is virtually impossible to satisfy complex forms of social preference, and most people end up in less than full accord with what their agents (institutions) are doing.

It would seem that we are back to a theory of strain and deep instability. Yet the same circumstances seem to lead to conservatism and stability for a second line of theorists, the Marxist rational choice school.[65] They ask why the working class prefers continuity (capitalism) to change (socialism). The answer is that, given an existing pattern of income distribution, the very high transactions costs of organizing a fragmented working class, and the risks of failure due to free rider problems (defection), it is rational, from the standpoint of most existing workers, not to risk what they have in the struggle for a transition to socialism. Again, the problem is one of forming encompassing coalitions, but here asymmetry of resources is added to the equation.

The principal-agent literature has explored the pioneering thought of Arrow and produced many valuable insights. But its equations result in radical swings between pessimism and optimism, because outcomes are extremely sensitive to small assumptions. At the same time, they are totally insensitive to anything resembling recursively formed group identity, the practical goals of human collective activity, or the role of independent reflection and action in generating new rounds of precedent and convention.

The point of departure for the economic historian Douglass North is the existence of high transactions costs, and his theoretical assumption is that principals' and agents' particular interests are to survive, rather than to maximize their own or society's "global" interests.[66] As a consequence, social coordination in one period ultimately becomes institutional sclerosis in another. Only when exogenous factors (that is, events contrary to the intentions of interested actors or, in the terminology of rational choice theory, "counterfinal" outcomes) disrupt the continuation of the existing order is it possible to reshape institutions and restore efficient forms of economic coordination. Therefore, the only good institutions are meta-rules to prevent sclerosis, such as perfected property rights, which promote continuous competition and disrupt the survival strategies of particular interest groups. Competition is the medicine for the disease of sclerosis.

North constructs a coherent theory of coordination within the Market World. According to this theory, it is useless to construct institutions that correct failures of commitment over time, because all coordination is instantaneous: an optimal economic history is a succession of instantaneous "market" optima. To realize these optima, individuals must be protected from barriers which might be placed in the path of their exercise of sovereignty. Only the State, acting to maintain market action, especially by perfecting property rights and their transferability, is viewed as absolutely necessary. The paradox here is very strong, although not always well understood in the literature: only a return to instantaneity can allow a real historical dynamic in the economy to unfold.

The Limits of Contemporary Institutionalism

In their sensitivity to collective action, uncertainty, and diversity of situations, both the New Institutional Analysis and New Institutional Economics versions of contemporary institutional analysis represent major advances for social science. They go beyond the inability of orthodox economics to deal with real institutions, and beyond the tendency in much of social science to relegate problems of action to theories of norms or supra-individual structures.

But both approaches have positive assumptions and normative ambitions that limit their explanatory power. Their theoretical architecture combines suppositions about human behavior with respect to a diversity of objective situations (and objects and group structures) that make it possible to predict outcomes in the form of resulting efficient, or blocked, institutional arrangements: for the New Institutional Economics, the organization of production systems, firms, and contracts; for the New Institutional Analysis, overall growth-maximizing institutional environments or failures thereof. The theories have strong, substantive views about what elements constitute optimal institutions; they imitate closely the economic outcomes of perfect markets by compensating for the human failures that lead to market failures. They find unique correspondences between behaviors, objective situations, and efficient outcomes. Any deviations from such outcomes are attributed to institutional environments that block actors from attaining optima.

The New Institutional Analysis and the New Institutional Economics, much like neoclassical economics, arrogate to themselves a very strong normative vocation. They instruct us to create environments that eliminate the major classes of human failures or moral dangers, including credible political regimes, contractual environments (with their well-ordered rules and procedures), and, of course, de-bureaucratization (on the presumption that internalization creates disincentives to efficiency).[67] In the end, however, the theory leaves us far from its initial commitment to analyze the diversity intrinsic to the objects that define economic action, in a land where there is strong suspicion of anything that would seem to create ties between persons except those that closely imitate market competition. Anything else is bound to reproduce moral dangers.

As a result, both the New Institutional Analysis and the New Institutional Economics view the idea of resolving problems of human failure through collective action exclusively in terms of institutions that limit actors' ability to take advantage of their necessary interdependencies. Although the New Institutional Analysis correctly calls our attention, as social scientists, to the need to be hard-headed and realistic about the uncertainties of others' actions and the possibility of mutually damaging self-interested behavior, not to mention evil, it cannot analyze the existence of and bases for coordination between persons in the construction of social life.

Successful pathways to economic development are not merely the residual results of an absence of moral dangers and the presence of incentives, but the product of mobilizing resources and constructing coordination among persons based in different frameworks of action. Actors construct real worlds of production, with their corresponding products and frameworks of action, over many trajectories; these are at the root of a real diversity much greater than that incorporated in contemporary institutional analysis. Indeed, this is the process which contemporary institutional analysis would eclipse. But that view employs a rather simplistic psychology, leading to a normative and optimizing vision of the process of economic development, rooted in an unsustainable opposition between individuals and institutions.

14

TOWARD A THEORY OF CONVENTIONS, ECONOMIC ACTION, AND ECONOMIC DEVELOPMENT

From Concertation to Convention; From Convention to Action

One branch of the New Institutional Analysis does open up a fruitful line of inquiry, in the guise of the problem of *concertation*. It has been widely observed that certain patterns of interaction in economic life are stable not "in spite of" the actors' interests (as in the Marxist view of the risks of change, North's sclerosis, Olson's difficulty of collective action, or Arrow's social ordering), nor because they conform to actors' obvious interests. Concertation is most often seen as the outcome of accidental (or exogenous) and fortuitous circumstances, such as when small, homogeneous groups form coalitions or come together in the presence of external threats.

But some analysts see another possible route to concertation, one that concerns endogenous institutional innovations within the process of concertation itself.[1] These analyses take as their starting point Axelrod's[2] key observation that the best strategy in interaction for any particular group of actors is tit-for-tat, whether or not there are underlying distributional tradeoffs. In other words, concertation results from making current commitments involving sacrifices and risks with the prospect of realizing future gains jointly with others, but about which distributional conflicts may well arise. This notion of collective gains in spite of possible distributional conflict goes against the grain of most of the New Institutional Analysis.

Concertation is influenced by the ways actors judge the possible consequences of cooperation (in the language of the New Institutional Analysis, the "probabilities and utilities" they assign to different conditions). These actions include probing the intentions of other actors and devising strategies to influence those actors. Perceptions about the likelihood of cooperation are shaped in part on the basis of the degree of traditional knowledge of others and the degree of mutual acquaintance;[3] the "expected utilities" of cooperation grow greater as information increases and when a particular set of circumstances narrows the possible varieties of future action (such as opportunism or exploitation of short-term advantages).[4] In the course of interaction, actors may develop commitments to institutions themselves, a form of binding their future actions. Moreover, institutions may, by stabilizing certain kinds of risks, make principals more reliable supporters of their agents, hence increasing those agents' credibility with respect to the agents of other groups of principals. It can be shown, in other words, that learning is involved in chains of interactions which "endogenously" produce rules that actors agree to honor in the face of future uncertainties.

The problem of concertation of groups as formulated by the New Institutional Analysis can be more generally cast as the problem of *coordination of actors*. Game theory has shown that, when some conflict of interest exists—when one person gains more from a given outcome than another but both persons will benefit more from a common solution than if they act with no coordination at all—pure rational choice cannot predict the outcome. This is because the elements of interaction, reflexivity (forming beliefs about the choices others have made) and strategy (taking into account that others are forming beliefs about one's own choices) are involved. The outcomes are not predictable nor determinate from the outset.[5]

David Lewis was the first to explore systematically the possibility that when actors are faced with a recurrent problem of coordination, behavioral regularities can emerge simply as a consequence of repetition, where the regularity is progressively reinforced by that repetition.[6] Lewis shows that the outcomes are progressively "set" by interaction itself, as precedents set up rounds of reinforcing expectations that make given outcomes increasingly more rational. In other words, the chain of expectations is reproduced. These precedents, moreover, have a very wide range of potential origins: they may be explicit agreements but they may also be accidents; extraordinary actions at critical moments may highlight one option rather than another (for example, leadership). Small events may have big outcomes for coordination if they launch chains of interactions.[7]

These "conventional trajectories" do not reflect the best options at the outset, in the sense of the global optima proposed by much rational choice theory; rather, the "efficiencies" become progressively more established as repetitions of behavioral regularity increase, precisely because the consequences of belief become more reliable. In this view, social coordination is not a product of interaction among persons with given, fixed "portfolios" of interests, but a product of the sequence of interactions themselves. Our position draws on the lessons of Lewis, Axelrod, and others, but goes beyond their theme of "salience due to precedent."

Requirements for an Effective Theory of Economic Action

It is now clear that a good theory (perhaps "approach" would be more appropriate) of economic coordination and institutions should be quite different from the contemporary institutionalist efforts while incorporating some of their basic intuitions. The four key qualities of such a framework can now be made explicit.[8]

Realism and Indeterminacy. Hypotheses in social science are normally formulated in one of two ways: deduction, whereby a model is constructed on the basis of assumptions, developed according to a series of logical propositions, and, ideally, tested empirically; or induction, where rigorous empirical observation makes it possible to formulate hypotheses judged to describe the observed reality in lawful form. The analysis outlined in this book incorporates elements of both, but is confined to neither. It is inductive in seeking to understand situations of action from "within," in the sense that it seeks hypotheses which closely follow those situations as they are lived, perceived, and interpreted by the actors themselves: this is how we have defined possible worlds of production. It is deductive in seeking to identify the empirically observable consequences of different situations.

The non-determinate character of actions is the keystone of a viable theory, because that is what actors face in reality: situations which involve uncertainty. Actors do, of course, follow those routines that allow them to avoid posing questions about what to do, but routines themselves must have origins and those are not routinized. Moreover, even in day-to-day interactions, uncertainty is actively present in numerous situations—for example, when there are tensions between different possible analyses of a given situation, and thus between different types of possible action, or when an actor is faced with responses or behaviors of others that are inconsistent with his or her expectations. For economic actors, these fundamental uncertainties can only be relieved through simultaneous action and deduction. It is just this complex opening and closing of action possibilities that we have attempted to theorize as the multiplicity of possible worlds of production.

Many different contemporary economic phenomena call for this theoretical perspective of economic realism and indeterminacy: the development of the assets-objects of the economy; institutional arrangements; and "strong competition" based on product differentiation, technological change, and asymmetric signals and incentives. In all these circumstances, coordination among actors plays an important role—in mobilizing resources, processing signals, responding to incentives, and making choices which drive the objects-assets of the economy down certain pathways rather than others. This is the essence of a complex pragmatic which defines a world of production.

Behavioral Realism and Indeterminacy. The concept of "realism" includes many of the conditions identified in New Institutional Analysis research involving the problematic nature of coordination among actors and the probability of concertation, including risk and uncertainty, bounded rationality and incomplete information, interests (and their fragmentations and overlaps), principal-agent relationships and group size, and transactions costs. But while the New Institutional Analysis assigns preeminent importance to individual interests, behavioral realism and indeterminacy require that interests be placed in the context of interactions and prior experiences. These experiences are the results of boundedly rational choices which are in turn caught up in continuously forming circles of expectations; as a result, interests (preferences) are themselves highly endogenous and open to continuous transformation. Behavioral indeterminacy means that in modeling the probabilities of behaviors that will trigger coordination (in our terms, access to possible worlds of production), or behaviors that block coordination or impede transitions from one set of coordination behaviors to a better set, we must take care to stay within the context of the action frameworks and situations of the actors at hand.

Experience, or more exactly the learning of which actors are capable, is key to the way actors interpret data, although such learning does not exist a priori but appears only in some concrete situations. Such acts of interpretation are analogous to the root process underlying many important technological innovations: they depend on widely available knowledge, but do not necessarily follow from it. They require a final, interpretative synthesis which leaps from one paradigm to another. Behavioral realism and its correlate, indeterminacy, are concerned with sorting out configurations of meanings at least as much as they are with the structures of interest so dear to neo-institutionalist thought.[9]

Endogeneity and Historicity. Third, a viable framework must be able to understand endogeneity in both the economic (objects; technology) and the behavioral (coordination) spheres. As we have seen, many dimensions of economic organization are interdependent, sometimes cumulative, and often unpredictable. So, in many senses, are patterns of coordination: the mechanism driving coordination path dependency is not increasing returns, but salience due to precedent,[10] combined with and continuously transformed by reflective interpretation and interaction. Objects and conventional patterns of coordination interact in complex ways.

Diachronic Analysis. This fourth property of a framework puts endogenously generated path-dependent phenomena in the context of the larger environment and the tests it imposes upon them.[11] What is the nature of the developmental dynamic of real worlds of production? Can we discover general lessons about the "growth" process, its historical character, for these conventional systems? Economic analysis normally considers the effects of history as the results of previous periods of accumulation of physical and human "capital" and in terms of formal organizational structures of production and markets. It is this accumulation which determines, at each moment, the capacities and possibilities of the economy at hand. From the perspective of the real worlds of production, however, things are much more complex.

Obviously, conventions will have significant effects on economic performance. Sooner or later, forms of coordination may face external tests, and will do well or poorly. In the medium run, one possible outcome is what New Institutional Analysis theorists identify as sclerosis, which may lead to blocked development. We may actually enlarge the area of circumstances in which sclerosis may develop beyond those envisioned by North by taking into account the diversity of possible worlds, their products, and the action problems associated with them. At any given moment, in any given real world, there exist certain "costs" of access to other possible worlds. When actors of that real world expect such costs to be very high, not just in short-term pecuniary ways but in terms of identities, they may generate negative self-selection processes in the medium term, closing themselves into the existing world. In a sense, this analysis in terms of accessibility costs is a reinterpretation of the notion of institutional sclerosis, but using a much more varied palette as it draws on the multiplicity of possible worlds on which economic development may be based.

The range of self-selection processes is enlarged not only in the negative sense of sclerosis, but in the positive sense of innovation. Positive selection is largely a function of whether existing conventions and institutions have the capacity to adjust accessibility to different possible worlds of production. These conventions define the inner and outer margins of efficient change in any given time period for a group of products and for the competences and actions of persons and the objects they employ in production. As a result, in the medium to long run, conventions select for economic specializations of the territories (localities, regions, nations) over which they operate, through sustained patterns of success and failure.[12] But they do more than this: successful systems of conventions, that is, successful real worlds, "invent" the de facto best products and processes in the sectors in which they operate. Hence, they play a strong role in describing the evolutionary path of those sectors *tout court*. They produce the supplies of certain objects that lead to the "social construction of markets."[13] The economic tests of those sectors are thus themselves path-dependent and subject to strong influence by the generation of products, technologies, and practices from specific conventional systems. It is in this sense that actions, as embodied in conventions, produce the pathway of development of the economy.

The Foundations of Worlds of Production: Categories of Analysis

A framework which meets the requirements set out above must employ analytic categories quite different from those used in much of economics and even much of economic sociology. Figure 14.1 depicts these categories: in the left-hand column, the categories of action of possible worlds of production; in the middle, the conventions and resources which provide access to possible worlds—what institutionalism calls the "environments" actors draw upon in constructing real worlds of production; in the right-hand column, the specific quotidian routines and procedures mobilized in the acts of production and exchange, which make up a model of production.

The figure should be read both from left to right in terms of the passage from possible worlds and from right to left in terms of the unending circle of concrete influences on the possible. Each column may also be read from top to bottom as a logical (but not historical) construct, where—for example—in any given real world of production and exchange (right-hand column), conventions of labor are incorporated in conventions of productivity and both form part of the substance of a successful real product.

Categories of Action. Three categories of action in possible worlds of production emerge from our discussion of economic and behavioral realism, indeterminacy, and endogeneity.

Interpretative activity is the basis for the actions of persons (always

	Categories of Analysis	
Possible Worlds: Categories of Economic Action	The Passage to Reality: Access to Possible Worlds	Real Worlds: Models of Production
Interpretative Activity	**Conventions of Identity**	**Competences to Identify Relevant Actions**
(interests, knowledge, rights, entitlements, duties, norms, time, risks, discounting, capacities, etc.)	resources offered capacities-efforts rights defined duties defined	judgments salience of objects persons
Interaction-Coordination	**Conventions of Participation**	**Conventions of Productivity, Labor and Product Qualities**
probing learning strategies mutual knowledge	numbers entry power compromise rules-contracts loyalty exit	equivalences distributional arrangements roles prices productivity skills efforts capacities
Work and Exchange: Realization of Product	**Resource Endowments**	**Products**
Coherence Qualities of Coherence	physical capital human "capital" organizations market/state institutions income levels	

Figure 14.1   Categories of analysis.

300

situated in a given context of interactions) which generate the conventions of production and exchange, that is, the routines and expectations under which production and exchange are carried out in a coordinated fashion. The activity of work and exchange carried out in this context is key to realizing the product: that activity is founded on the respect of norms of quality and performance, that is, in relationship to an expectation of the real tests which the product will undergo.

We replace the standard focus of economics on "choice" and of institutional analysis on "interest" with interpretative activity; and we substitute its counterpart, "reasonable action," for the standard focus on rationality, maximization, or optimization.[14] Reasonable action has qualities partially defined by the objects at hand, and it unfolds in the course of interactions, through the hypotheses, revisions, and adjustments put forth by actors drawing on different action frameworks. Where interactions are repeated, we can discern never-ending chains of expectation formation and regularities in the ways in which people interpret information. These give concrete content to such dimensions of calculation as interests, rights and entitlements, norms and duties, horizons of time-risks-discounting, understanding of capacities, and perception of distributional issues. They define what is considered reasonable, so that reasonability itself can be regarded as a precedent-dependent phenomenon. The task of analysis here, as we demonstrated in Chapters 6 through 8, is essentially to sort out the chains of meaning and determine their social grounding and import.[15] In this assertion we explicitly reject three other perspectives: the behaviorist approach, which sees people as mere reactors to stimuli; the idealist view, which sees them as motivated exclusively by ideas, tastes, and preferences; and the cognitivist approach (so dear to most of the New Institutional Analysis), which sees action as the product of mental phenomena that can be analyzed by formal methods similar to those of mathematics and logic.

A second domain of action is that of *interaction-coordination*. Though, as we have seen, the New Institutional Analysis has revealed much about certain empirical regularities in individual and group interactions, its approach of "games among rational actors" has two essential flaws: its cognitivist view (rational action as a formal structure), and its exclusion of path dependency and endogenously transforming experience chains. The elements of interaction that we have singled out—including strategy, probing, mutual acquaintance, traditional knowledge, and leadership—affect the extent to which underlying "structural" conditions (included in both game theory and historical studies) are actually understood and, hence, acted upon.[16]

The third category of action is that of *immediate work and exchange.* In decentralized capitalist economies, ex post tests of performance always (but not exclusively) serve as indicators of competitiveness. These tests are implemented in many ways: in product markets, through different price tolerances (or through patterns of entry); in financial markets, through different tolerances for profit rate, growth, or market share according to the sector and the nation; in central banks and government decisions about macroeconomic policy based on different acceptable interactions between income, output, growth, and distribution. There is frequently debate about how well existing rules provide correct and fair tests in relation to some set of legitimate economic goals, that is, to a notion of the economic common good, especially when it comes to defining the legitimacy of macroeconomic objectives.

Conventions, Institutions, and Economic Process: A Series of Research Programs

The rows and columns of Figure 14.1 describe several different circles of coordination, each affording a partial view of the economy as a complex, open-ended system, somewhat analogous to the way in which partial equilibrium models in economics section out a piece of the whole system for close, bounded scrutiny.

Let us now look across the first two rows of Figure 14.1, within each domain of action, but over time. Our studies of worlds of production (Chapters 6 through 8) revealed that, at the level of daily coordination and in establishing conventions of specific worlds of production, actors seem to draw on differentiated propensities to coordinate (and different qualities of coordination), which we labeled the conventions of identity and participation.

In real time, of course, actors' identities are part of a never-ending biographical circle of day-to-day interpretations and interactions along a pathway chiseled out of experiences in work; and conventions of participation are results of collective understanding (and sometimes formalization) of past interactions. At any given moment, however, actors hold identities and act within an interpretative framework which defines reasonable action.[17] Students of comparative industrialization now generally agree that there are important differences in the ways in which key economic groups are constituted, even among economies of similar levels of income and development.[18] Yet the notion of identity has not made its way as a central analytical category into much economic thought.[19] Moreover, the underlying categories of these analyses are typically taken as fixed and self-evident: examples include "labor markets," the "banking system," or even "entrepreneurs" and "the working class." A more general formulation of the problem takes, as its point of departure, the formation of identities and builds on that to the notion of regularized interactions as conventions of participation.

The cell of the middle column of Figure 14.1 represents the results of previous rounds of economic accumulation, notably of physical and human capital and formal organizational structures. These determine basic resource mobilization capacities at any given moment. Normally, analyses of economic development take history into account by looking exclusively at these accumulated results of past efforts, yet the evidence suggests that this approach is woefully inadequate: think of the success stories of the German or Japanese economies in building up from a destroyed productive base in the postwar period; in contrast, consider the incapacities of many Third World economies in spite of abundant resources, or the downward spirals of certain other economies in the face of past glories.

Some institutional analysis in economics or economic sociology calls our attention to the roles of rules, government institutions, or forms of private sector organization in economic development.[20] But they usually run up against the same problem: having specified these forces, the analysis cannot show why they exist as they do in some places and not others, and why they are so imperfectly imitatable. The question of "intangible" factors in development, though often posed in the institutionalist literature, is rarely given the prominence it deserves, while the importance of tangible resource endowments is frequently exaggerated, although they are deprived of any substantive content by abstracting them as "assets."

Conventions, Selection, and Pathways to Economic Development

Figure 14.2 depicts a matrix of interactions with high levels of vertical and horizontal recursiveness.[21] To consider this as a framework for analyzing economic development, think of the right-hand column as multi-sectoral.

The economy is a complex open system moving forward through time, with three pairs of evolving constitutive relationships (identity–labor; participation–productivity; and resources/objects/structures–profits/performance). These pairs are internally recursive, but they also have strong influences on each other through the real worlds of production constructed at any given moment. The pathway of economic development is built out

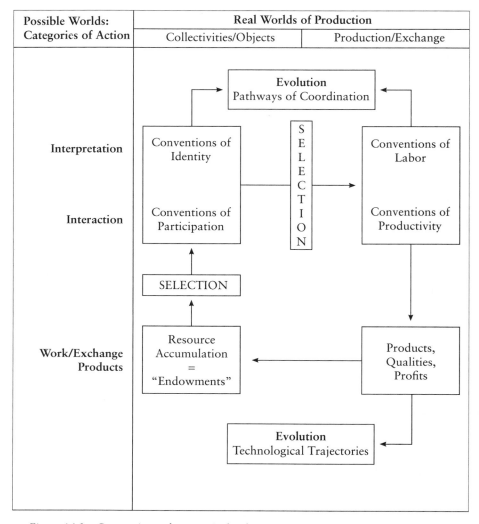

Possible Worlds: Categories of Action	Real Worlds of Production	
	Collectivities/Objects	Production/Exchange

Figure 14.2 Conventions of economic development.

of this complex open system with autonomous but interconnected domains of action.

Two pairs of primary "weak-form" selection processes are at work in constituting real worlds of production: the constraints imposed by the range of technological possibilities for a given type of product, with the corresponding range of possibilities for productivity and asset configurations; and constraints coming from existing conventions of identity and participation. They are described in Chapters 2, 3, and 9.

Two long-term trajectories or pathways interest us here. First we ask how pathways of coordination, that is, evolving coordination patterns, come about through feedback from real worlds of production, which themselves reflect prior selection pressures. Coordination and production have a highly recursive relationship, with tendencies toward stability, but multiple points of openness. The second concerns the better-known "path dependency." We have qualified this notion in technology ("technological trajectory"), observing that the tendency toward lock-in due to increasing returns is relative to the rate of technical progress and product differentiation within a given technological paradigm (see Chapter 1). Path dependency in conventions and organization is strongly shaped by routinization and precedent, but is opened up, to varying degrees, by interpretative activity and the degree of access that actors have to different possible worlds of production. Selection pressures in the economy are thus based not simply on technological factors, but on the extent to which conventions push for change or lock-in, and the directions in which they push. In other words, the coordination framework plays a key role in defining the substantive content of technological and organizational pathways and the extent to which they are used, adopted, and modified by particular firms, regions, or nations.

The Aims of a Social Science of Conventions

The tasks described here are priorities for economic analysis as a theorized, but interpretative and empirical, activity. Unless we sort out the multiple configurations of meaning for economic actors, we will not understand the nature of economies fundamentally characterized by dynamics, diversity, and non-equilibrium processes. Yet we do not propose separating these configurations from material objects or from external forces: they are subject to tests; they do better or worse faced with these tests; they adjust in different ways faced with the results of such tests.

Such an approach presents substantial methodological problems, for the microscopic study of conventions does not permit the construction of economic laws with greater and greater generality. Rather than attempting to follow a rising curve of cumulative findings, this approach attempts to break the domains of action and coordination into a disconnected yet coherent sequence of probes, some aiming for greater breadth, others for greater depth.[22] Such studies build on other studies, not in the sense that they take up where others leave off, but in the sense that, better informed and better conceptualized, they plunge more deeply into the same things. The method is not parsimonious, but it does offer the possibility of appreciating the diversity, multiplicity, and richness of action frameworks in modern economies. This lack of parsimony is surely a reasonable price to pay.

NOTES

1. Action and Diversity versus Models of Growth

1. Marglin and Schor, 1990.
2. Chandler, 1966; Galbraith, 1967.
3. Boyer and Coriat, 1986; Best, 1990.
4. Lafay and Herzog, 1989.
5. Greenaway and Milner, 1986; Gerstenberger, 1990.
6. Amendola, Guerrieri, and Padoan, 1991.
7. Amendola, Guerrieri, and Padoan, 1991.
8. Pavitt and Patel, 1990.
9. Vernon, 1979.
10. Amendola, Guerrieri, and Padoan, 1991.
11. Krugman, 1990.
12. Coriat, 1990; Dertouzos, Lester, and Solow, 1990.
13. Dosi, Pavitt, and Soete, 1990; Amendola, Guerrieri, and Padoan, 1991; see also Gibbons and Metcalfe, 1986.
14. Freeman, 1991: 372.
15. The standard approach in economics is to view these forces—factor costs, organizational capabilities, and so forth—in relation to a single continuum of best practices: those which maximize or impede maximization of productivity, minimize or impede minimization of costs. Yet, despite a very large volume of research, the relationship between productivity, income and growth is inconclusive (Dollar and Woolf, 1988; see also Robinson, 1956; Hodgson, 1988; Mokyr, 1990). Naturally, there is a rough correlation between high levels of aggregate productivity and high levels of income on the globe, but research has never been able to separate result from cause. For example, in both Adam Smith (1776) and Stigler (1951) the relationship is reversed, as it is in Romer (1986, 1990), although orthodoxy continues to repeat that productivity maximization is the root cause of income growth. As we have noted, technology

gaps are often responsible for the highest rates of income per unit of investment, since absolute advantages are rewarded through quasi-rents. Indeed, those activities in capitalism with the highest price-cost ratios (and hence the highest potential for capital accumulation and presumably for further supply-creating investment and demand-generating income) are often the activities without the highest standard factor productivities, precisely because they operate according to different pricing rules from those governing perfect competition (Robinson, 1956; Kaldor, 1972; Harris, 1978). In other words, short-term income growth of any specific firm, region, or nation is often maximized under conditions where productivity—in the standard sense of money output per unit of input—is not maximized; it is the secondary consequences of these same, non-maximizing technological innovations which generate the possibility of "long-term" average productivity improvements through diffusion. (On innovation, see David, 1975; Nelson and Winter, 1982; Dosi, 1988; Amendola and Gaffard, 1991. See also Perroux, 1950, on diffusion channels and the discussion in Sheppard, Webber, and Rigby, 1991 on average productivity improvements.) A paradox exists: some people have to "break the rules"; for the system to progress, some actors must violate equilibrium (Young, 1928; Kaldor, 1972).

Overall levels of output growth, in turn, may be exogenous, in the case of tradeable products, that is, they may be dependent on income levels and elasticities in buying areas (where, again, technology gaps are critical in producing income-maximizing outputs), but highly endogenous and not directly dependent on productivity in the case of domestic demand. This is because demand is related not strictly to aggregate income levels, but to long-run trends in income distribution (in concert with returns to foreign trade, in part determined by absolute advantages); these, in combination with income elasticities, will determine output levels (Robinson, 1956; Harris, 1978; Dosi, Pavitt, and Soete, 1990).

The strong possibility exists that maximizing standard, Ricardian, allocative efficiencies in an economy (through standard factor productivity maximization and determination of output) could work counter to maximizing income growth: in part because they would detract from development of more income-maximizing absolute advantage activities, in part because they might counteract long-term income distribution strategies that would maximize elasticity of growth for the "right" (income-maximizing) products. In other words, Ricardian efficiencies may not be compatible with dynamic Schumpeterian efficiencies or growth efficiencies (Schumpeter, 1934). And it is dynamic income growth, in turn, which generates the scale effects that have been demonstrated to be the single greatest key to average productivity growth (Romer, 1986). There is thus no single criterion which allows us to judge that best practice, even in limited comparative advantage terms, consists of the maximization of standard factor productivity. In technical terms, economics attempts to deal with this problem under the "reevaluation of prices" problem, that is, weighting output values so as to reflect quality changes (Gordon, 1986). This is an interesting measurement technique, and it shows that productivity is not always what it seems, but it does not get at the problem from the standpoint of what economic actors do or should be doing, which is not always to maximize money output per unit of currently valued money input, but often to defy that "rule" in favor of allocational inefficiencies.

16. Amable, 1990; Dosi, Pavitt, and Soete, 1990.
17. This distinction between "weak" and "strong" competition is used in Storper and Walker, 1989.
18. Dosi, 1987; Amendola and Gaffard, 1990; Arthur, 1994.
19. Chapter 2 gives a detailed discussion of product qualities and technology.
20. Dosi, Pavitt, and Soete, 1990.
21. Dosi, Pavitt, and Soete, 1990.
22. Dosi and Orsenigo, 1985; Amendola and Gaffard, 1990.
23. See, *inter alia:* Schumpeter, 1934; Solow, 1957; Rosenberg, 1982; Dosi, 1988; Amendola and Gaffard, 1990; Lundvall, 1990a, 1990b; Mokyr, 1990. See also Romer (1990) for an orthodox approach which nonetheless recognizes the central role of knowledge.
24. Cohendet, Llerena, and Sorge, 1991.
25. Silverberg, Dosi, and Orsenigo, 1988; Dosi, Pavitt, and Soete, 1990.
26. Dosi and Orsenigo, 1985: 13. A clear early statement on this can also be found in Kaldor, 1972.
27. David, 1975, 1986; Nelson and Winter, 1982; Dosi and Orsenigo, 1985; Foray, 1991; Arthur, 1994.
28. To put it more formally, this means that there is no single "absorbing state" which, given sufficient intensity of competition, all choices save the optimum will fail, faced with a survival test.
29. Amendola and Gaffard, 1990, 1992; Bruno, 1992.
30. Dosi and Orsenigo, 1985.
31. This observation is made in Piore, 1992.
32. Recently, the "classical revival" in growth theory, based in Chicago, has depicted growth as a consequence of Smithian-Stiglerian dynamics (Romer, 1986; Lucas, 1988; contrast them to Arrow, 1962, or, at a more historical-empirical level, Rosenberg, 1982, and Mokyr, 1990). Growing markets (we are not told why they grow in the first place) make possible an increasing division of labor, which in turn increases the possibility of efficient specialization of outputs. In the Chicago interpretation, specialization leads to increasing returns at the level of the economy as a whole, but on the basis of perfect competition at the level of particular firms. Patterns of specialization are global competitive optima.
33. Moore, 1966; see the discussion of Italy in Chapter 5 for more detail.
34. Sabel, 1982; Hall, 1988; Amsden, 1990.

35. As in the approach known as the "économies de la grandeur." See Boltanski and Thévenot, 1987, 1991.
36. Wacquant, 1993: 3.
37. Always according to a particular pathway, of course. Such a pathway often appears, retrospectively, to have been predestined or predetermined, although in reality its realization is usually quite tortuous and not at all self-evident at the outset.
38. Lewis, 1969.
39. Lewis, 1969: 42.
40. Turner (1994) is the latest example of the "anti-practice" position in social science.
41. Thévenot, 1989a, 1989b, 1989c.
42. Hardin, 1995; Sugden, 1993.
43. Wacquant, 1993: 4.
44. Nonetheless, we openly acknowledge our debt to the work on the politics of economics and economics based in politics. Without the inspiration of these lines of reflection, it would be difficult today to root economic and social thought in a recognition of diversity.
45. Different components of profitability correspond to these different systems, as do specific expectations of actors with respect to profit levels.
46. See Lewis, 1986.
47. In another domain, the world of art (described by H. Becker, 1976), artists, spectators, critics, and others compete to construct reputations. The resulting "economic value" of works of art thus seems to have much in common, at least at first, with the Interpersonal World.

2. *Possible Worlds of Production*

1. Knight, 1921.
2. Knight, 1921: 233.
3. Knight, 1921: 205.
4. Knight, 1921: 241. Emphasis ours.
5. Polanyi, 1962: 52–53.
6. Marschak, 1968; see Williamson, 1985: 3.
7. "Indeed, in some cases and for some purposes, nearly the whole income of a business may be regarded as a quasi-rent, that is an income determined for the time by the state of the market for its wares, but with little reference to the cost of preparing for their work the various things and persons engaged in it." (Marshall, 1890: 626).
8. Knight, 1921: 258.
9. Hayek, 1945.
10. Taylor, 1972.
11. Haudricourt, 1987; Landes, 1992.

12. Marxist "labor process" studies in the 1970s emphasized the "real" versus the "formal" subsumption of labor to capital. These scholars, especially Braverman (1974), identified this as *the* unique pathway of development of capitalist labor relations, but we see it as a particularity of one world of production. Braverman and his contemporaries wrote with the postwar push of mass production in mind. Numerous other scholars have criticized that theory as an oversimplification, notably Sabel (1982).

13. Gibbons and Metcalfe, 1986; Coriat, 1990, 1991.

14. This definition must be distinguished from another used in industrial economics, where the term "economy of scope" refers to both the range of products and the number of phases in a complex production process within an integrated firm (in the sense of vertical integration). Even though "economies of scope" is used to describe both, they lead to entirely different organizational outcomes: when there is vertical integration and many phases, the product will tend to be standardized and its production rooted in scale economies, unlike the situation with economies of variety.

15. Aoki, 1990; Amendola and Gaffard, 1991.

16. See, for example, Chandler, 1966.

17. Lewis (1969) describes a coordination sequence in which everything depends strictly on mutual anticipations; in such a situation, the smallest doubt that paralyzes a single actor suffices to destroy coordination, like a house of cards. But this is not true when a convention of standardization is in place.

18. Akerlof, 1970.

19. This communicational paradox is one of the key concepts in Habermas, 1976. See the earlier section on specialization versus standardization.

20. Or, more generally, the different kinds of expression, whether verbal or physical, which contribute to action and communication.

21. Marshall, 1890, vol. 4: 271 (chap. 10: "The Concentration of Specialized Industries in Particular Localities").

22. Actors in such a system develop, nonetheless, a savoir-faire and a certain common language. But both are limited to the collectivity formed by the firm and cannot be transferred to other firms. This is the same as the notion of specificity formalized in human capital theories, and is similar to the notion of idiosyncrasy developed in Doeringer and Piore (1971) and later used by Williamson (1985) in a much more restricted way. Doeringer and Piore (1985), in a new preface to their book, note that productive know-how is "analogous to a language, rather than a production function, a property inherent in groups rather than individuals."

23. As in the many jokes and caricatures of the "mad inventor:" we never know until the last minute whether he is a genius or a fool.

24. Even when there is implicit—and sometimes explicit—control of peers with respect to work rules.

25. Cornu (1980) extends this from consumer products to the objects used in

work, in describing how retired shipfitters become once again fully aware of their skills when surrounded by machines and tools from their former trade. Latour (1985) calls attention to the mnemonic functions of material objects in scientific-intellectual work.

26. Searle, 1977.

3. Firms, Profits, Work, and Innovation

1. The literature on the borders of the firm has affirmed that the firm is not a basic, but rather a derivative, unit of economic analysis. See Dosi and Salvatore, 1992.
2. Cohendet and Llerena, 1989.
3. Hart, 1937. Compare this to the notion of adaptation to an optimal, fixed output level, as in Stigler, 1951.
4. Arrow, 1962, 1968, 1972; Weitzman, 1979.
5. Stigler, 1939.
6. Fraser, 1984.
7. Coase, 1937.
8. Yet, as we shall see, such non-market forces cannot be accounted for satisfactorily by the existing neo-institutionalist theories in economics. They require a theory of conventions.
9. Hyman and Streeck, 1988.
10. Piore and Sabel, 1984; Becattini, 1987; Storper and Scott, 1989.
11. Dosi, Pavitt, and Soete, 1990.
12. Gold, 1964; Bellofiore, 1985.
13. The result is a corollary relative to the statistical observation of models of production implemented by firms. The firm's navigation between these different constraints contributes to the determination, for the ratios in Figure 3.3, of the ensemble of values which show the firm's position with respect to models of production. The values of these ratios, contributing to the firm's returns, must a priori be distributed statistically along the two axes in such a way that one represents the theoretical force of the market and the other the production process. These values should also be grouped coherently in ways that reflect the different ensembles we call "models of production." Finally, it should be possible to discern distortions or tensions among models in the form of incoherent combinations of values of different ratios. We provide numerous examples of this in Chapter 4.
14. In a situation of total, perfect capital mobility, with one uniform interest rate and so forth, this would not be true. But even orthodox approaches to vintage capital and lagged capital mobility models show that uniform profit rates do not exist. We go beyond such reasoning here to suggest that, in fact, actors do not use the profit rate as a guide in all cases, but only in certain particular, constructed circumstances. The rate of interest, moreover, no more defines a

hierarchy of choices than does the rate of profit, in that there are many other intervening factors, among them the framework of action at hand.

15. Chapters 4 and 6 discuss this issue, with considerable detail for the French case.

16. See especially Reynaud, 1990, 1992.

17. Marshall, 1890, vol. 6, chap. 6: 560.

18. The existence of personal autonomy makes neoclassical labor economics, which considers the worker as an instrument that responds predictably to stimuli, unacceptable. The idea that problems of information cannot be reduced either to imperfections or to insufficient quantity of information is beginning to gain ground. Favereau (1989) notes that the notion of the incomplete labor contract concerns, in the first place, the historical attempt to "extend" and "perfect" the labor relation, an attempt destined to failure from the outset.

19. Knight, 1921: 241–243.

20. Identifying productivity with a particular observable criterion such as "direct labor productivity" would thus contradict this meaning.

21. We owe this observation to Ned Lorenz.

22. Affichard, 1986.

23. This corresponds to the "lower primary segment" of the internal labor market, defined by Piore, 1975.

24. Much of the literature, such as Williamson (1985) and Freeman and Medoff (1984), argues that relative stability of employment relations is a consequence of firm-specific skills and bilateral monopoly for workers and employers, and thus it is high in mass production situations. We may observe, first, that in recent years this situation seems empirically to be disappearing, even in capital-intensive consumer durables industries, with employment reductions and apparent generalization of skills required (or deskilling). This suggests that the typical postwar employment relation in manufacturing was an evolved convention, perhaps based on worker bargaining power in the external labor market (that is, the threat of strikes and their effects in disrupting production), but that the skills argument was not particularly credible. Much of the labor queue and labor market segmentation literature also implies that ascribed characteristics, not skills, were at issue.

25. Ewald, 1986.

26. Marglin, 1974.

27. Williamson, 1985, emphasizes the terms "organization" and "role." We should remember that he links both to "marketable." (1985: 209).

28. Smith observed: "The wages of labour vary according to the small or great trust which must be reposed on the workman. The wages of goldsmiths or jewelers are everywhere superior to those of many other workmen, not only of equal, but of much superior ingenuity: on account of the precious metals with which they are intrusted. We trust our health to the physician; our fortune and

sometimes our life and reputation to the lawyer and attorney. Such confidence could not safely be reposed in people of a very mean or low condition." (Cited in Klein and Leffler, 1981: 618.)

It is in this light that we employ the term "market" to describe labor activity in this world, while conceding that this is completely opposite to standard usage. See also Stinchcombe on "craft labor."

29. Aoki, 1990.
30. See the discussion of Italy in Chapter 6.
31. Lundvall, 1990a, 1990b, 1992.
32. Amendola and Gaffard, 1990.
33. Johnson and Lundvall, 1992; see also Rosenberg, 1982; von Hippel, 1987; Teece, 1988, 1989; Hakansson, 1989.
34. Richardson, 1972.
35. Mowery, 1988; Mytelka, 1990.
36. Patel and Pavitt, 1991; De Vet, 1993.

4. Situating Firms in Worlds of Production

1. This analysis section owes much to the case studies and data analysis carried out by Karine Daniel, Isabelle Dussouet, Pascal Griot, Lucie Nicolas, Pierre Prada, Olivier Riou, Stephane Rouze, Luc Tessier, François Treuil, and Cecile Vessin. Luc Tessier also assisted with analysis of the files of the National Employment Fund. A number of detailed case studies were prepared in the course of this work; some of them are briefly summarized in the "Illustrations" accompanying this chapter.

   The research was supported by the Ministry of Labor, Employment, and Training, and by financing from the PIRTTEM program of the CNRS, as well as the Commissariat Général du Plan. We thank the ANVAR, the Délégation à l'Emploi and the firms which provided us with information. We also thank Florence Bouchet and Robert Weisz for providing eight case studies of firms in the Provence-Alpes-Côte d'Azur region which were included in the FIM sample. A preliminary version of the results of this study was published in *Travail et Emploi*, 2 (1992). Other useful sources include Kerscher and Nenot, 1989; Callens, 1990; Bouillaget, 1991.
2. Evidence of this dynamism can be found in the increase in "intangible" investments, such as software (from 6% in 1980 to 11% in 1985), R&D expenses (from 9% to 13%), and advertising (6% to 8.5%). *Source:* Ministry of Industry and Foreign Trade, 1992.
3. Boulin and Taddei, 1989.
4. Balut, 1990; Villeval et al., 1992.
5. Celerier and Kirsch, 1990: 125.
6. Salais and Tessier, 1991.

5. Identifying Real Worlds of Production in
France, Italy, and the United States

1. Onida, 1980; Porter, 1990; Colombo, Mariotto, and Mutinelli, 1991.
2. PBTL industries were separated from others using a variety of criteria applied to U.S. 4-digit census sectors. HTI industries were defined as those 4-digit sectors with greater than 25% scientists and engineers in their workforces. The DIC industries were defined on the basis of the diversity of their products. We used an index developed for the U.S. Census Bureau (Gollop and Monahan, 1982) to rank manufacturing establishments on the basis of their level of product diversification for the years 1963, 1967, 1972, 1977, and 1982. We defined DIC industries as those having a product diversification greater than the U.S. all-industry average in 1982, or those with a rapidly increasing index of diversification.
3. PMMs will have a smaller role in each nation's trade than the other two groups in any case, because the definition used restricts it to a small number of subsectors. If this analysis were expressed in terms of location quotients, PMMs would appear more important in the figure.
4. Sforzi, 1990.
5. Two other sets of cases were studied (they may be found in Salais and Storper, 1993). Both appear in the middle section of Table 5.6, as leading national complexes which fall just under the cutoff for international specialization. The *système sud* refers to the growth of selected areas of southern France where attempts have been made to hive off parts of French high technology specialties in order to create new centers. Though these places are subject to a double set of constraints—the organization of French high technology in general and its concentration in Paris in particular—it is clear that different conventions of participation and identity are at work in southern France than in the Ile de France. A third set of cases involves the French territorial periphery: such diverse venues as the "new west" (Vendée, parts of Bretagne) and the eastern axis of France, from the Haute Savoie to the Jura and Franche-Comté. Here, a few fashion- or craft-based forms of production are doing well, faced with vigorous international competition. All are marked by strong family-based solidarities or community-based hierarchies, and by their traditional resistance to integration into the Paris-based national system.

6. France: Innovative Real Worlds of
Fashion and High Technology

1. We have drawn most heavily on the work of Montagne-Villette (1987) in this section. Other references include Nystrom, 1928; Simon, 1931; Guilbert and Isambert-Jamoti, 1956; Prevost, 1957; Latour, 1961; Barthes, 1967; Elias,

1974; Battiau, 1976; Duroselle, 1980; Delbourg-Delphis, 1981; Conseil Economique et Social, 1982; Goncourt, 1982; Zeitlin and Sabel, 1985; Green, 1986; Guillon and Taboada-Leonetti, 1986; Herpin, 1986; Manusardi, 1986; Prevot, 1986; Saglio, 1986; Saint-Geours, 1986; Zarca, 1986; Commissariat Général du Plan, 1987; Farault, 1987; Lipovetsky, 1987; Jacomet, 1989; Waldinger et al., 1989; Roche, 1990.

2. Montagne-Villette, 1987; Jacomet, 1989.
3. Waldinger et al., 1989.
4. Boissonade, 1931.
5. See, *inter alia,* Goncourt, 1982.
6. Prevost, 1957.
7. Lipovetsky, 1987.
8. We have drawn most heavily on the work of Carroué (1988) in this section. Other references include Tocqueville, 1956; Schattschneider, 1960; Shonfield, 1965; Servan-Schreiber, 1968; Paxton, 1973; Reynaud, 1975, 1988; Friedberg, 1976; Zysman, 1977, 1986; Suleiman, 1979; Levy-Leboyer, 1980; Bauer and Cohen, 1981; Berger, 1981; Savary, 1981; Coing, 1982; Boniface and Heisbourg, 1983; Fontanel, 1983; Lauber, 1983; Lemettre, 1983; Mercier and Segrestin, 1983; Stoffaes, 1983; Carroué, 1984, 1986, 1988; Malkin, 1984; Boucheron, 1985; Hayward, 1985; Salomon, 1985; Cavard, 1986; Conseil Economique et Social, 1986; Gourevitch, 1986; Maurice, Sellier, and Silvestre, 1986; Sallez, 1986; Veltz, 1986; Bourdon, 1987; Cohen, 1987; Grando and Verdier, 1987; Guichard, 1987; INSEE, 1987a, 1987b, 1988; Lakota and Milelli, 1987; Swyngedou and Anderson, 1987; Beckouche, 1988, 1990; Hall, 1988; Lehoucq and Strauss, 1988; Moulaert, Chikhaoui, and Djellal, 1988; Scott, 1988b; Veltz et al., 1988; Pottier, 1989; Amable, 1990; Bourdieu, 1990; Chapman, 1990; Pavitt and Patel, 1990; Lyon-Caen, 1991.
9. Pavitt and Patel, 1990: 12.
10. Pavitt and Patel, 1990: 7.
11. S291 = 2911: telecommunications; 2912: medical instruments; 2913: instrumentation, industrial automation, etc.; 2914: professional materiel; 2915: passive components (condensors, resistors, etc.); 2916: active components (semiconductors, tubes).
12. Carroué, 1988.
13. The Hauts de Seine can probably be considered the "brain" of the entire French national high technology economy; with 18% of national high technology employment, and almost 30% of regional employment, it includes such high technology zones as La Defense, Rueil, and Nanterre.
14. Scott, 1988b.
15. Carroué, 1986.
16. To provide just a few examples: ABG Semca/Thomson, 66%, Aerospatiale, 49%; Electronique Dassault, 77%; Turbomeca, 59%; SNECMA, 28%.

17. Crouzet, Dassault, Veyrpic, Air Liquide, Merlin Gerin, Thomson, Pompes Guinards, Cime Bocuse/Pechiney.
18. Skocpol, 1979.
19. Hall, 1988.
20. Bourdieu, 1990.
21. Carroué, 1988: 12.
22. Salomon, 1985.
23. Hall, 1988: 153.
24. Hall, 1988: 157.
25. Shonfield, 1965: 128, 137; in Hall, 1988.
26. Birnbaum, 1977.
27. Dagnaud, 1984.
28. Bauchet, 1986.
29. *Le Monde,* Saturday January 21, 1995, p. 15: "La haute technologie française doît se financer aux Etats-Unis."
30. Carroué, 1984, 1988.

7. Italy: Interpersonal Action and the Division of Labor

1. Brusco, 1982; Garofoli, 1983a, 1983b; Piore and Sabel, 1984; Zeitlin and Sabel, 1985; Bellandi, 1986; Becattini, 1987, 1988a; Sforzi, 1990; Goglio and Sforzi, 1991.
2. Del Monte, 1986.
3. Nuti, 1989; Sforzi, 1990.
4. Much of this analysis has been inspired by the "Florentine School" of economists and geographers and the "Emilian School" of social scientists. Both emphasize the historically constructed patterns of behavior which have underpinned industrial development in NEC Italy, though neither is responsible in any way for the analysis here.
5. Onida, 1980; Porter, 1990; Colombo, Mariotto, and Mutinelli, 1991.
6. Storper and Harrison, 1991.
7. Bagnasco, 1977, 1985; Garofoli, 1983a, 1983b, 1988; Capitani and Garofoli, 1985; Dematteis, 1985; Bellandi, 1986; Becattini, 1987, 1988b, 1989a, 1989b; Sforzi, 1990; Dematteis and Ferlaino, 1991; Goglio and Sforzi, 1991.
8. Stigler, 1951; Nuti, 1989.
9. Lorenzoni, 1980, 1983, 1986; Bursi, 1982, 1989; Brusco, 1983; Enrietti, 1983; Fua, 1983, 1985; Bellandi, 1986; ISTAT, 1986; Russo, 1986; Becattini, 1988a; Scarpitti, 1988, Cappiello, 1989; Courault and Romani, 1989; Goodman and Bamford, 1989; Tinacci Mosello, 1989.
10. Michaelson, 1989.
11. Belussi, 1990.
12. Del Monte, 1986: 33–34.

13. Del Monte, 1986.
14. Cori and Cortesi, 1977; Brusco, 1983; Bellandi, 1986, 1988, 1989; Becattini, 1989a, 1989b; Bianchi, 1989; Dei Ottati, 1991.
15. Lugli and Tugnoli, 1991.
16. Bursi, 1982.
17. Stigler, 1951; Contini, 1984; Nuti, 1984, 1986, 1988; Contini et al., 1987.
18. Bartolini, 1989.
19. Lorenzoni, 1980; Becattini, 1984, 1989a; Bellandi, 1986; Del Monte, 1986; Dei Ottati, 1987; Bianchi, 1989; Lazerson, 1989, 1990; Prosperetti, 1989; Rey, 1989; Amin and Robbins, 1990; Belussi, 1990.
20. Bellandi, 1989.
21. Belussi, 1990.
22. Cappecchi, 1990a.
23. Bursi, 1982. This process has been documented in great detail for the ceramic tile equipment industry of Sassuolo (Bursi, 1982; Russo, 1986).
24. Belussi, 1990.
25. Cappecchi, 1990a, 1990b.
26. Balestri, 1982.
27. Frey, 1975; Solinas, 1982; Barca, 1989; Bartolini, 1989; Brusco and Pezzini, 1990; Brutti, 1990; Carboni, 1990.
28. Bellandi and Trigilia, 1990.
29. Forlai, 1989; Forlai and Bertini, 1989; Prosperetti, 1989.
30. As revealed in the detailed data of the Unione Industriale Pratese. Balestri, 1991b.
31. Balestri, 1982, 1990; Bursi, 1982; ISTAT, 1986; Russo, 1986; Belussi, 1987, 1990; Regalia, 1987; Cappecchi, 1989; Bellandi and Trigilia, 1990; Lugli and Tugnoli, 1991.
32. This allows us to refute directly the often-made claim that postwar Italian industrialization provides evidence of a double tradeoff, between the Industrial Triangle and NEC Italy, and between mass and flexible production on the grounds that in the 1970s the NEC region grew more rapidly than the Triangle on the basis of flexible rather than mass production. The growth of the NEC region's *decentramento produttivo* was fully compatible with the growth of mass production in Milan and Turin in the 1950s and much of the 1960s because the two areas were specialized in different industries.
33. Another statement frequently made in the literature (for example, Goodman and Bamford, 1989; Amin and Robbins, 1990) is that these production systems were based directly on traditional practices involving artisanship, pride of craft, and so on, and that this is the essential basis of their existence in the 1960s and 1970s. Tuscany and Emilia, however, have histories riven with discontinuities, disruptions, conflicts, and institutional innovations, suggesting that to equate their success directly with tradition is simplistic.

34. Zaninotto, 1978; Nuti, 1986, 1988; Forlai, 1989; Forlai and Bertini, 1989; Prosperetti, 1989; Rey, 1989; Balestri, 1991b.
35. Moore, 1966.
36. Berger, 1981; Carboni, 1991.
37. Such worlds are analyzed in detail in Salais and Storper, 1993 (the French version of this book).
38. Giddens, 1984; Shils, 1981.
39. Not only is it difficult to speak of a national set of conventions of participation in a country as diverse as Italy, but even at the level of NEC Italy there are important inter-regional and inter-communal variations in history, structure, and functioning of economic participation. There are many Italian "success stories of local development" (Camagni and Cappello, 1990), not just one. We are not trying to efface such differences, but rather to trace a broad story line which, to varying degrees, applies to the specific cases.
40. Banfield, 1958; Almond and Verba, 1963; Pye and Verba, 1965; Moore, 1966; Berger, 1980; Verba, 1982; Fua, 1983, 1985; Carboni, 1990, 1991; Todd, 1990.
41. Becattini, 1987.
42. Todd, 1990.
43. Salvestrini, 1965; Tinacci Mosello, 1983; Cappecchi, 1990b.
44. Cappecchi, 1990b.
45. Becattini, 1975, 1978; Brusco, 1982, 1983; Fua and Zacchia, 1983; Fua, 1985; Dei Ottati, n.d.; Cappecchi, n.d., 1989.
46. Paci, 1973.
47. Becattini's 1987 interpretation is thus at odds with that of Barca, 1989.
48. Rey, 1989.
49. Solinas, 1982.
50. Dei Ottati, 1987; Cappecchi, 1990a, 1990b.
51. Trigilia, 1990.
52. Brutti, 1990: 3.
53. This failure to analyze labor from both "external" and "internal" perspectives marks much non-Italian writing about labor in the Third Italy. British critics of the Third Italy, in particular, stress what they see as the exploitive nature of wage-labor conditions and picture the family as inherently regressive and oppressive (Amin and Robbins, 1990). On the first point, they ignore the workers' own interpretative framework; on the second, they assume that the family is the nuclear family, saddled with obligations but containing no opportunities. Often, they make empirically untenable claims by confusing Emilia-Romagna and Tuscany with other areas of Italy, where different conditions obtain (Paci, 1980), and virtually all tend to assume, but do not demonstrate, that the family in Third Italy oppresses women, even though local scholars of other subjects assert otherwise (see especially Pesce, 1990).

54. Le Play, 1879; Becattini, 1975; Ardigo and Donati, 1976; Berger, 1980; Paci, 1980; Kertzer, 1984; Giovannini, 1987; Pesce, 1990; Ritaine, 1987, 1989; Todd, 1990; Paloscia, 1991.
55. Brusco, 1982; Bursi, 1982, 1989.
56. Becattini, 1984; Bagnasco and Trigilia, 1985; Trigilia, 1985; Barbagli, Cappechi, and Cobalti, 1988.
57. Bellandi, 1992 (personal communication).
58. Mutinelli et al., 1991.
59. Russo, 1986; Bursi, 1982.
60. Becattini, 1984; Bagnasco, 1985; Trigilia, 1985; Bordogna, 1987; Perulli, 1987; Scarpitti and Trigilia, 1987; Scarpitti, 1988; Becattini, 1989a; Ritaine, 1989.
61. Trigilia, 1990.
62. Trigilia, 1986a, 1986b, 1990.
63. The term is used by Trigilia (1990), who borrows it from Dore's (1986a) characterization of the negotiated character of Japanese production systems.
64. The Bridge, 1988.
65. Perulli, 1988.
66. Trigilia, 1986a, 1986b.
67. Lazerson, 1989.
68. Respectively, the Sabatini Laws; Laws 374/76, 675/77, 46/82; and the Marcora Law.

8. California High Technology: The Intellectual World in a Market Context

1. Habbakuk, 1962; Fishlow, 1965; Rosenberg, 1972; Hounshell, 1984.
2. Fishlow, 1965; Rosenberg, 1972; David, 1975; Temin, 1975.
3. Fishlow, 1965; Rosenberg, 1972.
4. Brown (1995) shows that there was adaptation to the special traction needs of users in the design of locomotives, sometimes including the need for great durability. But most of the adaptation was in the general direction described here. We thank Phil Scranton for pointing this out to us.
5. Elkin, 1987.
6. Leontief, 1953; Hartz, 1955; Habbakuk, 1962; Landes, 1970; Mansfield, 1972, 1981; Rosenberg, 1972; Di Tella, 1982; Hounshell, 1984; Bellah et al., 1985; Markusen, 1985; Scott, 1986, 1990; Scott and Angel, 1987; Florida and Kenney, 1988, 1990; Nelson, 1988; Ramo, 1988; Saxenian, 1988, 1990, 1991; Kelley and Brooks, 1989; de Vet, 1990; Dertouzos, Lester, and Solow, 1990; Lederman, 1992; de Vet and Scott, 1992.
7. Hartz, 1955; Wiebe 1975; Bellah et al., 1985; Todd, 1990; Jencks, 1994.
8. Ramo, 1988.
9. Nelson, 1988.

10. Other conditions which facilitate entrepreneurial activity in the United States, despite the overwhelming importance of the large-firm sector, are well known and include the well-developed and highly fluid capital market, as well as relatively low "social wage" and overhead costs (Bucaille and Beauregard, 1987; Hickmann, 1989).

11. Donald Douglas independently experimented to invent the DC-3, the first "mass market" civilian airliner, in Santa Monica in the 1930s; Shockley, Terman, and others operated in the same fashion in Silicon Valley in the 1950s.

12. Angel, 1989; de Vet, 1990.

13. Hartz, 1955; Bellah et al., 1985; Markusen, 1985; Scott, 1986; Scott and Storper, 1987; Ramo, 1988; Scott, 1988a, 1988b; Gordon, 1989; de Vet, 1990; de Vet and Scott, 1992.

14. Scott, 1988a, 1988b.

15. de Vet, 1990.

16. Ramo, 1988.

17. de Vet 1990; Saxenian, 1990.

18. Thernstrom, 1964; Molotch, 1976; Clark, 1985; diLellio, 1987; Ely, 1987; Scott and Storper, 1987; Davis, 1988; Glasmeier, 1988; Manzagol, 1989; Scott and Paul, 1990; Markusen, Hall, and Deitrick, 1991; Bloch, 1992.

19. The clearest example of this is the Irvine family in Orange County, California. See Molotch, 1976; DiLellio, 1987.

20. See the detailed case studies of the high technology industries in Grenoble and Toulouse in Salais and Storper, 1993a: 231–274.

21. Thernstrom, 1964.

22. Earle, 1990.

23. Hartz, 1955; Bellah et al., 1985.

24. Chandler, 1966, 1977; Vernon, 1966; Galbraith, 1967; Kendrick, 1973; Mensch, 1979; Norton and Rees, 1979; Hekman, 1980; Hekman and Strong, 1981; Scranton, 1983, 1986; Hounshell, 1984; Noyelle and Stanback, 1984; Markusen, 1985; Clark, Gertler, and Whiteman, 1986; Cohen and Zysman, 1986; Markusen, Hall, and Glasmeier, 1986; Messine, 1987; Stowsky, 1987; Hyman and Streeck, 1988; Nelson, 1988; U.S. Congress Office of Technology Assessment, 1988; Gordon, 1989; Hickmann, 1989; Kelley and Brooks, 1989; Dertouzos, Lester, and Solow, 1990; Bass, 1991.

25. Cusumano, 1985; Dore, 1987a, 1987b; Aoki, 1988; Sabel et al., 1989.

26. Saxenian, 1994.

27. Stowsky, 1987.

28. Christopherson, 1994.

29. Bass, 1991.

30. Hickmann, 1989. Recent research on turbulence via entry and exit confirms this. See Baily, Hulten, and Campbell, 1992; Baldwin and Gorecki, 1990; and Alexander, 1994.

31. Kelley and Brooks, 1989.
32. Lieberman, 1988; for an excellent study of California failure in this regard, see Stowsky, 1987.
33. Lazonick, 1990.
34. Aoki, 1990; Coriat, 1990; Sabel et al.,1989.
35. Storper, 1985b.
36. Cohen and Zysman, 1986.
37. Florida and Kenney, 1990.

9. *Selection, Stability, and Transformation of Real Worlds of Production*

1. Bourdieu, 1990.
2. Pye and Verba, 1965; Sapelli, 1981; Verba, 1982; Trigilia, 1986a; Perulli, 1987; Golden, 1988; Regini, 1988; Cappecchi, 1989; Brusco and Pezzini, 1990; Brutti, 1990.
3. Hickmann, 1989.
4. Nuti, 1989.
5. Sabel et al., 1989; Cooke and Morgan, 1994.
6. Harrison, 1989.
7. Callon, 1986.

10. *States and Institutions as Conventions*

1. See, *inter alia*, Rawls, 1971; Nozick, 1974; Hirst, 1990; Millon-Delsol, 1992.
2. This includes some of the "constitutional environments" said to be linked to economy growth (Scully, 1992). This approach is criticized in Putnam, 1992.
3. In French political philosophy, "l'état subsidiaire" signifies a state which, rather than positioning itself above society and economy, the classical Cartesian-Colbertist conception, is instead a situated, involved party. The notion of subsidiarity is also employed in much liberal Christian philosophy.
4. Hirst, 1990.
5. Foucault, 1973; see also Dreyfus and Rabinow, 1982.
6. Which in itself is denied by extreme forms of so-called "situatedness" such as libertarianism.
7. Bellah et. al, 1985. This is closely argued in Walzer (1983) as well.
8. Wolfe, 1989.
9. Tocqueville, 1956.
10. Kant, 1976.
11. Fainstein, 1994: 21.
12. Rawls, 1971: 251.
13. Simmel, 1950: 73.
14. Fainstein, 1994: 23.

15. On versions of Protestant thought, see McIntyre, 1984; Walzer, 1983; Fox, 1988; Hauerwas, 1988; Lasch, 1991; on communitarianism, see Etzioni, 1988.
16. West, 1991.
17. West, 1991.
18. Flyvberg, 1992.
19. Piore, 1992.

11. State Intervention: A Critique of the French Case

1. Hirsch, 1991.
2. d'Iribarne, 1989.
3. Marsden, 1989.
4. Paxton, 1973.
5. d'Iribarne, 1989.
6. Zysman, 1977; Cohen, 1969.
7. Saglio, 1988.
8. Saglio, 1988.
9. Jobert and Tallard, 1991; Lanfranchi and Coutrot, 1991; Morin, 1991; Turquet, 1992. There exists in France a set of norms (for example, regulations on minimum wage, working time, and the like) called "public social order" that cannot be abrogated, even in favor of workers. The Council of the State (*Conseil d'Etat,* March 22, 1973) defined the "public social order" as "an ensemble of provisions which guarantee minimal social rights to workers, which can in no case be violated or reduced, but which do not interdict improvements nor addition of guarantees not foreseen, whether this be in legislative, regulatory, or conventional form" (Rotschild-Souriac, 1991).
10. Drawn from Didry and Salais, 1991, who investigated the collective labor agreements signed in 1936, using the labor press and reports of the Conseil d'Administration of firms affected by the strike wave as their principal empirical evidence.
11. Philip, 1937; Sewell, 1980; Siwek-Pouydessau, 1991.
12. Kolboom, 1986.
13. Which was widely publicized via the union press. See the article "Une Convention Type" in *Union des Métaux,* June–July 1936.
14. Didry and Salais, 1991.
15. Retière, 1990.
16. Affichard, 1986.
17. Marsden, 1986.
18. But for reasons having to do with macroeconomic regulation of the labor market.
19. Guibert, Laganier, and Volle, 1971; Bony and Eymard-Duvernay, 1982.
20. Fourquet, 1980.

21. Keynes, 1936, chap. 12.
22. Meny, 1992.
23. Rosanvallon, 1990.
24. See Chapter 6, where we discuss this.
25. For an explanation of grands corps and grandes écoles, see Bourdieu, 1990, and Boltanski, 1982.
26. See Chapter 10 for a discussion of the notion of patrimony.
27. Law of 1945.
28. Article L431-4 of the Labor Code, 1982.
29. The French term "personnel" is a false cognate in English: it refers to a community of persons, hence our translation as "members."
30. Bué and Rossi, 1991.
31. Articles L 219-9 and L 132-26 of the Labor Code.
32. For example, the existence of a special authorization for women to work at night in a given branch of the economy eliminates any legal right for unions to oppose night work within a specific firm in that branch (Bué and Rossi, 1991).
33. Morin, 1991.
34. Gremion, 1987; Boy, 1987.
35. Gerbaux and Muller, 1989.
36. Chevallier, 1985: 333.
37. Gerbaux and Muller, 1989.
38. Sueur, 1987: 420.
39. Ganne, 1985.
40. Meny, 1992; Lavialle, 1992.
41. It is frequently invoked today as the role of the European Community, another level which supplements the nation-state. This interpretation is widespread in France, which is not surprising given the strength of the convention of the external state. Paradoxically, it is the French version of the external state which, applied in Brussels, would most call into question the existence of a French state, by relegating it to intermediate status.

12. Competitiveness, Situated States, and Real Worlds in Three Countries

1. This is a vast debate. See, *inter alia,* North and Thomas, 1973, vs. Marx and Moore, 1966.
2. Tyson, 1987, 1990; Dertouzos, Lester, and Solow, 1990; Coriat and Taddei, 1991; Porter, 1990; Reich, 1991; Krugman, 1994.
3. Romer, 1986.
4. Porter, 1990.
5. Dertouzos, Lester, and Solow, 1990; Coriate and Taddei, 1991.
6. Forlai and Bertini, 1989.
7. Colombo, Mariotto, and Mutinelli, 1991; ERVET, 1991.

8. Balestri, 1991a, 1991b.
9. A number of observers hold that these systems must, inevitably, lose some of their interpersonal character: either they will become successful large firms obeying the universal laws about abstraction of qualities of actors and products or, worse, where existing firms and localities cannot discover ways to produce efficiently in existing localities, they would become "bodiless heads" for systems located elsewhere: shoes and textiles might be designed in Tuscany, but production would be externalized. Local economies would become tertiarized at the expense of direct production activity. Bianchi, 1987; Bianchi et al., 1988; Harrison, 1989a; Gaeta, 1985.
10. As of this writing, the principal issue is how to define an industrial district, which raises the problem of whether abstract national criteria or more flexible local criteria are to be applied. This point was made in a conversation with Mario Pezzini, July 1993.
11. Scarpitti, 1988; Bellandi and Trigilia, 1990; SPRINT, 1990, 1991; NOMISMA, 1991.
12. Lassini, 1985; Gobbo, 1989; Regini and Sabel, 1989; Carboni, 1990; Bigarelli and Crestanello, 1991.
13. Linhart, 1991.
14. Florida and Kenney, 1988, 1990.
15. Scott, 1993.
16. Dertouzos, Lester, and Solow, 1990.
17. Fishlow, 1965; Rosenberg, 1972.
18. Porter, 1990.

13. A Critique of Contemporary Institutionalism

1. Williamson, 1985.
2. Williamson, 1992: 21.
3. Williamson, 1992: 22.
4. See, *inter alia:* Coase, 1937; Stigler, 1961; Williamson, 1975, 1985; Goldberg, 1980; MacNeil, 1981; Barzel, 1982; Cheung, 1983; Singh, 1985; Dow, 1987; Stiglitz, 1987; Englander, 1988.
5. Williamson, 1985: 74.
6. Seravalli, 1992: 5.
7. Seravalli, 1992.
8. Alchian and Demsetz, 1972; Barzel, 1982; Singh, 1985.
9. Seravalli, 1992.
10. Alchian and Demsetz, 1973; Klein, Crawford, and Alchian, 1978; Grossman and Hart, 1986. Early contributions to the economics of property rights include Coase, 1959, 1960; Alchian, 1961; and Demsetz, 1967.
11. Barzel, 1982: 36.
12. Piore, 1992. See also the vast literature on the history of mass production,

which goes against the grain of the transactions cost interpretation of mass production as an optimal combination of resources: for example, Hounshell, 1984; Zeitlin and Sabel, 1985; and especially Scranton, 1986. On the history of engineering, see Landes, 1970.

The simplest and most orthodox of these accounts notes that costs of production dominate costs of transactions over time. In a domain of established technological competence, for instance, transactions are likely to become more standardized over time and their costs diminish through learning; in other words, high transactions costs are a temporary effect of technological change (Langlois, 1991). Likewise, underlying "substantive" technological and cognitive factors can, even in the absence of asset specificity, generate uncertainty that encourages vertical integration: again, production considerations dominate.

Langlois (1991) complements but enriches the analysis of Stigler (1951), who developed a neo-Smithian conception of the division of labor in production, in which capacity increments under conditions of growth (hence uncertainty) are added in the form of external suppliers until either the situation is stabilized and the risks associated with integration decrease, or when capacity can be added capacity either internally or in the form of consolidated additional establishments. The capacities to interlink production units increase in concert, and therefore the organization of the economy is essentially a function of growth-driven economies/diseconomies of scale and scope. For a similar argument, see Scott, 1988a. The analysis thus far remains mechanical and neo-Smithian (specialization-growth-interlinkage), though it does suggest ways in which the dynamic of production drives and shapes transactions and not, principally, the other way around, as the transactions cost economics notion of "adaptive economizing" would suggest.

13. Richardson, 1972.
14. Mariotti and Caincara (1986) demonstrate this principle clearly in an empirical examination of the textile-clothing industry: know-how is stage specific, but can be transferred across product lines, which impedes vertical integration and forces producers to rely on complementary talents of other firms. Pursuing the question somewhat differently, Dosi and Salvatore (1992: 178) show that the desire to control assets may play a strong role in determining the firm's vertical scope, but have no logical connection to its horizontal boundaries. Foray (1990) argues that the only compelling case for vertical integration is that of similar and complementary activities. In all these cases, asset configurations are not only driven by the scale of operation, but involve definite qualities of the assets with no straightforward correspondence to scale.
15. See especially Dosi and Salvatore, 1992. But see also Arrow, 1972.
16. Teece, 1988; Cohendet, Llerena, and Sorge, 1991; Lundvall, 1990a, 1990b; Foray, 1991.
17. Arrow, 1972.

18. Young, 1928.
19. Kaldor, 1972. Storper (1989) analyzes Young's idea of external economies, as having less to do with the question of the appropriability of returns than with the permanently upsetting, disequilibrium nature of the economic process. Kaldor captures this notion quite well; as we explained earlier, in referring to external economies as something like "external interdependencies over time," with no global optimum. The Chicago "classical revival" growth theorists use Young as a point of reference, but their message is quite different from ours. They focus on the question of returns and not on the processal dynamic, but we believe Young's idea of external economies had little to do with the notion of returns. Hence, the Chicago School's label "classical" is not merited; their approach is rigorously neoclassical, concluding as it does that external interdependencies are compatible with perfect competition (Lucas, 1988).
20. Amendola and Gaffard, 1990.
21. Piore, 1992.
22. Foray and Garrouste, 1990. See Varela, 1990.
23. See the classic statements by March and Simon, 1958; Penrose, 1959. Much of this has gone out of fashion, but it seems to us highly relevant. We might also think, in this regard, of some of the early writings on action (although without their functionalism): see Merton, 1936; Parsons, 1937.
24. We thank Erik Kwok for inspiring this discussion. See Kwok, 1990; also, in the same spirit, Imai and Itami, 1984.
25. This is in addition to our critique above, that asset forms are not associated in any clear fashion with forms of control. See also Dore, 1987a, 1987b; Johanson and Mattson, 1987; Lieberman, 1988; Asanuma, 1989; Powell, 1990.
26. For example, those who argue that Japanese firms have lifetime employment because of specific human capital. This is a tautology, where specificity is both cause and effect. See Dore, 1987a, 1987b; Aoki, 1988.
27. On Germany, see Sabel et al., 1989; on Italy, see Chapter 5 of this book.
28. We analyze these industries in Chapters 4 and 5.
29. Becker, 1976; Schelling, 1978. For a variety of critiques, see Titmuss, 1970; Granovetter, 1985; Sen, 1985; Hindess, 1988; Thévenot, 1989b; Sabel, 1993b.
30. Granovetter, 1985. See also Ouchi, 1981.
31. Sen, 1977; Thévenot, 1989a; Lorenz, 1991; Sabel, 1993b.
32. The New Institutional Economics utilitarianism in particular has been labeled an "undersocialized" view of the influences on economic choices, to the detriment of a reasonable analysis of human actions as "embedded in" and learned from the environment (Granovetter, 1985). See also the excellent discussion in Bromley (1989), which attempts to deal not only with embedded routines but also with the role of values, in the sense of what he calls "rights and entitlements" in institutions. Much of what we have said about the construction of conventions in Chapter 2, and in our empirical analyses, exemplifies such embeddedness, in our view. Motivations include not only maximization, but

often survival (at the expense of maximization; see North, 1981). Under some circumstances, in other words, total maximization of wealth implies the destruction of some organizations or redistribution of income and resources, and those individuals or organizations who would lose will block maximization. In other cases, organizations are not in the game for profit maximization but for market share or growth (see the numerous studies of the Japanese firm, for example, Aoki, 1988; Prestowitz, 1988). Such motivations might also be rooted in social norms, cultural values, principles of justice, and so on, which enable or constrain competition and cooperation, consensus formation, loyalty, trust, suspicion, mutual obligations, individualism, collectivism, paternalism, and so on (see Almond and Verba, 1963; Moore, 1966; Fox, 1974; Sen, 1982; Young, 1990). To this complexity of human motivations, we must add the complexity of routes by which organizations and other collective agents pursue them: strategies of organizations, involving complex internal relationships and external linkages, and involving both short- and long-run considerations, with varying mixtures of risk and uncertainty, all come into play in the behavioral "cocktail" that emerges (see also Ben-Porath, 1980).

33. Arrow, 1951; Schelling, 1978; Hindess, 1988. See Azariadis (1981) for a counter view; and the early statement of Parsons (1937), and criticism of it, in Turner (1985, 1988).

34. We take this to be one of the underlying messages of Liebenstein (1976), although he did not state it in this way. See also Polanyi (1944).

35. To emphasize: we put aside the question of motivations in the following section, and deal only with claims about the coordination of actors.

36. For a good explanation of this difference, see Bromley, 1989.

37. Merton, 1936; Parsons, 1937, 1951.

38. Geertz, 1973: 201. One of the well known and ultimately inconclusive battles over these two extremes was fought out over explaining peasant behavior (a supposedly "simple" test case): see Popkin, 1979.

39. Tilly, 1984.

40. For valiant but, in our opinion, not fully successful attempts, see Calhoun, 1988. See also the papers in Taylor, 1988; and Moore, 1966; Dawley, 1976; Elster, 1978, 1982, 1989; Hindess, 1988.

41. For the critique of Marxism's totalizing, see Thompson, 1978. For a discussion of Foucault, see Dreyfus and Rabinow, 1983.

42. Barnes and Sheppard, 1991.

43. Coase, 1960; Olson, 1971; Alchian and Demsetz, 1972; Becker, 1976; Becker, 1985; Singh, 1985.

44. Stigler, 1961; Liebenstein, 1976; North, 1981; Pratt and Zeckhauser, 1985; Langlois, 1986.

45. North and Thomas, 1973; North, 1981.

46. Przeworski, 1985; Schelling, 1980; Lange, 1984a.

47. Lange, 1984, 1988. See also Keohane, 1984, for a discussion of concertation at an international scale.
48. Stigler, 1974a, 1974b; Riker, 1980; Cheung, 1983; Pratt and Zeckhauser, 1985.
49. North and Thomas, 1973; North, 1981.
50. Olson, 1971.
51. Elster, 1989. Or, in another domain, see Fox, 1974. See also Hirschman's (1970) critique of the idea that market or contractual "exit" is the only possible rule for efficient social interaction.
52. Przeworski and Wallerstein, 1982; Marin, 1983; Katzenstein, 1984; Maurice, Sellier, and Silvestre, 1986; Lange, 1988; Moene and Wallerstein, 1992.
53. See especially Buchanan and Tullock, 1965; Buchanan, 1975. But also see Alchian and Demsetz, 1972; Becker, 1976, 1983; Peltzman, 1984; Stiglitz, 1987. Related comments and viewpoints include Schotter, 1981, and Perrow, 1986.
54. See the following subsection for a definition of this problem.
55. Moe, 1987.
56. Schelling, 1978, 1980; Sabel, 1992. The early institutionalists attempted to capture this difference by labeling normal contracts "commodity transactions" and rule-setting processes "institutional transactions."
57. Granovetter, 1985. See also March and Simon, 1958; Sen, 1985; Marsden, 1986; Lorenz, 1991.
58. Arrow, 1951. See also Riker, 1980; Schepsle and Weingast, 1981.
59. Moe (1987) has a good review of this literature. See also Alt and Schepsle, 1990.
60. March and Olson, 1984; Pratt and Zeckhauser, 1985.
61. For an interesting discussion of such a problem with respect to labor unions, see Sabel (1981) and, somewhat differently, Pizzorno (1978).
62. See text at notes 38 and 45.
63. See text at note 47 and references thereto.
64. This is, of course, Arrow's seminal point (1951). See also Elster, 1978, 1982, 1984.
65. Notable works here include the contributions in Roemer, 1986, as well as Roemer, 1982; see also Przeworski, 1985; and the critique in Carling, 1986.
66. North, 1981.
67. Williamson, 1992: 74.

14. Toward a Theory of Conventions, Economic Action, and Economic Development

1. Lange, 1988.
2. Axelrod, 1984.
3. Many of these factors are discussed in our case studies in Chapters 6 through

8. See especially our comparison of conventions of identity and participation in Chapter 9.

4. Even relatively orthodox theorists admit this: see Azariadis, 1981.

5. Lewis, 1969. See also Axelrod, 1984.

6. Lewis, 1969.

7. Much in the same way that "small" technological choices may have important long-term effects on technological trajectories. See also the discussion on technological-organizational trajectories in Chapter 1.

8. We thank Sandy Jacoby for his insights on the qualities an adequate theory should have: Jacoby, 1989. These conditions are also inspired by the "old" institutionalism: Commons, 1924, 1934, 1950; Bush, 1987. See also the review in Hodgson, 1988.

9. Geertz, 1973.

10. Lorenz, 1991: 9.

11. One of the seminal points made by Commons, 1934. See our discussions of self-selection in Chapters 1 and 2. We agree with Foray's (1991) point about the openness of these processes but see no reason why openness must necessarily take the form of multiple equilibria.

12. See our discussions in Chapters 1, 3, and 5.

13. A phrase borrowed from Bagnasco, 1985: "la costruzione sociale del mercato."

14. See Thévenot, 1989a, 1989b, 1986.

15. An excellent discussion of interpretative activity is Clark's 1985 analysis of how judges interpret laws according to what are, in effect, conventions that are not parts of the law. See also Kripke, 1982, and Giddens, 1984, for linguistically based perspectives; on labor markets, see Sabel, 1982; Jacoby, 1983. A different approach is taken by Etzioni, 1988, who speaks of morality rather than interpretation.

16. For some contemporary sociological discussions which attempt to go beyond Parson's intentionalism and functionalism, with a core focus on interaction as the basis of action, see Turner, 1985, 1988, and the papers in Alexander et al., 1987. Note that they explicitly try to get away from earlier classificatory schemes of action as falling into different kinds of modalities (ceremonial, etc.), as in Ayres and Veblen (see Bush, 1987).

17. The early institutionalists had a convenient terminology for these *durées,* cast in the language of transactions: commodity transactions, the daily flow of goods and services in the economy, "work out" and "implement" coordination among actors in the form of concrete activity. But these theorists pointed out that most of these commodity transactions did not in any way affect the basic institutional order. Rather, the establishment of this order seemed to result from critical episodes in which agreements are secured about rules of the game (Commons, 1950; Bush, 1987).

These observations are salient to the analysis of conventions, but only with some important modifications. Rather than concentrating on "constitutional" events, in the sense of episodes in which explicit agreements are secured to establish explicit rules (for example, as in Sabel, 1992), we concentrate on rounds of expectations and practices as they form patterns of identity and participation. Participation is heavily affected by constitutional events, of course, but the latter is a subset of the former, not the other way around.

18. The classic statement is Polanyi, 1944. Various applications include Bendix, 1956; Cole, 1979; Morishima, 1982; Maurice, Sellier, and Silvestre, 1986; Dore, 1987a, 1987b; Becattini, 1989a; Dei Ottati, 1991.

19. A number of major studies have, in effect, focused on identity and participation without employing our theoretical architecture—see Almond and Verba, 1963, or Rokkan, 1970—but these were not applied specifically to economic analysis.

20. There is a vast body of literature on this topic. For a review, see North, 1981 (although we do not endorse his conclusions).

21. We are aware of problems of time in economic analysis. See Currie and Steedman, 1990, for an overview, as well as the insights of the evolutionary school (Nelson and Winter, 1982; Arthur, 1994), and other recent contributions such as those found in Maddison, 1991.

22. This idea is inspired by Geertz, 1973.

REFERENCES

Affichard, J. 1986. "L'homologation des titres et diplômes de l'enseignment technologique, une transformation pour donner valeur d'Etat à des formations spécifiques." In R. Salais and L. Thévenot, eds., *Le Travail: Marchés, règles, conventions*. Paris: Economica: pp. 139–159.

Akerlof, G. 1970. "The Market for 'Lemons': Quality Uncertainty and the Market Mechanism." *Quarterly Journal of Economics*, 89: 488–500.

Alchian, A. 1961. *The Economics of Property*. D-2316. Santa Monica, Calif.: Rand Corporation.

Alchian, A., and H. Demsetz. 1972. "Production: Information Costs and Economic Efficiency." *American Economic Review*, 62: 777–795.

——— 1973. "The Property Rights Paradigm." *Journal of Economic History*, 33: 16–27.

Alexander, J., B. Giesen, R. Much, and N. Smelser, eds. 1987. *The Micro-Macro Link*. Berkeley and Los Angeles: University of California Press.

Alexander, L. 1994. "Technology, Economic Growth, and Employment: New Research from the Department of Commerce." Paper presented at Conference on Employment Growth in a Knowledge-Based Economy, OECD, Copenhagen, November 7–8.

Almond, G., and S. Verba. 1963. *The Civic Culture: Political Attitudes and Democracy in Five Nations*. Princeton: Princeton University Press.

Alt, J., and K. Schepsle, eds. *Perspectives on Positive Political Economy*. Cambridge: Cambridge University Press.

Amable, B. 1990. "National Learning Effects, International Specialization and Growth Trajectories." OECD Technology-Employment Programme Conference, Paris, June.

Amendola, M., and J. L. Gaffard. 1990. *The Innovative Choice: An Economic Analysis of the Dynamics of Technology*. Oxford: Blackwell.

——— 1991. "Creation of Technology and Criteria of Efficiency." Paper presented to Management of Technology colloquium, Paris, May 17–28.

—— 1992. "Reflections on Growth and Dynamics: The Analytical Meaning of Innovation Systems." Paper presented to the international workshop "Systems of Innovation." Bologna, October 4–6.

Amendola, M., P. Guerrieri, and P. C. Padoan. 1991. "International Patterns of Technological Accumulation and Trade." Paper presented at European Association for Research in Industrial Economics (EARIE) conference, Ferrara, September 1–3.

Amin, A., and K. Robins. 1990. "Flexible Specialisation and Small Firms in Italy: Myths and Realities." In F. Pyke, G. Becattini, and W. Sengenberger, eds., *Industrial Districts and Inter-Firm Cooperation in Italy.* Geneva: ILO, pp. 185–219.

Amsden, A. 1990. *Asia's Next Giant.* New York: Oxford University Press.

Angel, D. 1989. "The Labor Market for Engineers in the US Semi-conductor Industry." *Economic Geography,* 65: 999–112.

Aoki, M. 1988. *Information, Incentives and Bargaining in the Japanese Economy.* Cambridge: Cambridge University Press.

—— 1990. "Toward an Economic Model of the Japanese Firm." *Journal of Economic Literature,* 28: 1–27.

Ardigo, A., and P. Donati. 1976. *Famiglia e Industrializzazione.* Milan: Franco Angeli.

Arrow, K. J. 1951. *Social Choice and Individual Values.* Cambridge: Cambridge University Press.

—— 1962. "The Economic Implications of Learning by Doing." *Review of Economic Studies,* 29: 154–174.

—— 1968. "Optimal Capital Policy with Irreversible Investment." In J. N. Wolfe, ed., *Value, Capital and Growth.* Chicago: Aldine, pp. 1–20.

—— 1972. *The Limits of Organization.* New York: Norton.

Arthur, W. B. 1994. *Increasing Returns and Path Dependence in the Economy.* Ann Arbor: University of Michigan Press.

Asanuma, B. 1989. "Manufacturer-Supplier Relationships in Japan and the Concept of Relation-Specific Skill." *Journal of the Japanese and International Economies,* 3: 1–30.

Axelrod, R. 1984. *The Evolution of Cooperation.* New York: Basic Books.

Azariadis, C. 1981. "Self-fulfilling Prophecies." *Journal of Economic Theory,* 25: 380–396.

Bagnasco, A. 1977. *Tre Italie.* Bologna: Il Mulino.

—— 1985. "La Construzione Sociale del Mercato: Strategia di Impresa e Esperimenti di Scala in Italia." *Stato e Mercato,* 13: 9–45.

Bagnasco, A., and C. Trigilia, eds. 1985. *Società e Politica nelle Aree di Piccola Imprese. Il Caso Delle Valdesa.* Milan: Franco Angeli.

Baily, M. N., C. Hulten, and D. Campbell. 1992. "Productivity Dynamics in Manufacturing Plants." *Brookings Papers on Economic Activity,* Microeconomics, pp. 187–267.

References

Baldwin, J. R., and P. Gorecki. 1990. "The Contribution of the Competitive Process to Productivity Growth: The Role of Firm and Plant Turnover." Ottawa: Research Paper No. 23D, Business and Labor Market Research Group, Analytical Studies Division, Statistics Canada.

Balestri, A. 1982. "Industrial Organization in the Manufacture of Fashion Goods: The Textile District of Prato 1950–1980." M.A. thesis, University of Lancaster.

———— 1990. *Cambiamento e Politiche Industriali nel Distretto Tessile di Prato.* Milan: Franco Angeli.

———— 1991a. *Gestione Economica e Struttura Finanziaria di un Gruppo di Imprese Tessili Pratesi negli Anni Otanta.* Prato: Unione Industriale Pratese, Uffico Studi.

———— 1991b. *La produzione di Impianti e Macchinari Tessile nell'Area Pratese.* Prato: Unione Industriale Pratese.

Balut, M. E. 1990. "Le recours à une formation homologuée dans un mode de gestion de la main d'oeuvre," in "L'avenir du niveau V (CAP-BEP)." *Collection des Etudes du CEREQ,* 56: 127–133.

Banfield, E. 1958. *The Moral Basis of a Backward Society.* New York: Free Press.

Barbagli, M., V. Cappechi, and A. Cobalti. 1988. *La Mobilità Sociale in Emilia Romagna.* Bologna: Il Mulino.

Barca, F. 1989. "Modèle de spécialisation flexible des PME et écart de rémunération." In M. Maruani, E. Reynaud, and C. Romani, eds., *La flexibilité en Italie.* Paris: Syros, pp. 239–251.

Barnes, T., and E. Sheppard. 1991. "Is There a Place for the Rational Actor? A Geographical Critique of the Rational Choice Paradigm." Paper presented at Association of American Geographers meeting, Miami, April.

Barthes, R. 1967. *Le système de la mode.* Paris: Point.

Bartolini, S. 1989. "Elementi di una microfondazione della teoria dei distretti industriali." Unpublished paper, University of Pisa.

Barzel, Y. 1982. "Measurement Cost and the Organization of Markets." *Journal of Law and Economics,* 25: 17–38.

Bass, S. 1991. "Prospects for Local Industrial Policy in the Age of the Keiretsu: Japanese Direct Investment in Southern California's Biotechnology Industry." M.A. thesis, University of California, Los Angeles.

Battiau, M. 1976. *Les industries textiles de la région Nord-Pas-de-Calais: étude d'une concentration géographique d'entreprise et de sa rémise en cause,* 2 vols. Lille: Société Géographique Lilloise.

Bauchet, P. 1986. *Le plan dans l'Economie Française.* Paris: Presses de la Fondation Nationale des Sciences Politiques.

Bauer, M., and E. Cohen. 1981. *Qui gouverne les groupes industriels?* Paris: Seuil.

Becattini, G. 1975. *Lo Sviluppo Economico della Toscana.* Florence: Guaraldi.

———— 1978. "The Development of Light Industry in Tuscany: An Interpretation." *Economic Notes,* 7: 107–123.

335

——— 1984. "L'Ambiente: Ospite Scomodo della Política Industriale." *Economia e Política Industriale,* 43: 3–8.

——— ed. 1987. *Mercato e Forze Locale: Il Distretto Industriale.* Bologna: Il Mulino.

——— 1988a. "Italian Industrial Districts: Problems and Perspectives." *Studi e Discussioni.* Florence: University of Florence, Department of Economics.

——— 1988b. *Modelli Locali di Sviluppo.* Bologna: Il Mulino.

——— 1989a. "Riflessione sul Distretto Industriale Marshaliano come Concetto Socio-Economico." *Stato e Mercato,* 25: 111–128.

——— 1989b. "The Marshallian Industrial District as a Socio-Economic Notion." In F. Pyke, G. Becattini, and W. Sengenberger, eds., *Industrial Districts and Inter-Firm Cooperation in Italy.* Geneva: ILO.

Becker, G. 1976. *The Economic Approach to Human Behavior.* Chicago: University of Chicago Press.

——— 1983. "A Theory of Competition Among Pressure Groups for Political Influence." *Quarterly Journal of Economics,* 98: 371–400.

——— 1985. "Public Policies, Pressure Groups, and Deadweight Costs." *Journal of Public Economics,* 28: 329–347.

Beckouche, P. 1988. "L'industrie électronique française: les régions face à la transnationalisation des firmes." Ph.D. diss., University of Paris I, Paris.

——— 1990. "High Tech française et territoire: un double clivage." In G. B. Benko, ed., *La dynamique spatiale de l'économie contemporaine.* Paris: Editions de l'Espace Européen, pp. 191–214.

Bellah, R., et al. 1985. *Habits of the Heart: Individualism and Commitment in American Life.* Berkeley: University of California Press.

Bellandi, M. 1986. "The Marshallian Industrial District." *Studi e Discussioni,* 42. Florence: University of Florence, Department of Economics.

——— 1988. "Economia di Scala e Costi di Transazione." *Studi e Discussioni,* 45. Florence: University of Florence, Department of Economics.

——— 1989. "The Role of Small Firms in the Development of Italian Manufacturing Industry." In E. Goodman and J. Bamford, eds., *Small Firms and Industrial Districts in Italy.* London: Routledge, pp. 31–52.

Bellandi, M., and C. Trigilia. 1990. "Come Cambia un Distretto Industriale: L'industria Tessile di Prato." Florence: University of Florence, Department of Economics.

Bellofiore, R. 1985. "Money and Development in Schumpeter." *Review of Radical Political Economics,* 17: 21–40.

Belussi, F. 1987. "Benetton: Information Technology in Production and Distribution: Case Study of the Innovatrice Potential of Traditional Sectors." *SFRU Occasional Paper Series,* 25, University of Sussex.

——— 1990. "Innovation Diffusion, Innovation Acquisition and Path Dependency in Traditional Sectors: An Empirical Investigation for the Veneto Region of Italy." Verona: European Institute of Technology.

References

Bendix, R. 1956. *Work and Authority in Industry.* New York: Wiley.

Ben-Porath, Y. 1980. "The F-Connection: Families, Friends and Firms in the Organization of Exchange." *Population and Development Review,* 6: 1–30.

Berger, S. 1980. "Reflections on Industrial Society: The Survival of the Traditional Sectors in France and Italy." In S. Berger and M. Piore, *Dualism and Discontinuity in Industrial Societies.* New York: Cambridge University Press, pp. 88–131.

—— 1981. "Lame Ducks and National Champions: Industrial Policy in the Fifth Republic." In W. G. Andrews and S. Hoffman, eds., *The Fifth Republic at Twenty.* Albany, N.Y.: SUNY Press, pp. 292–310.

Best, M. 1990. *The New Competition: Institutions of Industrial Restructuring.* Cambridge: Polity Press.

Bianchi, P. 1987. "Intermediaries and Structural Change in Small Firm's Area: The Italian Experience." Paper presented at New Technologies and New Intermediaries conference, Stanford Center for European Studies, Stanford, Calif., June.

—— 1989. "Riorganizzazione Produttiva e Crescita Esterna dell'Imprese Italiane." In M. Regini and C. Sabel, eds., *Strategie di Riaggiustamento Industriale.* Bologna: Il Mulino, pp. 39–61.

Bianchi, P., M. G. Giordani, and F. Pasquini. 1988. "Industrial Policy in Italy at a Local Level." Paper presented at Regional Science Association 28th European Congress, Stockholm, August.

Bigarelli, D., and P. Crestanello. 1991. "Casi Concreti di Sviluppo Local: Il Caso di Carpi." IRIS Conference "Possibilitá e Limiti dello Sviluppo Locale." Prato, September 16–21.

Birnbaum., P. 1977. *La Logique de l'Etat.* Paris: Fayard.

Bloch, R. 1992. "The Making of an Outer City: Industry, Culture and Land in Oakland City, Michigan." Ph.D. diss., University of California, Los Angeles.

Boissonnade, P. 1931. *Colbert: le triomphe d'Etatisme, la fondation de la suprématie industrielle de la France et la dictature du travail 1661–1683.* Paris: Rivière.

Boltanski, L. 1982. *Les cadres: La formation d'un groupe social.* Paris: Les Editions de Minuit.

Boltanski, L., and L. Thévenot. 1987. *Les économies de la grandeur.* Cahiers du Centre d'Etudes de l'Emploi, 31. Paris: Presses Universitaires de France.

—— 1991. *De la justification.* Paris: Gallimard.

Boniface, P., and F. Heisbourg. 1983. *La puce, les hommes et la bombe.* Paris: Hachette.

Bony, D., and F. Eymard-Duvernay. 1982. "Cohérence de la branche et diversité des entreprises: étude d'un cas." *Economie et Statistique,* 144: 13–25.

Bordogna, L. 1987. "Strategies of Flexibility: Enterprises, Trade Unions, Local Governements: The Case of Montedison Petrochemical Plan in Ferrara." Contribution to colloquium on New Technologies and New Forms of

Industrial Relations, MIT Conference Center, Endicott House, Cambridge, Mass.

Boucheron, J. M. 1985. "Rapport pour la commission de la Défense Nationale." Assemblée Nationale, no. 275, 21st session ordinaire 1984–1985, Paris.

Bouillaguet, P. 1991. "Les politiques de l'emploi: orientations et bilans (1975–1991)." Rapport pour l'emploi, Commission des Comptes de la Nation, July 2.

Boulin, J. Y., and D. Taddéi. 1989. "Les accords de réduction et réorganisation du temps de travail." *Travail et Emploi*, 40: 33–51.

Bourdieu, P. 1990. *La noblesse d'Etat*. Paris: Gallimard.

Bourdon, F. 1987. "Influence de la Recherche-Développement sur le système productif." *Révue d'Economie Régionale et Urbaine*, 2: 181–202.

Boy, L. 1987. "Entreprises en difficulté: la recherche d'un consensus autour du thème de l'entreprise." In A. Pirovano et al., *Changement social et droit négocié (De la résolution des conflits à la conciliation des intérêts)*. Paris: Report to the Commissariat général du Plan, March, pp. 42–88.

Boyer, R., and B. Coriat. 1986. "Technical Flexibility and Macro Stabilization." *Ricerche Economiche*, 11: 771–835.

Braverman, H. 1974. *Labor and Monopoly Capital: The Degradation of Work in the 20th Century*. New York: Monthly Review Press.

Bridge, (The). 1988. "Italian Textile Workers: Innovation and New Industrial Relations." Rome: The Bridge Association.

Bromley, D. 1989. *Economic Interests and Institutions*. Oxford: Basil Blackwell.

Brown, J. K. 1995. *The Baldwin Locomotive Works*. Baltimore: Johns Hopkins University Press.

Bruno, S. 1992. "Innovative Systems: The Economics of Ex-ante Cooperation." Paper presented to the international workshop "Systems of Innovation," Bologna, October 4–6.

Brusco, S. 1982. "The Emilian Model: Productive Decentralization and Social Integration." *Cambridge Journal of Economics*, 6: 167–184.

——— 1983. "Flessibilitá e Solidità del Sistema: L'esperienza Emiliana." In G. Fua and C. Zacchia, *Industrializzazione Sensa Fratture*. Bologna: Il Mulino, pp. 180–210.

Brusco, S., and M. Pezzini. 1990. "Small Scale Enterprise in the Ideology of the Italian Left." In F. Pyke, G. Beccatini, and W. Sengenberger, eds., *Industrial Districts and Inter-Firm Cooperation in Italy*. Geneva: ILO, pp. 20–35.

Brutti, P. 1990. "Industrial Districts: The Point of View of the Unions." Contribution to Colloquium on Industrial Districts and Local Economic Regeneration, ILO, Geneva, October 18–19.

Bucaille, A., and B. Costa de Beauregard. 1988. *Les Etats: acteurs de la concurrence industrielle*. Centre de Prospective économique. Paris: Economica.

Buchanan, J. 1975. *The Limits of Liberty*. Chicago: University of Chicago Press.

References

Buchanan, J., and G. Tullock. 1965. *The Calculus of Consent.* Ann Arbor: University of Michigan Press.

Bué, J., and D. Rossi. 1991. "Les accords dérogatoires et le travail de nuit des femmes: le passage d'une interdiction légale à une autorisation contractuelle." Presentation to colloquium, "Les conventions collectives." Paris, May 23–24.

Bursi, T. 1982. *Il Settore Meccano-Ceramico nel Comprensorio della Ceramica: Struttura e Processi di Crescita.* Milan: Franco Angeli.

——— 1989. *Piccola e media impresa e politiche di adattamento: Il distretto della maglieria di Carpi.* Milan: Franco Angeli.

Bush, P. D. 1987. "The Theory of Institutional Change." *Journal of Economic Issues,* 21: 1075–1115.

Calhoun, C. 1988. "The Radicalism of Tradition and the Question of Class Struggle." In M. Taylor, ed., *Rationality and Revolution.* Cambridge: Cambridge University Press, pp. 129–175.

Callens, S. 1990. "Essai sur les logiques économiques liées aux initiatives pour l'emploi." *Dossier de Recherche* 28, Centre d'Etudes de l'Emploi, Paris.

Callon, M. 1986. "Eléments pour une sociologie de la traduction." *L'Année Sociologique,* 36: 169–208.

Camagni, R., and R. Capello. 1990. "Towards a Definition of the Manoeuvering Space of Local Development Initiatives: Italian Success Stories of Local Development, Theoretical Conditions and Practical Experience." In W. Stohr, ed., *Global Challenge and Local Response: Initiatives for Economic Regeneration in Contemporary Europe.* London: Mansell, pp. 328–353.

Capitani, G., and G. Garofoli. 1985. "Industrializzazione e Terziarizzazione Diffusa in Lombardia." In R. Innocenti, ed., *Piccola Città e Piccola Impresa: Urbanizzazione, Industrializzazione e Intervento Pubblico nelle Aree Periferiche.* Milan: Franco Angeli, pp. 119–148.

Cappecchi, V. (n.d.). "Les facteurs de développement d'une économie régionale." Bologna: University of Bologna, unpublished manuscript.

——— 1989. "Petite entreprise et économie locale: la flexibilité productive." In M. Maruani, E. Reynaud, and C. Romani, eds., *Le flexibilité en Italie.* Paris: Syros, pp. 271–286.

——— 1990a. "L'industrializzazione a Bologna nel Novecento: dal Secondo Dopoguerra ad Oggi." *Storia Illustrata di Bologna,* 9/V: 161–180.

——— 1990b. "L'industrializzazione a Bologna nel Novecento: Dagli inizi del Secolo alla Fine della Seconda Guerra Mondiale." *Storia Illustrata di Bologna,* 18/IV: 341–360.

Cappiello, M. A. 1989. "I Distretti Industriali Calzaturieri della Toscana." Manuscript. CNR Project on Industrial Systems, Rome.

Carboni, C. 1990. *Lavoro Informale ed Economia Diffusa: Costanti e Trasformazioni Recenti.* Rome: Editions Lavoro.

——— 1991. "The Realms of Social Inequalities: Social Stande, Class and Citizenship in Western Advanced Society." Working paper, Department of Political Science, Ancona, Italy.

Carling, A. 1986. "Rational Choice Marxism." *New Left Review,* 160: 24–62.

Carroué, L. 1984. "L'électronique professionnelle en région parisienne. Recherche à propos d'un tissu industriel régional." *Analyses de l'Espace,* 3–4: 22–44.

———— 1986. "Technologies nouvelles, modernisation et dépendances extérieures: la bureaucratique en France." *Bulletin de l'Association géographique française,* 63: 251–255.

———— 1988. "Les industries électriques et électroniques en France." Doctoral thesis, University of Paris I, Paris.

Cavard, J. C. 1986. "Industrie de haute technologie et politique départementale de l'innovation dans la couronne parisienne septentrionale." *Bulletin de l'Association géographique française,* 63: 227–238.

Caves, R., and M. Porter. 1979. "From Entry Barriers to Mobility Barriers." *Quarterly Journal of Economics,* 91: 241–261.

Célérier, S., and E. Kirsch. 1990. "Les CAP par unités capitalisables: une modalité de requalification ouvrière." L'avenir du Niveau V (CAP-BEP). *Collection des Etudes du CEREQ,* 56: 117–126.

Chandler, A. 1966. *Strategy and Structure: Chapters in the History of the Industrial Enterprise.* Cambridge, Mass.: MIT Press.

———— 1977. *The Visible Hand: The Managerial Revolution in American Business.* Cambridge, Mass.: Harvard University Press.

Chapman, H. 1990. *State Capitalism and Working Class Radicalism in the French Aircraft Industry.* Berkeley: University of California Press.

Cheung, S. 1983. "The Contractual Nature of the Firm." *Journal of Law and Economics,* 26: 1–22.

Chevallier, P. 1985. *Eléments d'Analyse Politique.* Paris: Presses Universitaires de France.

Christopherson, S. 1994. "Rules as Resources in Investment Location Decisions." Paper presented to Innis Centennial Symposium, Toronto, September.

Clark, G. L. 1985. *Judges and the Cities.* Chicago: University of Chicago Press.

Clark, G., M. Gertler, and J. Whiteman. 1986. *Regional Dynamics: Studies in Adjustment Theory.* Boston: Allen and Unwin.

Coase, R. 1937. "The Nature of the Firm." *Economica,* 4: 386–405.

———— 1959. "The Federal Communications Commission." *Journal of Law and Economics,* 2: 1–40.

———— 1960. "The Problem of Social Cost." *Journal of Law and Economics,* 2: 1–40.

Cohen, J. 1987. "Emploi de haute technologie et technopoles: Paris Sud dans le contexte régional et national." Contribution to colloquium "Villes et Technopoles," Toulouse, Septeember.

Cohen, S. 1969. *Modern Capitalist Planning: The French Model.* Cambridge, Mass.: Harvard University Press.

References

Cohen, S., and J. Zysman. 1986. *Manufacturing Matters*. New York: Basic Books.

Cohendet, P., and P. Llerena. 1989. "Flexibilités, risque et incertitude dans la théorie de la firme: un Survey." In P. Cohendet and P. Llerena, eds., *Flexibilité, information et décision*. Paris: Economica, pp. 7–71.

Cohendet, P., P. Llerena, and A. Sorge. 1991. "Modes of Usage and Diffusion of Science and Technology: Valorizing Diversity." Paper presented at the International Symposium Europe-USA, Management of Technology, Paris, May.

Coing, H. 1982. *La ville, marché de l'emploi*. Grenoble: Presses Universitaires de Grenoble.

Cole, R. 1979. *Work, Mobility and Participation: A Comparative Study of American and Japanese Industry*. Berkeley and Los Angeles: University of California Press.

Colombo, M. G., S. Mariotto, and M. Mutinelli. 1991. *The Internationalization of the Italian Economy*. Politecnico di Milano, Consorzio Universitario in Ingegneria per la Gestione d'Impresa, Milan.

Commissariat Général du Plan. 1987. "Perspectives d'évolution de l'industrie textile française." Rapport du Comité "Prospective des échanges internationaux." Paris.

Commons, J. R. 1924. *The Legal Foundations of Capitalism*. New York: Macmillan.

——— 1934. *Institutional Economics: Its Place in Political Economy*. New York: Macmillan.

——— 1950. *The Economics of Collective Action*. New York: Macmillan.

Conseil, Economique et Social (République Française). 1982. "Le devenir des industries du textile et de l'habillement." *Journal Officiel*, February 25.

——— 1986. "Les prêts et aides aux entreprises." *Journal Officiel*, Brochure 4049.

Contini, B. 1984. "Dimensioni di Impresa, Divisione del Lavoro e Ampiezza del Mercato." *Monetà e Credito*, 148: 371–437.

Contini, B., U. Colombino, L. Treves, and M. Vitelli. 1987. "New Forms and New Areas of Employment Growth: Final Report for Italy." Brussels: Report to the Commission of the European Communities.

Cooke, P., and K. Morgan. 1994. "The Regional Innovation System in Baden-Württemburg." *International Journal of Technology Management*, 9: 1–36.

Cori, B., and G. Cortesi. 1977. *Prato: Frammentazione e Integrazione di un Bacino Tessile*. Turin: Fondazione Giovanni Agnelli Editore.

Coriat, B. 1990. *L'atelier et le robot*. Paris: Christian Bourgois.

——— 1991. *Penser à l'envers*. Paris: Christian Bourgois.

Coriat, B., and D. Taddei. 1991. *Made in France*. Paris: Economica.

Cornu, R. 1980. "Comment accommoder les rivets de Port-de-Bouc." *Technologies, Idéologies, Pratiques*, 2, Nos. 3 and 4.

Courault, B., and C. Romani. 1989. "La flexibilité productive en question: le modèle italien à l'épreuve des études comparatives." Contribution to the First Conference of the European Association of Labour Economics (EALE), Turin, September 8–10.

Currie, M., and I. Steedman. 1990. *Wrestling with Time: Problems in Economic Theory.* Ann Arbor: University of Michigan Press.

Cusumano, M. 1985. *The Japanese Automobile Industry.* Cambridge, Mass.: Harvard University Press.

Dagnaud, M. 1984. *L'élite rose.* Paris: Ramsay.

David, P. 1975. *Technical Choice, Innovation and Economic Growth: Essays on American and British Experiences in the 19th Century.* Cambridge: Cambridge University Press.

———— 1986. "Understanding the Economics of Poverty: The Necessity of History." In W. Parker, ed., *Economic History and the Modern Economist.* Oxford: Basil Blackwell.

Davis, M. 1988. "The Political Economy of Late-Imperial America." *New Left Review,* 165:51–83.

Dawley, A. 1976. *Class and Community: The Industrial Revolution in Lynn.* Cambridge, Mass.: Harvard University Press.

Dei Ottati, G. (n.d.). "Prato: 1944–1963. Reconstruction and Transformation of a Local System of Production." Florence: University of Florence, manuscript.

———— 1987. "Distretto Industriale, Problemi della Transazione e Mercato Communitario: Prime Considerazioni." *Economia e Política Industriale,* 51: 93–122.

———— 1991. "Il Finanziamento dello Sviluppo Locale." Contribution to colloquium "Possibilità et limiti dello sviluppo locale." Istituto di Ricerche sociali (IRIS), Prato, September.

Delbourg-Delphis, M. 1981. *Le chic et le look.* Paris: Hachette.

Del Monte, A. 1986. "Job Generation in Small and Medium-Sized Enterprises: Italy." Naples: University of Naples, manuscript.

Dematteis, G. 1985. "Contro-Urbanizzazione e Deconcentrazione: un Salto di Scala nell'Organizzazione Territoriale." In R. Innocenti, ed., *Piccola Città & Piccola Impresa: Urbanizzazione, Industrializzazione e Intervento Pubblico nelle Aree Periferiche.* Milan: Franco Angeli, pp. 101–118.

Dematteis, G., and F. Ferlaino, eds. 1991. *Le Aree Metropolitane Tra Specificità e Complementarietà.* Turin: Istituto Richerche Economico-Sociali del Piemonte.

Demsetz, H. 1967. "Toward a Theory of Property Rights." *American Economic Review,* 57: 347–359.

Dertouzos, M., R. Lester, and R. Solow. 1990. *Made in America: Regaining the Competitive Edge.* Cambridge, Mass.: MIT Press.

DeVet, J. M. 1990. "Innovation and New Firm Formation in Southern California's Medical Device Industry." Master's thesis, University of California, Los Angeles.

———— 1993. "Globalisation and Local and Regional Competitiveness." *STI Review* 13, Paris, OECD.

DeVet, J. M., and A. J. Scott. 1992. "The Southern Californian Medical Device Industry: Innovation, New Firm Formation and Location." *Research Policy,* 21: 145–161.

References

Didry, C., and R. Salais. 1991. "L'écriture des conventions. Entre le métier et l'industrie, un moment critique : les conventions collectives 1936–1937." Contribution to colloquium "Les conventions collectives." Paris, May.

DiLellio, A. 1987. "Changing Citizenship in 'High Tech' Communities: The Case of Dallas (US) and Grenoble (France)." Paper presented at the International Conference on Technology, Restructuring and Urban Regional Development, Dubrovnik, June.

D'Iribarne, P. 1989. *La logique de l'honneur: gestion des entreprises et traditions nationales.* Paris: Seuil.

Doeringer, P., and M. Piore. 1971. *Internal Labor Markets and Manpower Analysis.* Lexington, Mass.: Heath.

———— 1984. *Internal Labor Markets and Manpower Analysis,* 2nd ed. New York: Sharp.

Dollar, D., and E. Woolf 1988. "Convergence of Industry Labor Productivity among Advanced Economies 1963–1982." *Review of Economics and Statistics,* 80: 549–558.

Dore, R. 1986. *Flexible Rigidities: Industrial Policy and Structural Adjustment in the Japanese Economy, 1970–80.* London: Athlone.

———— 1987a. *Taking Japan Seriously.* Stanford: Stanford University Press.

———— 1987b. *British Factory/Japanese Factory: The Origins of National Diversity in Industrial Relations.* Berkeley and Los Angeles: University of California Press.

Dosi, G. 1987. "Institutions and Markets in a Dynamic World." SPRU Discussion Paper 22, Brighton.

———— 1988. "Sources, Procedures and Microeconomic Effects of Innovation." *Journal of Economic Literature,* 25: 1120–1171.

Dosi, G., and L. Orsenigo. 1985. "Order and Change: An Exploration of Markets, Institutions and Technology in Industrial Dynamics." SPRU Discussion Paper 32, Brighton.

Dosi, G., K. Pavitt, and L. Soete. 1990. *The Economics of Technical Change and International Trade.* New York: New York University Press.

Dosi, G., and R. Salvatore. 1992. "The Structure of Industrial Production and the Boundaries Between Firms and Markets." In M. Storper and A. Scott, eds., *Pathways to Industrialization and Regional Development.* London: Routledge, pp. 171–193.

Dow, G. 1987. "The Function of Authority in Transaction Cost Economics." *Journal of Economic Behavior and Organization,* 8: 13–38.

Dreyfus, H., and P. Rabinow. 1982. *Michel Foucault: Beyond Structuralism and Hermeneutics.* Chicago: University of Chicago Press.

Duroselle, B. 1980. *Les métiers de la mode et de l'habillement.* Paris: Marcel Valtat.

Earle, C. 1990. *Geographical Inquiry and American Historical Problems.* Stanford, Calif.: Stanford University Press.

References

Elias, N. 1974. *La société de cour*. Paris: Editions Calmann-Levy.

Elkin, S. L. 1987. *City and Regime in the American Republic*. Chicago: University of Chicago Press.

Elster, J. 1978. *Logic and Society: Contradictions and Possible Worlds*. Chichester: Wiley.

———— 1982. "Sour Grapes: Utilitarianism and the Genesis of Wants." In A. Sen and B. Williams, eds., *Utilitarianism and Beyond*. Cambridge: Cambridge University Press, pp. 219–238.

———— 1984. *Ulysses and the Sirens*. New York: Cambridge University Press.

———— 1989. *The Cement of Society*. Cambridge: Cambridge University Press.

Ely, J. 1987. "Post Fordist Restructuring in the Federal Republic of Germany and the United States: The Role of the New Social Movements." Paper delivered at the Sixth International Conference of Europeanists, Washington, D.C., October 31.

Englander, E. 1988. "Technology and Oliver Williamson's Transaction Cost Economics." *Journal of Economic Behavior and Organization,* 10: 339–354.

Enrietti, A. 1983. "Indústria Automobilistica: la 'Quasi-Integrazione verticale' come modello interpretativo del rapporti tra le imprese." *Economia e Politica Industriale,* 38: 39–72.

ERVET (Ente Regionale per la Valorizzazione Economica del Territorio). 1991. "Acquisizione e Fusioni in Emilia Romagna," *ERVET Materiali* 26, Bologna.

Etzioni, A. 1988. *The Moral Dimension: Toward a New Economics*. New York: The Free Press.

Ewald, F. 1986. *L'Etat-providence*. Paris: Fayard.

Fainstein, S. 1994. "Justice, Politics and the Creation of Urban Space." New Brunswick, N.J.: Rutgers University Center for Urban Policy Research, working paper 71.

Farault, F. 1987. *Histoire de la belle jardinière*. Paris: Belin.

Favereau, O. 1989. "Marchés internes, marchés externes." *Revue Economique,* 40: 273–328.

Fishlow, A. 1965. *American Railroads and the Transformation of the Antebellum Economy*. Cambridge, Mass.: Harvard University Press.

Florida, R., and M. Kenney. 1988. "High Technology Restructuring in the US and Japan: Flexible Specialization vs. 'Structured Flexibility.'" School of Urban and Public Affairs (SUPA) Working Paper 88-15. Pittsburgh: Carnegie-Mellon University.

———— 1990. *The Breakthrough Illusion: Corporate America's Failure to Move from Innovation to Mass Production*. New York: Basic Books.

Flyvberg, B. 1992. "Power Has a Rationality That Rationality Does Not Know." Aalborg, Denmark: University of Aalborg, unpublished paper.

Fontanel, J. 1983. *L'économie des armes*. Paris: La Découverte/Maspéro.

References

Foray, D. 1990. "The Secrets of the Industry Are in the Air: 'Eléments pour un cadre d'analyse du phénomène du réseau d'innovateurs.'" Paper delivered at the Colloquium "Networks of Innovators," Montreal, May 1–3.

——— 1991. "Dynamique économique et nouvelles exigences de l'investigation historique: 'Learning to Love Multiple Equilibria.'" *Révue Economique*, 2: 301–312.

Foray, D., and P. Garrouste. 1990. "Changements technologiques et stabilité des formes productives: éléments de dynamique industrielle." *Economie appliquée*, 43: 51–73.

Forlai, L. 1989. "Prospettive del conto terzismo nel quadro del evoluzione del modello pratese." Internal document, Bologna, NOMISMA.

Forlai, L., and S. Bertini. 1989. "Evoluzione e prospettive del distretto pratese. Alcune considerazione teoriche." Rome: Report of the National Research Council, *Sistema delle Imprese*.

Foucault, M. 1973. *Madness and Civilization*. New York: Vintage.

Fourquet, F. 1980. *Les comptes de la puissance. Histoire de la comptabilité Nationale et du Plan*. Paris: Encre (Recherches).

Fox, A. 1974. *Beyond Contract: Work, Power, and Trust Relations*. London: Faber.

Fox, R. W. 1988. "The Liberal Ethic and the Spirit of Protestantism." In C. Reynolds and R. Norman, eds., *Community in America*. Berkeley: University of California Press, pp. 238–249.

Fraser, R. W. 1984. "Demand Fluctuations, Inventories and Flexibility." *Australian Economic Papers*, June, pp. 105–111.

Freeman, C. 1991. "Networks of Innovators: A Synthesis of Research Issues." *Research Policy*, 20: 350–375.

Freeman, R., and J. Medoff. 1984. *What do Unions Do?* New York: Basic Books.

Frey, L., ed. 1975. *Lavoro a Domicilio e Decentramento Produttivo*. Milan: Franco Angelli.

Friedberg, E. 1976. "L'Etat and l'industrie en France." Paris: Rapport CSO-CORDES.

Fua, G. 1983. "Rural Industrialization in Later Developed Countries: The Case of Northeast and Central Italy." *Banca Nazionale del Lavoro Quarterly Review*, 147 (Rome), pp. 351–377.

——— 1985. "Les voies diverses du développement en Europe." *Annales Economies, Sociétés, Civilisations*, 3: 579–603.

Fua, G., and C. Zacchia, eds. 1973. *Industrializzazione Sensa Fratture*. Bologna: Il Mulino.

Gaeta, L. 1985. "Le Difficoltà dell'Imprese Emiliano-Romagnole delle Confezione: una Crisi di Comparto o l'Emergere dei Limiti del Piccolo e Bello?" Carpi: CITER.

Galbraith, J. K. 1967. *The New Industrial State*. Boston: Houghton Mifflin.

Ganne, B. 1985. "Du notable au local: transformations d'un modèle politique." *Les Annales de la Recherche urbaine,* 28: 23–32.

Garofoli, G. 1983a. "Aree di Specializzazione Produttive e Piccole Imprese in Europa." *Economia Marche,* II, 1, pp. 3–43.

—— 1983b. "Le Aree-Sistema in Italia." *Politica ed Economica,* XIV, 11, November.

—— 1988. "Modelli Locali di Sviluppo: Tipologia di Aree e Politiche di Intervento." University of Pavia, Department of Economics.

Geertz, C. 1973. *The Interpretation of Cultures.* New York: Basic Books.

Gerbaux, M., and P. Muller. 1989. *Les entrepreneurs ruraux: Agriculteurs, artisans, commerçants, élus locaux.* Paris: L'Harmattan.

Gerstenberger, W. 1990. "Reshaping Industrial Structures." Presentation to the OECD colloquium, Technology-Employment Programme, Paris, June.

Gibbons, M., and J. Metcalfe. 1986. "Technological Variety and the Process of Competition." Paper presented to the Conference on Innovation Diffusion, Venice, June.

Giddens, A. 1984. *The Constitution of Society: Outline of the Theory of Structuration.* Cambridge: Polity Press.

Giovannini, P. 1987. "La Societá Toscana e le Sue Trasformazioni." In Istituto Gramsci Toscano, Verso una Riflessione sul Modello Toscano di Sviluppo, Atti del Seminario Tenutosi a Firenze nell'aprile 1987, pp. 31–52.

Glasmeier, A. 1988. "Factors Governing the Development of High Tech Industry Agglomerations: A Tale of Three Cities." *Regional Studies,* 22: 287–301.

Gobbo, F., ed. 1989. *Distretti e Sistemi Produttivi all Soglia Degli Anni'90.* Milan: Franco Angeli.

Goglio, S., and F. Sforzi. 1991. "Le Differenziazione Regionali in Italia." University of Trento, Economic Development Research Group.

Gold, B. 1964. "Industry Growth Patterns: Theory and Empirical Results." *Journal of Industrial Economics,* 13: 53–73.

Goldberg, V. 1980. "Relational Exchange: Economics and Complex Contracts." *American Behavioral Scientist,* 23: 337–352.

Golden, M. 1988. *Austerity and Its Opposition: Communism, Corporatism, and the Italian Labor Movement.* Ithaca, N.Y.: Cornell University Press.

Gollop, F. M., and J. L. Monahan. 1982. "From homogeneity to heterogeneity: an index of diversification." Washington, D.C: U.S. Bureau of the Census, unpublished report.

Goncourt, E. de. 1982. *La femme du XVIIIe siècle.* Paris: Flammarion (originally published in 1962).

Goodman, E., and J. Bamford, eds. 1989. *Small Firms and Industrial Districts in Italy.* London: Routledge.

Gordon, R. J. 1986. "Why US Wage and Employment Behavior Differs from that in Britain and Japan." *The Economic Journal,* 92: 13–44.

References

——— 1989. "Global Networks and the Innovation Process in High Technology SMEs: the Case of Silicon Valley." In D. Maillat and J. C. Perrin, eds., *Entreprises innovatrices et réseaux locaux*. Paris: Economica, pp. 195–222.

Gourevitch, P. 1986. *Politics in Hard Times: Comparative Responses to International Economic Crises*. Ithaca, N.Y.: Cornell University Press.

Grando, J. M., and E. Verdier. 1987. "Le secteur de l'électronique professionnelle: entreprises et emplois." Joint publication: Centre d'Etudes de l'Emploi/CEREQ/Service d'Etudes et de Statistiques industrielle du ministère de l'Industrie, Paris.

Granovetter, M. 1985. "Economic Action and Social Structure: The Problem of Embeddedness." *American Journal of Sociology*, 93: 481–510.

Green, N. 1986. "Immigrant Labor in the Garment Industries of Paris and New York: Variations on a Structure." *Comparative Social Research*, 9: 231–244.

Greenaway, D., and C. Milner. 1986. *The Economics of Intra-Industry Trade*. Oxford: Basil Blackwell.

Grémion, C. 1987. "Decentralization in France: A Historical Perspective." In G. Ross, S. Hoffmann, and S. Malzacher, eds., *The Mitterand Experiment: Continuity and Change in Modern France*. New York: Oxford University Press, pp. 237–247.

Grossman, S., and O. Hart. 1986. "The Costs and Benefits of Ownership: A Theory of Vertical and Lateral Integration." *Journal of Political Economy*, 94: 691–719.

Guibert, B., J. Laganier, and M. Volle. 1971. "Essai sur les nomenclatures industrielles." *Economie et Statistique*, 20: 23–36.

Guichard, O. 1987. "La France doît cultiver ses points forts." *Politique Industrielle*, 8: 115–122.

Guilbert, M., and V. Isambert-Jamati. 1956. *Travail féminin et travail à domicile*. Paris: Editions du CNRS.

Guillon, M., and I. Taboada-Leonetti. 1986. *Le triangle de Choisy: un quartier chinois à Paris*. Paris: L'Harmattan.

Habbakuk, H. 1962. *American and British Technology in the 19th Century*. Cambridge: Cambridge University Press.

Habermas, J. 1976. *Connaissance et intérêt*. Paris: Gallimard. (Originally published in Germany, 1968.)

Hakansson, H. 1989. *Corporate Technological Behavior: Cooperation and Networks*. New York: Routledge.

Hall, P. 1988. *Governing the Economy: The Politics of State Intervention in Britain and France*. Oxford: Polity Press.

Hardin, R. 1995. *One for All: The Logic of Group Conflict*. Princeton, N.J.: Princeton University Press.

Harris, D. 1978. *Capital Accumulation and Income Distribution*. Stanford: Stanford University Press.

References

Harrison, B. 1989. "Concentration without Centralization: The Changing Morphology of the Small Firm Industrial Districts of the Third Italy." Paper presented at the International Symposium on Local Employment, National Institute of Employment and Vocational Research, Tokyo.

Hart, A. G. 1937. "Anticipations, Business Planning and the Cycle." *Quarterly Journal of Economics*, 273–297.

Hartz, L. 1955. *The Liberal Tradition in America*. New York: Harcourt, Brace, Jovanovich.

Haudricourt, A. G. 1987. *La technologie, science humaine. Recherches d'histoire et d'ethnologie des techniques*. Paris: Editions de la Maison des Sciences de l'Homme.

Hauerwas, S. 1988. "A Christian Critique of Christian America." In C. H. Reynolds and R. Norman, eds., *Community in America*. Berkeley: University of California Press, pp. 250–268.

Hayek, F. 1945. "The Use of Knowledge in Society." *American Economic Review*, 35: 519–530.

Hayward, J. 1985. *The State and the Market Economy: Industrial Patriotism and Economic Intervention in France*. Brighton: Wheatsheaf.

Hekman, J. S. 1980. "Can New England Hold Onto Its High Technology Industry?" *New England Economic Review*, March–April: 35–44.

Hekman, J., and S. Strong. 1981. "The Evolution of New England Industry." *New England Economic Review*, March–April: 35–46.

Herpin, N. 1986. "L'habillement, la classe sociale et la mode." *Economie et Statistique*, 188: 35–54.

Hickmann, R. 1989. "The Job Creation Process: Implications for Regional Economic Development." Report to the Ministère du Travail et des Affaires Sociales Françaises, Paris.

Hindess, B. 1988. *Choice, Rationality and Social Theory*. London: Unwin Hyman.

Hirsch, J. P. 1991. *Les deux rêves du commerce: Entreprise et institutions dans la région lilloise 1760–1860*. Paris: Editions de l'Ecole des Hautes Etudes en Sciences Sociales.

Hirschman, A. 1970. *Exit, Voice, and Loyalty: Responses to Decline in Firms, Organizations, and States*. Cambridge, Mass.: Harvard University Press.

Hirst, P. Q. 1990. *Representative Democracy and Its Limits*. Oxford: Polity Press.

Hodgson, G. 1988. *Economics and Institutions: A Manifesto for a Modern Institutional Economics*. Oxford: Polity Press.

Hounshell, D. 1984. *From the American System to Mass Production, 1800–1932*. Baltimore: Johns Hopkins University Press.

Hyman, R., and W. Streeck, eds. 1988. *New Technologies and Industrial Relations*. Oxford: Basil Blackwell.

Imai, K., and H. Itami. 1984. "Interpretation of Organization and Market." *International Journal of Industrial Organization*, 2: 285–310.

References

INSEE. 1987a. "Statistique et indicateurs des régions françaises. Annexe au projet de loi de finances pour 1988." Paris: Collections de l'INSEE.

———— 1987b. "Les industries électroniques et électriques." *Vue sur l'Economie Aquitaine,* 25: 20–26.

———— 1988. "Grandes firmes industrielles et sous-traitance." *Statistiques et Etudes,* no. 2.

ISTAT. 1986. "Indagine sulla Diffusione dell'Innovazione Technologia nell'Industria Manifatturia Italiana." *Notiziario,* June, 4–41.

Jacoby, S. 1983. "Industrial Labor Mobility in Historical Perspective." *Industrial Relations,* 22: 261–282.

———— 1989. "Learning from the Past: The New Institutional Labor Economics and the Old." Working Paper 173, UCLA Institute of Industrial Relations, Los Angeles.

Jacomet, D. 1989. *Le textile-habillement: une industrie de pointe.* Paris: Economica.

Jencks, C. 1994. *Rethinking Social Policy.* New York: Harper Collins.

Jobert, A., and M. Tallard. 1991. "Le rôle du diplome dans la construction des grilles de classification professionnelle." Presentation to colloquium, "Les conventions collectives," Paris, May.

Johanson, J., and L. Mattson. 1987. "Interorganizational Relations in Industrial Systems: A Network Approach Compared with the Transaction Cost Approach." *International Studies of Management and Organization,* 17: 34–48.

Johnson, B., and B. A. Lundvall. 1992. "National Systems of Innovation and Institutional Learning." Paper presented to the international workshop "Systems of Innovation," Bologna, October 4–6.

Kaldor, N. 1972. "The Irrelevance of Equilibrium Economics." *The Economic Journal,* 82: 1237–1255.

Kant, I. 1976. *Critique of Practical Reason.* New York: Garland.

Katzenstein, P. 1984. *Small States in World Markets.* Ithaca, N.Y.: Cornell University Press.

Kelley, M., and H. Brooks. 1989. "From Breakthrough to Follow-Through." *Issues in Science and Technology,* 5: 42–47.

Kendrick, J. 1973. *Post-War Productivity Trends in the United States.* New York: National Bureau of Economic Research.

Keohane, R. 1984. *After Hegemony.* Princeton: Princeton University Press.

Kerscher, N., and A. V. Nénot. 1989. "Délégation à l'Emploi et négociation des conventions du Fonds National de l'Emploi: la pratique des contreparties." *Droit Social,* 1 (special issue on restructuring of firms).

Kertzer, D. 1984. *Family Life in Central Italy, 1880–1910: Sharecropping, Wage Labor, and Coresidence.* New Brunswick, N.J.: Rutgers University Press.

Keynes, J. M. 1936. *The General Theory of Employment, Interest, and Money.* London: Macmillan.

References

Klein, B., R. Crawford, and A. Alchian. 1978. "Vertical Integration, Appropriable Rents and the Competitive Contracting Process." *Journal of Law and Economics,* 21: 297–326.

Klein, B., and K. Leffler. 1981. "The Role of Market Forces in Assuring Contractual Performance." *Journal of Political Economy,* 89: 615–641.

Knight, F. 1921. *Risk, Uncertainty, and Profit.* New York: A. H. Kelly.

Kolboom, J. 1986. *La révanche des patrons. Le patronat français face au Front Populaire.* Paris: Flammarion [originally published in German, 1983].

Kripke, S. A. 1982. *Wittgenstein on Rules and Private Language.* Oxford: Basil Blackwell.

Krugman, P. 1990. *Rethinking International Trade.* Cambridge, Mass.: MIT Press.

———— 1994. *Peddling Prosperity: Economic Sense and Nonsense in the Age of Diminished Expectations.* New York: W. W. Norton.

Kwok, E. 1990. "The Geography of Governance: A Comparative Study of the Japanese and US Semiconductor Industries." Dissertation proposal, Department of Geography, University of California, Los Angeles.

Lafay, G., and C. Herzog. 1989. *Commerce international: la fin des avantages acquis.* Paris: Economica.

Lakota, A. M., and C. Milelli (coords.). 1987. *Emploi, entreprises et équipements en Ile-de-France: une géographie de la turbulence.* Collection Reclus Modes d'Emploi, 10. Montpellier: Public Research Group "Reclus," Maison de la Géographie.

Landes, D. 1970. *The Unbound Prometheus.* London: Cambridge University Press.

———— 1992. "Homo Faber, Homo Sapiens: Knowledge, Technology, Growth and Development." Opening address, 18th Conference of the European Association for Research in Industrial Economics (E.A.R.I.E.), Ferrara, September.

Lanfranchi, N., and T. Coutrot. 1991. "Les logiques de branche en matière de négociation collective des salaires." Presentation to the colloquium, "Les conventions collectives." Paris, May.

Lange, P. 1984. "Unions, Workers and Wage Regulation: The Rational Bases of Consent." In J. Goldthorpe, ed., *Order and Conflict in Contemporary Capitalism.* New York: Oxford University Press, pp. 98–123.

———— 1988. "The Institutionalization of Concertation." Paper presented at conference on Micro-Foundations of Democracy, Chicago, April 29–May 1.

Langlois, R. 1986. "Rationality, Institutions and Explanation." In R. Langlois, ed., *Economics as a Process: Essays in the New Institutional Economics.* New York: Cambridge University Press, pp. 116–142.

———— 1991. "Transaction-Cost Economics in Real Time." University of Connecticut Working Paper 91-1501, Storrs, Conn.

Lasch, C. 1991. *The True and Only Heaven: Progress and Its Critics.* New York: Norton.

Lassini, A. 1985. *Gli interventi regionali per i servizi alle imprese.* Milan: Franco Angeli.

Latour, A. 1961. *Les magiciens de la mode*. Paris: Julliard.

Latour, B. 1985. "Les vues de l'esprit." *Culture Technique* (June 14): 4–29.

Lauber, V. 1983. *The Politics of Economic Policy: France 1974–1982*. New York: Praeger.

Lavialle, C. 1992. "De la fonction du térritoire et de la domanialité dans la genèse de l'Etat en France sous l'Ancien Regime." *Droits*, 15:19–32.

Lazerson, M. 1989. "A New Phoenix: The Return of the Putting-Out Mode of Production." ILO Workshop on Industrial Districts, Florence, April.

——— 1990. "Subcontracting in the Modena Knitwear Industry." In F. Pyke, G. Becattini, and W. Sengenberger, eds., *Industrial Districts and Interfirm Cooperation in Italy*. Geneva: ILO, pp. 108–133.

Lazonick, W. 1992. "Learning and the Dynamics of International Competitive Advantage." In R. Thompson, ed., *Learning and Technological Change*. New York: St. Martin's Press, pp. 172–197.

Lederman, L. 1992. "The Differing National Civilian Technology Strategies of Leading World Traders." *Technology Analysis and Strategic Management*, 4: 2.

Lehoucq, T., and J. P. Strauss. 1988. "Les industries françaises de haute technologie: des difficultés à rester dans la course." *Economie et Statistique*, 207: 15–22.

Lemettre, J. F. 1983. "Pour une politique du système industriel." *Révue d'Economie Industrielle*, 23: 66–78.

Leontief, W. 1953. *Studies in the Structure of the American Economy*. New York: Oxford University Press.

Le Play, F. 1879. *Les ouvriers européens*. Tours: Mame.

Levy-Leboyer, M. 1980. "The Large Corporation in Modern France." In A. Chandler and H. Daems, eds., *Managerial Hierarchies: Comparative Perspectives on the Rise of the Modern Industrial Enterprise*. Cambridge, Mass.: Harvard University Press, pp. 117–160.

Lewis, D. 1969. *Convention: A Philosophical Study*. Cambridge, Mass.: Harvard University Press.

——— 1986. *On the Plurality of Worlds*. Oxford: Basil Blackwell.

Liebenstein, H. 1976. *Beyond Economic Man: A New Foundation for Microeconomics*. Cambridge, Mass.: Harvard University Press.

Lieberman, M. 1988. "Learning, Productivity and US-Japan Industrial Competitiveness." In K. Ferdows, ed., *Managing International Manufacturing*. Amsterdam: North Holland, pp. 215–238.

Linhart, D. 1991. *Le torticolis de l'autruche. L'éternelle modernisation des entreprises françaises*. Paris: Seuil.

Lipovetsky, G. 1987. *L'Empire de l'éphémère: la mode et son destin dans les sociétés modernes*. Paris: Gallimard.

Lorenz, E. 1991. "Historical Dependency, Conventions and the Competitive Decline of the British Shipbuilding Industry." Paper presented at annual

Economic History Association conference, Boulder, Colorado, September 27–29.

Lorenzoni, G. 1980. "Lo Sviluppo Industriale di Prato." In *Storia di Prato (secolo XVIII–XX)*, vol. 3. Prato: Editions Cassa di Risparmio e Depositi, pp. 275–297.

———— 1983. "La costellazione di imprese, una base di indagine sui processi di sviluppo." *Economia e Politica Industriale*, 38: 52–78.

———— 1986. "Strategia e Flessibilità Organizzativa." *Economia e Politica Industriale*, 52: 141–162.

Lucas, R. 1988. "On the Mechanics of Economic Development." *Journal of Monetary Economics*, 22: 3–42.

Lugli, L., and S. Tugnoli. 1991. *L'articolazione Funzionale e Produttiva dell Aziende Meccaniche in Regione*. Bologna.

Lundvall, B. A. 1990a. "From Technology as a Productive Factor to Innovation as an Interactive Process." Paper presented at colloquium "Networks of Innovators," Montreal, May 1–3.

———— 1990b. "User-Producer Interactions and Technological Change." Paper presented at the OECD Conference, Technology-Employment Programme, Paris, June.

———— 1992. *National Systems of Innovation: Toward a Theory of Innovation and Interactive Learning*. London: Frances Pinter.

Lyon-Caen, A. 1991. "Grandeur and décadence de la loi professionnelle." Presentation to the colloquium "Les conventions collectives." Paris, May.

MacNeil, I. 1981. "The Economic Analysis of Contractual Relations." *Northwestern University Law Review*, 75: 1018–1062.

Maddison, A. 1991. *Dynamic Forces in Capitalist Development*. Oxford: Oxford University Press.

Malkin, D. 1984. "Mutations industrielles et IXe plan." *Révue Economique*, 35: 1091–1146.

Mansfield, E. 1972. "Contribution of R and D to Economic Growth in the United States." *Science*, 175: 477–486.

———— 1981. "Composition of R and D Expenditures: Relationship to Size of Firm, Concentration and Innovative Output." *Review of Economics and Statistics*, 63: 610–615.

Manusardi, G. 1986. *Dix ans avec Pierre Cardin*. Paris: Fanval.

Manzagol, C. 1989. "Réflexions sur les trajectoires d'une technopole: Phoenix." Paper presented to the International Conference "Les nouveaux espaces industriels." La Sorbonne, Paris, March.

March, G., and J. Olson. 1984. "The New Institutionalism: Organizational Factors in Political Life." *American Political Science Review*, 78: 734–749.

March, J., and H. Simon. 1958. *Organizations*. New York: Wiley.

Marglin, S. 1974. "What Do Bosses Do? The Origins and Functions of Hierarchy in Capitalist Production." *Review of Radical Political Economics*, 6:33–60.

Marglin, S., and J. Schor, eds. 1990. *The Golden Age of Capitalism*. New York: Cambridge University Press.

Marin, B. 1983. "Com'è Possibile la Collaborazione di Classe? Alcune Condizioni Politico-Istituzionali. L'Esperienza Austriaca." *Problemi Della Transizione,* 13.

Mariotti, S., and C. Caincara. 1986. "The Evolution of Governance in the Textile-Clothing Industry." *Journal of Economic Behavior and Organization.* 7: 351–374.

Markusen, A. 1985. *Profit Cycles, Oligopoly, and Regional Development*. Cambridge, Mass.: MIT Press.

Markusen, A., P. Hall, and S. Dietrick. 1991. *The Rise of the Gunbelt*. New York: Oxford University Press.

Markusen, A., P. Hall, and A. Glasmeier. 1986. *High-Tech America: The What, How, Where, and Why of the Sunrise Industries*. Boston: Allen and Unwin.

Marschak, J. 1968. "Economics of Inquiring, Communicating, Deciding." *American Economic Review,* 58: 1–18.

Marsden, D. 1986. *The End of Economic Man? Custom and Competition in the Labor Market*. New York: St. Martin's Press.

Marshall, A. 1890. *Principles of Economics,* 2 vols. London: Macmillan (9th ed., 1961).

Maurice, M., F. Sellier, and J. J. Silvestre. 1986. *The Social Foundations of Industrial Power: A Comparison of France and Germany*. Cambridge, Mass.: MIT Press.

McIntyre, A. 1984. *After Virtue: A Study in Moral Theory*. South Bend, Ind.: Notre Dame University Press.

Mensch, G. 1979. *Stalemate in Technology*. Cambridge, Mass.: Ballinger.

Meny, V. 1992. "La république des fiefs." *Pouvoirs,* 68: 17–21.

Mercier, M., and D. Segrestin. 1983. "L'effet territoire dans la mobilisation ouvrière. Essai d'analyse de situation complexe." *Révue française de sociologie,* 29: 61–79.

Merton, R. K. 1936. "The Unanticipated Consequences of Purposive Social Action." *American Sociological Review,* 1: 894–904.

Messine, Ph. 1987. *Les saturniens: quand les patrons réinventent la société*. Paris: La Découverte.

Michaelson, A. 1989. *Local Strategies of Industrial Restructuring and the Changing Relations between Large and Small Firms in Contemporary Italy: The Case of Fiat Auto and Olivetti*. Turin: Clerici Vagantes.

Millon-Delsol, C. 1992. *L'Etat subsidiaire*. Paris: Presses Universitaires de France.

Ministère de l'Industrie et du Commerce Extérieur. 1992. "Les nouvelles armes du défi industriel." Report of Preliminary Mission, April.

Moe, T. 1987. "Interests, Institutions and Positive Theory: The Politics of the NLRB." *Studies in American Political Development,* 2: 236–299.

Moene, K. O., and M. Wallerstein. 1992. "What's Wrong with Social Democracy."

Contribution to colloquium on Perspectives on Market Socialism, Berkeley, May 16–19, 1991.

Mokyr, J. 1990. *The Lever of Riches: Technological Creativity and Economic Progress.* New York: Oxford University Press.

Molotch, H. 1976. "The City as Growth Machine." *American Sociological Review,* 82: 309–332.

Montagne-Villette, S. 1987. "L'industrie de prêt-à-porter en France." Doctoral thesis, University of Paris I, Paris.

Moore, B. 1966. *Social Origins of Dictatorship and Democracy.* Boston: Beacon Press.

Morin, M. L. 1991. "Le dualisme de la convention collective. Aperçu historique." Presentation to the colloquium "Les conventions collectives," Paris, May.

Morishima, M. 1982. *Why Has Japan Succeeded?* Cambridge: Cambridge University Press.

Moulaert, F., Y. Chikhaoui, and F. Djellal. 1988. *Locational Behavior of French High Tech Consultancy Firms.* Lille: University of Lille I, Department of Economics.

Mowery, D., ed. 1988. *International Collaborative Ventures in Manufacturing.* Cambridge, Mass.: Ballinger.

Mytelka, L., ed. 1990. *Strategic Partnerships and the World Economy.* London: Frances Pinter.

Nelson, R. 1988. "Institutions Supporting Technical Change in the United States." In G. Dosi et al., *Technical Change and Economic Theory.* London: Pinter, pp. 312–329.

Nelson, R., and S. Winter. 1982. *An Evolutionary Theory of Economic Change.* Cambridge, Mass.: Harvard University Press.

NOMISMA. 1991. *Strategie e Valutazione nelle Politica Industriale.* Milan: Franco Angeli.

North, D. 1981. *Structure and Change in Economic History.* New York: Norton.

North, D., and R. Thomas. 1973. *The Rise of the Western World: A New Economic History.* Cambridge: Cambridge University Press.

Norton, R., and J. Rees. 1979. "The Product Cycle and the Spatial Decentralization of American Manufacturing." *Regional Studies,* 13: 141–151.

Noyelle, T., and T. Stanback. 1984. *The Economic Transformation of American Cities.* Totowa, N.J.: Rowman and Allanheld.

Nozick, R. 1974. *Anarchy, State, and Utopia.* New York: Basic Books.

Nuti, F. 1984. "Demandes, division du travail entre firmes: Notes sur la structure interne des secteurs traditionnels de l'industrie italienne fortement ouverts sur l'extérieur." In *Politiques Industrielles,* pp. 167–182.

—— 1986. "Differenti approcci al tema dei distretti industriali: Analisi di alcuni elementi di fatto e di principio trascurati dalla letteratura." In *Atti del Convegno "rapporti fra le imprese e nei sistemi produttivi di settore nei distretti industrial."* Pisa.

———— 1988. "Trasformazioni strutturali delle piccole e medie imprese nei distretti industriali." In *Atti Convegno, "Contesto competitivo e trasformiazioni strutturali delle piccole e medie imprese nei distretti industriali e nei rapporti di subfornitura."* Milan: Catholic University.

———— 1989. "I Distretti dell'industria manifatturiera." Rome: Report to national research council, *Sistema delle Imprese.*

Nystrom, P. 1928. *The Economics of Fashion.* New York: The Ronald Press.

Olson, M. 1971. *The Logic of Collective Action: Public Goods and the Theory of Groups.* Cambridge, Mass.: Harvard University Press.

Onida, F. 1980. "Esportazioni e Struttura Industriale dell'Italia negli Anni 70." *Economia Italiana,* 1: 97–139.

Ouchi, W. 1981. *Theory Z: How American Businesses Can Meet the Japanese Challenge.* Reading, Mass.: Addison-Wesley.

Paci, M. 1973. *Mercato del Lavoro e Classi Sociali in Italia.* Bologna: Il Mulino.

———— 1980. *Famiglia e mercato del lavoro in un'economia periferica.* Milan: Franco Angeli.

Paloscia, R. 1991. "Agriculture and Diffused Manufacturing in the Terza Italia: A Tuscan Case Study." In S. Whatmore et al., eds., *Rural Enterprise: Shifting Perspectives on Small-Scale Production.* London: D. Fulton, pp. 34–57.

Parsons, T. 1937. *The Structure of Social Action.* New York: The Free Press.

———— 1951. *The Social System.* New York: The Free Press.

Patel, P., and K. Pavitt. 1991. "Large Firms in the Production of the World's Technology: An Important Case of Non-globalization." *Journal of International Business Studies,* First Quarter: 1–21.

Pavitt, K., and P. Patel. 1990. "L'accumulation technologique en France: Ce que les statistiques des brevets tendent à montrer." *Révue d'Economie Industrielle,* 51: 1–50.

Paxton, R. O. 1973. *La France de Vichy.* Paris: Seuil.

Peltzman, S. 1984. "Constituency Interest and Congressional Voting." *Journal of Law and Economics,* 27: 181–210.

Penrose, E. 1959. *The Theory of the Growth of the Firm.* Oxford: Basil Blackwell.

Perroux, F. 1950. "Economic Space: Theory and Applications." *Quarterly Journal of Economics,* 64: 89–104.

Perrow, C. 1986. "Economic Theories of Organization." *Theory and Society,* 18: 11–45.

Perulli, P. 1987. "Flexibility Strategies: Employers, Trade Unions and Local Government: The Case of Modena Industrial Districts." Contribution to colloquium, "New Technologies and New Forms of Industrial Relations," MIT Conference Center, Endicott House.

Pesce, A. 1990. "Un'Altra Emilia Romagna: elementi per una storia sociale della differenza sessuale." In Commissione per la Realizzazione della Parita Fra Uomo e Donna, Regione Emilia Romagna, *Un'Altra Emilia Romagna.* Milan: Franco Angeli, pp. 17–130.

Philip, A. 1937. "The Renewal of Collective Labor Agreements." Lectures given at the Institut Supérieur Ouvrier. Published in the series *Education Syndicale,* Paris.

Piore, M. 1975. "Notes for a Theory of Labor Market Stratification." In R. Edwards, M. Reich, and D. Gordon, *Labor Market Segmentation.* Lexington, Mass.: D. C. Heath, pp. 125–150.

——— 1992. "Technological Trajectories and the Classical Revival in Economics." In M. Storper and A. Scott, eds., *Pathways to Industrialization and Regional Development.* London: Routledge, pp. 157–170.

Piore, M., and C. Sabel. 1984. *The Second Industrial Divide.* New York: Basic Books.

Pizzorno, A. 1978. "Political Exchange and Collective Identity in Industrial Conflict." In C. Crouch and A. Pizzorno, eds., *The Resurgence of Class Conflict in Western Europe since 1968.* London: Macmillan, pp. 277–298.

Polanyi, K. 1944. *The Great Transformation.* New York: Holt, Rinehart and Winston.

Polanyi, M. 1962. *Personal Knowledge: Towards Post-Critical Philosophy.* New York: Harper and Row.

Popkin, S. 1979. *The Rational Peasant: The Political Economy of Rural Society in Vietnam.* Berkeley and Los Angeles: University of California Press.

Porter, M. 1990. *The Competitive Advantage of Nations.* London: Macmillan.

Pottier, C. 1989. "The Location of High Technology Industry in France." In M. J. Breheny and R. McQuaid, eds., *The Development of High Technology Industries: An International Survey.* London: Routledge, pp. 192–222.

Powell, W. 1990. "Neither Market nor Hierarchy: Network Forms of Organization." *Research in Organizational Behavior,* 12: 295–336.

Pratt, J., and R. Zeckhauser. 1985. *Principals and Agents.* Boston: Harvard Business School Press.

Prestowitz, C. 1988. *Trading Places: How We Allowed Japan to Take the Lead.* New York: Basic Books.

Prévost, J. C. 1957. *Le Dandyisme en France, 1817–1839.* Geneva: Droz.

Prévot, V. 1986. *Géographie du textile.* Paris: Masson.

Prosperetti, L. 1989. "Dynamique de la productivité dans l'industrie et rôles des petites et moyennes entreprises." In M. Maruani, E. Reynaud, and C. Romani, *La flexibilité en Italie.* Paris: Syros, pp. 307–317.

Przeworski, A. 1985. *Capitalism and Social Democracy.* Cambridge: Cambridge University Press.

Przeworski, A., and M. Wallerstein. 1982. "The Structure of Class Conflict in Democratic Capitalist Societies." *American Political Science Review,* 76: 215–238.

Putnam, R. 1992. *Making Democracy Work.* Princeton: Princeton University Press.

Pye, W., and S. Verba. 1965. *Political Culture and Political Development.* Princeton: Princeton University Press.

References

Ramo, S. 1988. *The Business of Science*. New York: Hill and Wang.

Rawls, John. 1971. *A Theory of Justice*. Cambridge, Mass.: Harvard University Press.

Regalia, I. 1987. "The Sesto San Giovanni Area: Decline or Industrial Readjustment?" Contribution to colloquium, "New Technologies and New Forms of Industrial Relations," MIT Conference Center, Endicott House, February.

Regini, M., ed. 1988. *La sfida della flessibilità: impresa, lavoro e sindacati nell fase "post-fordista."* Milan: Franco Angeli.

Regini, M., and C. Sabel, eds. 1989. *Strategie di riaggiustamento industriale*. Bologna: Il Mulino.

Reich, R. 1991. *The Work of Nations: Preparing Ourselves for 21st Century Capitalism*. New York: Alfred Knopf.

Retière, J. N. 1990. "La manufacture des Tabacs de Nantes, 1857–1914. Les monographies d'entreprise." Paris: CNRS Research Group "Institutions, Emploi et Politique Economique," Working Paper 90-03.

Rey, G. 1989. "Profile and Analysis, 1981–85." In E. Goodman and J. Bamford, eds., *Small Firms and Industrial Districts in Italy*. London: Routledge, pp. 69–93.

Reynaud, B. 1990. "Les modes de rémunération et le rapport salarial." *Economie et Prévision*, 92–93: 1–14.

——— 1992. *Le salaire, la règle et le marché*. Paris: Christian Bourgois.

Reynaud, J. D. 1975. *Les syndicats en France*. Paris: Seuil.

——— 1988. "La négociation des nouvelles technologies: Une transformation des règles du jeu." *Revue Française de Science Politique*, 38: 5–22.

Richardson, G. B. 1972. "The Organization of Industry." *The Economic Journal*, 82: 883–896.

Riker, W. 1980. "Implications of the Disequilibrium of Majority." *Science Review*, 71: 432–447.

Ritaine, E. 1987. "Prato ou l'exaspération de la diffusion industrielle." *Sociologie du Travail*, 29: 139–156.

——— 1989. "La modernité localisée? Leçons italiennes sur le développement régional." *Revue Française de Science Politique*, 39: 155–177.

Robinson, J. 1956. *The Accumulation of Capital*. London: Macmillan.

Roche, D. 1990. *La culture des apparences. Une histoire du vêtement, XVIe–XVIIe siècles*. Paris: Fayard.

Roemer, J. 1982. *A General Theory of Exploitation and Class*. Cambridge, Mass.: Harvard University Press.

——— 1986. *Analytical Marxism*. Cambridge: Cambridge University Press.

Rokkan, S. 1970. *Citizens, Elections, Parties*. New York: McKay.

Romer, P. 1986. "Increasing Returns and Long-Run Growth." *Journal of Political Economy*, 94: 1002–1037.

——— 1990. "Endogenous Technological Change." *Journal of Political Economy*, 98: S71–S102.

References

Rosanvallon, P. 1990. *L'Etat en France de 1789 à nos jours.* Paris: Seuil.

Rosenberg, N. 1972. *Technology and American Economic Growth.* New York: Harper and Row.

———— 1982. *Inside the Black Box: Technology and Economics.* Cambridge: Cambridge University Press.

Rotschild-Souriac, M. A. 1991. "Autonomie de la négociation d'entreprise." Contribution to the colloquium "Les conventions collectives." GRECO "Relations professionnelles." May 23–24, Paris.

Russo, M. 1986. "Technical Change and the Industrial District: The Role of Inter-Firm Relations in the Growth and Transformation of Ceramic Tile Production in Italy." *Research Policy,* 14: 329–343.

Sabel, C. 1981. "The Internal Politics of Trade Unions." In S. Berger, ed., *Organizing Interests in Western Europe.* New York: Cambridge University Press, pp. 209–244.

———— 1982. *Work and Politics: The Division of Labor in Industry.* New York: Cambridge University Press.

———— 1993a. "Constitutional Ordering in Historical Context." In F. Scharpf, ed., *Games in Hierarchies and Networks.* Boulder: Westview Press.

———— 1993b. "Elaborer la confiance: de nouvelles formes de coopération dans une économie volatile." In D. Foray and C. Freeman, eds., *Technologie et Richesse des Nations.* Paris: Economica, pp. 419–450.

Sabel, C., G. Herrigel, R. Deeg, and R. Kazis. 1989. "Regional Prosperities Compared: Massachusetts and Baden-Wurttemburg in the 1980s." *Economy and Society,* 18: 374–403.

Saglio, J. 1986. "Petites et moyennes entreprises industrielles et environnement urbain." In *France, Plan Urbain, Commissariat Général du Plan, Mutations Economiques et Urbanisation.* Paris: La Documentation Française, pp. 204–250.

———— 1988. "La concurrence: une règle du jeu économique parmi d'autres." Lyon: GLYSI/CNRS, Maison Rhône-Alpes des Sciences de l'Homme.

Saint-Geours, J. 1986. "Une vision culturelle de l'industrie." *Politique Industrielle,* 2: 13–26.

Salais, R., and M. Storper. 1993. *Les Mondes de Production: Enquête sur l'Identité Economique de la France.* Paris: Editions de l'Ecole des Hautes Etudes en Sciences Sociales.

Salais, R., and L. Tessier. 1991. "Modernisation des entreprises et recours au Fonds National de l'Emploi entre 1982 et 1988." Research report for Ministère du Travail, de l'Emploi et de la Formation Professionnelle, July.

Sallez, A. 1986. "Planification spatiale et planification stratégique." *Révue d'Economie Régionale et Urbaine,* 3: 301–317.

Salomon, J. J. 1985. *Le Gaulois, le cow-boy et le samouraï: rapport sur la politique française de technologie.* Paris: Ministère de l'Industrie et de la Recherche.

References

Salvestrini, A.. 1965. *I moderati Toscani e la classe dirigente italiana, 1859–1876*. Florence: Olschki.

Sapelli, G., ed. 1981. *La classe operaia sotto il fascismo*. Milan: Franco Angeli.

Savary, J. 1981. *Les multinationales françaises*. Paris: Presses Universitaires de France.

Saxenian, A. 1988. "Regional Networks and the Resurgence of Silicon Valley." Institute of Urban and Regional Development Working Paper 508, University of California, Berkeley.

—— 1990. "The Origins and Dynamics of Production Networks in Silicon Valley." Institute of Urban and Regional Development Working Paper 516, University of California, Berkeley.

—— 1991. "Contrasting Patterns of Business Organization in Silicon Valley." Institute of Urban and Regional Development, Working Paper 535, University of California, Berkeley.

—— *Regional Advantage: Culture and Competition in Silicon Valley and Route 128*. Cambridge, Mass.: Harvard University Press.

Scarpitti, L. 1988. "Una rassegna ragionata della letteratura sulle aree ad economia diffusa e sui distretti industriali." Rome: ENEA Dir. Centrale Studi.

Scarpitti, L., and C. Trigilia. 1987. "Strategies of Flexibility: Firms, Unions and Local Governments: The Case of Prato." Contribution to colloquium on New Technologies and New Forms of Industrial Relations, MIT Conference Center, Endicott House.

Schattschneider, E. 1960. *The Semisovereign People*. New York: Holt, Rinehart and Winston.

Schelling, T. 1978. *Macromotives and Microbehavior*. New York: Norton.

—— 1980. *The Strategy of Conflict*. Cambridge, Mass.: Harvard University Press.

Schepsle, K., and B. Weingast. 1981. "Structure-Induced Equilibrium and Legislative Choice." *Public Choice*, 37: 503–519.

Schotter, A. 1981. *The Economic Theory of Social Institutions*. New York: Cambridge University Press.

Schumpeter, J. 1934. *The Theory of Economic Development*. Cambridge, Mass.: Harvard University Press.

Scott, A. 1986. "High Technology Industry and Territorial Development: The Rise of the Orange County Complex, 1955–1984." *Urban Geography*, 7:3–45.

—— 1988a. *Metropolis: From the Division of Labor to Urban Form*. Berkeley and Los Angeles: University of California Press.

—— 1988b. *New Industrial Spaces: Flexible Production and Regional Economic Development in the USA and Western Europe*. London: Pion.

—— 1990. "The Aircraft Industry in Southern California: The Early Years." UCLA Papers in Economics and Human Geography, 2, Los Angeles.

—— 1993. *Technopolis*. Berkeley and Los Angeles: University of California Press.

359

Scott, A. J., and D. Angel P. 1987. "The U.S. Semi-conductor Industry: A Locational Analysis." *Environment and Planning A,* 19: 875–912.

Scott, A. J., and A. Paul. 1990. "Collective Order and Economic Coordination in Industrial Agglomerations: The Technopoles of Southern California." *Environment and Planning C: Government and Policy,* 8: 179–193.

Scott, A. J., and M. Storper. 1987. "High Technology Industry and Regional Development: A Theoretical Critique and Reconstruction." *International Social Science Journal,* 112: 215–232.

Scranton, P. 1983. *Proprietary Capitalism.* New York: Cambridge University Press.

———— 1986. *Figured Tapestry.* New York: Cambridge University Press.

Scully, G. W. 1992. *Constitutional Environments and Economic Growth.* Princeton: Princeton University Press.

Searle, J. 1977. *Speech Acts.* London: Cambridge University Press.

Sen, A. 1977. "Rational Fools: A Critique of the Behavioral Foundations of Economic Theory." *Philosophy and Public Affairs,* 6: 317–344.

———— 1982. *Choice, Welfare, and Measurement.* Cambridge, Mass.: MIT Press.

———— 1985. "Goals, Commitment and Identity." *Journal of Law, Economics and Organization,* 1: 341–356.

Seravalli, G. 1992. "Subcontractors' Relationships: A Suggested Research Outline." Berkeley: University of California, Institute of Urban and Regional Development, Working Paper.

Servan-Schreiber, J. J. 1968. *The American Challenge.* New York: Atheneum.

Sewell, N. 1980. *Work and Revolution in France: The Language of Labor from the Old Regime to 1848.* New York: Cambridge University Press.

Sforzi, F. 1990. "The Quantitative Importance of Marshallian Industrial Districts in the Italian Economy." In F. Pyke, G. Becattini, and W. Sengenberger, eds., *Industrial Districts and Interfirm Cooperation in Italy.* Geneva: ILO, pp. 75–107.

Sheppard, E., E. Webber, and D. Rigby. 1991. "Technical Change." Manuscript, University of Minnesota, Minneapolis.

Shils, E. 1981. *Tradition.* Chicago: University of Chicago Press.

Shonfield, A. 1965. *Modern Capitalism.* London: Oxford University Press.

Silverberg, G., G. Dosi, and L. Orsenigo. 1988. "Innovation, Diversity and Diffusion: A Self-Organization Model." *Economic Journal,* 98: 1032–1054.

Simmel, P. 1950. *The Sociology of Georg Simmel,* p. 73.

Simon, P. 1931. *Monographie d'une industrie de luxe: la haute couture.* Paris: Seuil.

Singh, N. 1985. "Monitoring and Hierarchies." *Journal of Political Economy,* 93: 599–609.

Siwek-Pouydessau, J. 1991. "Les statuts des personnels dans le secteur public." Presentation to the colloquium "Les conventions collectives," Paris, May.

Skocpol, T. 1979. *States and Revolutions.* Cambridge, Mass.: Harvard University Press.

References

Smith, A. 1776. *The Wealth of Nations* (1937 ed.). New York: Modern Library.

Solinas, G. 1982. "Labor Market Segmentation and Workers' Careers: The Case of the Italian Knitwear Industry." *Cambridge Journal of Economics,* 6: 331–352.

Solow, R. 1957. "Technical Change and the Aggregate Production Function." *Review of Economics and Statistics,* 39: 312–320.

SPRINT (Sistema Pratese Innovazione Technologiche). 1990. "Rapporto sul Sistema Economico Pratese." Prato: Sprint.

———— 1991. "La Congiuntura a Prato nel II trimestre 1991." Prato: Sprint.

Stigler, G. 1939. "Production and Distribution in the Short Run." *Journal of Political Economy,* 47: 305–327.

———— 1951. "The Division of Labor Is Limited by the Extent of the Market." *Journal of Political Economy,* 69: 213–215.

———— 1961. "The Economics of Information." *Journal of Political Economy,* 70: 94–105.

———— 1974a. "The Theory of Economic Regulation." *Bell Journal of Economics and Management Science,* 2: 3–21.

———— 1974b. "Free Riders and Collective Action: An Appendix to Theories of Economic Regulation." *Bell Journal of Economics and Management Science,* 2: 359–375.

Stiglitz, J. E. 1987. "The Design of Labor Contracts: The Economics of Incentives and Risk Sharing." In H. Nalbantian, ed., *Incentives, Cooperation, and Risk Sharing.* Totowa, N.J.: Rowmann and Littlefield, pp. 48–68.

Stoffaes, C. 1983. *Politique industrielle.* Paris: Droit.

Storper, M. 1985a. "The Spatial and Temporal Constitution of Social Action: A Critical Reading of Giddens." *Society and Space,* 3: 407–424.

———— 1985b. "Oligopoly and the Product Cycle." *Economic Geography* 61: 260–282.

———— 1989. "The Transition to Flexible Specialisation in the US Film Industry: External Economies, the Division of Labor and the Crossing of Industrial Divides." *Cambridge Journal of Economics,* 13: 273–315.

Storper, M., and B. Harrison. 1991. "Flexibility, Hierarchy and Regional Development: The Changing Structures of Production Systems and Their Forms of Governance in the 1990s." *Research Policy,* 21: 407–422.

Storper, M., and A. J. Scott. 1989. "The Geographical Foundations and Social Regulation of Flexible Production Complexes." In J. Wolch and M. Dear, eds., *The Power of Geography: How Territory Shapes Social Life.* London and Boston: Unwin Hyman, p. 21–40.

Storper, M., and R. Walker. 1989. *The Capitalist Imperative: Territory, Technology, and Industrial Growth.* Oxford: Basil Blackwell.

Stowsky, J. 1987. "The Weakest Link: Semi-conductor Production Equipment, Linkages and the Limits to International Trade." Berkeley Roundtable on the International Economy (BRIE), Working Paper 27, Berkeley.

References

Sueur, P. 1987. *Histoire du droit public francais*. Paris: Presses Universitaires de France.

Sugden, R. 1993. *Rationality, Justice, and the Social Contract*. Ann Arbor: University of Michigan Press.

Suleiman, E. 1979. *Les élites en France. Grands corps et grandes écoles*. Paris: Seuil.

Supiot, A. 1989. "Déréglementation des relations de travail auto-règlementation de l'entreprise." *Droit Social*, 3: 195–205.

Swyngedou, E., and S. Anderson. 1987. "Le schéma spatial de la production de haute technologie en France." *Révue d'économie régionale et urbaine*, 2: 321–349.

Taylor, F. W. 1972. *Principles of Scientific Management*. Westport, Conn.: Greenwood Press Publishers.

Taylor, M. 1988. *Rationality and Revolution*. Cambridge: Cambridge University Press.

Teece, D. 1988. "Technological Change and the Nature of the Firm." In G. Dosi et al., eds., *Technical Change and Economic Theory*. London: Pinter.

——— 1989. "Competition and Cooperation in Technology Strategy." Berkeley: University of California, School of Business Administration.

Temin, P. 1975. *Causal Factors in American Economic Growth in the 19th Century*. London: Macmillan.

Thernstrom, S. 1964. *Poverty and Progress: Social Mobility in a Nineteenth Century City*. Cambridge, Mass.: Harvard University Press.

Thévenot, L. 1986. "Economie et formes conventionnelles." In R. Salais and L. Thévenot, eds., *Le travail. Marché, règles, conventions*. Paris: Economica, pp. 195–217.

——— 1989a. "Economie et politique de l'entreprise; économie de l'efficacité et de la confiance." In L. Boltanski and L. Thévenot, eds., *Cahiers du Centre d'Etudes de l'Emploi*, 33, special issue on "Justice et justesse dans le travail." Paris: Presses Universitaires de France, pp. 135–207.

——— 1989b. "Reasonable Action in a Complex Universe: Critical Deliberation within a Plurality of Coordinative Conventions." Contribution to Stanford-Paris summer seminar, Stanford, Calif., May 10.

——— 1989c. "Equilibre et rationalité dans un univers complexe." *Révue Economique*, 40: 147–197.

Thompson, E. P. 1978. *The Poverty of Theory and Other Essays*. New York: Monthly Review Press.

Tilly, C. 1984. *Big Structures, Large Processes, Huge Comparisons*. New York: Russell Sage Foundation.

Tinacci Mosello, M. 1983. "Modernitá e tradizione di un sistema industriale locale: il modello pratese della 'fabbrica diffusa' e la sua evoluzione storica." *Atti del XXIII Congresso Geografico Italiano*, VII, vol. II, Catania, pp. 294–305.

References

———— M. 1989. "Innovative Capacities of Industrial Districts. Hypothesis and Verification: The Case-Study of Prato in Tuscany." *Studi e Discussioni,* 59. Florence: Department of Economics, University of Florence.

Titmuss, R. M. 1970. *The Gift Relationship.* London: Allen and Unwin.

Tocqueville, A. de 1956. *Democracy in America.* New York: Penguin.

Todd, E. 1990. *L'invention de l'Europe.* Paris: Seuil.

Trigilia, C. 1985. "La regolazione localistica: economia e politica nell'aree di piccola imprese." *Stato e Mercato,* 14: 181–228.

———— 1986a. "Small Firm Development and Political Subcultures in Italy." *European Sociological Review,* 2: 161–175.

———— 1986b. *Grandi partiti e piccole imprese.* Bologna: Il Mulino.

———— 1990. "Italian Industrial Districts: Neither Myth nor Interlude." Paper delivered to conference on Industrial Districts and Local Economic Regeneration, Geneva, October 18–19.

Turner, J. H. 1985. "The Concept of Action in Sociological Analysis." In G. Seebass and R. Toumea, eds., *Analytical and Sociological Theories of Action.* Dordrecht, Holland: Kluwer.

———— 1988. *A Theory of Social Interaction.* Stanford: Stanford University Press.

Turner, S. P. 1994. *The Social Theory of Practices: Tradition, Tacit Knowledge and Presuppositions.* Cambridge: Polity Press.

Turquet, P. 1992. "Analyse économique des syndicats: Application au cas des négociations collectives françaises dans la décennie quatre-vingt." Doctoral thesis, University of Rennes, I.

Tyson, L. 1987. *Creating Advantage: Strategic Policy for National Competitiveness.* Berkeley: Berkeley Roundtable on the International Economy.

———— 1990. *Who's Bashing Whom? Trade Conflict in High Technology Industries.* Washington, D.C.: Institute for International Economics.

U.S. Congress, Office of Technology Assessment. 1988. *Paying the Bill: Manufacturing and America's Trade Deficit.* Washington, D.C.: U.S. Government Printing Office.

Varela, F. 1990. *Autonomie et connaissance. Essai sur le vivant.* Paris: Seuil.

Veltz, P. 1986. "L'espace des industries électriques et électroniques." *Les Annales de la Recherche Urbaine,* 29: 69–77.

Veltz, P., et al. 1988. "Nouvelle économie, nouveaux territoires." Caisse des Dépôts et Consignations, Actes du Colloque Economie et Territoire "Vers une nouvelle dynamique du développement local." Paris.

Verba, S., ed. 1982. *The Civic Culture Revisited.* Toronto: Little Brown.

Vernon R, 1966. "International Investment and International Trade in the Product Cycle." *Quarterly Journal of Economics,* 80: 190–207.

———— 1979. "The Product Cycle Hypothesis in a New International Environment." *Oxford Bulletin of Economics and Statistics,* 4: 255–267.

Villeval, M. C., ed. 1992. *Mutations industrielles et reconversion des salariés.* Paris: L'Harmattan.

References

Von Hippel, E. 1987. *The Sources of Innovation*. New York: Oxford University Press.

Wacquant, L. J. D. 1993. "On the Tracks of Symbolic Power: Prefatory Notes to Bourdieu's 'State Nobility.'" *Theory, Culture, and Society*, 10: 1–19.

Waldinger, R., H. Aldrich, R. Ward, et al. 1989. *Ethnic Entrepreneurs: Immigrant Business in Industrial Societies*. Newbury Park: Sage Publications.

Walzer, M. 1983. *Spheres of Justice: A Defense of Pluralism and Equality*. New York: Basic Books.

Weitzman, M. C. 1979. "Optimal Search for the Best Alternative." *Econometrica*, 47: 641–654.

West, C. 1991. *The Ethical Dimensions of Marxist Thought*. New York: Monthly Review Press.

Wiebe, R. 1975. *The Segmented Society: An Introduction to the Meaning of America*. New York: Oxford University Press.

Williamson, O. 1975. *Markets and Hierarchies: Analysis and Antitrust Implications*. New York: The Free Press.

——— 1985. *The Economic Institutions of Capitalism: Firms, Markets, Relational Contracting*. New York: The Free Press.

——— 1992. "The Economic Analysis of Institutions: In General and with Respect to Country Studies." Paris: OECD, Division of Science, Technology, and Industry, unpublished paper.

Wolfe, A. 1989. *Whose Keeper? Social Science and Moral Obligation*. Berkeley: University of California Press.

Young, A. 1928. "Increasing Returns and Economic Progress." *The Economic Journal*, 38: 527–542.

Young, I. 1990. *Justice and the Politics of Difference*. Princeton: Princeton University Press.

Zaninotto, E. 1978. "Struttura tecnologica, professionalità, decentramento produttivo: ipotesi interpretative del caso veneto." *Economia e Politica Industriale*, 18: 147–165.

Zarca, B. 1986. *L'artisanat français: Du métier traditionnel au groupe social*. Paris: Economica.

Zeitlin, J., and C. Sabel. 1985. "Historical Alternatives to Mass Production: Politics, Markets and Technology in Nineteenth Century Industrialization." *Past and Present*, 108: 113–176.

Zysman, J. 1977. *Political Strategies for Industrial Order: State, Market and Industry in France*. Berkeley: University of California Press.

——— 1986. *Governments, Markets, and Growth*. Ithaca, N.Y.: Cornell University Press.

NAME INDEX

SUBJECT INDEX

absolute advantages, 10
action, capacities for, 215–233
action frameworks, 39, 197–203
aerospace industry, 130–146
Aerospatiale, 142
agency, 215
agglomeration, geographical, 180
Airbus Industrie, 256
artisans, 170
assets: specificities, 246; complementarities, 246, 277–278; learning, 246–247;
  similarities, 277–278; appropriability
  of, 278
automobile industry, 53
autonomy, 213–214

Bell Laboratories, 74
Benetton, 255, 257
best practice, 10
biotechnology industry, 180, 186
Boeing, 179
Bologna, 193
Boston, 182
brand names, 150
Bretton Woods treaty, 4
Bull, 142
"buy American" campaign, 216

California, 174–188, 199–201
capacities for action, 251
Cap Gemini Sogeti, 141
Catholicism, 13, 220
choice, consumer, 301
Choletais (France), 244

citizenship, 213
clothing industry, 117–130; in Paris,
  117–130; in Emilia-Romagna, 149–173
CNA (Italy), 190
coalitions, 285, 289–290
codification, 37
cognitive frameworks, 178, 197
common good, 170–171, 208–209, 213,
  218; interventionist, 209; liberal, 209,
  210–212; American, 212; French,
  224–245
communication, 36
communitarianism, 217
comparative advantages, 8–9
competitiveness, 98, 246–265; in Italy,
  252–256; in France, 256–260; in U.S.,
  261–265
complexity, 9–12
concertation, 285, 294
confidence, 214
conflict, 202
conservatism, 183
consumer-producer relations, 29
consumers, 29, 52
consumer tastes, 64
contracts, 74–75, 181, 183
convention (definition of), 16, 17; emergence, 17–18; as hypothesis, 17–19;
  evolution, 18–19
conventions of identity (definition of), 23
conventions of participation (definition
  of), 23
cooperation, 294
coordination, 14

367

dination, 207; as conventions, 207–208; New Institutional Analysis, 269–270; New Institutional Economics, 272–283, 269–270, 301–302; and assets, 269, 271; and uncertainty, 271; and action frameworks, 271; and transactions costs, 272–277; environments, 280. *See also* firms
intangible factors, 303
inter-firm relations, 168–171
interpersonal relations, 72, 74, 119–130, 141–143, 149–173, 169, 199
interpretation, 202, 299, 301
Italy, 98, 102, 108–111, 149–173, 178, 180, 188, 192, 194, 200, 202

Japan, 71–73, 162, 185, 199, 248, 262, 303
judgment, 49, 57

keiretsu, 72, 199
Keynesianism, 247

labor conventions, 57–62, 171–172; in Industrial World, 60; in Market World, 61; in Interpersonal World, 61; in Intellectual World, 62
liberalism, 73, 213, 218, 265
localism, 216–217
Los Angeles, 180
loyalty, 193

Mafia, 163
market failure, 185
market fluctuations, 27, 40
Marxism, 283–284, 290
Matra, 142
maturity (of industries), 177
mechanical engineering industry, 151
medical instruments industry, 180, 181, 186
membership, 189, 199
middle classes, 163
military industrial production, 195
Minneapolis, 182
models of production: definition of, 44; routines, 45–46; Industrial, 47; Market, 47; Marshallian, 48; Innnovation, 49
Modena (Italy), 149–173, 193
moral hazard, 184–185, 283

nativism, 216
networks, 48, 116, 141, 170–171
New Institutional Analysis, 283–293, 301–302
non-economic forces, 13

Olivetti, 255
opportunism, 184–185, 194, 212, 283
Orange County (California), 181, 262

Paris, 182
participation, conventions of, 163–173, 189–203, 215; definition, 23
path dependency, 12, 65, 197–203, 305
persons. *See* interpersonal relations; identity, conventions of
petite bourgeoisie, 163
Plan, the, 78, 141–142, 145–146. *See also* France
political subcultures, 170
positivism, 39
possible worlds of production: action frameworks, 19–20, 39–40; Market, definition, 20, 34–35; Interpersonal, definition, 20, 35–36; Industrial, definition, 21, 32–34; Intellectual, definition, 21, 36–37; boundaries between, 40–42
postmodernism, 220
Poujadism, 216
pragmatics, 14, 39, 277
pragmatism, 222
Prato (Italy), 149–173, 193, 253, 254
precedent, 295–296
predictability, 45
principal-agent theory, 288–291
producer/financial services industry, 186
product, 37; centrality of to economic analysis, 15; dedicated, 29; generic, 29; qualities, 29, 53, 71, 197–198; nature of, 37–38
product life cycle, 176, 187
production flexibility, 155
productivity conventions, 58–61
profitability, 50–56, 159; in Marshallian model, 51; in Market model, 51; in Industrial model, 51; in Innovation model, 51; and industrial organization, 53. *See also* quasi-rents
Protestantism, 13, 162–163, 220
proximity, geographical, 71, 115. *See also* regions
public choice, 287–288